Hunting the Ethical State

Hunting the Ethical State

The Benkadi Movement of Côte d'Ivoire

JOSEPH HELLWEG

The University of Chicago Press Chicago and London

JOSEPH HELLWEG is assistant professor of religion at
Florida State University.

The University of Chicago Press, Chicago 60637
The University of Chicago Press, Ltd., London

Printed in the United States of America

20 19 18 17 16 15 14 13 12 11   1 2 3 4 5

ISBN-13: 978-0-226-32653-5 (cloth)
ISBN-13: 978-0-226-32654-2 (paper)

ISBN-10: 0-226-32653-5 (cloth)
ISBN-10: 0-226-32654-3 (paper)

Library of Congress Cataloging-in-Publication Data
Hellweg, Joseph.
Hunting the ethical state : the Benkadi movement of Côte d'Ivoire / Joseph Hellweg.
p. cm.
Includes bibliographical references and index.
ISBN-13: 978-0-226-32653-5 (cloth : alk. paper)
ISBN-10: 0-226-32653-5 (cloth : alk. paper)
ISBN-13: 978-0-226-32654-2 (pbk. : alk. paper)
ISBN-10: 0-226-32654-3 (pbk. : alk. paper)
1. Crime prevention—Côte d'Ivoire—Citizen participation—History—20th century. 2. Social movements—Côte d'Ivoire—History—20th century. 3. Hunting customs—Côte d'Ivoire. 4. Africans—Côte d'Ivoire—Rites and ceremonies. 5. Sacrifice—Social aspects—Côte d'Ivoire. 6. Islamic occultism—Social aspects—Côte d'Ivoire. 7. Côte d'Ivoire—History—1993–
I. Title.
DT545.84.H45 2011
966.6805'2—dc22   2011000119

♾ The paper used in this publication meets the minimum requirements of the American National Standard for Information Sciences—Permanence of Paper for Printed Library Materials, ANSI Z39.48-1992.

For my parents, Raymond and Dorothy Hellweg,
with love, joy, and gratitude

And for those who have perished or suffered from the violence in Côte d'Ivoire in 2010 and 2011 following presidential elections, this book is also for them, with the hope that again, one day soon, Côte d'Ivoire will flourish in peace

Contents

Illustrations

Table

Figures

Note on Names, Tense, and Orthography

Because the Benkadi movement was at the center of a national controversy in the 1990s, I have given pseudonyms to villages and to those persons mentioned in this book who are still living and who played key roles in Benkadi's organization beyond the national limelight. I have used the real names of all those who played public roles in hunters' lives and in Benkadi. My host, Dramane Coulibaly, is a case in point. He was a prominent hunter in northwestern Côte d'Ivoire but quite critical of Benkadi in private.

I have chosen to write most of this book in the past tense to avoid problems associated with the ethnographic present (Fabian 1983), and because I mostly describe past events. I mean in no way to imply that the people I describe here no longer perform the practices that I document.

When I offer a parenthetical transcription of a plural word in the Julakan language of northwestern Côte d'Ivoire, I do so without using the "y" that Matt Carr has adopted as the plural marker. Citing M.-J. Derive (1985), Carr (1995a: 7) writes, "It has been noted that in Manding dialects the 'plural' denotes plural as opposed to non-plural, rather than plural as opposed to singular." Therefore, the "singular" form of a word may also indicate its plural as opposed to its "non-plural" meaning.

I rely on two systems of orthography for non-English words in this book: French and simplified phonetic. Simplified phonetic transcriptions almost always appear italicized to transcribe words from Julakan. For the names of most

Table 1 Pronunciation Guide for French and Julakan Vowels and Consonants

Morpheme	Approximate American English Equivalent	Transcription System
Vowels:		
a	like the *o* in "fond"	French and phonetic
e	like the *e* in "grey"	Phonetic
é	like the *e* in "grey"	French
ε	like the *e* in "bed"	Phonetic
i	like the *i* in "machine"	French and phonetic
ô	like the *o* in "rope"	French
o	like the *o* in "rope"	Phonetic
ɔ	like the *ou* in "bought"	Phonetic
ou	like the *oo* in "boot"	French
u	like the *u* in "dune"	Phonetic
Consonants:		
c	like the *tch* in "catch"	Phonetic
di	like the *j* in "jar" when followed by a vowel	French
g	like the French *r*	Phonetic
gb	like the *gb* in "tugboat" as a single sound	Ivoirian French and phonetic
n	Only the *n* at the start of a word or between vowels is pronounced in French and Julakan. Otherwise, when *n* follows a vowel at the end of a word, it nasalizes the previous vowel in both French and Julakan.	French and phonetic
ŋ	like the *ng* in "ring"	Phonetic
ʃ	like the *sh* in "shy"	Phonetic
ti	like the *tch* in "catch" when followed by a vowel	Ivoirian French

people and places, I have followed Ivoirian French style, using French accents where appropriate. When I was unsure about how a French-speaking Ivoirian would spell a name, or when the French spelling seemed too difficult to pronounce in English, I either invented my own spelling in Ivoirian French, as with the personal name "Chémon," or used the anglicized version, as in the case of the ethnic term "Sénoufo," which became "Senufo." Any consistent approach to orthography proved impossible. I saw no benefit to anglicizing all Ivoirian terms. The ethnic and linguistic term "Bété," for example, seemed best left in its French spelling.

Table 1 indicates American English pronunciations that approximate those of French and/or phonetic characters used in this book. I indicate whether the character in question is used in the French or phonetic system or both in the far right column under "Transcription System."

Acknowledgments

It is a pleasure to thank publicly those whose support, guidance, and assistance made this book possible. In Côte d'Ivoire, Dramane Coulibaly, Madénba Traoré, Drissa Koné, and Moussa Fofana made me feel at home in Nienesso, Niamasso, Odienné, and wherever we traveled together. The Ministry of Higher Education and Scientific Research of Côte d'Ivoire graciously allowed me to pursue my research in Denguélé, and Dr. François Assi Adopo of the University of Abidjan's Institute of Applied Linguistics generously affiliated me with the institute for the duration of my work. The Fulbright Foundation funded my dissertation fieldwork in Côte d'Ivoire, and the Carter G. Woodson Institute for African-American and African Studies at the University of Virginia funded the writing of the dissertation on which this book is based. I thank them all and am forever in their debt.

At the University of Virginia, my doctoral committee made writing a dissertation an intellectual adventure in the best sense of the phrase. David Sapir encouraged me to focus my interests on performance and ritual and gave me his unfailing support. Kandioura Dramé suggested Côte d'Ivoire to me as a research site before I had ever considered it. Roy Wagner challenged me to think in bolder theoretical terms. Hanan Sabea reminded me that dozos never spoke with only one voice. And my committee chair, Susan McKinnon, challenged my thinking in ways that changed who I am and the way I see the world for the better. Her ideas on culture, kinship, hierarchy, and power and her critical responses to my writing stand as models to me for how to be a scholar, teacher, and advisor. I will always be grateful to her.

Beyond my committee, Edith Turner hosted me as a boarder in her home while I was a graduate student and tutored me on the primacy of rapport in research. Joseph Miller made me an apprentice of African history. And Dell Hymes introduced me to ethnopoetics. I dedicate chapter 8 to his memory.

At Florida State University, Michael Uzendoski has been an invaluable friend and colleague. He read and critiqued this manuscript while we were both affiliated with the Department of Anthropology. Dianna Bell, a doctoral student in the Department of Religion, also read and critiqued my manuscript. It has been a pleasure to teach, work, and learn with them both, along with my wonderful colleagues in the Religion Department. They remind me each day that academic life can be both humane and rewarding. I thank Adam Gaiser in particular for his help with the Qur'anic references. At Strozier Library, Lisa Vernon, Andrés Ruiz, and Job Jaime created several of the figures for this book. Malcolm Shackelford, ever attentive, helped me with photographs. In the final days of preparing this book, several friends at Florida State provided much-needed help at the hour when I most needed it. Susan Minnerly proofread and corrected the manuscript. Dianna Bell and James Broucek helped prepare the index. And Tyler Monsein checked and corrected the references. Responsibility for any errors, however, is mine.

Florida State University also provided me a leave of absence from 2008 to 2010, for which I would like to thank Dean Joseph Travis. During this time, I was able to teach and do research as a Fulbright Scholar at the Universities of Kankan, Guinea, and Bamako, Mali. It was in Kankan that I completed most of the revisions for this book. Andrew McLean, Molly Sanchez-Crowe, and Serge Akhani of the United States Embassy in Conakry, Rector Moriah Conté of the University of Kankan, and Oury Labé Diallo, the director of the university's American Reading Room, made it possible for me to complete my revisions in the best conditions.

Also in Tallahassee, I have depended on Urmilla Deshpande's boundless friendship, sizzling wit, merciless editing, loving family, and unfailing help with maps and illustrations on more occasions than she may care to remember. She has taught me much about both writing and friendship along the way. She is my sister, and I am hers!

I owe my continuing involvement with West Africa to those who helped me learn to speak Julakan years ago. At the University of Virginia, Ellen Contini-Morava guided my first study of Mande grammar. Kassim Koné taught me introductory Bamanankan at Indiana University, and Moussa Coulibaly, a teacher *hors pair,* tutored me in Tagbusikan at the University of Abidjan. Grants from Dean Robert Huskey at the University of Virginia and from the Rotary Foundation made my initial stays in Abidjan possible. Cassian Braconnier sent me an early, unpublished version of his Wojɛnɛkakan dictionary. And Matt Carr of Serving in Mission (SIM) gave me his grammar and dictionary of Wojɛnɛkakan. He and his wife Brenda and their SIM colleagues, Paul and Jenny Manson, Mark and Nancy Rogers, Barbara Tschetter, and Chuck and Lois Forster, became dear and indispensable friends.

While I was an undergraduate at Carleton College, Jackson Bryce, Van Dusenbury, Chérif Keïta, Nader Saiedi, Steve Caton, and my advisor, the late Paul Riesman, encouraged my interests in Africa, anthropology, and social theory. They were teachers whose guidance I am still trying to deserve. While at Carleton, I had the unenviable job of packing the books in Paul Riesman's office into boxes after his untimely death. This book is part of a conversation that I wish I could have continued with him in person.

Conversations I sustain are with James Zolnowski and fellow Africanist, Fr. Jack Schuler—both in St. Louis. They help me understand the meaning of what I have learned.

I also remain indebted to all those in Côte d'Ivoire who assisted me with my research. Faya Dev first told me to go to Odienné. And the following persons offered their guidance and warmest hospitality in Abidjan, Korhogo, Odienné, and Yamoussoukro: Claude Franck About and his wife Ange, Indran and Ruth Amirthanayagam, the late Samka Bamba, Alain Bambara, the Bathily family, Simone Brown, Bro. Arthur Cherrier and the Marianist Community of Notre Dame d'Afrique, the Coulibalys in Nienesso, the Diocese of Odienné, Diomandé Symphor, Beth Duff-Brown, Abdoulaye and Lamine Doumbia, the late Inza Fanny, Prince Ouédji Firmin, Alice Henry, the staff of the Hôtel les Frontières, Marie-José Hourantier, Youssouf Kaloulé, Ibrahima Kamagaté, Adama Koné, Koné Adama, Sarata Koné, the Konés of Niamasso, Fr. Damien Kono of Cameroon, the late Ahmadou Kourouma, his wife Christine, Fr. Céléstin N'Dri, Tiécoura Ouattara, Denguélé's Peace Corps volunteers, Haywood and Sabine Rankin, Fr. Morel of INADES, Fr. Bernard Rauch, Daniel Reed, Van Reidhead, the Rotaract Club of Odienné, Lamine Savané, Abiba Sawadogo, James Silkensen, Fr. Ivano Tosolini, Ali Touré and family, the staff of the Yankadi, Lily Yeh, Zerbo Zangoulé, Abass Zein, and Solange Zougou.

In addition, special words of thanks go to David Brent and Laura Avey at the University of Chicago Press for their editorial assistance, to the book's two anonymous readers whose criticisms improved it tremendously, and especially to Maia Rigas, whose incomparable copyediting made this a better book. And also to the Centre de Cartographie et de Télédétection of Côte d'Ivoire for permission to base figure 4 on a map that the center produced; to Florian Serfaty of Group Jeune Afrique for granting permission to model figure 5 on a map in *Jeune Afrique l'Intelligent*; to Lily Yeh and Ouédraogo Yilémnabin Richard for the use of their photos; and to Kate Browne who helped me find the first four words of this book's title.

Finally, I thank my Aunt Mary Anne Lynch, B.V.M., who started me thinking about the world; my brother and sister, James and Julia, and their families, who have remembered me from afar; Diadié Bathily and Drissa Koné, who befriended me in Côte d'Ivoire and beyond; and above all, my parents, who crossed vast distances—cultural, geographical, and linguistic—to visit me during my fieldwork and to whom I dedicate this book.

ONE

Mestizo Dozos: Sacrifice, Shape-Shifting, and the State

Hunters in a State of Flux

This book explores how poor, politically marginalized, mostly Muslim West African men used ritual sacrifice to fight crime in the country of Côte d'Ivoire in the 1990s. When police failed to quell a national crime wave, initiated hunters, called *dozo*s, assumed unofficial police roles. They did so according to the imitative logic by which they blended into the forest to kill game and made a place for themselves as hunters in Islam.[1] Because hunters often slay game in ways not considered ritually pure (halal), hunting presents an inherent challenge for Muslims. Dozos reconciled such contradictions through their rituals. They made sacrifices to their tutelary spirit, Manimory,[2] to recreate the offerings that enabled him to fuse with the forest and become omnipresent and all-powerful within it. His transformation confirmed his status as a Muslim saint. Their synthesis of hunting and Islam gave them a model for resolving other challenges to their hunting roles. This study explains how the dozo ritual ethos and its associated practices, together called *dozoya*, informed their new security roles and how the development of their new security roles can, in turn, inform the nature of politics and anthropology in Africa.

Dozo Encounters of My First Kind

On the night of December 30, 1993, I was traveling by bus along the highway between the northern city of Korhogo and the coastal metropolis of Abidjan (see fig. 1). I had been studying Julakan, the most widely spoken language after French in Côte d'Ivoire, and doing research on francophone theater in Abidjan, Côte d'Ivoire's economic capital, since October. But when Côte d'Ivoire's legendary first president, Félix Houphouët-Boigny, died on December 7, actors stopped performing during the two-month-long mourning period, leaving me with no plays or rehearsals to attend. So when an Ivoirian reggae singer and friend, Faya Dev, invited me for the New Year to visit his hometown of Katiola, four hundred kilometers to the north of Abidjan, I agreed. It was my first trip to "the Great North" (*Grand Nord*).

En route, police and gendarmes stopped the bus at multiple roadblocks. The glow of their kerosene lamps announced their checkpoints from afar. A movable, retractable lattice of metal spikes showed drivers where to stop at the entrance and exit of each town. At every checkpoint, our driver turned on the cabin lights to stir sleeping passengers awake before he disembarked with his papers and several hundred francs CFA in hand with which to placate authorities.[3] A short while later, a uniformed agent boarded the bus and said, "Bon soir, mesdames, messieurs. Les papiers, s'il vous plaît"—"Good evening, ladies and gentlemen. Papers please." He slowly worked his way to the back of the bus, checking each person's identity card and my passport.[4] He did so ostensibly to identify illegal immigrants, smugglers, and criminals, but profit was as pertinent a motive. Those without papers went outside where, some told me later, they tendered cash to reenter the bus. Otherwise, the police would have detained them at the checkpoint when the bus left.

Several hours into the trip, while an Alpha Blondy cassette was playing loudly over the speakers, our driver stopped at a dark, isolated spot on the road, far from any checkpoint and for no apparent reason. He turned off the engine and the music, leaving us wide awake and silent.

Seconds passed without the usual formalities. The driver stayed seated. No one boarded the bus. Curious passengers peered silently through the foggy windows. I overheard two of them whisper to each other that bandits had blocked our way. A man next to me, perhaps sensing my confusion, explained that thieves routinely stopped buses at gunpoint along this highway to rob passengers. He more than satisfied my curiosity. All

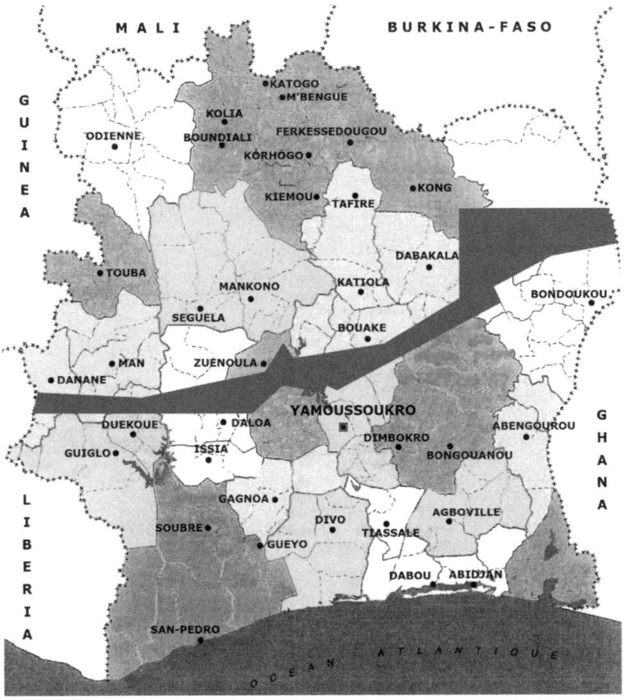

1 Map of Côte d'Ivoire. The black bar across the map denotes the buffer zone that French troops secured to block the rebel advance during the 2002 to 2007 rebellion. Map by Urmilla Deshpande, based on a 1997 map by the Ivoirian Centre de Cartographie et de Télédétection, used with permission.

discussion ceased when a passenger seated toward the front of the bus announced the approach of several armed men. Where were the police now when we needed them?

Then suddenly, a passenger exclaimed in a loud whisper, "Les dozos!"—"The dozos!"

My anxiety turned back to confusion. "Les dozos?"

I had never heard the word. But now I could hear the armed men outside, invisible from my seat, speaking calmly to the driver through his window. Then without further ado, the driver started the engine, and the "dozos" let us proceed. No money changed hands, no papers were checked. I turned, baffled, to my fellow traveler. He said that hunters—"dozos"—had been patrolling highways for some time to quell banditry and that they were now collaborating with state police agents to provide security.

Benkadi on the Road

Dozos called their security movement *Benkadi*,[5] which means "Agreement is sweet" in the Mande languages referred to collectively as Julakan, whose native speakers call themselves Jula.[6] As members of Benkadi, dozos manned security patrols, captured criminals, and restituted stolen goods to crime victims across the country. They did so as hunters, sorcerers, and healers with a history of sustaining reciprocity with non-dozos by sharing game meat, protecting farmers' fields from vermin, shielding non-dozos from sorcerers, and healing illnesses with plants from the forest. As members of Benkadi, they drew on their hunting, occult, and healing skills to track and capture thieves, repel the sorcery that criminals used, and enforce basic public health measures. They treated Côte d'Ivoire's crime wave as a symptom of a larger moral disorder that threatened community well-being, requiring a comprehensive, ethical cure that they articulated through ritual.

Dozos' initiatory sacrifices bound them to non-dozos through the vows that dozos made to their patron spirit, Manimory, against lying, stealing, committing adultery, and betraying other dozos. As long as dozos respected these taboos and made sacrifices to Manimory, he would protect them on the hunt. Because dozos' initiatory vows linked their hunting success to their moral conduct beyond the hunt, their sacrifices to Manimory offered a means for reflecting on parallel but contrasting domains: the hunt and everyday life. Their ritual activity was therefore ethical activity because it offered guidelines for moral action in multiple arenas.[7] When criminals violated the standards that dozos upheld for themselves, overwhelming dozos' communities and the country as a whole, dozos felt personally implicated in the crisis and entitled to act. Because they responded to a national crime wave through principles that structured their hunting lives, their ethical position became a political one, exemplifying the cultural pluralism inherent wherever precolonial institutions like *dozoya* coexisted side by side with those bequeathed by colonialism (see Ayittey 2006).

In contrast to the moral deontology of Côte d'Ivoire's written laws, dozos grounded their sense of legality in an ethic of virtue (see MacIntyre 1984).[8] Although non-dozo men also hunted, healed, made sacrifices, and in some cases, unofficially policed villages and neighborhoods, dozos performed these activities according to a distinctive, though far from static or uncontested, dozo ethos encoded in their sacrifices.[9] They used the ethical state they cultivated to reform what they saw as the Ivoirian state's immoral abandonment of the poor to crime. As organic intellectuals (see Gramsci 1971; Feierman 1990; Hountondji 1977, 31; Mudimbe 1991, 49), they used ritual's transformative symbols and practices to assume new identities as quasi-state agents.[10] Their sacrifices affirmed a cosmopolitan, mestizo vision (Piot 1999, 22–23; Amselle 1998, xix) of social responsibility as compelling as that of any nongovernmental organization (NGO), political party, or government. Although most dozos were nonliterate peasants or urban shantytown residents, they organized Benkadi along bureaucratic lines to collaborate unofficially with state security forces to patrol rural roads and highways as well as villages, towns, and cities. Restructuring their ritual ties as bureaucratic ones transformed their largely Muslim, Mande- and Syenara-speaking ritual hunting network into a national, francophone security force.

Benkadi grew to include tens of thousands of armed men, at which point state officials began to perceive it as an opposition militia organized in support of Muslim politician and former prime minister Alassane Ouattara. Consequently, the state began to repress Benkadi in 1996 and banned its activities in southern Côte d'Ivoire in 1998 (Bassett 2003, 15–18). In 2002, when former Ivoirian soldiers failed in their attempt at a coup d'état but managed to occupy all of northern Côte d'Ivoire, many dozos joined them. Within a decade, dozos had transformed themselves from hunters to auxiliary police to enemies of the state. Anthropological interest in Benkadi therefore lies, at least in part, in explaining how and why dozos altered their relationship to the state so dramatically in so little time, particularly given the ritual basis of their movement.

Although occult practices like ritual, sorcery, and witchcraft may challenge, resist, or subvert state power (Balandier 1970; Binsbergen 1981; Jean Comaroff 1985; Fernandez 1982; Lanternari 1963), the state may just as easily employ occult discourses to consolidate power (A. Cohen 1981; Stoller 1995; Taylor 1999). Indeed, I shall argue that ritual enabled dozos to occupy a "third space" (Bhabha 1994, 36–38) somewhere in between and beyond the dichotomies of state and civil society (see Ferguson 2006, 89, 97–103).[11] They assumed state prerogatives while violating national law according to a savvy analysis and engagement of the state's faults, potential, and vulnerabilities. Benkadi can therefore illuminate anthropological discussions of state power, ritual movements, mimetic creativity, the ethics of sacrifice, the nature of agency, and parastatal violence in Africa and beyond, six themes to which I now turn in greater detail.

Hunting, Modernity, and the State, or What's Neo- about Neoliberalism?

Benkadi's success reflected the general weakening of the postcolonial state in Africa. Since the end of the Cold War, several African states have "imploded under the combined effects of economic crisis, neo-liberal programs of structural adjustment and the loss of legitimacy of political institutions" (Bayart, Ellis, and Hibou 1999, 19; Rothberg 2003; Zartman 1995). In response, ruling elites consolidated networks of support, bought off opponents, commandeered state resources, manipulated markets, broke laws, dismantled bureaucracies, held creditors at bay, and allied with national or international corporations to privatize public services (Azam 2006; Ayittey 1999; Boone 2003a, 2003b; Reno 1998, 15–23). Even when the resulting "arbitrarily and poorly bureaucratized" states failed "to conform to . . . Western notions of political modernity" (Chabal and Daloz 1999, 4), they managed to retain power for elites in times of state contraction (14), preventing political rivals from mounting effective opposition.

Elites filled the "dangerous vacuum" that emerged "around the edges" of the state (Richards 1996, 36) through clientage. Africa's colonial administrations had similarly relied on nonstate institutions (Rodney 1973, 164–165), cutting "deals with local strongmen [and] tolerating their use of delegated state authority for private gain in exchange for their loyalty and help in reigning in administrative costs" (Reno 1998, 21; see Ferguson 2006, 100). Under colonialism, European and American companies assumed client roles as "good partners . . . not only for the revenues they generated but also for taking over local administrative tasks in return for privileged access to resources or markets" (Reno 1998, 21). After independence, elites retained this "bifurcated" strategy by sustaining civil law and state police protection for affluent urbanites on whom lower-class elites depended for support, while minimizing such services for villagers and those living in periurban settings (Mamdani 1996, 16–34, 52–61). Members of the underclass—and especially ethnic, regional, or religious minorities—were often victimized by police abuse and were left vulnerable to crime (Salih 2001, 25, 29–30, 46). If African states became "*vacuous* and *ineffectual*" after the Cold War, it was not because they "did not consolidate, as was once expected, on the foundation of the colonial legacy" (Chabal and Daloz 1999, 14, emphasis in original), but because they did.

In prewar Sierra Leone, for example, public services shrank in proportion to state retraction (Richards 1996, 36). Officials let client businesses monopolize the exploitation of natural resources in return for carrying out "many of the more complicated tasks of the state (like organizing communications, schooling and medical services)" (35). In prewar Liberia, the state delegated to "chiefs and district commissioners . . . extensive powers of coercion and patronage which they could then use to enhance their own standing through the manipulation of informal networks" (Ellis 1999, 212; see Crowder and Ikime 1970).[12] Elites in Burkina Faso, Côte d'Ivoire, Guinea, and Mali similarly outsourced police-, military-, and conservation-related services to initiated hunters (Bassett 2003, 2004; Ferme and Hoffman 2004; Hagberg 2004; Hellweg 2004; Leach 2000; K. Traoré 2004) whose status grew as a result.

Ritually based security movements like Benkadi (Bassett 2003; Ferme 2001a, 26–30; Hagberg 1998; Hellweg 2006; Richards 1996, 182–183) flourished elsewhere in Africa as well: the Bakassi and Egbesu Boys in Nigeria (Omeje 2005; Meagher 2007; Smith 2004), Sungusungu in Tanzania (Abrahams 1987; Fleischer 2000; Heald 2005), and PAGAD in South Africa (Knox and Monaghan 2003, 44–47). These movements articulated impoverished people's desperation between the global, neoliberal dynamics emerging within urban areas, on one hand, and contrasting ritual, religious, and often rural-based discourses of power, on the other (Comaroff and Comaroff 2001, 310–311). While the emergence of dozos as organized actors in cities and nation-states was new, the structural contradictions of their positions were not. As they attempted to "reform . . . the bifurcated" postcolonial state, they linked "the urban and the rural—and a whole series of related binary opposites such as rights and custom, representation and participation, centralization and decentralization, civil society and community—in ways that," for the most part "have yet to be done" (Mamdani 1996, 34) by politicians, policy makers, and NGOs.

Rituals, Resistance, and Reform

Anthropologists, historians, and sociologists have long focused on African ritual discourses as means for resolving such dichotomies. In the 1950s and 1960s, when African states were becoming independent, scholars criticized studies that depict rituals as static means for maintaining bounded, homogenous social groups. New voices testified to the ways that ritual provoked participants to critique and modify the structures that governed daily life (Richards 1956; Turner 1967). Ritual's syncretic capacities seemed to make life more comprehensible and manageable under rapidly changing, often paradoxical circumstances (Balandier 1957).

They helped oppressed populations to vent their frustrations (Gluckman 1963, 126–132 passim; I. Lewis 1989; Turner 1968) and to organize protonationalist rebellion (Ranger 1967, 381), ethnic emancipation (Schoffeleers 1972, 92), anticapitalist resistance (Linden and Linden 1974, 132; Binsbergen 1981, 290; cf. Hobsbawm 1959), and anticolonial revolt (Fuglestad 1975, 210; Lan 1985; Lanternari 1963, 19–62; Stoller 1989a).[13] New interest in Marxism and Antonio Gramsci (1971) recast ritual as a means of subverting hegemonic discourses by altering the meanings of their terms (Hall and Jefferson 1976; Hebdige 1979; Scott 1977, 1985).[14] Jean Comaroff (1985), for example, showed how South African initiated churches used ritual to resist the state. Tswana Christians recontextualized Christian signifiers within precolonial ritual practices and, in doing so, implicitly and unconsciously subverted the colonial and neocolonial power associated with Christian signs and symbols.

Theorists have analyzed such conjunctures of ritual traditions and modern ideologies in terms of the interplay between social structures and the events and behaviors that challenge, reinforce, or undermine them (Sahlins 1981, 5, 33, 50, 54; see also Bourdieu 1977, 78–87; Certeau 1984, 55, 57; Giddens 1979, 70; 1984, 25, 139–141; Ortner 1984, 144–157). As people follow patterns of thought and action amid circumstances resistant to them, people will alter those structures. The new structures then shape new forms of action, which will change again in response to new circumstances.

In the case of Benkadi, dozos reproduced their ethos of *dozoya*—or "what dozos do"—amid rising crime, amplifying those aspects of *dozoya* that were useful for providing security. Dozo initiations, for example, formerly followed a long hunting apprenticeship in rural areas. But in cities and towns, they were reduced to ritual sacrifices alone to recruit Benkadi members who wanted to man security patrols rather than hunt. As a result, a new, literate, francophone bureaucracy of dozo presidents, secretaries-general, and treasurers arose alongside a preexisting dozo hierarchy of mostly nonliterate, often nonfrancophone dozo chiefs. Thanks to these new officers, Benkadi succeeded in pursuing its security efforts with the tacit approval, and later suspicion, of literate, francophone police and state officials.

Shape-Shifting as Strategy

Elsewhere in West Africa, beyond Côte d'Ivoire, hunters underwent similar transformations in relation to the state. In Sierra Leone, *kamajor* hunters supported President Tejan Kaba in a civil war in which their loyalty to the state, respect for the laws of war (Ferme and Hoffman 2004, 79), and occult claims to repel bullets and disappear in battle (Ferme 2001a, 27, 223; Richards 1996, 171, 182) came under scrutiny. When the state made them its primary army, *kamajor*s gained a say in state policy (Leach 2000, 587–588), compromising the state sovereignty they supposedly defended. In Guinea, *donso* hunters guarded national parks at the request of international donor agencies in an arrangement that left critics worrying that *donso*s might become a power unto themselves (591–593).[15] They nearly did when former president Lansana Conté asked them to guard Guinea's border with Sierra Leone against rebel incursions (585).[16] Meanwhile, in Mali, elites ingratiated themselves with *donso*s to attract funding from donors who saw hunters as indigenous development agents. *Donso*s liked the idea, exchanging their "symbolic capital" for aid and state favor (K. Traoré 2004, 101–102). And in Burkina Faso, demographic pressures, regional migration, climatic shifts, and conflicting patterns of land use brought ethnic Senufo and Mossi farmers into conflict with Fulbe agropastoralists, with Senufo *donso*s resorting to violence against Fulbe herders and threats to authorities to keep quiet about *donso* exactions (Hagberg 1998, 121–126, 226–236; Hagberg 2004, 42–43, 52–57, 65–67). In each case, hunters altered their historical identities in contexts of political, economic, and environmental change.

Bassett (2003, 7–8, 25–26) has argued similarly for dozos in Côte d'Ivoire, suggesting that ecological changes due to overhunting reoriented dozos' ritual ethos, triggering Benkadi's rise. Unable to bag game, dozos hunted criminals, according to Bassett (2003, 4–7, 22–25), as if they were game. Quoting Ellis and ten Haar (1998, 193), Bassett (2003, 2) claims that the Ivoirian state's inability to "'fulfill its expected functions in regard to . . . law and public order'" pushed dozos to revive "'traditional' religious beliefs and practices . . . in the context of . . . social, political, and economic change" (cf. Meagher 2007). For Bassett, Benkadi dozos continued to hunt, but in a new environment and with new prey. They adjusted their pursuits in response to changes that would otherwise have compromised their identity.

I argue in contrast that dozos saw Benkadi and their ethos, *dozoya,* as related but distinct phenomena. As senior dozo (*dozoba*) Dramane Doumbia, once explained to me, "Benkadi is not *dozoya.* It is something dozos do."[17] Since *dozoya* means "what dozos do," his statement was something of a paradox: How could Benkadi be "something dozos did" without being *dozoya?* I infer that dozos perceived the pursuit and capture of thieves and the restitution of stolen goods as analogous and parallel to, rather than identical with, their stalking, killing, and redistribution of game. The challenge for anthropology, and for social theory, is to explain why.

Structure, Agency, Oscillation

Sociologist Franco Crespi (1992, 134) finds contemporary theory wanting in precisely this respect. Its explanations of transformations, like those that generated Benkadi, privilege the interaction of agents and structures as the motors of change. But the "recognition of the interplay between actors and structures is not sufficient to ground a theory of action," Crespi writes. "To say that action produces structures and is, in turn, conditioned by [them] does not explain the reasons for this interaction nor why action has an ambivalent attitude towards these structures." In other words, contemporary social theory describes how rather than why people suffer tensions between structure and practice.

Crespi (1992, 134) locates this dialectic between action and structure within persons themselves, rather than beyond them. Critical personal reflection, he writes, "negate[s] the objectivated forms" of structured relations, "showing that the Self is constructed through the dialectic between identification with and differentiation from" structures. "The individual," he argues, "appears both as a product of society and as a potential active producer of new meanings and new practices by shifting from one . . . form of determinacy" to another. For Crespi, alternating between one's personal prerogatives and one's social obligations is less a predetermined struggle between agency and structures than the nature of power itself, that is, the ability to self-consciously shape this struggle. According to Crespi, power is the "capacity to deal with the unavoidable contradictions of the relation between action and norms" (Crespi 1992, 95), between one's ability to alter one's role and the role as historically constituted. I argue that dozos relied on sacrifice to negotiate this relation, that is, to alter their performance of *dozoya* in accord with their changing awareness of historical circumstances.[18]

In West Africa, Amselle writes, "Social status or position is constantly subject to transaction. Far from being fixed entities embedded in immutable categories, [roles] are renegotiated continually according to . . . prevailing situations." Benkadi's emergence from *dozoya* in the 1990s reflected a history of such negotiation. Consider that thirteenth-century dozo, Sunjata Keita, unified the segmented polities of the western Sudan into the centralized polity of Mali or that, centuries after Mali had fragmented, dozos fought as soldiers in armies commanded by the ruler of Segou or by the warlord Samory Touré (Amselle 1998, 105, 108) until these armies dispersed under French colonialism. As soldiers in precolonial polities and as hunters in colonial and postcolonial states, dozos have fluctuated between state and segmentary organization as "two poles of the same hierarchized space" (Amselle 1998, 116). When dozos in Côte d'Ivoire reorganized their village and city-based ritual networks into Benkadi, they centralized once more.

Dozos also moved between the pragmatics of hunting and the rules of Islam. One of their most potent hunting strategies was to blend into the forest through sorcery in order to ambush prey. But after killing game, most dozos, being Muslim, tried to slit the animal's throat. Likewise, after their all-night funeral sacrifices for dead dozos, which some Muslims condemned as *shirk*, or "idolatry," dozos respectfully removed their amulet-laden shirts (*dozodɛrɛkɛ*) to avoid any such confusion and said their morning Muslim prayers at about 5:00 a.m. They claimed that Manimory, as a Muslim saint (*waliju*), was descended from Abraham, Ishmael, and Esau, although he reportedly sacrificed his first wife and first son before vanishing in the forest to become omnipotent and omnipresent within it. Dozos revered Manimory, too, as if he were a Sufi saint in ritual areas called *danguns*, the spot of his own sacrifices and disappearance.[19]

These histories, practices, and narratives located *dozoya* between segmentary and state organization, the forest and domesticity, paganism and Islam, local orality and scriptural literacy (Amselle 1998, 161).[20] According to Amselle (xi–xii), such oscillation between contrasting domains reflects the fundamental hybridity of West African identity: "[T]he relationship between these elements must not be conceptualized in terms of oppositions and cleavages, but rather in terms . . . of multi-belongingness." Traversing diverse terrains for centuries, dozos posited "an originary mixture," or "syncretism," at the heart of *dozoya* (120, 161).

The history of their transformation involved more than the imitation of the forest, Islam, or Ivoirian police—more than the blurring of differences between some original and a copy (Taussig 1993, xiii, xviii, 47, 121).[21] Through initiation, dozos gained the trust of colleagues who taught them how to blend into the forest through stealth and sorcery, following Manimory, so they could stalk their prey unseen. Through sacrifice, dozos created a relationship to what they imitated that was analogous to Manimory's position vis-à-vis the forest: that of an equal, not a copy. They may have violated Islam in some people's eyes by honoring Manimory, but they gave Manimory a Muslim pedigree in doing so. They may have set aside hunting to capture criminals, but they asked for

Manimory's protection while on patrol through the offerings they made to him for safety on the hunt.

Dozos made Manimory indistinguishable from the forest, *dozoya* tantamount to Islam, and hunting akin to policing. They transformed their encompassed status in the forest, in Islam, and under state authority into an encompassing one. Through mimesis, they enveloped within their range of prerogatives a mastery over the forest, a form of Muslim piety, and the adoption of state security roles. In doing so, they undermined the hierarchies that distinguished original from copy, insider from outsider, superior from subordinate.[22] Their transformations were *retro*mimetic. Instead of dissolving differences between originals and copies, they refashioned the original as the copy and the copy as the original.[23]

For dozos, true Islam was that which canonized Manimory. True *dozoya* was that which dozos used while policing. Such equations premised dozos' comfort in the forest, Islam, and the state on Manimory's original mimetic acts. Dozos approached these milieus as media by which to realize Manimory's feats anew using their "traditional" ritual ethos as a "modern" model for social transformation (see Scott 1998, 331). *Dozoya* comprised a kind of *mētis*, or "knowledge that [could] come only from [the] practical experience" of hunting (Scott 1998, 6)—from the ability to integrate so well into one's environment on its own terms as to pass imperceptibly through it. What made *dozoya* so contemporary was its history of success (323–324) at adapting to unforeseeable situations before which the state's pretense of enforcing a "predictable, routinized" kind of security, "ordered in advance and down to the smallest detail," made no sense (314). Dozos began instead "with the unpredictable . . . and then devise[d] the techniques and equipment (from an existing repertoire, to be sure)"—of *dozoya*—"(but one invented largely by [them])" (314). If sacrifices to Manimory structured dozos' approach to policing and hunting, then to understand Benkadi's security activities, one must first understand dozos' sacrificial relation to the hunt.

The Ethics of Sacrifice

To ensure success on the hunt, dozos sacrificed domestic items like kola nuts, chickens, and goats that also figured in non-dozo sacrifices. Gifts of kola nuts mediated marriages and accompanied the naming rituals (*dentɔgɔla, denkunli*) that introduced newborns to their families and neighbors.[24] Chickens served as gifts for important visitors. Goats substituted for sheep in Muslim sacrifices for the holy day of Tabaski (Eid al-Adha).[25] Dozos sacrificed these same items—kola nuts, chickens, and goats, but never sheep—at their initiations and in rituals meant to protect them from hunting hazards and the souls of dead dozos. In doing so, they destroyed metonyms of domestic life in dozo contexts, just as Manimory did in dozos' tales of his sacrifices. This was the case, I argue, because dozo sacrifice linked dozos and non-dozos in a reciprocal cycle of exchange.

After hunting and at dozo funerals, dozos distributed game meat to family members, neighbors, friends, dozos mentors, and even strangers. They called these gifts *sacrifices* in French and *saraka* in Julakan,[26] from the Arabic *sadakat,* meaning "alms" (Delafosse 1955, 627) or "charity."[27] Dozos' symbolic destruction of their relations with non-dozos for safe and successful hunting compelled them to return the favor by sharing game meat after each hunt and at the death of each dozo, making the dozo role a locus of moral responsibility.

For dozos, sacrifice was a "technology of the self" (Foucault 1988; Laidlaw 2002) through which they formed themselves as ethical agents in relation to hunting and comparable pursuits. It enabled them to anticipate and avoid the negative consequences of violating their reciprocal relations with others (Hellweg 2009, 41). Through sacrifice, dozos subjected themselves and their actions to recurring, critical scrutiny. When they destroyed signifiers of their relations to non-dozos, they enacted a "forced intention" (Frankl 1959, 194) to transgress those relations, dramatizing the hazards they faced on the hunt and that might prevent them from providing non-dozos with game meat, medicinal plants, or protection from crop damage or sorcery. These hazards included game run amok, poisonous snakes, sharp rocks and branches, other hunters' "friendly fire," and the fires hunters lit in the dry season to clear the forests of dry grass. By calling such dangers to mind, dozos could better avoid or avert them so as to avail non-dozos to the fruits of dozo hunting and analogous dozo pursuits.

Following the rise of crime in Côte d'Ivoire in the 1990s, a new analogy for hunting arose. When highwaymen began seizing cash crops that northern farmers sent southward by truck for sale, dozos intervened,[28] protecting these crops from human interlopers just as they killed pests in farmers' fields and offered game meat to non-dozos. *Dozoya* did not mandate the analogy between killing animals and policing, but the analogizing practice of sacrifice made it possible. Because sacrifice protected dozos when they hunted for the benefit of non-dozos, it also protected them when they used their guns to protect non-dozos from crime. Without dozo ritual, Benkadi would not have existed. Benkadi was the product of dozos' response to crime as apperceived and interpreted through sacrifice. For this reason, sacrifice, as a moral means of evaluating and responding to crises, is a main focus of analysis in this book, one with a clear precedent in the anthropological literature.

Sacrifice between Structure and Agency

Anthropologists have long depicted sacrifice as a means of managing moral relations between sacrifiers and others. Hubert and Mauss (1964, 13) and Durkheim (1965, 377–392) describe sacrifice as modifying the condition "of the moral person who accomplishes it" (Hubert and Mauss 1964, 39). They affirm that sacrifiers "imparted to the victim something of [their] own personality" (39) so that sacrifiers and spirits "fused together" in the offering (32, 44). Then, when sacrificers immolated the victim, the spirits retreated, leaving some of their power for sacrifiers in the victim (50–60), which sacrifiers then consumed. Each party acquired something of the other's potential (61–76), enhancing her or his ability to act through a kind of contractual agreement (100) that reaffirmed the existing order (102).

Evans-Pritchard (1956, 199) similarly describes sacrifice as effecting a "change of status or relationship" through a bargain with spirits to free a person from illness, misfortune, or possession in exchange for a victim's immolation (208, 225, 260). For Evans-Pritchard, the victim symbolizes the sacrifier's "inner state" (276, 279), which dies "with the victim" (281) as a substitute for the afflicted sacrifier. Spirits remove illness in exchange for the sacrifier's symbolic death, having no material interest in the offering (277) per se. Objectifying the intention to die in the afflicted's place is enough (279).

Because spirits move both within and beyond persons—causing illness or other afflictions—the ritual agreements that regulate spirits' activities encompass all areas of human experience, including health, work, and reproduction. Lienhardt (1961, 63, 81, 85, 90–93) thus defines spirits or "Powers" as "configurations of experience contingent upon [sacrifiers'] reaction to their . . . environments," both natural and social (147). Humans regulate these environments through sacrifice because it mobilizes the moral relations among participants necessary to dispel attitudes that might prevent them from confronting misfortune together (294). By "imaging . . . the grounds of suffering in a particular Power, [sacrifiers] grasp its nature intellectually in a way which satisfies them, and thus to some extent transcend and dominate it," freeing them "symbolically" from what they might otherwise have to passively endure (170; cf. Beidelman 1966, 545; Hutchinson 1985, 630–631) by filling them with suprahuman power (Heusch 1985, 211, 213; Bloch 1992).[29]

Sacrifiers reconfigure their agency in the face of affliction, grounding action in the intentions they express to spirits. As the chief dozo of the village of Somokoro explained, "Everything lies in your thoughts (*miriya*) . . . in your heart (*dusukun*). It's you who says what you have to say [to Manimory]. Then, when you kill the chicken, it is you who eats it . . . [Manimory] takes the chicken and kola nuts, but through your intentions (*hakiri*)."[30] For sacrifiers, spirits like Manimory exemplify "types of action and . . . the efficacy of the collective evaluations and reactions made possible by those types" (Valeri 1985, 22, 346). Spirits index the cultural idioms that structure sacrifiers' agency (346). If, as Lienhardt, argues, and as Valeri paraphrases it, "divinities make it possible to *interpret* the experience from which they are derived," then "they cannot be considered simple images or reflections of experience; they must add something to it—be concepts and not just images" (346). Spirits, and the sacrifices made to them, comprise a classificatory system on which human action depends for its meaning and enactment (see Sahlins 1976, 22–23). Dozos drew on sacrifice accordingly as a template for their security work. In the 1990s, they introduced Benkadi to Manimory in the context of sacrifices intended for protection on the hunt. As their concerns changed, so did the intentions they expressed to Manimory, expanding the range of their roles.

Sacrifice fashioned dozo roles as anything but static and unchanging. Dozos modeled themselves as "partible" persons (Strathern 1988, 185), "fractal" pluralities (Wagner 1991; see also Gable 1996, 105–106; Mead 1934, 164–173), and "dividuals" (Evans-Pritchard 1956, 281). By offering spirits an intentional part of themselves in their victims, they acted as a "conjunction and disjunction of spaces, human and non-human" (Heusch 1985, 213; see Piot 1999, 19) in which "spirits precede[d]—and exceed[ed]—social relations" (Piot 1999, 154). Their sacrificial offerings simultaneously embodied their relations with non-dozos and with spirits (see Godelier 1999, 104–105; Mauss 1967, 11; Piot 1999, 117–119; Strathern 1988, 178). When they killed, cooked, and ate their gifts to Manimory in the *dangun*, they did more than symbolize concepts (Valeri 1985), they consumed symbolized relations. They fashioned themselves as a protective link between non-dozos and Manimory, capable of responding to anything that threatened the generalized "agreement" (*bɛn*) they sustained between these parties—the *bɛn* of Benkadi.

If dozos restructured their agency through sacrifice to respond to emergent threats, it follows that they perceived what social theorists call "structures"—ecological, demographic, and sociopolitical relations—through the idiom of spirits (Fortes 1980, x–xi). Manimory and the spirits of deceased dozos represented dozos' relations with the forest, Islam, and the state in ways that defined their agency in these domains. Dozos in turn perceived their own persons, whom social theorists call "agents," more as structures, shared through sacrifice and gift giving with a plurality of actors, both humans and spirits. For these reasons, dozo sacrifice and Benkadi require a theory of action from beyond the dialectics of structure and practice or the related dichotomies of culture and personality (Benedict 1934; Holland et al. 1998, 270), structure and process (Turner 1967, 112–113; Turner 1969), norms and action (Parsons 1968, 76–77), structure and event (Sahlins 1981, 5, 33, 50, 54), or discourse and practice (Certeau 1984, 48).

In most social theory, structures constrain, provoke, or enable agents' actions, while agents accommodate, resist, or alter structures. Dozos modeled Benkadi differently. The spirits of Manimory and deceased dozos—consubstantial with categories of action (Valeri 1985)—regulated dozos' agency in ways that opened them to change. To paraphrase Piot (1999, 18), dozos did not just "have" relations with spirits; they *were* those relations. In order to redefine themselves as unofficial police, they reoriented their responsibilities to non-dozos by modifying their intentional relations to Manimory.

Dozos' power resulted less from controlling or resisting external forces (see Lukes 2005, 30) than from restructuring the internal relations that governed their persons and reflected their responsibilities to others (Ollman 1971, 15–16, 260). Dozo personhood as a microcosm of society (see Douglas 1966, 115–128 passim) became a locus for social change. In the Ivoirian political climate of the 1990s that stigmatized dozos and other Julakan-speaking, northern-descended Muslims on ethnic, regional, and religious grounds, dozos shifted shape to circumvent their marginalization in these realms (Hellweg 1997; Leach 2000), just as they did in the forest and in Islam, where they faced comparable risks from hunting hazards, purity laws, and accusations of blasphemy. By becoming unofficial police, they fulfilled their protective historical roles while attempting to enfranchise themselves and their communities in the Ivoirian nation-state. They transformed their pursuit of a personal ethical state into the hunt for a political one.

Dozo Violence

But dozos were far from ethical or heroic in all that they did. Their lapses into gratuitous violence undermined their plausibility as unofficial police.[31] As security agents and then as soldiers in Côte d'Ivoire's 2002–2007 rebellion, dozos committed atrocities against the same people they were ostensibly trying to protect or collaborate with in the 1990s: women, the poor, immigrants, Ivoirian citizens, and police. Their crimes included documented cases of rape, murder, and beatings. These acts paralleled similar abuses by state security forces (United States Department of State 1997, 1998, 1999), mirroring a generalized climate of cruelty and lawlessness in Côte d'Ivoire.[32] But dozo violence resulted from more than the pragmatics of controlling crime. Dozos had historically used violence to reestablish social order (see Bird and Kendall 1980; McNaughton 1988).

As for the violence of dozo sacrifices, it conveyed a morally ambiguous message: within violent domains like the forest, one must behave violently. But when dozos violated social norms, as in the mythical killings of Manimory's wife and child or in the real case of an incestuous rape committed by a dozo (see chap. 4), they turned to sacrifice to resolve the resulting problems (*namara*). Manimory appears to have sacrificed himself after he killed his family. And when dozos died, their colleagues made sacrifices to resolve any outstanding disputes or grievances involving the dead. In each case, non-dozos benefited in some way, not because of or in spite of dozo violence, but in response to it, due to the ritual sacrifices it triggered. Granted, dozos made no attempt to criticize their own violence in terms of human rights discourse (see Engelke 1999), and the problem of generalized violence in Côte d'Ivoire was one that they alone could not solve.

Dozos used violence for what Benjamin (1978, 87–288) has called its "law-preserving" and "lawmaking" character. They offered an alternative means of law enforcement as well as laws of their own that did not depend on the state but drew their ultimate authority from dozos' potential for violence (Weber 1964, 154). When dozos began protecting communities from bandits, they collaborated with local and regional authorities, often bringing suspects to police and gendarmes. The result was a tacit contract in which the threat of violence by dozos complemented the threat of violence by the state, preserving state laws already in place. But as Benkadi spread across the country, dozos began to inflict violence in the purported service of their own "lawmaking" capacity when they felt that civilians or police failed to recognize their new authority. This earned Benkadi a sinister reputation akin to the one Benjamin (1978, 283–284) attributes to exceptionally successful criminals in whom "violence confronts the law with the threat of declaring a new law."

I explain Benkadi as dozos' attempt to deal with the consequences of the state's mismanagement of violence in relation to law. In the 1990s, Ivoirian presidents increasingly ruled Côte d'Ivoire as a "state of exception" beyond the bounds of the constitution (Agamben 2005). They did so to recapture the authority of Côte d'Ivoire's recently deceased founding president Félix Houphouët-Boigny. Meanwhile, structural adjustment in the 1990s left the state with so few resources that it all but abdicated its law-preserving function, opening a space for others to assume it for themselves and for dozos to pursue the lawmaking use of violence in those areas where state police maintained a negligible presence, as in the far northwestern Denguélé prefecture where I based my research. It was here that Benkadi originated.

Meetings with Remarkable Dozos

I made my first trip to Denguélé and its regional capital Odienné in August 1994. It was a town of about 50,000 at the time. I had abandoned a study of francophone theater in Abidjan due to various political and personal circumstances. On the advice of a friend, Ivoirian reggae singer Faya Dev, I traveled to Odienné to study performance there. While on a bus to Odienné for the first time, a fellow traveler insisted that I meet an eighty-year-old French Catholic priest in Odienné who reportedly spoke Julakan and Syenara and who might be able to help with my research. The next day, my traveling companion and I walked together to the missionary's home. There we found a forty-something, Evangelical Protestant "church-planter" from New Zealand. He, his Australian wife, and their four children had been living in Odienné for nearly six years. I soon explained my interest in performance, and they invited me to return the next day to meet a local Jula convert to their church who they said knew a local "griot."

The following day they introduced me to Drissa Koné, a confident, charismatic young man known for his hunting skills and command of the regional language, Wojɛnɛkakan, which most of Denguélé's residents called "Julakan." I took an immediate liking to him. He explained that Dramane Coulibaly, a renowned "hunters' griot" (*griot des chasseurs*), was a friend of his and that he would introduce me to him (see fig. 2). A few

2 My host (*jatigi*), Dramane Coulibaly (*foreground*), singing. He is accompanied by his friend and my research collaborator, Drissa Koné. Dramane wears an amulet-laden dozo shirt, or *dozodɛrɛkɛ*, intended to protect him from attacks of sorcery. Drissa wears the trademark tricorne dozo hat called a *namaturu*, or "hyena's crest," resembling a hyena's ears and hackles. Hyenas, although no longer present in Denguélé, are known to be ferocious hunters. Photo by Ouédraogo Yilémnabin Richard, San-Pédro, 3 August 1996.

days later, while accompanying the missionaries to a funeral in Drissa's village of Niamasso, seventeen kilometers west of Odienné, Drissa adopted me into his family. From then on, people in Denguélé called me Youssouf Koné.

For the remainder of August, through September, and into October, I consulted libraries and archives in Abidjan to learn more about Odienné and dozos. In October, I moved my belongings to Odienné by *dyna*,

3 The principle road through downtown Odienné that runs past the main market, looking southward in 1997. All photos by the author unless otherwise noted.

the taxi-vans that crisscrossed Côte d'Ivoire's extensive network of rural highways (see fig. 3). Having learned that Odienné's Catholic church rented rooms, I took one and kept it as a pied-à-terre in town. I spent the next three months studying Wojɛnɛkakan as best I could with no grammar or dictionary and getting to know Drissa and other Odiennéka, as Denguélé's residents call themselves after the name of their capital and its precolonial polity.

At the time, Drissa was working in the local rice-packing plant south of town along the highway and renting a room in the home of his former high school English teacher. He had lived previously in an uncle's compound, but when Drissa converted to Christianity, his uncle asked him to leave. Eventually, his former English teacher did the same, claiming that Drissa's refusal to pray as a Muslim was having a bad influence on his children. Drissa then found a room on the grounds of the missionaries' church. Every morning, I met him on my moped and drove him to work at the rice-packing plant. And every afternoon, I met him at the plant to drive him home. Meeting him regularly gave structure to my life while I waited for him to introduce me to his friend, the singer Dramane Coulibaly. Having lived in Abidjan for several months, I knew the wisdom of meeting new acquaintances in the presence of a trusted intermediary, or *sababu* in Julakan. Being introduced to Dramane by someone whom he already trusted would inspire more trust in me on Dramane's part. For this I was willing to wait.

Then finally, on the evening of November 18, 1994, the time had come. I picked Drissa up at work, and he directed me back to the paved highway away from town until we arrived at the police checkpoint. Here we stopped to show our identity papers, indicate our destination, and explain our reasons for traveling. We then drove seventeen kilometers south to the village of Nienesso and to Dramane Coulibaly's compound.

Dramane greeted us warmly. He wore a sleeved, ankle-length *boubou* robe of lustrous, dark-blue, jacquard-weaved *bazin* cloth and the kind of short, brimless, circular hat that Muslim men affect. As a courtesy, he spoke the "commercial Jula," or Tagbusikan, that I had studied in Abidjan and invited Drissa and me to eat dinner with him.[33] We ate at dusk with his sons and grandson in silence on the small cement porch in front of his rectangular, thatch-roofed, mud-brick house. His three wives, his daughter, and his sons' wives and daughters ate separately. We ate with our hands from two bowls filled with salty, spicy dipping sauce and thick, gelatinous, cornmeal patties (*kabato*), which had turned green from added cassava.

"Dɔ di?" Dramane asked, after we had finished eating and washed our hands with water poured from a striped plastic kettle (*selidaga*).[34] "What news?"

Drissa turned to me and repeated the question like a good *sababu*.

Looking at Drissa, I explained that I had come to Abidjan to study Julakan and then to Odienné to study Wojɛnɛkakan and learn about Dramane's singing.

Drissa turned to Dramane and translated into Wojɛnɛkakan the response I had just given in Tagbusikan, adding that he wondered whether Dramane might sing briefly for us. Dramane obliged on condition that his apprentice, Abou Touré, whom Drissa quickly fetched from the nearby village of Kahandara, accompany Dramane on the dozos' six-stringed, kora-like instrument called the *dozongɔnun*. When Abou arrived, we all entered Dramane's house where Dramane sang for Drissa and me in a riveting, mellifluous voice. Afterward, Dramane explained that he sang at dozo funerals and at other dozo events, and he told us to return the next day so he could sing more songs for us. We did, and a month later, he invited us to accompany him to a dozo funeral in the nearby village of Ziévasso.[35] From then on, Drissa and I accompanied him to record his performances at singing engagements across Denguélé and throughout Côte d'Ivoire.

Situating Denguélé

Denguélé is Côte d'Ivoire's northwestern-most administrative unit, one of a total of sixteen administrative regions (*préfectures*) in the country. It borders Guinea to the west and Mali to the north. The region's residents live in a transitional zone of forested savanna between the Malian Sahel and what remains of the rain forests of southern Côte d'Ivoire. The area is ideal for cultivating cashews, mangoes, cassava, millet, papaya, rice, soy beans, and yams.

The year split evenly into a rainy season lasting roughly from May to October and a mostly dry season during the remaining six months. In December, the cool, dry, northerly Harmattan winds blew beneath hazy skies depositing a fine layer of Saharan dust day after day, even over the surfaces of closed interiors. And men burned the grass that had grown tall in the forest during the rainy season. Winds carried the ash over great distances, sometimes depositing it in the form of white flakes falling gently from the sky like snow. Then came the relatively cool months of January and February before the heat returned with sharply rising temperatures in March and April that seemed to provoke small flies to sting from their own discomfort. In May, the rains began in earnest, making travel difficult over the dirt roads that linked Denguélé's villages to its prefectural capital, Odienné (see fig. 4).

These roads also linked Denguélé to Guinea and Mali westward and northward, respectively, and to the Ivoirian town of Boundiali to the east. The paved highway ran southward through the cities of Touba, Man, Duékoué, and Bouaflé to the political capital, Yamoussoukro and, farther south, through Toumodi, to Abidjan, the country's economic hub. In the 1990s, four different bus companies and an assortment of *dyna*s ran from Odienné to Abidjan and to Côte d'Ivoire's second-largest city, Bouaké. Travelers could also take the postal van south to the city of Man and east to Korhogo. Buses, vans, and bush-taxis linked Odienné to almost every major destination in Côte d'Ivoire, Guinea, Mali, and beyond. They rarely left with an empty seat.[36] Like most Ivoirians, Odiennéka had family, friends, and business to attend to across the country.

Odienné, Denguélé's capital, was a typical prefectural center: home to a regional hospital, a clinic run by Italian nuns, two state high schools, a state technical school (since destroyed during political protests), a private high school, several grade schools, a post office, hotels, and headquarters for police, gendarmes, customs agents, and the Water and Forest police (Les Eaux et Forêts) who guarded Côte d'Ivoire's natural resources. The

4 Map of the Denguélé region of northwestern Côte d'Ivoire including those places mentioned in this book. Map by Urmilla Deshpande, based on a 1997 map by the Ivoirian Centre de Cartographie et de Télédétection, used with permission.

colonial-era town center sat amid a grid of crumbling paved roads and manufactured earthen-brick (*géobeton*) or cinder-block buildings with corrugated metal roofs. Neighborhoods to the east housed many of the city's Ivoirian and expatriate professionals in *villas*, painted cinder-block houses with electricity, running water, and walled enclosures. Other professionals lived scattered across town. The rest of Odienné's neighborhoods featured a mix of cinder-block buildings and clusters of mud-brick, thatch-roofed homes more typical of villages. Those who could afford electricity and running water had them. Others relied on covered pumps or open wells in their compounds, or they lived near others who did.

Denguélé's majority Jula population (Launay 1982, 13) and Islam's long history in the region dated from precolonial migrations of Jula traders and Muslim scholars from Mali and other Mande areas to this originally non-Muslim, Senufo region. During my stay, even the most remote of Denguélé's villages contained a small mosque, and the vast majority of Odiennéka, both urban and rural, practiced Islam. Many Odiennéka also performed divination, masked dances, *dozoya*, sacrifices for ancestors, or other practices judged illicit by some Muslims. Christianity, in contrast, had a minimal presence, mostly in Odienné, which hosted several African initiated churches, an Evangelical church, and a Catholic diocese.[37]

Hunting *Dozoya*

Early in 1995, I decided I wanted to live part-time in Nienesso to keep better track of Dramane's performance schedule. When I asked him in January whether this was possible, he let me stay in his house while he was away in Abidjan singing for dozos. When he returned, we made plans for my house, and I eventually paid for the materials and labor to build it near his compound. When the house was completed in April, I began to divide my time between Odienné, Nienesso, and the various locations where Dramane sang. While accompanying Dramane, I began to meet dozos involved in Benkadi. I then started to travel across the country—to Abidjan, Duékoué, Ferkessédougou, Korhogo, San-Pédro, and Yamoussoukro—to attend Benkadi events beyond Denguélé. Drissa accompanied me. For the next two and a half years, we attended gatherings with and interviewed dozos throughout Côte d'Ivoire and observed and recorded their rituals, musical performances, and security activities until the end of my stay in December 1997. Drissa had led me to Dramane, and Dramane to other dozos. Dozos made contacts with each other in the same way, through trusted *sababu*s, maintaining a vast dozo network that assembled locally for colleagues' funerals and regionally and nationally for Benkadi meetings.

Eventually, Dramane asked whether I wanted to be initiated as a dozo. Although I had never killed game for him or accompanied him on the hunt as a typical apprentice might have done, I had assumed personal and financial responsibility for his hernia operation after he complained of severe abdominal pain while singing in the remote village of Dioulatiédougou. I also took members of his family and other Nienesso residents to the hospital for treatment in recognition of their hospitality. Dramane said he considered these services equivalent to those of a hunting apprentice and arranged for my initiatory sacrifice in Nienesso in 1996. By that time, Benkadi had become a topic of national interest, and I had begun to wonder what inspired dozos to fight crime. My initiation and participation in dozo rituals gradually revealed the extent to which sacrifice energized dozos' security work as well as their hunting.

Outline of the Book

I begin my exploration of Benkadi in chapter 2 by describing the colonial roots of political and socioeconomic instability in Côte d'Ivoire as the background of Benkadi's emergence. This instability gave dozos an opportunity to carve a niche for themselves in national life even as a growing wave of ethnocentric nationalism increasingly stigmatized northern-descended Jula and Syenara-speaking Muslims as second-class citizens.

Chapter 3 shifts focus to the local context of dozo life in Denguélé. It describes how dozos assumed ethical responsibilities toward non-dozos at their dozo initiations. Parallels between dozo and non-dozo rituals further reveal how dozos defined dozo rituals as variations on the ritual ties that bound non-dozos to each other. As a result, dozos and non-dozos considered *dozoya* and non-dozo life as interrelated parts in a long-term cycle of exchange.

In chapter 4, I examine dozo rituals in further detail, focusing on a range of dozo sacrifices. Dozos performed seasonal sacrifices to protect themselves while hunting. The more I participated in such sacrifices, the more I noticed dozos' security-related concerns appearing beside their hunting-related preoccupations in these rituals. I infer that dozos perceived their police roles in the same sacrificial terms that defined their hunting roles.

Consequently, Manimory, to whom dozos dedicated their sacrifices, played a central role in all dozo preoccupations. Chapter 5 compares contrasting narratives about his life to account for his ability to assure dozos' well-being in the forest, Islam, and the state. His descent from Muslim prophets and his sacrifices and disappearance in the forest offered dozos a model for assimilating to areas where their opponents—whether game, their Muslim critics, criminals, or state officials—challenged their legitimacy or undermined their communities' safety.

Dozos' initiatory relationship to Manimory forged the common ties that structured Benkadi's national dozo network, which chapter 6 explores. As if following Manimory's example, dozos adapted themselves to the state's bureaucratic modus operandi as unofficial police. Through Benkadi, they created a parallel hierarchy of literate francophone organizers and organizations alongside their historically oral and Julakan- and Syenara-speaking networks, allying themselves with two major national bureaucratic organizations in the hopes of gaining official approval for Benkadi's activities.

Meanwhile, Benkadi security patrols drew as much on dozos' hunting habits as on their bureaucratic skills, as chapter 7 explains. Dozos called on the same sorcery and hunting strategies that they used to catch game in the forests to immobilize and capture criminals in cities and towns. Their methods sometimes led to extravagant violence, in contrast to the more peaceful means that Benkadi used as a whole, and in particular in Denguélé, where dozos organized trials and imposed fines for criminals after having acquired the tacit approval of local authorities to do so. Such approval contributed almost as much as the dozos to Benkadi's success.

Beyond dozos' collaborations with local officials, their praise-singers proved to be their most important interlocutors. Chapter 8 highlights these singers' performances at both dozo funerals and Benkadi meetings. Because Benkadi patrols required the same guns, sorcery, and stealth that dozos used while hunting, hunting songs also evoked the use of these skills against crime. Musicians voiced non-dozos' expectations of dozo protection and checked dozos' excessive arrogance as hunters or police by reminding them that their ultimate aim was to kill game in the forest.

Chapter 9 concludes this book by arguing that dozos' controversial attempts to confront crime in Côte d'Ivoire foreshadowed greater tensions to come. After the state outlawed Benkadi in southern Côte d'Ivoire in 1998, many dozos joined the 2002 rebellion that split the country in two along roughly the same line of demarcation that the state had used to curtail Benkadi's activities in 1998. Ironically, dozos's collaboration with the state resulted in conflict with it. But whether for or against the state, Benkadi revealed that ordinary people with extraordinary vision could reshape a nation by transforming themselves through ritual. I will begin their story by tracing Benkadi's origins to the political economy that characterized the colonial and postcolonial history of Côte d'Ivoire.

TWO

Criminal Instability: History, Identity, and Mimesis in a State of Exception

Imitation as Politics

Dozos' adopted their new police roles in the context of a broader historical transformation of the Ivoirian state. Since independence in 1960, Côte d'Ivoire had been a model of apparent economic and political stability. It had suffered no coups d'état, and its principle exports of cocoa and coffee had assured relative prosperity. By the 1990s, all this had changed. The country's founding president, Félix Houphouët-Boigny, was gravely ill, cocoa and coffee prices had fallen since the 1980s, multiparty democracy was revealing deep political cleavages among elites, and crime was rampant. Faced with these challenges, new president Henri Konan Bédié, who came to power immediately after Houphouët-Boigny's death, refounded the Ivoirian state on revisionist principles. He insinuated that his and Houphouët-Boigny's ethnic Baoulé leadership had its basis in the cultural geography of colonial Côte d'Ivoire. This retromimetic strategy—which tried to assure Bédié an invulnerability that antedated Houphouët-Boigny's—came with a double price. Because the state now lacked the economic resources to assure the public services it had formerly provided, it turned to help from nonstate agents even while projecting a renewed autonomy. Bédié also divided the country along ethnic and religious lines by rewriting Ivoirian law to support his implicit contention that southern Christians had greater legitimacy as Côte d'Ivoire's rulers because of their precolonial location in what became the focus of French agricultural production in Côte d'Ivoire.

This chapter explains how Bédié's new approach to power paved the way for Benkadi's rise and fall. Bédié mimicked Houphouët-Boigny's former authority by rewriting Ivoirian laws while Benkadi mimicked Ivoirian security agents. Both drew upon the same mimetic strategy to adapt to the withering of state power in the era of structural adjustment. Their mutual implication in the same global and national political and economic circumstances elicited parallel mimetic responses, complementary in their ends, divergent in their idioms.[1] Following Tsing (2005, 7–8, 267, 270), I consider such mimesis an "engaged universal,"[2] an ideology, prerogative, or strategy deployed simultaneously by state and nonstate agents—in this case, to appropriate the power of the state that Houphouët-Boigny had created.[3] The "awkward, unequal, unstable, and creative qualities of interconnection across difference," or "friction" (Tsing 2005, xi, 4–6), that framed the state's and Benkadi's respective uses of mimesis emerged within a shared political and cultural order.

Dozos and a State of Collapse

In the 1990s, Côte d'Ivoire, like other African states, underwent a post–Cold War transition to greater meddling by international institutions in its affairs, a situation that Mbembe (2001, 74) has called "fractionated sovereignty." This transition coincided with the state's retreat from "formal international markets," its "integration into circuits" of global crime, and the "emergence of multiple forms of *private indirect government*" (80, emphasis in original) in which nonstate authorities or state agents acting independently of the state performed functions that the state could no longer fulfill—often with the state's overt or tacit approval (67). In Côte d'Ivoire, as elsewhere, a "*direct link* [now existed] *between, on the one hand, deregulation and the primacy of the market and, on the other, the rise of violence and the creation of private military, paramilitary, or jurisdictional organizations*" (78–79, emphasis in original). Benkadi was a case in point.

Côte d'Ivoire had become particularly uncertain after Houphouët-Boigny's death. His loss triggered such a fierce struggle for succession among the country's elites that his constitutionally appointed successor, former president of the National Assembly Henri Konan Bédié, altered the Electoral and Nationality Codes to exclude his political rival, Alassane Ouattara, from running for president. Bédié tried to appropriate Houphouët-Boigny's former authority by creating an ersatz legitimacy for his regime premised on excessive legalism. This recourse to legality mirrored a "general preoccupation in the postcolonial world with 'the law' and the citizen as *legal* subject . . . a preoccupation growing in counterpoint to, and deeply entailed in, the rise of the felonious state, private indirect government" (Comaroff and Comaroff 2006, 20), and multiparty democracy (see Comaroff and Comaroff 2006, 2; Mbembe 2006, 309, 311). Crime rose, in turn, thanks to an increasingly underfunded, underequipped, and underpaid police force. Police turned to racketeering to offset poor salaries, and private security companies began protecting those who could pay for their services. Vigilante groups did the same for those who could not.

A volatile situation resulted from which emerged unexpected forms of organization and alliance (see Mbembe 2001, 77), in this case, between a segmenting state and the dozos' private security initiatives. As the state retracted in the face of economic stagnation and multipartyism, dozos concentrated their authority to take advantage of the state's retreat. Dozos and the state were imitating each other's organizational strengths, shifting between centralized and segmentary forms of organization (see Amselle 1998, 116) to adapt to the indeterminacies of global economics and national politics.

The logic of state atrophy across Africa was, as Mbembe (2001, 80) described it, as mimetic and ambiguous as the logic of dozo centralization:

> A formal budget is prepared, but it is executed and adhered to on purely contingent and informal criteria. There is a proliferation not of independent power centers but of more or less autonomous pockets in the heart of what was, until recently, a system . . . They form links in an unstable chain where parallel decisions coexist with centralized decisions, where everything and its opposite are possible. In this situation, proper procedures are frequently by-passed, rules chopped and changed, and then usually bent, and actions are structurally unpredictable—a combination of situations in which nothing gets done, and sudden, erratic, accelerated movements, unforeseen consequences, and paradoxical outcomes.

In this environment, officials represented the state while working beyond its laws, increasingly mirroring, albeit unintentionally, dozos' attempts to do the same.

What Amselle (1998, 116) observed about precolonial West Africa applied to the Ivoirian state and dozos in the postcolonial era: "We should see segmentary societies as the product of state societies and analyze the reproduction of the former as part of the latter . . . the state and the segmentary are merely two poles of the same hierarchized space." The state's neglect of crime and its neoliberal willingness to cede responsibility to nonstate actors (see Ferguson 2006, 205) made Benkadi as much the product of the state as its nemesis. My goal in this chapter is to uncover dozos' nearly century-long involvement with the state, from colonial to postcolonial times, to show that long before Benkadi, the destinies of dozos and the state were already intertwined.

Markets, Migrations, and Muslims

After World War I, France's minister of colonies Albert Sarraut reformed the French colonial administration to increase revenues from the colonies "to recharge a weakened France" after the war (Toungara 1980, 267). He reduced the autonomy of colonial administrators in favor of a more centralized approach to management. Previous policies had failed to make trade between France and its colonies profitable. Sarraut proposed a plan of "increased regional specialization" in agricultural production to solve the problem. "Cocoa was to be promoted in Ivory Coast, cotton in the Niger valley, and oil and timber in West and Central Africa" (268). Later, coffee and wood were added to cocoa as important Ivoirian exports.

The project became law in April 1921, but by the end of that year, a financial crisis robbed France of the money to initiate it (Toungara 1980, 268). Even with insufficient funds, officials from the governor general to local administrators pursued the plan as best they could by mobilizing "more forced labor, more intensive agriculture, and increased taxation" (268–269). Administrators all but coerced peasants to cultivate cash crops to pay colonial taxes, incorporating them into the asymmetric relationships of world market exchange. In return for cash crops and, to a lesser extent, "gathered produce," France offered peasants "imported 'trade goods'—such things as textiles, hardware and low-quality tools" (Suret-Canale 1988, 220; Toungara 1980, 267):

> Peasants and colonial agents exchanged their products at rural warehouses under demeaning conditions. There was a personal poll tax, payable in cash, which the producer had to find from the sale of his crops; and there were various forms of forced labour or compulsory cultivation, the sale price being fixed according to price lists established by administrative diktat" (Suret-Canale 1988, 220).

African peasants made little profit while "commercial establishments known as 'trading houses'" reaped fortunes. Colonial traders benefited "not because of the volume of their business but because of the size of their profit margins, their investment being minimal" (221).

In 1929, on the eve of the Great Depression, France tried again to increase its colonies' profitability. It based its "'Great Colonial Loan Acts'... upon the assumption that enough resources were now available in the [metropole] to finance African development . . . and that such development would provide the basis for further metropolitan growth." Under the plan, "loans and grants offered to African colonies . . . were designed to improve infrastructure (particularly transport) and thus to increase production of exports" (Austen 1987: 199), but the Depression eroded any potential profits. In the end, "the problems of the home economies far exceeded any relief which could come from contracts for colonial projects and the world demand for all African commodities (except gold) plummeted sharply" (199). In response, the French—like other Europeans—enforced protectionist trade policies with their colonies, and administrators channeled capital they had once directed toward infrastructures "to increase [African peasants'] commercial cultivation efforts" (203). Lacking the capital to expand infrastructure, France intensified preexisting policies of taxation, intimidation, and forced labor.

After World War II, France again faced the need for resources for postwar reconstruction. This time administrators intervened in the private sector (Antoine et al. 1987, 19). If the empire was to endure, France's colonies and their commercial agents had to produce more "efficiently" (Antoine et al. 1987, 19; Gbagbo 1982, 65, 66). To this end, governor André Latrille of Côte d'Ivoire tried from 1943 to 1945 and again from 1946 to 1947 to correct disparities in production between African- and French-run cash-crop plantations. Between 1944 and 1945, African-run plantations generated 95 percent of all cocoa production and 82.78 percent of all coffee production (Gbagbo 1982, 65–66). French-run plantations accounted for the rest.

Latrille decided that the colony's economic future lay in enhancing African rather than French production. In May 1945, under pressure from aspiring politicians like the young Félix Houphouët-Boigny and other members of the nascent African Agricultural Union (Syndicat Agricole Africain; Benot 1989, 43–44; Duprey 1962, 222–228), Latrille allowed African producers with two or more hectares of coffee or three or more hectares of cocoa to join the union, freeing them from forced labor (Duprey 1962, 226). Gradually Latrille began replacing forced with voluntary labor (Gbagbo 1982, 67). In 1945, he allocated a grant, first requested by white farmers at advantageous rates (Duprey 1962, 225), to all planters, whether black or white, at the same rates and without insisting on the original plantation surface requirement of 25 hectares. Latrille judged that "it [was] not logical to help" a minority of white "colonists alone by taking money from a [colonial] budget, 83% of which [was] supplied by" industrious African producers "excluded from this help" (Gbagbo 1982, 67–68).

Jean Rose, the leader of the French Chamber of Agriculture in Côte d'Ivoire, resisted Latrille's reforms. In late 1945, he managed to have Latrille removed from office on suspicion of being a communist (Duprey 1962, 227–228). But Latrille's successor, de Mauduit, undid Rose's hopes of rigging the election of an Ivoirian representative to France's new Constituent Assembly, proposed by Charles de Gaulle in Brazzaville in 1944 to give colonized peoples a voice in revising colonial policies in a French commonwealth. Houphouët-Boigny won Côte d'Ivoire's seat (Duprey 1962, 228–230). On April 5, 1946, due mostly to Houphouët-Boigny's efforts, the first Constituent Assembly abolished forced labor in the colonies (Benot 1989, 34, 53–54). After Latrille learned of the assembly's decision during his second appointment as governor from 1946–1947, he began encouraging voluntary labor migration from colonial Côte d'Ivoire's northern regions into the rich agricultural areas of the south to compensate for the loss of forced labor. His initiatives would have far-reaching consequences for Ivoirian demography, economics, and politics.

Latrille's Corridor

Latrille relied on the rail line leading from Bobo-Dioulasso in contemporary Burkina Faso to the coastal city of Abidjan in Côte d'Ivoire to facilitate migrants' southward movement. From 1932 to 1947—during which time future president Henri Konan Bédié and future prime minister Alassane Ouattara were born (in 1934 and 1942, respectively)—Burkina Faso was part of Côte d'Ivoire and known as "Upper," or *Haute*, Côte d'Ivoire (Amin 1973, 49).

Latrille, as governor of the entire colony, opened a workers' hostel in Bobo-Dioulasso to process southward-bound workers. To ensure their smooth reception in the south, he "created employment offices" in the populous, working-class Abidjan districts of Adjamé and Treichville to provide new arrivals access to public services (Gbagbo 1982, 68). In Abidjan and in the northern Ivoirian city of Ferkessédougou, the first major railway stop after Bobo-Dioulasso, Latrille "opened hostels, where workers were fed and lodged" (68), and he opened similar hostels in the cities of Agboville, Bouaké, and Dimbokro because of their proximity to the rail line, and in Daloa because of its proximity to Côte d'Ivoire's plantations in the western center of the country. For "manual laborers coming from Ouagadougou," Upper Côte d'Ivoire's other major city, "he put into circulation two trucks assuring free service between Ouagadougou and Bobo-Dioulasso" (68) to bring workers to Bobo's railroad station. "For workers coming from middle Côte d'Ivoire (the regions of Korhogo and Bouaké)," he provided free rail transportation and offered "special provisions of gasoline . . . to facilitate the transportation of workers by road" (68). His migratory corridor began in Côte d'Ivoire's uppermost reaches and ran southward along the rail line into "Lower," or *Basse*, Côte d'Ivoire. Here planters could find the workers they needed in hostels, and laborers could find jobs at employment offices.

Latrille's replacement of forced local laborers with voluntary migrant labor increased the number of workers on Ivorian plantations by 20 percent and Ivorian economic productivity as measured in total exports by 25.7 percent in 1946 and 11.81 percent in 1947 (Gbagbo 1982, 74, 75). After the construction of Abidjan's Vridi Canal from 1936 to 1950, which made Abidjan's port more accessible to the Atlantic, "the exported value of [cocoa, coffee, and wood] nearly tripled" (Bonnassieux 1987, 17). And by 1960, coffee, cocoa, and wood represented 50 percent, 23.3 percent, and 16.9 percent, respectively, of the total value of all exports (Antoine et al. 1987, 21). Between 1948 and 1956, administrators also improved roads to facilitate the flows of workers and agricultural produce within the interior of Côte d'Ivoire, especially along the "Cocoa Route" between Abidjan and Abengourou and along the "Coffee Route" between Abidjan and Gagnoa (Antoine et al. 1987, 19). Ironically, although Houphouët-Boigny's and Latrille's reforms led to political independence, they also assured the country's longtime vulnerability to world market fluctuations (Amin 1967; 1973, 59–60; Wallerstein 1964; Zartman and Delgado 1984).[4]

Jula in Côte d'Ivoire

Evidently, the agricultural prosperity of southern Côte d'Ivoire on which the country based its postindependence success depended on northern-originated labor from West Africa's savanna and Sahel regions (see A. Touré 1985, 16–17). Before independence, migration ran southward from the independently administered French colonies of Upper Volta

(Haute Volta, formerly Upper Côte d'Ivoire), Soudan (Mali), and Guinea. For centuries, these areas had lain in the sphere of Mandenkan and Gur speakers and Muslim cultural and political influence, linked together by trade routes plied by Muslim Mande merchants, called *jula* in northern Mande languages. Mandenkan-speaking groups residing in, around, and between the northern Ivoirian towns of Kong, the site of a precolonial polity (Mundt 1987, 58–59; Launay 1992, 50), Korhogo (Launay 1992, 51), Ferkessédougou, Katiola, Odienné, Mankono, Séguéla (see Launay 1982, 2–3), Bondoukou, and Touba used this same word to identify themselves in ethnic terms. In Côte d'Ivoire, the term *jula* has a long, complex history linked to colonialism, precolonial migration, and Islam.

Before colonialism, Mandenkan-speaking traders circulated across what is today northern Côte d'Ivoire, dominating long-distance commerce because of their linguistic and cultural links to the wider Mande world whose inhabitants had long managed trade networks linking the Sahara to the forests of southern Côte d'Ivoire (Launay 1992, 49, 53–56; Toungara 1980, 54–59).[5] Well before colonial migrations, Mandenkan-speaking Muslims had been coming southward into Ivoirian forests to conduct trade. Because they practiced Islam, they monopolized long-distance trade with "Muslims outside the region" (Launay 1992, 56). Odienné's founding Kamagaté clan, for example, arrived in Denguélé as part of the Mande trade diaspora at some point around 1760, expelling Odienné's indigenous, non-Muslim, Syenara-speaking inhabitants (O'Sullivan 1976, vi–vii) to establish a lasting political and economic presence in northwestern Côte d'Ivoire.

In the colonial era, French military campaigns extended the Jula presence southward. By the end of 1898, the French had defeated and captured Samory Touré, who had led his soldiers—dozos among them (Y. Cissé 1994, 28)—in conquests across Guinea, Mali, Burkina Faso, and northern Côte d'Ivoire (Person 1968). Between 1908 and 1916, Lieutenant Governor Angoulvant "pacified" the remaining resistance in Côte d'Ivoire's southern forests (Weiskel 1981). The results were surprising. "Instead of disturbing trade as so many French merchants had feared the pacification encouraged more frequent passage of traders . . . Instead of stopping at Minignan and Samatiguila [trading centers to the north of Odienné], traders continued [southward] on to Man, Daloa, Tiassale and beyond to purchase kola nuts" (Toungara 1980, 206). Even peasants turned to trade since it had become "less dangerous since the pacification, and more lucrative due to the establishment of markets by the French administration" (263). Some traders left Odienné and returned after short absences, while others "settled near [colonial administrative] posts and railroad stations, where they made important profits as intermediaries between European merchants and African consumers" because they traveled farther into the interior than Lebanese or European merchants (263). Their presence in Abidjan, Bondoukou, Bouaké, Dabakala, Daloa, Ferkessédougou, Gagnoa, Katiola, Man, Touba (263–264), and San-Pédro grew, creating a regional network of Jula settlements beyond their original northern enclaves well before independence.

After the declaration of Côte d'Ivoire as a French colony in 1893, young Odiennéka migrated farther south to "the new towns of the coastal areas" (Mundt 1987, 59) to find paid work to meet the demands of French taxation. "French requisitions of crops, men, and taxes" (Toungara 1980, 261) and the return of sick laborers from the south had weakened local production, compromised public health, lowered birth rates, increased mortality, and further increased youthful wanderlust. As a result, "many villages were almost deserted, practically void of life . . . Some relatives even begged young people to leave to seek work elsewhere to help supplement the family income" (261–262). Between 3,000 and 4,000 men were migrating annually to earn money in the southern forest zone in "public works, on plantations, and in nascent factories around Abidjan. After a prolonged absence, the family sent a wife to join the young man; and later, a younger brother joined him" (262). Jula migrants arrived and started families in the forest zone to meet the demand for labor, not only to pay taxes but to fulfill family obligations. The colonial experience taught generations of West Africans how to exploit state imperatives for the benefit of domestic projects while using domestic networks to adapt to state obligations.

By independence, Jula migrants had altered Ivoirian demographic patterns. The word *jula*, or *dioula* in French, now assumed numerous linguistic, ethnic, professional, and religious connotations beyond its original meaning of "trader," making the word "contextually defined" and "ambiguous" (Launay 1992, 59):

> One could . . . be identified as "Dyula" [Jula], not only in Korhogo [and throughout northern Côte d'Ivoire], but also in the new and fast-growing communities in the south of Côte d'Ivoire, where many Dyula from Korhogo had emigrated during the first half of the twentieth century. In the south, all Manding-speaking Muslim immigrants were known as "Dyula," whether they were from Guinea, Mali, or Upper Volta [Burkina Faso]. In short, the "Dyula" were a highly heterogeneous community of "outsiders" linked by a common language and a common religion. (Launay 1992, 65)

Because these migrants spoke Mandenkan, either as a mother tongue or lingua franca, and because they occupied similar positions in the colonial economy, southerners began to refer to them all as "Jula." Suddenly, Islam and Mandenkan became salient markers of identity, overwhelming formerly pronounced cultural, linguistic, and regional differences. "Jula" now meant those northern-descended Muslims from within and beyond the Ivoirian colony—and later state—who had come south for economic reasons. Migrants and immigrants—including many dozos—came south as farmers and laborers, assuming new roles, forging new ethnic identities (Dozon 1987), and settling in new areas in response to the state's dictates. After independence, they remained in the south, albeit on increasingly contested grounds.

"Unity, Discipline, Work"[6]

After independence in 1960, President Houphouët-Boigny hoped to sustain the economic niche that northern migrants had occupied before independence, given their substantial contribution to Côte d'Ivoire's "economic miracle," *le miracle ivoirien*. From 1963 to 1965, he proposed granting dual nationality to all immigrants residing in Côte d'Ivoire (Amondji 1984, 310–311). Opposition in the National Assembly defeated the proposal, but by 1965, non-Ivoirian Africans "represented ¼ of the total population; 35 to 40% of active masculine manual laborers; half of the manual laborers in urban zones, where they occupied 60% of urban jobs outside of government; [and] ½ to ⅔ of rural manual labor on plantations" (309). The economic capital of Abidjan reflected these shifts. "In 1978, one could count only 35% of Abidjan's population as native to the city, of which the majority were children; in the 15 to 59 year age groups, only one individual out of every 10 had been born in Abidjan," and "more than 38 percent of the [city's] inhabitants . . . [were] not Ivoirian" (Antoine et al. 1987, 11). The "flow of foreigners to Ivory Coast [was] not only one of the [Ivoirian] 'miracle's' consequences, it was one of its pre-conditions" (309).

In 1975, Burkinabes comprised the majority of these laborers.[7] Malians and Guineans formed the second- and third-largest migrant populations, respectively (A. Touré 1985, 16). Throughout the 1990s and into 2001, these rankings remained unchanged (Institut National de la Statistique 1996, 41, 43; Fall et al. 2001, 9). Northern Mandekan- and Gur-speaking areas of West Africa contributed Côte d'Ivoire's largest immigrant populations. Even within Côte d'Ivoire, the largest number of labor migrants came from the north (Institut National de la Statistique 1996, 43).

Houphouët-Boigny welcomed them all as long as they were willing to work. "Work will be voluntary," he declared, but "there will be no place for lazy people or parasites in Côte d'Ivoire" (Amondji 1984, 278). Henceforth, he ruled, all the nation's resources escaped the "obligations of customary law and private privileges." They now served the state and its development goals. He asserted the state's right of eminent domain over all "the riches above and below our soil not yet appropriated and which, because of this, can be profitably used for the good of the nation and for those exploiting them" (279). Labor for the nation's welfare, and agricultural labor in particular, became a means by which Ivoirians and non-Ivoirians could claim residency if not citizenship in southern Côte d'Ivoire. As a result, Côte d'Ivoire overtook Ghana in the 1970s as the world's largest cocoa producer. In 1977, cocoa prices soared (Economist Intelligence Unit 1989, 66). Prices for coffee had climbed the previous year (Gbagbo 1991, 93).

Côte d'Ivoire capitalized on its lucrative cocoa harvests through its "Stabilization Fund" (*Caisse de stabilisation*), a state-run commodity price regulating agency. When Côte d'Ivoire sold cocoa on the world market, the fund paid cocoa producers world market price for their crops. When that price surpassed the fund's "reference export price," producers made up the difference with a "compensatory payment" to the fund. Such payments provided the state a source of revenue when world prices swelled. When prices fell below the reference price, the fund lost money to producers, paying them the difference between the world market and reference prices (United Nations Conference on Trade and Development 1991, 20–21).

From 1976 to 1977, commodity rallies inspired hopes that Côte d'Ivoire would emerge as an economic success story (Gbagbo 1991, 93). They also marked the last time for the next decade and a half that the state would accumulate more revenue and provide more subsidies than it spent (88–89). From the late 1970s to the early 1990s, Côte d'Ivoire's economy followed the downward spiral of cocoa and coffee. Even then, when world cocoa prices fell by almost 50 percent in 1978, cocoa cultivation remained relatively profitable. Houphouët-Boigny continued to stake his country's future on agriculture.[8] Ivoirian farmers intensified production and expanded areas under cultivation until 1986 (Economist Intelligence Unit 1989, 1, 67).

But in the 1980s, world cocoa prices kept falling due to overproduction

(Economist Intelligence Unit 1989, 1). Cocoa and coffee sales increased mildly from 1977 to 1983, but so did real losses. The consequences reverberated into the 1990s, "provoking a cascade of chain reactions" that diminished the quality of Ivoirian life in all sectors by all indicators (Antoine et al. 1987, 39):

> Living standards fell almost continuously from 1978 to 1993, eroding average per capita incomes on average by 45%. The burden . . . cut across all groups—indigenous Ivoirians, non-indigenous Ivoirians and migrants, urban and rural, middle class and poor . . . They include[d] falling real incomes and personal consumption, deteriorating public services and a lack of opportunity for young people starting their working lives. (World Bank 1996, 1)

By 1990, the miracle had tarnished. Côte d'Ivoire's economic crisis would soon provoke a political one.

On April 30, 1990 (Koudou 2005, 40), on the heels of François Mitterrand's call in La Baule, France, for multiparty democracy across Africa, Houphouët-Boigny approved the formation of new political parties apart from his own Democratic Party of Côte d'Ivoire (Parti démocratique de Côte d'Ivoire [PDCI]; Akindès 2004, 19; Zolberg 1964, 81–146).[9] That same year, Houphouët-Boigny appointed Alassane Ouattara, a Julakan-speaking Muslim, as prime minister.

Once in office, Ouattara began implementing the World Bank's structural adjustment policies (Campbell 1995; Ridler 1993), privatizing state industries, reducing transportation subsidies for students, lowering new teachers' salaries,[10] and requiring immigrants to purchase residency cards (*cartes de séjour*) to remain and work in the country.[11] Following the presidential elections of 1990, which Laurent Gbagbo lost to Houphouët-Boigny, Gbagbo channeled popular dissatisfaction with Ouattara's policies into massive demonstrations led by his new party, the Ivoirian Popular Front (*Front Populaire Ivoirien* [FPI]).

If Ouattara gave voice to a growing Ivoirian xenophobia by implementing residency cards, then Gbagbo further articulated it. During the protests, he demanded an end to international interference in the economy, called for abrogating the right to vote to foreigners who had had the privilege until then (Dozon 2000, 49; see Crook 1997, 222–223), and accused Ouattara of being a Burkinabe (Zoro-Bi 2004, 47–49). Ouattara repressed the demonstrations. In "February 1992 virtually the whole FPI leadership was arrested and jailed on the basis of a thoroughly illiberal law, hastily passed by the Ouattara government, which made the organizers of demonstrations liable for anything that happened during the demonstration" (Crook 1997, 223–224; see Koudou 2005, 41, 47–48). Violence and the reckless manipulation of Ivoirian law in a time of economic crisis threatened to undermine Côte d'Ivoire's transition to multiparty democracy from the start.

Houphouët-Boigny, Bédié, and Ouattara

On the morning of Tuesday, December 7, 1993, Radio France Internationale announced on its second FM broadcasting day in Abidjan that Félix Houphouët-Boigny, long ill, had died at approximately 6:30 a.m. GMT that morning, on the thirty-third anniversary of Ivoirian independence.[12] He died in Yamoussoukro, his native village (*Fraternité Matin* 1993b, 1). But from May 14, 1993, up until just before his death, he had been absent from the country, residing at the Hôpital Cochin in Paris (I. Cissé 2007, 41, 50). Prime Minister Ouattara had ruled constitutionally in his absence, but the constitution counted the president of the National Assembly, Henri Konan Bédié, as Houphouët's successor. Already before Houphouët's death, France was urging Ouattara to submit to a "constitutional" succession and await the next elections to run for president (Soudan 1993, 15; Limam 1993, 20). Houphouët died amid this uncertainty. Bédié and Ouattara learned of his death within fifteen minutes (Placca 1994, 17). They arrived at the presidential palace in Abidjan for Bédié's summary inauguration, which ended with a cold handshake between the two (Placca 1994, 17).

Later that day, following a meeting of Ouattara's government from 5:00 to 6:00 p.m., communications minister Auguste Miremont cited a constitutional precedent that called on the Supreme Court "to make an official declaration of a vacancy in the executive office" before the new president could properly assume power. Ivoirian Radio and Television (Radio et Télévision Ivoirienne [RTI]) ran the announcement at 6:00 p.m. (Placca 1994, 19). That same day, Ouattara announced the appropriate steps for a constitutional succession in a letter to the Supreme Court's president: "Conforming to the dispositions of article 11 of the constitution and article 20 of law no. 78–663 of August 5, 1978, concerning the organization of the Supreme Court, I have the honor of submitting to your jurisdiction the responsibility of certifying the vacancy of the office of president of the republic."[13] Because the constitution provided that no succession could occur until after the Supreme Court had officially recognized the previous president's inability to hold office (Limam 1993, 18–20),[14] Ouattara was implying that Bédié had perpetrated a nonviolent coup d'état.

At the time, only five out of eight Supreme Court judges were seated on the bench. Three judges had departed, and their seats had yet to be filled—among them, the president of the court, its "chief justice" (Limam 1993, 18). Ouattara was trying to use the impasse to challenge the validity of Bédié's inauguration. Because "the certification of a vacancy could take a certain [amount of] time—just enough, for example, to create confusion to block the system . . . the prime minister could, in the name of the common good, resolve to pursue the mission with which Félix Houphouët-Boigny had [already] entrusted to him" (Placca 1994, 18). For over two hundred days before Houphouët's death was announced, Ouattara had held executive power according to article 24 of the constitution. The article stipulated that the president could delegate certain of his powers to the prime minister and that the "prime minister stands in for the president of the republic when the president is absent from the national territory" (Aggrey 1995a, 13)—in a European hospital, in this case. But once the president died, the legitimacy of Ouattara's executive power came into question. Because the Supreme Court could do nothing to resolve the matter—neither Houphouët-Boigny nor Ouattara had appointed new justices—the situation's complications proved so intractable that the only solution was an improvised one.

On December 7, Ouattara stationed members of the national police at the RTI station in Abidjan to prevent Bédié from entering the studios. He assigned a journalist loyal to him to read the 8:00 p.m. news. Shortly after the news began, Bédié and thirty red beret gendarmes entered the station. They met no resistance. A journalist described the scene that followed:

> The anchorman, dressed in mourning, is calmly finishing the day's headlines when the one who already considers himself president of the republic arrives on stage and sits down next to the anchorman.
>
> Someone slips the anchorman three messages of condolence addressed to Henri Konan Bédié, chief of state. [The anchorman] stumbles a bit, quite a bit in fact, in announcing his surprise guest's appearance: "The president of the Assem–, the president of the Repu–, President Henri Konan Bédié speaks to you." (Placca 1994, 18)

Bédié then read the following statement:

> The constitution, our supreme law, confers on me, in this dramatic situation, responsibilities that weigh heavily upon me, responsibilities of a chief of state. I will assume

them in line with their inspiration [Félix Houphouët-Boigny], and the country shall be governed . . . for all—Ivoirians and foreigners living on our soil.

To this end, I ask everyone to place themselves at my disposition. In sadness and mourning, in affection and in remembrance, may Côte d'Ivoire come together in unity. That is what I ask of her today in the name of our dear and illustrious deceased. (*Fraternité Matin* 1993c, 32)

Then, as if to rebuke Bédié for his immediate assumption of presidential power, someone at the station aired the minister of communication's earlier announcement (Placca 1994, 19). Bédié's camp riposted by ordering the station to run a report of Bédié's visit that day to the private residence of the papal nuncio to meet with the ambassadors of France, Great Britain, and the United States to receive their condolences for Houphouët-Boigny's death and congratulations for his inauguration (19). The fact that Bédié's succession occurred beyond the constitution's purview seemed a minor concern.

On the afternoon of the next day, Wednesday, December 8, Ouattara's advisors met in Abidjan's affluent Cocody district to consider the possibility of calling Ouattara's supporters into the streets of Côte d'Ivoire's northern towns to demonstrate in his favor. One influential advisor assured Ouattara that he could count on the national support of Jula bus company owners "because, when all is said and done, this coup d'état will have ended with the ousting of one of their own" (Placca 1994, 19).[15] But after Ouattara met with members of the military, he began receiving resignations from members of his cabinet before resigning by communiqué. He arrived at Bédié's home in Cocody in shirtsleeves and in a small car to conclude matters. He insisted the media not be present. The meeting lasted only a few minutes.[16] Just after noon on December 9, Albert Aggrey, secretary general of the Ivoirian government, announced the government's collective resignation in the presence of the prime minister at his office in Abidjan's Plateau district (Doualy 1993, 3).[17]

Further ethnic repercussions soon followed. "After 1994, after Ouattara left, all [Muslim] northerners lost important jobs," noted Ivoirian sociologist Abdou Touré. "I was fired from UNESCO, Ali Coulibaly was fired as the main television broadcaster, General Abdoulaye Coulibaly was fired as air force commander. We were replaced by Baoules," members of Houphouët-Boigny and Bédié's ethnic group.[18] Generals Robert Guéï and Lansana Palenfo were also fired (Keiffer 2000, 36; Langer 2004, 27).[19]

In October 1994, Ouattara's supporters formed a new opposition party, the Rally of Republicans (Rassemblement des Républicains [RDR];

Crook 1997, 225). They proposed Ouattara as their candidate for the 1995 presidential elections. Although the party declared no particular ethnic affiliation—their founders' origins cut across Ivoirian ethnicities (226–227)[20]—the majority of its supporters were Jula- and Gur-speaking Muslims of northern descent.

Writing Ivoirianness

The Bédié regime responded to the RDR's emerging opposition by revising Côte d'Ivoire's nationality and electoral codes to bar Ouattara from running for president, reinforcing the perception that political alliances and rivalries coincided with ethnic, regional, and religious ones. According to article 6 of the new nationality code, "Is Ivoirian: 1—the legitimate or legitimated child, born in Ivory Coast, except if her or his two parents are foreigners" (Aggrey 1995b, 5). By these criteria, Ouattara, the legitimate child of a mother from the Denguélé village of Gbéléban, qualified as Ivoirian.[21] But Bédié accused Ouattara of having a Burkinabe father (I. Cissé 2007, 57–58). And article 48 of the nationality code also stated, "Loses Ivorian nationality, the adult Ivoirian who voluntarily acquires a foreign nationality, or who declares recognition of such a nationality." The Bédié regime claimed that Ouattara, although born in Côte d'Ivoire in 1942, had assumed Voltaic (Burkinabe) nationality to pursue his education in economics in the United States and to work in the Central Bank of West African States (Banque Centrale des États d'Afrique de l'Ouest [BCEAO]; Zoro-Bi 2004, 52–53; International Monetary Fund n.d.). By this logic, Ouattara had abjured his Ivoirian citizenship. He could have reclaimed it, according to the new code, if he had taken steps much earlier. "During a period of fifteen years," the code stated, "beginning at registration on the census charts, the loss is subordinate to the authorization of the government by decree made by report of the chancellor, minister of justice, on the recommendation of the minister of public health and the minister of national defense" (Aggrey 1995b, 11). That fifteen-year period had elapsed. Ouattara's time had run out.

The coup de grâce came in the new electoral code:

> The presidential candidate must be Ivoirian by birth, born of a father and a mother themselves Ivoirian by birth. The candidate must never have renounced his Ivoirian nationality . . . The candidate for election as president of the republic must reside in Côte d'Ivoire. This residency must have been continuous during the five years preceding the election. This last condition is not required of those nationals chosen by the

State of Côte d'Ivoire to serve in international or multinational organizations. (Aggrey 1995c, 6)

The electoral code disqualified Ouattara as a presidential candidate on three grounds. First, although Ouattara was an Ivorian citizen in the minimal sense of having one legitimate parent of Ivoirian nationality, he needed two such parents to be a presidential candidate, each of whom in turn had to have had at least one parent of Ivoirian nationality. Given his and his parents' birth under French colonial rule, this appeared to be impossible since, at the time, Côte d'Ivoire lacked political sovereignty and "Ivoirians" lacked citizenship of any sort, being pure "subjects" (see Mamdani 1996). Second, Ouattara had at one point held a Voltaic diplomatic passport. From this, the Bédié regime inferred that Ouattara had accepted Burkinabe citizenship, implying a renunciation of Ivoirian nationality.[22] Third, presidential candidates needed to live continuously in Côte d'Ivoire for five years prior to elections unless representing Côte d'Ivoire's national interests in an international or multinational organization. Ouattara violated these criteria because he had worked in a personal capacity as deputy managing director at the International Monetary Fund from 1994 until 1999 (International Monetary Fund n.d.).

Bédié's new nationality and electoral codes raised personal recriminations to the level of legal precedent, just as Ouattara had done in imprisoning Laurent Gbagbo and attempting to bar Bédié's succession. But Bédié's changes required additional post facto rationalization to disguise their arbitrariness. Increasingly, the Ivorian state was becoming a "state of exception" (Agamben 1998, 15; 2005, 50–51; Benjamin 1968, 257) in which Bédié simultaneously affirmed and abrogated the validity of the juridical order he ostensibly upheld.[23] Neither Houphouët-Boigny nor Bédié ever suspended the constitution, but they never needed to do so.[24] Houphouët-Boigny had enforced revisions to Côte d'Ivoire's 1958 and 1960 constitutions so that they favored the executive (Zolberg 1964, 255–268),[25] and Bédié now ruled beyond the purview of state law, given the strictly unconstitutional way in which he came to power.

He handily won the 1995 presidential elections, which the RDR and FPI boycotted together and in which dozos played an unexpected role. In the north central city of Korhogo, dozo organizer and businessman Édouard Coulibaly turned a September 1995 dozo meeting into a pro-Bédié rally. It was rumored that he "had received a large sum of money from the PDCI to support Bédié's candidacy" (Bassett 2004, 39). The Bédié regime also recruited northern dozos to guard polling places from opposition protestors on election day. In the town of M'Bengué, they "shot one dead

5 Ethnolinguistic map of Côte d'Ivoire, by Andrés Ruiz, based on a map in *Jeune Afrique l'Intelligent* (2189–2190), 22 December–4 January, 41, used with permission of Groupe Jeune Afrique.

and wounded two" (39). Benkadi made its first appearance as a political militia at the request of the PDCI, not the RDR.

Then, in 1996, a little over a year later, Bédié abandoned his strategy of northern accommodation in favor of an antinorthern form of revisionist history known as *ivoirité*, or "Ivoirianness." Prominent Ivoirian intellectuals supportive of the new regime championed the ideology to help justify Bédié's changes to Ivoirian laws. They traced the birth of Côte d'Ivoire as a nation to its establishment as a colony by France in 1893 (Niangoran-Bouah 1996, 46–47),[26] attributing an idealized stability to its population.

By the late nineteenth century, they claimed, proto-Ivoirians had settled the Ivoirian region into five culturally distinct areas: Akan in the southeast and center, Krou in the western center and southwest, southern Mande in the west, northern Mande in the northwest and central north, and Gur across the north and northeast (Adiaffi 1996, 68; Niangoran-Bouah 1996, 48–49; see fig. 5). These ethnic enclaves supposedly served as lasting geographical references by which to arbitrate claims of regional autochthony, national citizenship, and immigrant status (Bombet 1996, 139–141; Loucou 1996, 20–21; Niangoran-Bouah 1996, 48–51). In contrast, proponents of *ivoirité* classed Burkinabe, Malian, and Guinean immigrants and northern Ivoirian migrants as outsiders in southern Côte d'Ivoire who upset the nation's ethnopolitical order. These same authors ignored that migrants had been moving southward from the Sahel and from northern Côte d'Ivoire since before independence and that their southern presence contributed to national prosperity.

Meanwhile, disputes over land tenure were arising between northern-descended immigrants and migrants and those southerners from whom they had rented and in some cases been given land. Such arguments increasingly led to conflict (Toungara 2001, 67–68; Woods 2003). Houphouët-Boigny's dream of a peaceful, prosperous, Akan-dominated, multiethnic republic could not withstand the successive assaults of xenophobic anti-immigrant sentiment and the ethnicization of politics.

Crime Stories from Côte d'Ivoire: Banditry, Ethnicity, and Police

Accompanying the rise in political acrimony in Côte d'Ivoire was a simultaneous increase in crime in response to the country's growing economic woes.

In February 1994, France devalued the franc CFA, the common currency of its former West African colonies. Overnight, the fixed exchange rate of fifty francs CFA per French franc fell to one hundred. France argued that the change would stimulate Ivoirian exports and generate economic growth. But although commodity exporters subsequently saw increased profits, "the rise in per capita incomes was too small to yield generalized improvements in living standards" (World Bank 1996, 2). The result was greater poverty.

Growing regional instability, along with increasing poverty, stimulated crime. In 1987, after the assassination of Burkina Faso's president

Thomas Sankara, armed supporters of his fled to Côte d'Ivoire (Brunie n.d.a, ii–iii), bringing their arms with them.[27] Civil war broke out subsequently in Sierra Leone and Liberia, encouraging arms movements across the Ivoirian border in increasing numbers through illegal trade.[28] The surge in arms coincided disastrously with diminishing educational (Gnonsoa 1991) and economic opportunities (B. K. 1994; F. N. 1995) in Côte d'Ivoire.

After the devaluation, new venues for illicit financial gain proliferated. Trafficking in stolen car and moped parts and related items grew exponentially along with the rise in prices for cars and other imports due to the weakened CFA franc (B. K. 1994; Badié 1994). An intensified drug trade across Côte d'Ivoire, Ghana, and Nigeria simultaneously spawned addicts compelled sometimes to satisfy cravings through crime (*Fraternité Matin* 1991; Akrou 1991; L. Kouassi 1991a, 1991b; Barry 1992; Kam 1992; S. Koné 1993). Haphazard urban expansion, continued urban migration and immigration (Moussa 1992; *Fraternité Matin* 1993a), delinquency, the education system's failure to retain students (Gnonsoa 1991), and unemployment (F. N. 1995) all added to the growing list of circumstances contributing to heightened insecurity. From 1991 to 1994, crime and banditry rose 36 percent in Côte d'Ivoire, notably in Abidjan (*Jeune Afrique*, 13–19 April 1995) as growing numbers of youths, in their early teens and up through their thirties, turned to crime to make a way for themselves (Y. I. 1994; F. Ibo 1995; Lébry 1995; Vauguy 1995).

Bandits working unchecked on Côte d'Ivoire's highways brought the issue of crime to national attention, laying bare the state's inability to solve the problem due to political distractions and financial difficulties. Ivoirians called these bandits "road cutters" (*coupeurs de route*) because they "cut" or blocked roads with logs, rocks, tires, or other detritus and then waited, guns in hand, to ambush vehicles and their passengers (L. Kouassi 1993d). No other crime so captured national attention or challenged the mettle of state security forces, for Ivoirians valued their mobility given their long history of migration. Northern cotton, peanuts, and cashews, central and southern cocoa and coffee, and timber from throughout the country moved over Côte d'Ivoire's highways to ports in San-Pédro and Abidjan. One needed only to visit the bus stations in Abidjan's Adjamé district to observe the constant flow of bus, van, and car traffic that linked Abidjan to the Ivoirian interior and beyond, day in, day out, all year long. Every urban area had its own bus station(s), and road cutters left no region untouched (Hégaud 1994; N'Guessan 1994; Diaby 1994). They operated across the country, in the center (Kakapé 1994; N'Guessan 1994), western center (F. Bamba 1994; W. Kouamé 1994), north (L. Kouassi 1993d; Assi 1997; N'Guessan 1994; Diaby 1994; *La Voie* 1995b), northeast (*Fraternité Matin* 1994b), northwest (*Fraternité Matin* 1994a), and west (N'Guessan 1994).

Journalist Lobo Kouassi (Kouassi 1994b) described the road cutters' work:

> With some variation, the scenario . . . is always the same. Attacks occur at night between 8:00 p.m. and 5:00 a.m. . . . the barricades are placed at the summit of a hill or end of a turn, about ten kilometers from the nearest populated area. As soon as the vehicle is forced to stop, crooks in hoods emerge from the underbrush, flashlights on, weapons in hand.
>
> . . . their strategy, always the same, consists of ordering the driver at gunpoint to turn off the motor and give them the keys . . . [They] systematically search the passengers: money, watches, necklaces, jewels, packages and other merchandise are collected . . .
>
> And woe to those with nothing to offer. They strip them naked like worms and cruelly abuse them. Their crime complete, they disappear with one of the [commandeered] vehicles, which they abandon farther on . . .
>
> . . . The victims are usually left with wounds from bullets or restraining devices when the bandits fail to slaughter them on the spot . . .

Highwaymen also killed police, gendarmes, or other security agents who tried to stop their robberies or whom bandits ambushed at checkpoints (Kambiré 1994; *Fraternité Matin* 1994a).[29]

Journalists and authorities attributed such attacks to foreign, unsalaried Fulbe pastoralists who came to Côte d'Ivoire from Burkina Faso, Guinea, or Mali with their cattle, attracted by its richer vegetation and greater wealth (L. Kouassi 1993d, 1994c). In northern Côte d'Ivoire, these herders provided a valuable service by caring for the cattle of Senufo and Jula agriculturalists. In 1993, however, a former prefect of Korhogo, Issa Diakité, suggested publicly that a Fulbe herder might compensate for a lack of cash by "stealing the livestock he oversees, pillaging harvests and, finally, by raising barricades along roadways to strip travelers of their goods" (L. Kouassi 1994a). By the early 1990s, the dominant image of the highwayman in Côte d'Ivoire had become that of a northern foreigner, a Fulbe pastoralist (Lébry 1996), reflecting a confluence of economic, ethnic, and political fears. Lobo Kouassi (1994c) was among the few journalists who noted the participation of Ivoirians in such crimes. The Ivoirian north, increasingly othered as "foreign," was developing a criminal reputation.

In fact, violent crime was present throughout the country. Journalists wrote of a generalized "psychosis" (*Fraternité Matin* 1994b; Agence Ivoirienne de Presse 1995) and "permanent fear" (Diomandé 1991) of crime. Houphouët-Boigny had given security forces permission to shoot bandits on sight, and newspapers printed the names and photos of criminal suspects, dead or alive (L. Kouassi 1993e; Akpo Kouassi 1994). The majority of those so identified appear to have been of Burkinabe nationality, reinforcing perceived overlaps between northern, immigrant, and criminal identities. Ivoirians, as well as Ghanaians and Guineans, also made notable appearances in such newspaper reports (L. Kouassi 1994c). But given northerners' visibility and their disproportionate numbers among the Ivoirian migrant and immigrant population, southern Ivoirians began to consider revisions to immigration laws as an effective way to control crime (Moussa 1992).

The press and public also noted the inefficiency of Ivoirian security forces as a contributing factor to rising crime (*Fraternité Matin* 1993a; Assi 1994; N'Guessan 1994; Dacha 1994; B. K. 1994; Deh 1995; D. S. 1995). Journalists overtly accused Ivoirian police and gendarmes of failing to protect the public (Dacha 1994; Bobissi 1995). One described embattled Ivoirian security forces as an "embarrassment" (Diaby 1994). Another recounted how bandits had succeeded in tying up two policemen at a suburban Abidjan police headquarters while absent officers were likely extorting money from taxi and *gbaka* drivers at a nearby police checkpoint (Gbizihi 1994).[30] The incident confirmed the public's impression that security forces operated on the edges of legality, like the criminals they supposedly pursued.

On one trip I took by *dyna* from Odienné to Duékoué, a distance of about 400 kilometers, the vehicle crossed numerous police checkpoints. We left Odienné at 9:45 a.m. By 2:00 p.m., the following had happened: Security and customs officials had fined one man 5,000 francs CFA for transporting cloth from Guinea that he was to use as an engagement gift. Two people without proper identification paid agents 1,000 francs to be allowed to continue their trip, and the *dyna* driver reported paying 2,500 francs to various gendarmes, 1,000 to various police, 500 to customs agents, and another 1,000 to other miscellaneous authorities at each stop.[31] In no case, to my knowledge, did any agent make an official report of any violation for which the driver or passengers might have been fined. Such events were typical occurrences on Ivoirian bus trips.

French consultant Raymond Courchamp (1994) concluded that police corruption and inefficiency, in addition to incidents of arbitrary violence by police, had eroded their credibility as a security force. Everywhere in

Côte d'Ivoire, from the prime minister's office to the presidential palace to the street, the rule of law was receding (see Agamben 2005, 30–31).

Police and gendarmes argued in their defense that the state withheld the funds, equipment, and personnel necessary to combat crime (Abiali 1994; B. K. 1994; Badié 1994; F. Ibo 1995; Kohon 1995; Nawayou 1995; W. Kouamé 1995; *La Voie* 1995b). In 1996, Ivoirian minister of security Marcel Dibonan Koné tried to redress these grievances. He promised to increase pay, end racketeering, fix broken equipment, and purchase new supplies (L. Kouassi 1996c, 3). Most famously, he supplied police with bicycles to patrol neighborhood streets. But by 1997, ammunition, handcuffs, patrol cars, and two-way radios were still lacking in many stations, and officers were still extracting bribes from drivers at checkpoints (Kikié 1997, 12; Sangho 1997, 2).

Journalists took up the image of the bicycle (Assi 1994, 1; d'Almeida 1995, 10; Koffi 1997, 5) as a symbol of state ineptitude. One reporter questioned whether Minister Koné could make Côte d'Ivoire's third-largest city, Daloa, more secure:

> From one station to the next, it's the same old song: police cars are unusable because of the difficulty of getting spare parts when [the cars] break down . . . We know that when it comes to security . . . a regular police presence makes an impression on the criminal mind, and police patrols reassure the population. As for police in Daloa, their own private cars are their only means of transportation apart from a few recently delivered bicycles . . . Although they hesitated and grumbled at first, the police finally mounted their new vehicles. But . . . these are not the means of transportation [best suited] for staging successful dragnets. (Banto 1997, 4)

Bandits were taking advantage of police immobility by preying on cross-country travelers. Minister Koné was responding with too little too late.

Security forces made the best they could of the situation. They encouraged citizens to report crimes (Moussa 1992; Abiali 1992) and accustomed themselves to working alongside private security firms (*sociétés de gardiennage*) whose uniformed, baton-carrying agents had become a habitual presence near banks, stores, offices, and markets in Côte d'Ivoire's largest cities (*Le Jour* 1995),[32] although their presence did not always deter crime (D. S. 1995). Police and local officials also tolerated neighborhood vigilante patrols (*comités de surveillance*; Gooré-Bi 1993; Kohon 1995), whose requests for official recognition had gone unanswered by officials at the Ministry of Security since 1985 (N'Guessan, Zouzou, and Yoboué 1992). Journalists noted the illegality of such patrols (Akpo Kouassi 1994) but saw their rise as inevitable (Kwamkan 1991). As early as late 1983, at least one group of young men was patrolling Abidjan's Abobo district with whistles, clubs, and fists as weapons (N'Guessan et al. 1992). It was not long before the state's abdication of its security responsibilities opened the way for dozos to act.

Hunters and Police in a State of Exception

Benkadi came to prominence by fighting banditry in northern Côte d'Ivoire. Here bandits made their initial appearance along the paved two-lane highways that linked the northern cities of Ferkessédougou and Korhogo to Abidjan via Bouaké (L. Kouassi 1993d; Kambiré 1994; L. Kouassi 1994a; Diaby 1994; *La Voie* 1995a). In 1992, authorities reported thirteen highway robberies in the Korhogo region alone (L. Kouassi 1993d). After dozos in the area began cooperating with authorities to stop these crimes, dozos across the country set up checkpoints similar to those manned by police to monitor the roads that eluded police oversight (Hégaud 1994; L. Kouassi 1994a, 1994c).

This partnership between dozos and police reflected the desperation and negligence of a state whose new leaders lacked the means and interest to provide public security and consolidate power at the same time. Dozos capitalized on the opportunity. They assumed a national presence, drawing on cross-country links long established through patterns of labor migration and immigration and cemented through the ritual ties of shared initiation.

By assuming police roles to fight crime, dozos followed a mimetic strategy analogous to that pursued by the Bédié regime. So deeply had Houphouët-Boigny imbued Côte d'Ivoire with his identity and so intimately had Ivoirians identified with it,[33] that Bédié faced a daunting task in establishing his authority independent of Houphouët-Boigny's and beyond the reach of Alassane Ouattara. *Ivoirité* vitiated these problems by historicizing and writing into national laws the continuity between colonial and independent Côte d'Ivoire that Houphouët-Boigny had personified. Benkadi dozos similarly appropriated the prerogatives of state police to legitimize themselves as security agents just as the state was starting to discriminate against northern-descended Muslims.

While alive, Houphouët had been the architect, incarnation, and guarantor of Ivoirian sovereignty (Vogel 1991). Bédié now had to suffer the indignity of France's devaluation of the CFA franc—over which he had no control—and which France would never have attempted during Houphouët-Boigny's lifetime. *Ivoirité* offered Bédié a transhistorical legitimacy that harkened beyond Houphouët-Boigny's person and Côte d'Ivoire's now humiliating dependence on France to a precolonial precedent. *Ivoirité* posited that Côte d'Ivoire's regional ethnic order, which Bédié claimed to guarantee and defend, had crystallized before France's colonial arrival and Houphouët-Boigny's birth. Bédié premised his legitimacy on this order. Whereas Houphouët-Boigny had assured Ivoirian stability with constitutional law as a supplement, Bédié made legality—or its simulacrum (Comaroff and Comaroff 2006, 35)—the foundation of his authority.

Bédié's and dozos' uses of mimesis—from within the state to exclude Ouattara from power, and from beyond it to ally with the state as ersatz police—paralleled each other. The parallels are significant. They reveal that the state and dozos shared a common political logic belonging neither to tradition nor to modernity. The "magical" thinking of mimesis was as much at home in bureaucracy as in the bush (see Taussig 1993, 220–223). Dozos were less out of place in their unofficial police roles than they may have appeared. They and the state, after a shared history of colonial political economy, inhabited the same milieu: the globalizing world economy in which regional population movements followed the flows of cocoa and coffee, and strategies for domestic prosperity harmonized with the demands of state-managed production.

Many dozos and their families had moved south due to the political and economic dynamics of French colonialism and to Houphouët-Boigny's calls for agricultural development. Many belonged to unions and development-related hometown associations that had a "rich tradition of associational activity . . . since the 1920s" (Woods 1994, 467) and that operated according to the same bureaucratic principles and roles privileged by the state. Many dozos had also been educated, at least in part, in state-run schools. They had been juxtaposing their dozo identities alongside their identities as citizens and subjects of Côte d'Ivoire for decades. Benkadi merely confirmed at a national level the ability of dozos to do so. But differences between the way that dozos and the state used mimesis were as, if not more, important than the similarities.

THREE

Dozos at Home and on the Hunt

From Domesticity to *Dozoya*

In the 1990s, dozos were transforming themselves in ways that paralleled the state's transformation. Dozos were becoming quasi-official police by reinterpreting the notions of kinship, residence, and alliance that underlay their hunting rituals.

In Denguélé, dozos and non-dozos structured their lives according to the same spatial, economic, ritual, and organizational idioms and values. These principles shaped *dozoya* as a reciprocal relationship between dozos and non-dozos that was most visible in the ways that dozos shared game with members of their communities and applied their hunting-related skills to ends not immediately related to hunting, such as guarding crops, combating sorcerers, and healing illness. This chapter argues that dozos' potential to extend their hunting roles to non-hunting-related activities like Benkadi defined *dozoya* even before Benkadi emerged. Dozos already organized *dozoya* in terms of the patterns and strategies that governed daily life in Denguélé: the structure of family compounds, relations between mothers' and fathers' children, and age and gender hierarchies. Parallels also existed between dozo and non-dozo rituals in terms of the ethical obligations they entailed. Finally, dozos and non-dozos evaluated their own and each other's character and conduct in terms of the shared values of agreement (*bɛn*), humility (*majigiya*), and patience (*sabari*). Dozos fought crime because it undermined the mutual agreement that defined both dozo and non-dozo well-being.

Hunters and Dozos

In rural Denguélé in the 1990s, most men hunted, but being a dozo meant becoming a different kind of hunter. Men living in villages hunted to add meat to a diet of mostly rice, maize, yams, cassava, fonio millet,[1] greens, beans, garden vegetables, peanut sauce, and smoked fish. Boys were socialized into hunting from an early age, building toy guns out of palm fronds, hunting birds and lizards with slingshots, and burning patches of dry grass near their villages to force out rodents for beating or spearing. Odiennéka called all men who hunted *sogofagabaga* or *sogofagala*, "killers of game."

In contrast to this word for "hunter," which derives from the act of killing game, the word *dozo*, according to Dramane Coulibaly, derived from the verb *ka don*, "to enter," and the noun for "home" or "village," *so* (see fig. 6).[2] In Denguélé, dozos were those men who routinely reentered their villages or towns after hunting in the uninhabited areas beyond them, such as agricultural fields (*sɛnɛkɛyɔrɔ*), the forest (*tun*), and forested savanna (*brisa* or *wula*). Dramane's etymology reflected the way dozos moved between inhabited areas and the spaces beyond them, joining them as parallel but connected worlds.[3]

Dozos hunted just as non-dozo men did, but they also did more. Many used medicinal plants (*fla*), incantations (*yirisi*), and divination to heal.[4] As sorcerers (*subaga*), they used power objects (*jo* or *boli*) and incantations (*yirisi*) to protect themselves while hunting. They also used plants and incantations to repel a vindictive soul force called *nyama*. They claimed that *nyama* emanated from the game they killed. If unrepelled, it could deform, render sterile, or even kill a dozo or members of his family, including unborn children as well as anyone who consumed the tainted meat. In farmers' fields, dozos killed the monkeys, rats, and agoutis ("cane rats," *thrynonomys swinderianus*; Haltenorth and Diller 1977) that ate farmers' crops (see Leach 1994, 157). When necessary, they used sorcery to counteract the sorcery of other sorcerers, including those called *sogoyɛrɛma* who transformed themselves into animals to wreak havoc on humans or livestock (cf. Person 1968, 62).[5] In Denguélé, the word for sorcerer, *subaga*,[6] also meant "witch."[7] The word's lexical ambiguity reflects

6 A mother and child in a compound (*lu*) in the village of Niamasso. Photo by Lily Yeh.

the moral ambiguity of dozo power. As sorcerers, dozos could either help or, like witches, harm.[8] They were as capable of upsetting the established order as reaffirming it.

Every dry season, they and non-dozo hunters burned the tall grass that clogged the forest in the rainy months and hindered hunting in the dry ones. If the fires burned out of control, they could wound or kill hunters or enflame entire villages. I once accompanied several dozos and hunters as they left their village to burn nearby forest. They took well-worn paths, carrying guns slung over a single shoulder or, like a yoke, over both. As they walked, they passed grass that had grown thick, nearly two meters high. At a fork in their path, they separated, forming two groups. One lit a line of fire across one end of the forest. The other waited at the opposite end to kill the game flushed out by the flames. Drissa Koné shot and killed an antelope from atop a six-foot-tall termite mound as it fled toward us. He dressed it, and we found other dozos to help take it back to his village. Hours later, after the conflagration, he and I walked through the forest, a smoldering landscape of bare, blackened bark and ash. Mature trees survived with the soil enriched and forest cleared, even as smaller plants, saplings, animals, and insects had perished. The flames stimulated the sudden growth of new grass, whose green shoots I noticed emerging from the grasses' black stumps a few days later. Fulbe cattle herders started such fires in the dry season when other foliage for their cattle had dwindled. From managing controlled burnings on the outskirts of villages to prevent forest fires from reaching them (see Fairhead and Leach 1996, 194, 196) to collecting medicinal plants and dispatching shape-shifting sorcerers who attacked persons or herd animals, dozos availed non-dozos to the forest's resources while shielding non-dozos from its dangers (see fig. 7).

Dozos oscillated, and perceived themselves as oscillating, between domestic life and hunting in ways that gained power for them in both. Odiennéka expressed this dual sense of dozo belonging through narratives that told of dozo forebears founding hunting camps (*buguda*) where the hunting was good (O'Sullivan 1976, 68–69). After returning repeatedly to these camps, sharing them with other hunters, and settling them with their families, the founders attracted other settlers, creating new villages (*dugu* or *so*). Regardless of these stories' historical accuracy,[9] they show that Odiennéka located dozo power in the transformative margins between the familial and the arboreal. Cultural practice revealed multiple analogies between these realms.

7 Dozos hunting in the forest on the day of a dozo funeral (*kozi*) that I attended in Kouroukoro-Mafèlè in May 1997. Note the bark of the trees, blackened by previous forest burnings.

Compounds and Families: Life and the *Lu*

Most Denguélé dozos, whether they lived in villages or in the town of Odienné, grew up in an extended family compound, or *lu*. The word referred both to the family and the space its members inhabited.[10] Place and family converged in these concepts, reminiscent of the notion of the "house" as theorized by Lévi-Strauss (1982), Carsten and Hugh-Jones (1995, 15–16), Joyce and Gillespie (2000), and McKinnon (1991, 28–32; 1995, 173). In Nienesso, where I lived, and in other villages I visited, round and occasionally rectangular mud-brick houses with bamboo-framed thatched roofs delimited circular or elliptical courtyards or *lu kɔnɔ* (Arnaud 1980, 203), *kɔnɔ* being the Julakan postposition meaning "in," "inside," or "within." When one headed "home," one said, *N'watɔ lu kɔnɔ*, "I am going home [into the *lu*],"[11] to mean that one was returning not just to a place but to one's family. The word *lu* thus translates variously as "compound" (Missionnaire de la Congrégation du Saint-Esprit 1906, 144), "extended family compound" (Toungara 1980, 12), as both "compound" and "extended family" (Cotten 1969, 27; Leynaud and Cissé 1978, 203), "homestead" (O'Sullivan 1976, 69), "household" (see McCall 1995, 178), or simply "house" (D. Cissé 1970, 161–162).[12]

Scholars have also discussed Mande social organization in terms of lineages, interpreting the *lu* as a "minimal lineage" (Person 1968, 54) defined by patrilineal authority and descent (D. Cissé 1970, 64; Leynaud and Cissé 1978, 179, 203).[13] More recent studies have contested the use of lineage models and descent theory (Kuper 1988; McKinnon 2000), arguing that they impose the structures they purport to describe. "In African lineage-based societies, kinship is created not only out of descent but also out of ties to land and locality" (Carsten and Hugh-Jones 1995, 16). This, too, was the case in Denguélé.

The "head of a compound" (*lutigi*) and his resident siblings, children, and sons' children bore his and his father's *jamu*, or "family name," and saw their compound as their primary residence.[14] Yet each *lu* was a space of contrasting, intersecting, and overlapping affiliations, obligations, and tensions organized through ties to both men and women. Within the *lu*, the oldest physically and mentally sound male in residence who could trace an affiliation through his father (*facɛ*) to the previous compound head was its "owner" or "master," its *lutigi*.[15] When a *lutigi* died, the next oldest agnatically related male succeeded him—brothers first, adelphically, then sons—inheriting his belongings (cf. Cashion 1984, 1: 96; Leynaud and Cissé 1978, 171–172) and caring for his wife or wives, possibly through the levirate (see Toungara 1980, 13–14), a practice current during my stay. These practices testified to an age hierarchy also manifest in language. In Mandenkan, one could only refer to one's siblings by citing their ages relative to one's own, calling them "older" (*kɔrɔ*) or "younger" (*dɔgɔ*) sister (*kɔrɔmuso, dɔgɔmuso*) or brother (*kɔrɔcɛ, dɔgɔcɛ*). No abstract terms for "sibling," "sister," or "brother" unmarked for age existed.

Such conventions made Dramane Coulibaly's older brother Mamandou the head of the compound they shared after their father Chémon died.[16] Dramane respected Mamandou's authority but showed all the outward signs of being the *lutigi*. Dramane occupied his father's house in the compound's central courtyard. His reputation surpassed his brother's, and his children were more numerous and mostly older than Mamandou's. Dramane had lived longer in the compound and contributed more work to it than Mamandou, who had gone to work in Mali as a younger man. While Mamandou was away, Dramane established a reputation as a renowned hunter, singer, and healer. He traveled the country to perform for dozos, and his medical expertise drew clients from as far away as Abidjan. He, his family, and their compound expanded as a result, giving Dramane's portion of the compound a certain autonomy from his brother's, so much so that villagers referred to it as a compound in its own right (*Dramani ta lu*).[17]

The cooking shelter (*gbabugu*) of Dramane's first wife demarcated Dramane's part of the compound from his brother's.[18] Dramane's area centered on an ellipse formed by the two-chambered rectangular home of his father where Dramane lived in a room adjacent to that of his first wife, Jènèba. This house (*bon*, or *fibon*[19]) stood at the compound's eastern end facing west. A perpendicular line of houses ran westward at the northern edge of the compound. In this line stood the round mud-brick houses of Dramane's second wife, Madénba,[20] followed by the round house of his second son's wife, followed by the rectangular house of his second son. Closing off the compound and facing opposite Dramane's home stood the round house of his third wife and their daughter. North of Dramane's compound lived his eldest son in a rectangular house along with his second wife. This son's first wife lived with her children in a round house facing his. I lived in a round house north of this son's first wife. North of me stood three more houses belonging to a Malian family who had settled in Dramane's compound. The Malians and I were "foreigners," or "guests" (*lonan*), of Dramane's and, in turn, of Mamandou's.

But Dramane as the de facto *lutigi* was his compound's ultimate authority (see Toungara 1980, 12). Mamandou made no attempt to intervene in his affairs. Dramane organized agricultural labor, oversaw food distribution and the commercial activity of his wives, sons, and their wives, and managed the *lu*'s financial and other resources. Every year he sacrificed a ram for the Muslim feast of Tabaski (Mamandou made his own sacrifice) to recall Abraham's near sacrifice of his son Ishmael to Allah. Dramane also sacrificed chickens at the base of his house in his father's memory. Both sacrifices occurred in the same domestic space. In Dramane's compound, residence, labor, and ritual reflected and determined his authority as *lutigi*, regardless of his brother's seniority, not as an exception to Jula principles of affiliation but as their consequence. Fulfilling part of the requirements of being a compound head—sustained residency, supervision of work, and performance of sacrifices—meant sharing in some of their prerogatives. Odiennéka did not expect all principles of authority in compounds to hold in every situation. People had to choose among them, deciding which most applied at any given time, leaving room for interpretation, improvisation, and manipulation, for women as well as for men.

In a case of levirate I knew in Nienesso, relations soured between the deceased husband's younger brother (*bɛnɔgɔcɛ*) and his two nephews due to the uncle's bad temper. As I was entering their compound late one afternoon, the stepfather threw a hand plough (*daba*) at his oldest nephew, who had just returned from the fields. The nephew dodged the hoe, but his stepfather advanced to grab him by the testicles and berate him about problems beyond my comprehension. Several months later, the stepfather suddenly and mysteriously died. A neighbor of mine speculated that his wife had poisoned his food. Even if others suspected as much, Nienesso's chief (*dugutigi*) never called the woman to account, and no one reported the incident to the police. She never remarried. Although her oldest son was living in the compound and was, as a result, its *lutigi*, he was unmarried, and his mother remained the decision maker and money manager. Her long residency in the compound, accumulated work, and close ties to her sons gave her an autonomy to decide what was best for them all. Even if she was innocent of murder, its attribution to her and the lack of any serious accusations against her illustrated the power to which women could aspire within a compound.

In the cases just mentioned, people who were not *lutigi*s in any formal sense acquired power by acting like *lutigi*s. Dramane's brother, to whom the *lutigi* title formally belonged, exercised it in some but not in all ways. The *lutigi* role comprised qualities and responsibilities capable of partition among various persons rather than wholes belonging permanently and exclusively to any one.[21] By appropriating aspects of the *lutigi* role, those who mimicked it succeeded in establishing themselves as equals in some sense and—in Dramane's case—potentially superior in authority to the ostensible compound head. In domestic contexts, those excluded from the *lutigi* role according to some criteria could acquire aspects of *lutigi* authority according to others.

Houses in the *Lu*

Similar shifts in identity occurred in the ways women and children gained membership in their husbands' and fathers' compounds through marriage, birth, and naming rituals. Every person in principle belonged to two overlapping groups of kin. Children of the same father (*fadenma* or *fadenmalu*) and their descendents, both within and beyond the compound, formed a father's "house," or *fabon*. The word *bon* means "house," or "building," in Julakan. When the prefix *fa*, "father," or *ba*, "mother," precedes it, the word denotes those people affiliated as kin through a shared father or mother, respectively. Those children related through the same mother (*badenma* or *badenmalu*) formed a *babon*, "mother's house."[22] Children of fathers and mothers belonged simultaneously to fathers' and mothers' houses without contradiction, but not without tension.[23]

In compounds, children of polygynous unions coexisted as residents within the same father's house, but each also belonged to the house of her or his mother.[24] Children of the same father subdivided into different groups of mothers' children, each centered on a different wife of their father's. Fathers with more than one wife faced the challenge of how to treat the children of different mothers—as well as the mothers themselves—equally. Barring human perfection, no father could do so in all circumstances, potentially causing anxiety and rivalry among his different wives and their children.[25]

Odiennéka, like other Mandenkan speakers, use the word *fadenya* to name the sometimes contentious ways in which one relates to one's father and his children by mothers different from one's own. The term also connotes fighting, intrigue, and struggle in general (Bird and Kendall 1980, 15; Jansen and Zobel 1996, 3). In Wojɛnɛkakan, *fa* means "father," and *den* means "child" or "dependent"[26] The suffix *-ya* turns the phrase for "father's child" into a word denoting a state of being: the quality of being a "father's child." *Fadenya* thus translates as "father-childness" (Bird and Kendall 1980, 14) or "half sibling-ness" (Jansen and Zobel 1996, 3) a not altogether negative thing since it spurs children to competitive achievement (Bird and Kendall 1980, 15).

Dramane's three sons by his first wife, for instance, were quite diverse in their character and success. The oldest was an established tailor in Nienesso, the second-oldest was an accomplished hunter and singer, and the youngest had gone south to find work in a sugar-processing plant. They strove to be different, but I never saw them fight or disagree publicly, in accord with the tendency of *badenya*, the way they related as children of the same mother—in peaceful collaboration (see Bird and Kendall 1980, 14–16). In Mandenkan, *ba* means "mother," and *badenya*, "mother-childness." While *badenya* connotes harmony, it may also result in conformity (Bird and Kendall 1980, 14–16). And *fadenya* was a tendency, not a destiny, among siblings of different mothers.[27]

The same mix of competition and collaboration characterized Dramane's relationship with his older brother Mamandou, who had a different mother from Dramane. Mamandou's mother was senior to Dramane's, and these brothers' characters were as different as those of Dramane's sons, who shared a mother, but the public face of their relations was just as genial. Despite the fact that Mamandou had been away from his father's compound for decades, Dramane welcomed him as the head of the compound when Mamandou returned. In every decision I ever saw Dramane make concerning the compound, he deferred to Mamandou, humbling himself (*k'a yɛrɛ majigi*) as was expected of a younger sibling. Whenever I left Nienesso for Odienné, or Odienné for another Ivoirian city to meet dozos, Dramane insisted that I first receive Mamandou's permission to do so—which I did—before Dramane would acquiesce. With regard to sibling relations such as those between Dramane and Mamandou, one might say, *o fadenya a di* or *o fadenya bara ja*, "their *fadenya* is sweet," because they publicly cooperated. *Badenya* and *fadenya* were therefore tendencies between which people alternated in varying ways rather than reified principles that strictly determined how they behaved with certain people at all times.

The dynamics of kinship organization in Denguélé were as much means by which Odiennéka analyzed and strategized action as they were behaviors. Those whose lives they structured moved among them in ways as flexible as those in which Odiennéka belonged to both their fathers' and mothers' houses. The results could be unexpected: a junior brother could achieve a more secure position in his father's compound than his older brother, the son of their father's senior wife. A mother, as head of a "mother's house," could exercise the prerogatives of a *lutigi* within her deceased husband's *lu*, and sons of different mothers or the same mother could balance sibling rivalry and cooperation so adroitly as to compete with each other while visibly collaborating. In Denguélé's compounds,

Odiennéka drew analogies between contrasting forms of behavior and affiliation. To paraphrase Wagner's (1977) notion of "analogic kinship," a younger brother could be a different kind of older brother, a widow a different kind of *lutigi*, and "sweet" cooperation a different kind of *fadenya*. Rituals surrounding marriage, birth, and naming provided the foundations for these analogies, given the way these rituals analogized the distinct but complementary forms of membership involved in belonging to father's and mother's houses. In patrilineal Jula society, ties through women were as important as ties through men.[28]

Ritual, Gender, Space

Marriage negotiations in Denguélé occurred in the following manner: parents made a series of offerings of ten kola nuts (*woro*) each to the parents of their son's prospective fiancée. While the woman's parents were deciding how to respond, they might claim, according to convention, that mice had eaten the kolas, necessitating further offerings, up to a total of three.[29] The kola nuts could be of any color: red, white, or yellow. Successful attempts ended in the *worosiri*, or "kola tying" (*attachement de colas* in French). By this time, the suitor would have purchased a dozen or so tailored outfits and other gifts such as head scarves and makeup for his bride (*kɔnyɔ*) and gathered sufficient cash for his future in-laws or done sufficient farmwork in their fields.

The bride's family provided her with cooking pots and utensils with which she would cook for her husband and their children, relatives, and guests. At a wedding I attended in the town of Odienné, these gifts were prominently displayed in one of the rooms of the bride's family's home. There seemed to be more pots than the bride could possibly use, stacked in a display more typical of the small stores that sold these items than of a kitchen. That same evening, women covered the bride with a shawl and sang to her as she sat on a chair in the open air of her family's compound. An hour or two later, the groom arrived in a borrowed Mercedes driven by a chauffeur to accompany his bride to his parents' compound where they would begin their married life.

Villagers enacted this transition with great drama. In Niamasso, a bride waited along the dirt road on the village's outskirts for her husband to arrive to accompany her back to his village. She cried for the duration of the hour or so that she waited. Finally, male relatives and friends of the groom arrived on several mopeds, guns in hand, at which point the bride stopped crying, mounted one of the mopeds, and left amid a flurry of volleys fired by the departing men. New couples usually lived in the groom's father's compound unless the husband had established a home elsewhere, having found work in another location, for instance. Unless a vacant house (*bon* or *fibon*, "sleeping house") was already available in the groom's compound, the family and other villagers would build a new one for them. In a compound, each wife also had access to her own cooking tripod (*gbakuru*) made of three standing rocks on and within which she placed aluminum pots and wood, respectively, for cooking. If a man's multiple marriages or several men's single marriages resulted in welcoming more women into the compound than there were cooking tripods, more tripods appeared, one raised for each new wife. In polygynous marriages, additional wives required additional houses, one for each of them and their potential children.

When a wife joined and resided in her husband's compound, she initiated a reciprocal relationship that her work sustained and that, were she to have children, would assure her a place within their father's compound.[30] Wives gathered firewood, cooked, purchased food and condiments at the market, farmed, washed clothes, advised their husbands privately, swept the compound morning and night, and brought water to the compound from the nearest stream, well, pump, or faucet. Even if a woman had no children—as was the case for Dramane's second wife, Madénba, in what was her second marriage[31]—the quality of her work in the compound and, in Madénba's case, the evident intimacy and mutual respect that she and Dramane shared, assured her a lifelong place in his compound.

For women who had children in their husbands' compounds, the process of bringing them into their father's house was as much the result of ritual as of the act of birth. Wives kept their father's *jamu* for life, but their children took their father's. After the birth of a child, the midwives buried its placenta (*dozo*) outside the door of its mother's house[32]—to the right for girls, to the left for boys—establishing the child as a member of its mother's house (*babon*) and a resident in its father's compound (*lu*). Seven days later, parents held a naming ceremony for the newborn, variously called *denkunli*, "child's head shaving," *dennabɔ*, "bringing out the child," and *dentɔgɔla*, "child naming," in which all these acts occurred. The rite completed a child's entry into its father's house (*fabon*) and into the compound from its mother's home into which it was born.

One such ceremony I attended occurred at a friend's compound in Nienesso. That morning, the mother shaved her baby son's head and, for the first time since his birth, left her house with him. Guests who had assembled in the compound were given a dense paste of finely pounded, uncooked rice mixed with water (*malodɛgɛ*) and one or two kola nuts of any color. We ate the rice and chewed the kolas while the parents announced their son's personal name (*tɔgɔ*) to the small crowd. Before returning to our compounds, we offered benedictions in return: *Ala i den balo*, "May God nourish your child," *Ala kɛnɛya di*, "May God give [your child] health," *Ala ſi jan di*, "May God give [your child] long life." The event lasted for barely forty-five minutes, but the child was now a member of his father's compound and house and would later, we hoped, work within it. A midwife had buried his placenta outside his mother's house, one that his mother's family had acquired for her through marriage negotiations, one that his father and other men of the village had built, and one that his mother would maintain. This mother's child only fully became his father's after his mother had shaved his head of the hair that had grown during their seclusion together and after his father had provided guests with food and kolas before publicly naming him.

Through marriage, placental burial, and child naming, a husband's family exchanged a house and bridewealth for a woman's ability to transform and simultaneously assimilate to their compound through work and conjugality. Wives and mothers came from a different "category," *si*, than their husbands and children, what Odiennéka often translated as "lineage" (*lignage*) and which literally means "kind" or "type of human being."[33] Wives joined their husbands' compounds to live with them without ever becoming identical to them in terms of substance.[34] They retained their fathers' family names and could return to their own family compounds in case of divorce, whereas their children would likely remain with their father, having established residency in his compound and carrying his family name, both of which made them primarily his dependents (*den*), although they would, in principle, always be welcome in their mother's father's compound.[35] All children were thus as much members of their mothers' houses as their fathers'. Being a person implied fluctuating between both while negotiating the topography of daily life. Through ritual, women and children entered their husbands' and fathers' compounds as strangers and, as a result of ritual and reciprocity, became full members within them. Men accomplished analogous transformations through *dozoya*.

Initiating Dozos

Dozo initiation was a mundane affair in Denguélé.[36] It granted men access to dozo gatherings previously closed to them. What counted most was how men made use of this access. At dozo funerals, hunting sacrifices, and the meetings where dozos coordinated Benkadi activities, they exchanged hunting stories and techniques, knowledge of medicinal plants, hunting incantations, and other dozo lore.[37] In Côte d'Ivoire in the 1990s, dozos also taught each other and their apprentices how to organize and gain tacit approval for Benkadi security patrols and how to use occult devices and incantations to protect themselves from criminals. Although dozo expertise and the number of men seeking to become dozos expanded with Benkadi's security activities, an initiatory sacrifice remained the sole means of becoming a dozo.

I observed only two other dozo initiations (see chap. 4) besides my own. In one, dozos initiated two apprentices at once. In the other, a young man was initiated after his dozo father's death. Both initiations occurred without fanfare in the context of more important sacrifices. Although I make no claim for my initiation being representative of others, its ritual aspects resembled aspects of the other initiations and dozos' sacrifices I witnessed. I describe my initiation to contextualize those features of dozo initiations that Denguélé dozos acknowledged as required for any such initiation.

I had been waiting for my initiation for months since Dramane first suggested it. Then at last, on the evening of June 10, 1996, Dramane came to my house in Nienesso to tell me that I would "kill my chicken" (*ka n'ʃiʃɛ faga*) the next morning. I had already given him the red rooster (*manadunun*) and ten red kola nuts (*woro wulen*) that an apprentice must offer for the sacrifice.[38] To contract a marriage and elicit blessings and goodwill during a child's naming ritual, Odiennéka also offered kola nuts, though of any color, to the parents of their son's prospective fiancée and to neighbors, respectively. To become a dozo, either the candidate or the candidate's family provided the kolas and chicken. In all these cases, an exchange of kola nuts opened the way for future alliances and access to residential and ritual spaces: in the husband's or father's house, compound, and village on one hand, and in the company of dozos in Manimory's ritual residence, the *dangun*, on the other.[39]

Early the next morning, Nienesso's chief dozo (*dozokuntigi*), Ouassé Koné,[40] blew his hunting whistle (*dozoflɛ*) to summon a dozen senior dozos from Nienesso to his compound. From there, we walked together to the *dangun* on the outskirts of Nienesso where the village segued into forest and fields. In Jula, *dan* means "border," "frontier," "limit," or "threshold." *Kun*—or *gun* after a nasalized consonant—means "head" or "tip." *Dangun* translates roughly as the "tip of the limit," marking the point of contact between inhabited and uninhabited areas.[41]

Dramane led us to the *dangun* while singing, accompanied on the dozos' harp-lute (*dozongɔnun*) by his apprentice, Abou Touré. Together, we crossed the paved highway running northward to Odienné and southward to the cities of Touba and Man. We then took a path through grass on to the edge of the forest. Farther on, the path led to the villagers' fields.[42]

Within ten minutes, we arrived at the *dangun*. It stood near the path in full view. Several dozos cleared it of leaves, fallen tree limbs, and debris that had accumulated since the last sacrifice. Other dozos gathered twigs and placed them in a pile over which, after the sacrifice, they would roast the rooster that I had given to Dramane. Chief dozo Ouassé cleared debris off of the small mushroom-shaped termite mound, the *tiningun* (cf. Cuello and Robin 2005, 156–157), which stood as the *dangun*'s focal point, anchored to the trunks of two adjacent trees (see Keita 1985, 24).[43] Drissa Koné claimed that dozos named this kind of termite mound after Manimory's first wife, Ma Tinin, abbreviating her name to *Tinin* by removing the title "mother" (*ma*) and adding the suffix *-kun*, meaning "head" or "tip."[44] Dozos called the mound "Tènè's head," as if to imply that she, like Manimory, had been transformed in some way into a part of the forest as a result of her sacrifice. The mound was an extension of Ma Tinin—a point of contact between dozos and Manimory—no doubt because Manimory had sacrificed her in the first *dangun*.

After dozos finished preparing the area, Dramane asked me in front of the others why I wanted to "kill a chicken" (*ka ʃiʃɛ faga*). He had already taught me the correct replies, which suggested that his colleagues expected such questions to be asked at dozo initiations.[45] "Because I like what dozos do," I answered.[46] Dramane then asked me to cite the things dozos should avoid. "Dozos must not lie, steal, commit adultery, or betray other dozos," I said.[47]

With that, Ouassé Koné took one of the kola nuts that I had given to Dramane and which Dramane had given to him in turn and squatted before the termite mound. Ouassé split the nut in two along its line of cleavage and placed the halves into a small calabash bowl filled halfway with water. He placed the bowl and the chicken near the foot of the mound. Earlier, Dramane had tied the bird's legs together with a slim length of cloth to keep it still. Ouassé then drank water from the calabash and spit it out onto the termite mound before addressing Manimory. He spoke as if Manimory sat before us, as if they were talking face-to-face. He told Manimory that I was giving him the kola nuts and rooster because I wanted to be a dozo. Then he removed the kola nut halves from the bowl, put the bowl aside, and repeated to Manimory our reasons for coming to the *dangun*. He explained that he was about to throw the kola halves into the air and that, were I acceptable as an initiate, Manimory should show his approval by making the kola halves land one face up, the other face down (see Dieterlen 1988, 242).

Ouassé then threw the kola nut halves into the air (see Keita 1985, 33, 36), focusing his gaze on the ground where they would fall. Both landed face up. It appeared that Manimory had mixed feelings about me. But as in other dozo sacrifices I had observed, the conversation continued. Just as a suitor's parents could offer kola nuts to the parents of his prospective fiancée three times before facing rejection, Ouassé repeated the process. If Manimory continued to refuse, dozos would desist, but negotiate they would.

Once more, Ouassé spat water onto the termite mound, invoked Manimory, and tossed the kola nut halves. This time, both landed face down. What had I done wrong? Did Manimory dislike my lack of hunting experience? Did my intention to write about him and his followers upset him? What would happen if my initiation failed? Would I lose Dramane's trust? Would dozos refuse to talk to me? How could I do my research?

I suddenly understood why dozos spoke of Manimory as a living being. The spirit they posited before me could make or break my immediate future—and theirs. Manimory confronted the living as an invisible presence who would in part determine—whether I "believed" in him or not—the next several years of my life and the start of my academic career. His ritual invocation made him a real, vital presence to me and to all those who made sacrifices to him.

It took a third toss of the kola to end my anxieties. This time, one half landed face up, the other face down, at which point Ouassé and the other dozos blew their whistles to announce Manimory's approval. As in marriage, a further gift was required, in this case, a red rooster. In the final act of betrothal—the *worosiri*—a groom gives his bride clothes, makeup, and other small gifts. The dozo initiate's final gift, which followed a presentation of kola nuts, recalled the roosters that Dramane sacrificed to his father at the base of his house. Dozo initiations accomplished ends analogous to those that characterized non-dozo rites regulating marriage and residence. Sacrifices served to tie Odiennéka to particular places.

One of the dozos manning the cooking fire now came forward, took the rooster in hand, secured it gently beneath one of his feet, and cut its throat.[48] He quickly lifted the bird over the termite mound, spraying the spouting blood upon it. When the bloodflow ceased, he tossed the bird onto the ground, where it fluttered about until it landed on its back, slightly flapping its wings—an auspicious sign (see Keita 1985, 37). Before it could move again, Dramane secured it with his hands and told me to place my right hand on its upturned breast. I did so, tying myself to my offering and, through it, to Manimory and to the vows I had made. Meanwhile, the blood I had brought to the *dangun* trickled into the soil, connecting me to Ma Tinin and Manimory just as the burial of a child's placenta links it to its father's compound. The same tropes of kola nut sharing, food preparation, bloodletting, and attachment to location that establish *lu* membership established dozo identity. Sacrifice made kinship among dozos as palpable as that which joined them to their domestic families. I was now a *Manimoryden*, a "child" or "dependent of Manimory," in his and his wife's residence. In the *dangun*, dozos domesticated the forest.

To celebrate, Dramane and his apprentice Abou began to sing while the dozo who had cut the rooster's throat removed its feathers, letting them fall onto the bloody termite mound. He and another dozo cut and cleaned the carcass over a layer of fresh leaves that they had laid on the ground. They roasted the meat over an open fire in ways that recalled women's preparation and distribution of food in their husbands' compounds. Both acts of preparing and cooking food confirmed the preparers' belonging in the space where they made the food: dozos in *dangun*s, women in their husbands' compounds.

Then we ate the rooster and the remaining kola nuts together and threw the clean bones onto or next to the termite mound. Until rain or animals would wash or carry the blood and bones away, the spattered, littered mound would stand as a sign of dozos' alliance with Manimory. Our meal ended the event just as the sharing of rice paste and kola nuts marked a child's entry into his father's compound. Entering the *lu* and *dangun* occurred as analogous events ending in comparable outcomes. Ritual transformed unrelated people into allies joined by reciprocal moral obligations. Naming ceremonies and marriage gave children and wives rights to *lu* membership and obligations within compounds, and dozo initiation welcomed apprentices into the *dangun* in return for their initiatory vows.

Manimory's Children: Diversity in the *Dangun*

Although dozos claimed no agnatic connection to Manimory, he stood in relation to them like a father to his "children" (*den*). And they called his wife, "Mother Tinin." Leaves, or *yiriden* in Julakan, stand in a similar relation to trees (*yiri*), just as students, or *lekɔlden*, do to schools.[49] In

Julakan, *den* names someone or something that depends on another person or thing for its definition. Dozos promised Manimory to remain loyal to each other and to refrain from adultery, theft, and deceit to express and protect their dependence on him. Breaking these vows, they said, could provoke Manimory to block a dozo from killing game or leave him open to injury in the forest as a warning to atone for his offenses.

Being a dozo, therefore, meant being a good husband (*cɛ*), relative (*baden*), and friend (*tericɛ*). Dozos thus configured their relations with each other in ways that depended intimately on their relations with non-dozo kin, spouses, and affines. Practical analogies linked *dozoya* to these relations. Dozos confided hunting secrets to their wives, and their wives offered them their occult expertise in return, which sometimes included hunting secrets entrusted to them by their fathers, brothers, or past husbands. Adultery by a dozo or his wife could, in contrast, ruin a dozo's hunting. So closely related were hunting and domestic life, dozos claimed, that if a dozo fired on animals coupling in the forest and found that his wife had been injured in an accident the same day, it would indicate that she was committing adultery, as revealed through the forest's sexual symbols. This collusion and mutual understanding, or *bɛn*, among dozos and between dozos and their wives, kin, and other non-dozos mirrored the qualities that defined *bɛn* or the lack thereof more generally in Denguélé. Just as marriage and birth brought different kinds of people into shared residence in a compound, initiation brought men of diverse backgrounds into the *dangun*.

According to Youssouf Cissé (1964, 178), dozos considered themselves neither "Malinke, Bambara, Senufo, Bobo, Fula, white or black, even if they [were] a little bit of all of these." Differences of "class, birth, and origin [had] no weight or resonance. The descendants of nobles, slaves," occupational status groups (*nyamakala*), and foreigners could become dozos, even dozo chiefs (*dozokuntigi*; Y. Cissé 1994, 51). "Whereas in [Mande] society in general, ethnicity, age, noble birth, freeman status, occupational specialization, descendancy from former slaves, or circumcision [were] all hereditary determinants of status or political power, none of these distinctions appl[ied]" among dozos (Cashion 1984, 1: 102). Scholars have noted that dozos exhibit the accountability, honesty, humility, and trustworthiness (see Cashion 1984, 1: 102; Y. Cissé 1994, 51–52) of the "love and devotion . . . typical of the matricentric family," that is, of *badenya* (Y. Cissé 1964, 178; Leynaud and Cissé 1978, 171 n. 4; Y. Cissé 1994, 46).

Among dozos in Côte d'Ivoire, I met Mandenkan- and Gur-speaking men of Malian, Burkinabe, and Guinean nationality, as well as Muslims,

Christians, and autochthonous ritual practitioners, including a Catholic, Syenara-speaking dozo in Korhogo, an initiated Baoulé man in Odienné, and in Abidjan, a young woman who, although uninitiated, accompanied her father to dozo events in dozo dress.[50] Such exceptions were rare but testified to ritual's ability to integrate and juxtapose differences.

But tensions arose even among dozos. While visiting the north-central Senufo region of Côte d'Ivoire to attend a Benkadi meeting, for example, the Odiennéka dozos I accompanied despaired of trusting their Senufo hosts without overtly criticizing them. The latter had refused to share hunting secrets they had recorded from a local dozo with a tape recorder that an Odiennéka colleague had lent them. Dozos exhibited as much competition (*fadenya*) as they did cooperation (*badenya*).

Dozos were also as hierarchical as they were egalitarian. After initiation, a dozo measured his seniority as a dozo according to the length of time since his initiation rather than according to the time elapsed since his birth. "For example, a son (though it would be unlikely) could [become a dozo] before his father and . . . be senior to him. A younger brother [could] join before his elder and . . . be senior to him" (Cashion 1984, 1: 101–102; see Y. Cissé 1964, 186, cited in Cashion 1984, 1: 102). Initiation in the *dangun* reconfigured seniority in a new relation of dependence beyond, but reminiscent of, the kind that prevailed in compounds. Seniority in each space depended on the length of one's residency within it. The initiatory hierarchy determined succession among dozo chiefs just as adelphic and patrilineal succession regulated inheritance among compound heads. When Odienné's chief dozo, Soumaïla Fofana, died in 1997, for example, his lieutenant, Kanamankan Diarrassouba, took his place since Kanamankan had reportedly been initiated longer than any other dozo in Odienné.[51]

But, as in domestic life, seniority was only one criteria among many. A dozo's accumulated knowledge need not have corresponded to his length of time in the *dangun*. Since no dozo could determine another dozo's experience or power from outward appearances, and because dozos relied on each other to learn *dozoya*, they strove to treat all their colleagues as peers. They typically addressed each other as "teacher" or "master," greeting each other saying, *I ni ko, karnanmɔgɔ*, "You and your exploits, teacher," regardless of the addressee's age or seniority.[52] No initiate wanted to offend his seniors, or anyone, for that matter, who could withhold the sorcery that could either help him hunt or "tie him up" (*k'a siri*) to spoil his hunting. As a result, dozos' behavior reflected the same tensions between hierarchy and egalitarianism, conflict and conformity, and *fadenya* and *badenya* that marked everyday life.[53] Dozos appealed to the same virtue of patient humility, *sabari*, with which non-dozos maintain their agency in the face of conflicting demands.

Sabari

Odiennéka attribute a wide but consistent range of meanings to the word. They use it variously as a verb meaning "to calm oneself, patiently endure," or "pardon" as a means of imploring others similar to "please"; as the noun meaning "patience" or "resignation" (Braconnier 1999, 733; see also Braconnier and Diaby 1982, 99; Coulibaly and Haraguchi 1993, 129); and as the verb meaning "to be well brought up [or] to calm oneself, in speaking of a man upset by anger or emotion" (Missionnaire de la Congrégation du Saint-Esprit 1906, 157). Delafosse (1955, 614) traced the word's etymology to the Arabic *çabr* (*as-sabr*) and defined it as follows: "N[oun]. 'patience'. Excl[amation]. 'patience! calm down!' Intr[ansitive]. v. 'to be patient, to be calm, to be dignified in one's manners, to calm oneself, to wait patiently'. Tr[ansitive]. v. 'to calm.'"

Odiennéka may use the word in several ways on any given day. If one notices someone, either familiar or unknown, about to engage in embarrassing, rude, dangerous, or careless conduct that may later provoke shame (*malo*), one can approach the person and say, "Sabari" to mean something like, "Hey, watch what you're doing. Think about what you're saying. Be careful! Stop, for heaven's sake!" If one finds two people arguing with each other or fighting, one may yell "Sabari!" to break up the dispute. Or, after having done something awkward, one may use the word to say, "Sorry, I realize what I've done. I apologize." *Sabari* as a reply may atone for anything from bumping into someone in the market to having been caught stealing. It can plead helplessness when another person asks too much of one, such as when a policeman demands a bribe for a traffic violation one has not committed. The word may entreat others to bear hardships, such as the death of a loved one or loss of a job, with dignity and perseverance. "Try to understand me," the word implies, "and I will try to understand you, and we will work things out to everyone's satisfaction." The word appeals to an interlocutor's "awareness" of or "intent" (*hakiri*) to recognize an injustice, oversight, difficulty, or other breach of civility noticed by the speaker. The common Jula greeting *hɛrɛ bɛ*, "Is there peace?" or "All is well?" evokes the same serenity. Odiennéka also use the expression *I y'i jusu suma*, "Cool your heart," to reproach angry or upset people whose "hearts have heated up" (*mɔgɔ min jusu gbannin*).

Movaly Fofana, a young dozo musician from Denguélé, sang one night about *sabari* to dozos who had gathered to dance (*ka dozotɔrɔn kɛ*) in Odienné:

If you go on the hunt and kill nothing and return to the village empty-handed,
Sabari!
If when you return from the hunt empty-handed, villagers laugh at you and make fun of you and say you're worth nothing,
Sabari!
If you leave your village in search of knowledge, travel far, and return ignorant,
Sabari!
Calm yourself, or you will forever be fighting.[54]

Movaly reminded men that they could remain dozos even in the face of failing as hunters. A "real dozo" (*dozo yɛrɛyɛrɛ*; cf. Bassett 2003, 7), Movaly implied, mastered himself as much as he did the hunt so that when he failed in his objectives, he remained ready to try again. Such self-discipline was crucial if dozos were to balance the conflicting hierarchical and egalitarian aspects of their relationships with each other.

Dozos sought men and boys as apprentices, for example, to enhance their own status. Having an apprentice made a dozo a *karanmɔgɔ*. In Julakan, *karan* means "to study," and *mɔgɔ* means "person." The words form a compound noun that means "teacher," "master," or "mentor." Julakan speakers used the term to refer to and address Qur'anic teachers and Muslim occult experts (*marabouts*) as well as dozos. They referred to all these figures' apprentices as *karanmɔgɔden*, meaning "apprentice," "student," or "master's child."

Dozo mentors judged apprentices' worthiness for initiation according to their hunting skills and moral character. "A known womanizer would be rejected outright. Beyond this, the only other standard by which one would be judged [was] that of loyalty to brother hunters and the acceptance of [their] rules" (Cashion 1984, 1: 106; Y. Cissé 1964, 181; 1994, 55–56). These included the unspoken expectation that apprentices give their mentors gifts of game meat, accompany them while hunting to help them skin, clean, and carry their quarry, and make themselves available for other chores, such as helping to farm, caring for livestock, running errands, or helping their masters' wives with household tasks (Y. Cissé 1994, 56–57).

As Kanamankan Diarrassouba, Odienné's chief dozo (*dozokuntigi*), explained to me in Julakan on August 16, 1997,

> Your master, he's your "chief" . . . you don't lay your hands on his wife if you want him to bless you. You gather wood for him. You carry water for his wife. You wash his clothes. Anything he asks you to do, you do. Your master—the day he dies, or rather, while he still lives, when something bad is about to happen to you, you will escape it. Oh Allah! Oh Manimory! I washed my master's clothes, carried his water, gathered his firewood and gave it to his wife. When something bad is about to happen to me, Manimory prevents it altogether.

Dozo apprenticeships began much as Jula marriages did, with acts resembling bride service. By obeying a teacher, an apprentice proved himself worthy of learning, just as a suitor might work for his fiancée's parents to prove himself worthy of marriage. As a Malian proverb states, "To forge iron well, one must first heat it white" (Y. Cissé 1994, 57). Before a master sponsored an initiate, he tested the man's mettle. If the apprentice endured his master's tests, he established a relationship of agreement in which the master could share his dozo knowledge with the apprentice and give him his Muslim blessing (*duan*). It was in the best interests of dozos to respect (*ka bɔnya*) each other and humble themselves (*k'olugu yɛrɛma jigi*) in each other's presence in order to learn from each another and win their mentors' help and protection.

But mentors benefited as much from these relationships as pupils. If a dozo lived near his teacher, he offered him the three hindmost ribs on each side of any large game animal whenever he killed one. Dozos called these ribs the "vulture's wing" (*duangaman*), associating dozos with vultures, who see and take all as hunters.[55] Still, when a dozo found an apprentice, he gained more than a source of potential labor and game meat. He gained a dependent who would pay him public homage and from whom he might also learn. Drissa Koné told me, for instance, that when he was younger, several dozos in his village of Niamasso wanted to recruit him as an apprentice because of his hunting skills. Each competed for his allegiance, telling him how to use incantations and plants for hunting. Because Drissa's father forbade him from being initiated as a dozo, Drissa had long refused such overtures from senior dozos. In doing so, he acquired a substantial amount of dozo knowledge, which he subsequently shared with other mentors and colleagues.

Jula men could thus learn *dozoya* without being initiated, and potential initiates could undergo initiation after having acquired substantial knowledge. As in compounds, men's roles comprised bundles of responsibilities that even those usually excluded from a given role might acquire. Dozos knew that junior colleagues might possess more knowledge than their seniors. Dramane Coulibaly routinely made the point when he sang the following song at every dozo gathering I attended with him:

That which some know
That which some know, others do not
Everyone is not the same
That which some know
That which some know, others do not.
[*Dɔ ye dɔ lɔn*
Dɔ ye dɔ lɔn, dɔ ma o lɔn
Mɔgɔ byɛ tɛ kɛlɛn ye
Dɔ ye dɔ lɔn
Dɔ ye dɔ lɔn, dɔ ma o lɔn]

The song warned dozos to respect each other, for no two had the same knowledge or expertise.

Kanamankan Diarrassouba put it this way:

Take a child . . . you don't know who it is. You say to yourself, "That's a child." But it's not [just] a child, it's an important person because the things he has in him are not the things you have in you. [If] you see him, you should go up to him, give him gifts, then he'll tell you what he knows. That will make you wise. That will increase your knowledge. But the person who doesn't agree with anyone[56]—neither children nor adults—even if [he's] a chief, [he's] nothing . . . You aren't [even] a chief in that case, because a chief should see many things.

Because appearances can be deceiving, even the most self-assured dozo humbly approached others to gain their expertise.[57] Like non-dozos, dozos cultivated an ethical state somewhere between the independence and volatility of *fadenya* and the modesty and conformity of *badenya* that enabled them to resolve the challenges they faced in forests and at home.

Enter the *Dangun*, Enter the *Lu*

Dozos thus underwent their initiations using the same symbols of kolas, blood, and shared meals that made wives members of their husbands' compounds and children members of their mothers' and fathers' houses. In marriages, multicolored kolas and bride wealth went from the suitor's family to the bride's to ally them. In the case of dozos, red kolas and a red rooster went from the initiate and sacrificer to Manimory for similar purposes. After a child's birth, burying its placenta outside the home of its mother established it as a member of both its mother's house and its father's compound. Dozos likewise spilled a rooster's blood over a termite mound named after Ma Tinin to give the initiate a place in her husband's *dangun*. Kolas and uncooked rice announced a child's entry in its father's house, and the consumption of kolas and fowl won dozos a place in the *dangun*. Through sacrifice, dozos entered the *dangun* so they could, like Manimory, blend into the forest as he had, just as women and children gained access to domestic areas to which they had no inherent claim.[58] Ritual created reciprocal moral relations that did more than transcend differences between wives and husbands, mothers' and father's houses, or among dozos. It preserved and reinforced those differences, making them explicit so that participants could better negotiate their positions among them.

The sacrifices that dozos made, beginning with their initiations, completed a generalized cycle of exchange that began with a woman's marriage into her husband's compound and continued with a child's birth and naming. Those sons who became dozos later made return exchanges of game to their own and neighboring compounds, defining themselves as beholden to and, as a result, responsible for managing the moral reciprocity that regulated the domestic relations to which they contributed through hunting, healing, and guarding crops.

Being a spouse, parent, or child of any kind in Denguélé required one to judge repeatedly how best to reconcile contrasting forms of kin substance (*siya*), parental networks (*babon* and *fabon*), affiliative principles (*badenya* and *fadenya*), and hierarchy (agnatic affiliation versus length of residence). Dozos similarly negotiated the continuum between belonging in one's compound and belonging in the forest. A wife founded a mother's house through marriage and birth, enabling her children to belong to both matrilateral and patrilineal kin networks. A husband sustained his father's house through sacrifice, marriage, and naming rituals to assure his dependents a place in his compound and wider village. And dozos made offerings in the *dangun* to regulate reciprocal relations in their compounds and in the forest. They belonged to both domains no less than children belonged to mothers' and fathers' houses and wives to fathers' and husbands' compounds. The dozo role implied a masterful alternation between compounds and hunting grounds that generated authority in each. The next chapter explains how sacrifice articulated this authority.

FOUR

Sacrificing for Security

Ritual Agency

Through sacrifice, dozos shaped themselves as embodied relations of protective agreement (*bɛn*) between Manimory and non-dozos, incarnating a responsibility to protect non-dozos from harm. When dozos killed game, they shared the meat with neighbors and strangers. When they made offerings to Manimory for safety on the hunt, they sometimes invited non-dozo hunters to participate. They also made sacrifices to protect a dead dozo's family and hunters as a whole from the rupture in reciprocity between the forest and the community that his death implied. And, as unofficial police, they requested Manimory's protection on patrol through the same rituals with which they sought his protection on the hunt. This chapter shows that dozos joined security concerns to *dozoya* in the same way they linked other concerns to sacrifice not immediately related to their own safety on the hunt: namely, because their safety was already bound to that of non-dozos. In chapter 1, I argued that dozos destroyed symbols from non-dozo contexts to call to mind the harm that inattention to danger could cause to all those who relied on the game meat, medicines, and other services dozos offered. Here I document this connection. Dozos incorporated security concerns into their sacrifices to such an extent that almost every dozo sacrifice I attended from 1994 to 1997 made some reference to Benkadi.

I begin this chapter by conceptualizing sacrifice as a means by which dozos fashioned themselves as ethical agents. I then narrate a range of dozo offerings for hunting, policing, and other purposes, highlighting the notions of personhood and practices of divination that structured dozo offerings.

Other scholars have interpreted occult or ritual aspects of social movements in Africa and elsewhere alternately as "primitive" forms of social protest (Hobsbawm 1959, 150–174), ideological masks to mobilize public support (Smith 2004, 441), adaptations to modernity under the "guise" of tradition (Ferme 2001a, 223; see Comaroff and Comaroff 1993, xxx), symbolic explanations for emerging inequalities (Geschiere 1997, 11), or "atavistic" regressions to precolonial practices (Omeje 2005, 86). I argue instead that dozos used sacrifice as a contemporary idiom for adapting innovatively to the global tensions that sparked state retraction, economic decline, and social upheaval in Côte d'Ivoire (see Tsing 2005, 270). I contend that sacrifice structured *dozoya* as a moral response to danger, shaping dozo identity as an ongoing, protective response to changes along the border between domestic and nondomestic spheres that dozos have long secured from *nyama*, illness, and instability.

Dozos used sacrifice as what Foucault (1988) calls a "technology of the self" (Laidlaw 2002, 322–323). Through their initiations and subsequent hunting-related sacrifices, they either sought and achieved or failed to sustain the ethical self-mastery they ground in local cultural idioms of reciprocity with non-dozos. In Côte d'Ivoire, where *dozoya* assumed ethnic, regional, and religious overtones in the context of political rivalries that the state polarized in ethnic terms, dozos shaped Benkadi as a form of what Lonsdale (1992, 468) has called "moral ethnicity," a "popular critique of leadership that demands that power be linked with virtue" (Clough 2003, 263–264; see MacIntyre 1984). While President Bédié was framing Ivoirian national politics in ethnic terms to mimic and supersede Houphouët-Boigny's former authority, dozos were imitating the state to enfranchise themselves in the Ivoirian nation as members of an increasingly marginalized population. They took Houphouët-Boigny's call for productive labor as the hallmark of virtuous citizenship. To the extent that they made "of themselves a certain kind of person" through their sacrifices and the labor they organized—"because it [was] as such a person that, on reflection, they ought to live" (Laidlaw 2002, 327)—sacrifice fashioned dozos as ethical agents at a time of crisis that compromised their agency and the state's.

In their offerings to Manimory and at dozo funerals, dozos broke kola nuts, immolated roosters, and tossed both into the air to watch how they fell to divine whether Manimory or their dead dozo colleagues approved

8 A dozo lets the blood from the severed carotid arteries of a sacrificed rooster drip over the *tiningun* termite mound that stood as the centerpiece of Nienesso's *dangun*, Dec. 6, 1996.

of their intended actions, divining the kinds of persons and projects they ought to be and do within a moral community founded on an ethic of reciprocity (see Laidlaw 2002, 324; see fig. 8).[1] They did so by reconciling their intentions (*hakiri*) with Manimory's and with those of dead dozos. Living dozos sought these spirits' protection from forest hazards, the rancor of other dead dozos and, in the 1990s, banditry. Sometimes dozos made sacrifices to ensure protection from all these dangers simultaneously, classing them as analogous. Their novel categorization of policing reflected the sacrificial context of *dozoya*.

Sacrifice, *Dozoya*, and Manimory

Sacrifice modeled each dozo as an "internal relation" (Ollman 1971, 27, 49, 69)—a nexus of overlapping obligations to Manimory, dead dozos, and non-dozos. Dozos' offerings of kola nuts and roosters—and of goats at dozo funerals—defined the dozo role as "a social creation, not an individual one" (MacIntyre 1984, 129; see Lonsdale 1992, 466–468). Their sacrifices sustained "a relation . . . of contiguity, by means of a series of successive identifications" (Lévi-Strauss 1966, 225) of non-dozos' interests with dozos' and of dozos' intentions with spirits'. Their offerings symbolized these overlapping links, standing as metonyms of the relations through which dozos acquired them.[2]

Dozo initiates gave a red rooster and ten red kola nuts to their sponsor (*karanmɔgɔcɛ*) before initiation. They might acquire these gifts any number of ways: inheriting roosters from deceased relatives (fathers, mothers, or siblings), receiving them as gifts while visiting other villages, or buying them at markets. They might acquire kola nuts through familial sharing, gift giving, or purchase. Their offerings indexed their relations to kin and friends, or to the markets that the Jula diaspora had spread across West Africa (Griffith 1971, 167). As with roosters, "Giving kola nuts [was] always a sign of deference, respect or affection" (Dieterlen 1988, 241).

In Denguélé, an initiate's sponsor or local dozo chief sacrificed these items on the initiate's behalf in the *dangun* near their village, town, or city. Before killing the rooster, the sacrificer took one of the kolas, split it in two, and asked Manimory that the pieces land so as to show that he had accepted the offering. If they fell propitiously, a "throat cutter" (*kantɛgɛla)* slit the bird's neck and let it convulse on the ground. If it landed on its back, it confirmed Manimory's approval. Then the initiate and other dozos would roast and eat the rooster. Now the kolas and rooster embodied the initiate's ties to Manimory.

According to Denguélé Benkadi organizer Moussa Fofana, initiation created a protective "tie" (*ka lafyɛnli kɛ*) between new initiates, Manimory, and other dozos because the initiate vowed (*ka lafyɛngana kɛ*) to remain loyal to dozos and eschew adultery, lying, and stealing. He could then participate in dozo gatherings and cultivate dozos' trust. Should a dozo break his vows, Manimory would punish him with a series of "accidents" while hunting or with "mishaps" while on Benkadi patrols. These would increase in severity until proving fatal if the dozo made no sacrificial amends. Sacrifice premised dozos' relations with dozos and non-dozos on reciprocal links with the dead. Dozos brought slain game to the dead dozo's family at a dozo funeral to dissuade the dead dozo's spirit (*ya*) from spoiling the hunt, ruining his family's crops, or making his family's livestock ill out of hurt feelings over being forgotten by his colleagues (Hellweg 2004, 11). Indeed, *every* dozo sacrifice that I attended in Denguélé assured the well-being of non-dozos as well as dozos, especially when dead dozos seemed to threaten it.

The tales of Manimory that Denguélé dozos told illustrate this paradox. Manimory sacrificed his first wife and first son in the forest before returning to the same spot to abandon his hunting accoutrements and vanish (Hellweg 2006). Manimory the hunter became prey. Manimory the sacrificer became a victim. He became omnipresent and all-powerful within the forest as a result, able to help dozos fulfill non-dozos' expectations for meat, medicinal plants, and safety. His sacrifice of his wife and son imbued the forest with his presence so that he became indistinguishable from it, a perfect imitation. Dozos honored his accomplishment with further sacrifices, in imitation of the originals. They established the first *dangun* on the site of his disappearance, offering kola nuts there to secure his help while on the hunt. They then replicated the *dangun* near the villages, towns, and cities where they lived, mimetically extending Manimory's own mimetic power.

Every dozo sacrifice mimicked Manimory's sacrifice of his family. Dozos sacrificed gifts that embodied familial and social relations to help them feed their own families and others'. They related to non-dozos by destroying metonyms of their relations to them, performing paradoxical acts in which they intended, "even if only for a moment, precisely what [they] fear[ed]" (Frankl 1959, 196): damage to these relations through their failure to provide game, protect crops, expel *nyama*, or control the forest burnings they oversaw. Through sacrifice, dozos dramatized the destruction of these relations, and by extension themselves, to overcome their fear that hunting might result in death or serious harm to their families or colleagues. Such "forced intentions" of failure alleviated the "anticipatory anxiety" that might otherwise lead to actual inadequacy (193–204). Reenacting the destruction of Manimory's family symbolized dozos' obligations to non-dozos as an ongoing debt to them (see Eliade 1974), a responsibility to give back to their families the life that Manimory took from his.

When dozos aired their intentions to Manimory, they classified their contingent concerns—with forest dangers, *nyama*, shape-shifting sorcerers, the threat of dead dozos, and eventually crime—under the purview of *dozoya*. Manimory showed his approval or disapproval of these ends in the way dozos' offerings fell.[3] As a result, sacrifice reconciled dozos' desire to maintain their historical hunting roles with a simultaneous need—as indeterminate as the falls of roosters and kola nuts—to respond to threats similar but not identical to those they met while hunting. These threats elicited the deployment of *dozoya* because they menaced the moral reciprocity that *dozoya* upheld.

For dozos, sacrifice resolved "the unavoidable contradictions" (Crespi 1992, 95) between dozos' "need for identity and predictability" as hunters and their "opposed need for distanciation and difference" (93) as men who did more than hunt. Sacrifice moved dozos ritually "from one form of determinacy to another" (93)—from their hunting roles on one hand to their contingent, nonhunting roles as healers, soldiers, antisorcerers, and police on the other (see Gottlieb 1992, 14–16). Sacrifice created "moments of freedom" (Fabian 1998, 21) for dozos in which they could respond innovatively to unforeseen perils in the overdetermined realms of the forest and state.[4] Such moments were, to paraphrase Paul Riesman (1977, 141), "a necessary condition for [dozos'] participation" in Benkadi and for Benkadi's existence. The malleability of dozo roles preceded Benkadi, not the other way around. Understanding Benkadi therefore requires an ethnography of dozo sacrifice, starting with the sacrificial nature of the hunt.

Hunting as Sacrifice

Dozos practiced hunting as a form of sacrifice because they shared their kills with others.[5] When a dozo killed a large herbivore, such as an antelope, as I once watched Drissa Koné do, he removed its *nyama* by reciting an incantation, sprinkling the carcass with plant material, and cutting off and burying the tail. Then he dressed the meat and transported it back to his village with other dozos' help in order to distribute it for cooking and consumption. Drissa explained that he, like other dozos, gave most of the spine and base of the ribs (together called *kasamba*), along with part of the peritoneum (*kɔnɔgbolo*), to the first person he met after shooting a game animal,[6] and the lowest three pairs of ribs (*duangaman*) to his dozo mentor (*karanmɔgɔ*). To his neighbors or resident dozo musician (*dozongɔnunfɔcɛ*) he gave the meaty part of the forelegs (*kaba*). In his compound, his father took the tips of the ribs and the chest organs, including the lungs and heart (together called *sisi*) and liver (*byɛn*). He gave the lumbar vertebrae and kidneys (*kɔ*) to his mother if she was still alive or, if not, to his wife. If unmarried, he gave the neck (*kan*) to the sister-in-law (*ninmɔgɔ*), who washed his clothes and made his meals, in recognition

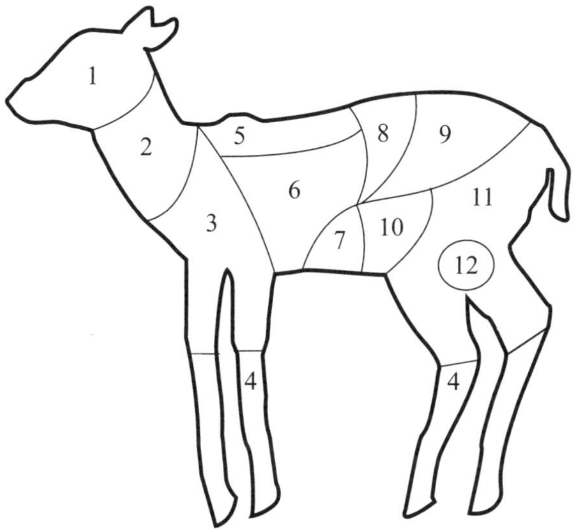

9 This image shows how dozos divided the bodies of the ungulates they hunted and of the goats they sacrificed. Diagram by Lisa Vernon.

of her work. If he was married, and his mother was still alive, he gave the neck to his wife. But if his mother had died, his wife received the lumbar vertebrae and kidneys, and he took the neck for himself. To his younger brother(s) went the animal's udders and surrounding flesh (*sundaga*) or the testicles and scrotum (*bara*).[7] He saved the haunches (*woro*) and stomach (*furu*) for his family and, for his children especially, the head (*kungɔlɔ*), shins and hooves (*gbɛnen*), and remaining intestines (*nogo*) (cf. Cuello and Robin 2005, 158). The carcass's division embodied the relations that consumed it (Douglas 1966, 114–115), revealing the giver as an intersection of obligations to multiple persons (see figs. 9 and 10).

The Julakan word most used for sacrifice, *saraka*, confirms the equation of sacrifice, hunting, and sharing (cf. Cuello and Robin 2005, 261–269). It derives from the Arabic *sadakat*, meaning "alms" (Delafosse 1955, 627; cf. Mauss 1967, 15–16) or "charitable offering," as opposed to the more official tithing or "almsgiving" denoted by the Arabic word *zakat* (*yaga* in Julakan). *Saraka* and its French gloss, *sacrifice*, both named a variety of offerings in Denguélé, including offerings to Manimory and food given to guests at funerals or to neighborhood children and beggars. Dozos used these words to name their distribution of game meat after the hunt. Dozo Samka Bamba,[8] born in Denguélé but living in Abidjan when I met him, called hunting a form of sacrifice when he compared

Head *Kungɔlɔ*

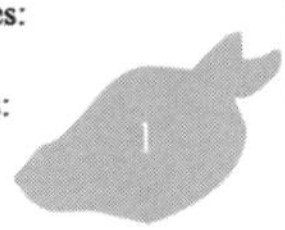

Distribution for Hunted Ungulates:
Dozo's Children

Distribution for Sacrificed Goats:
Junior Dozos

Neck *Kan*

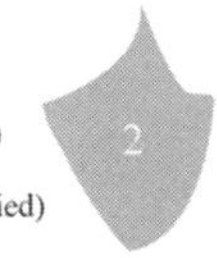

Distribution for Hunted Ungulates:
Sister-in-Law (if Dozo was unmarried)
Dozo's Wife (if his mother was alive)
The Dozo Himself (if his mother had died)

Distribution for Sacrificed Goats:
Dozo Singer

Shoulder *Kaba*

Distribution for Hunted Ungulates:
Neighbors or Dozo Singer

Distribution for Sacrificed Goats:
All Dozos

Hooves *Gbɛnɛn*

Distribution for Hunted Ungulates:
Dozo's Children

Distribution for Sacrificed Goats:
Junior Dozos

Spine, Peritoneum
Kasamba, Kɔnɔgbolo

Distribution for Hunted Ungulates:
First person met after striking the animal

Distribution for Sacrificed Goats:
All Dozos

Liver, Thoratic Cavity
Sisi, Byɛn

Distribution for Hunted Ungulates:
Father

Distribution for Sacrificed Goats:
Senior Dozos, Dozo Cooks

Stomach *Furu*

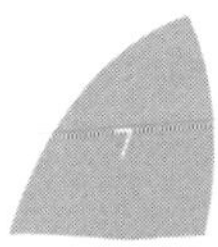

Distribution for Hunted Ungulates:
Dozo's Family

Distribution for Sacrificed Goats:
Junior Dozos

Lowest Long Two Pairs of Ribs
Duangaman

Distribution for Hunted Ungulates:
Dozo's Mentor

Distribution for Sacrificed Goats:
All Dozos

Back, Kidneys *Kɔ*

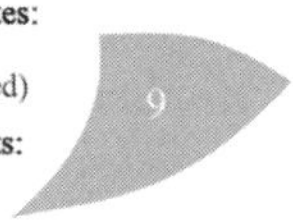

Distribution for Hunted Ungulates:
Dozo's Mother (if alive)
Dozo's Wife (if his mother has died)

Distribution for Sacrificed Goats:
All Dozos

Intestines *Nogo*

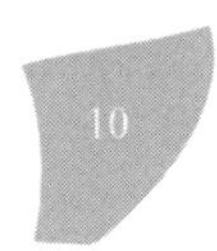

Distribution for Hunted Ungulates:
Dozo's Children

Distribution for Sacrificed Goats:
Junior Dozos

Haunches *Woro*

Distribution for Hunted Ungulates:
Dozo's Family

Distribution for Sacrificed Goats:
All Dozos

Udders/Scrotum, Testicles
Sundaga/ Bara

Distribution for Hunted Ungulates:
Younger Brother

Distribution for Sacrificed Goats:
Sacrificer

10 This table shows how dozos distributed the meat of the ungulates they hunted and of the goats they sacrificed. Numbers refer to those in figure 9. Table by Lisa Vernon.

it, in French, to commercial hunting. "If you kill [game]," he said, "and you distribute [the meat], then you have made a sacrifice. But if you sell [it] . . . you've done business, that's all." Another Denguélé-born dozo living near Korhogo, Mory Diakité, claimed that hunting absolved Muslim dozos of their sins (*hakɛ* or *jurumu*). He said that dozos had historically protected human beings, Allah's most precious creations, from predators that would otherwise have hunted them to extinction. Allah forgave their faults in return (see chap. 5; Hellweg 2004, 11).

Dozos classified damnation, other kinds of fire, dead hunters, death on the hunt, and criminals as problems that were amenable to sacrificial solution because sacrifice protected the reciprocal relations that these problems threatened. These relations were the primary causes of dozo action. Odiennéka referred to such causation as *sababuya*, or "relational causality."

Causal Relations

What anthropologist Michael Jackson writes about "intermediaries," or *sabu*, among the Kuranko of Sierra Leone applies equally well to the Julakan cognate, *sababu nyuman*, with which I've replaced the Kuranko word in the following passage by Jackson (1988, 199): "[I]f a person gives a . . . gift . . . to someone else, the gift improves the fortunes of the receiver and makes the donor his [*sababu nyuman*] ("good cause," i.e., the reason for the good fortune). Or, if a person introduces someone to a friend who is the means by which the friend finds good fortune, then that someone will be known [as a *sababu nyuman*]." A *sababu* is someone who brings good fortune to others by establishing relationships between them. Good fortune stems from relating a person to something or someone of value. *Sababuya*, the quality of being a *sababu*, implies a person conceived of as a relation between persons. The moral assumption is that people should create good relations between others, relations that Odiennéka would describe as "sweet" (*di*).

The quality of an Odiennéka's role as a *sababu* depended in part on one's "intentions," or *hakiri*—what Jackson (1988, 199) translates as "moral understanding" for the Kuranko cognate, *hankili*, and which Bailleul (2000a, 166–167) translates as "mind," "intelligence," "memory," "intention," "hope," "wisdom," and "reflection" for the Bamanakan cognate *hakili* (see Braconnier 1999, 281–282; Carr 1995b, 39; Coulibaly and Haraguchi 1993, 56).[9] In Denguélé, the notion of "moral understanding" implies an intent to act on it (see MacIntyre 1984, 59). Those dozos lauded as *mɔgɔ bɛrɛ*, or "real people," at their funerals were those who had practiced *mɔgɔya*, or "person[able]ness," while alive, what one might call "conviviality" (Overing and Passes 2000; Uzendoski 2005, 16–17). Jackson (1988, 201) similarly defines the Kuranko cognate, *morgoye*, as "mindfulness of others," adding that "a 'true person' is one who has harmonizes inner being . . . with social being" (201), internalizing moral relations as ethical obligations.

Dozos did just this in sacrifice, divining moral action by reconciling their personal intentions with the social expectations of non-dozos and spirits. In the forest, their fidelity to their wives, other dozos, Manimory, dead dozos, and dead dozos' families spurred them to hunt well, thereby sustaining these relations. If sacrifices regulated these ties, then hunting encompassed more than the forest, shaping dozos' relations beyond it.

The Egg of Uncertainty

In Denguélé, dozos opened the hunting season with offerings intended to protect all hunters from forest dangers. The first of these offerings was the *kalanvaŋ*. In Julakan, *kalan* denotes the spring released in a locally made artisanal musket when the trigger is pulled. The spring frees the gun's hammer, igniting powder to fire shot from the muzzle. *Faŋ* denotes a protective offering (the *f* is voiced after the *n* of *kalan*) (cf. Bailleul 2000a, 122), giving *kalanvaŋ*, meaning something akin to "trigger protection."[10]

On the morning of February 5, 1997, near the village of Nienesso, about seventy-five men and boys, dozos and non-dozos alike, piled guns, machetes, knives, and hand ploughs—anything that might kill game—on the other side of the highway from Nienesso, between the village and the *dangun*. The crowd fell silent as chief dozo Ouassé Koné lit both ends of a meter-long torch of dry grass. He held it in the middle where it was accented with green leaves from the *mana* tree. Then he lunged back and forth, waving the torch near the tools and weapons, asking Manimory and Nienesso's dead dozos to protect hunters from stray bullets, piercing branches, animals, snakes, and forest fires. The crowd shouted, *Yɔ, yɔ, yɔ, yɔ!* in response, and Ouassé threw the torch to the ground, whereupon an egg hidden at its center burst. Afterward, the participants gathered their guns and tools and returned to the village in good spirits.

Back in Nienesso, senior dozo Koné Youssouf talked about the egg: "People don't know what kind [of chick] it is," he said. "Is it male . . . female . . . white . . . black-and-white . . . red? No one knows . . . So it goes in the dry grass, and all [our problems] go with it." As a result, he said, "hunters should have no accidents . . . in the forest." I took him to mean that just as one could not know the gender or color of an unborn chick, one could never foresee the hazards one might face on the hunt. But hunters could anticipate them in the egg, which lay hidden in the torch's green leaves and dry grass, metonyms of the forests where dozos hunted. Like the torch's flames, gunfire and forest burnings ignited the forest, endangering hunters. Fire killed saplings, blackened bark, and sometimes burned whole villages, but the forest soon regenerated (see Fairhead and Leach 1996, 230). Dozos symbolized this rebirth with the green leaves near the center of the torch, which focused hunters on the perils they could meet in the forest (see Lienhardt 1985, 293), favoring their "real resolution insofar as it depend[ed] on the moral relations of the agents" (Valeri 1985, 347) and their ability to face what they feared (Frankl 1959, 193). By symbolically intending their injury and death in the egg's destruction, hunters prepared themselves for both.

Dozos described their sacrifices in just such terms. At a dozo sacrifice I attended in Odienné, thirty-one-year-old dozo Adama Fofana described dozo offerings in French as "a form of meditation." If you want to do something, he said, "you know you cannot do it without Manimory, so you come to the bush (*brousse*) to meditate." Back in Nienesso, dozo Doumbia Soungalo described the *kalanvaŋ* in like terms in Julakan:

> The bad things that can happen in the fields today, the egg will take them out of our way . . . It's a sacrifice [*saraka*] . . . it closes them . . . The chief dozo . . . called on the dead . . .We shouldn't have any problems in the forest now that the dry season [*tɛrɛma*] has begun . . . He put the egg in the grass with [our] problems. He names [our] problems while holding the [torch] in his hand.

Adama and Soungalo agreed: contemplating problems before they arose helped preempt them.

Chief dozo Ouassé demonstrated. "You hold [the torch] like this," he said, mimicking the way he had held it. "You throw it on the ground. [The egg] breaks."[11]

"And so, your problems 'break'?" I tentatively asked.

"Unh-HUNH!" replied in unison Ouassé, Youssouf, Soungalo, and another dozo seated with us. For dozos, sacrifice offered a determinate way to conceptualize the hunt's indeterminacy. By intending what they hoped to avoid, dozos hoped to avoid what they intended. When they destroyed the *kalanvaŋ*'s egg and torch, they anticipated their own injury and death. The egg—still invisible and unformed like dozos' fears—seeped into the ground like roosters' blood at initiations, making sacrificers' intentions one with the forest and Manimory. Their symbolic deaths resembled Manimory's sacrifices and disappearance within it, without requiring dozos to sacrifice their families or die as Manimory did.

Through the *kalanvaŋ*, dozos joined their awareness and intentions to the more encompassing ones they posited as Manimory's. They transferred his protection through ritual to the hunting implements lying in proximity to their offerings, transforming through "meditation" their vulnerable, external perspective on the forest into a protective, internal one for themselves and for non-dozos. As hunters, they were not the forest, but through sacrificial identification with Manimory, they were not separate from it, either (see Willerslev 2004, 638). In sacrifice, each dozo existed not only as "a 'me' but [as] a 'not not me'" (Schechner 1985, 112), viewing "nature not as ontologically separate from the human realm but as part of a larger domain of human sociality and experience" (Uzendoski 2005, 657), one they could view alternately as masters and victims, outsiders and insiders, just as Manimory did, who personified their "perspectivism" (Viveiros de Castro 1998).[12] This communion among dozos, Manimory, and non-dozos was more than abstract. Dozos claimed that Manimory communicated directly with them in dreams.

Dream Sacrifices

Odienné dozo Amara Koné told me in Julakan that Allah sent dreams (*kibaro*) to dozos in which Manimory told them to make sacrifices.[13] "Manimory cannot speak," he told me, but could communicate through images. Amara claimed that Manimory had told him in a dream that he and his dozo colleagues should collect a variety of roots, sacrifice two roosters and drain their blood over the roots, burn the roots, pound the charcoal to dust, and wash their bodies with an infusion made from the powder. In July 1996, a year before Benkadi patrols began in Odienné, Amara and his colleagues did so, claiming that the concoction would make them invulnerable to bandits' knives, bullets, and sorcery (Hellweg 2004, 11–12). Manimory himself had instructed dozos to apply *dozoya* to crime, to protect them on patrol as he did on the hunt, through sacrifice.

On December 23, 1996, Chief Dozo Soumaïla Fofana organized a similar sacrifice in response to a dream. A Malian colleague had dreamt that the spirit of a dead dozo had requested an offering to Manimory to protect the dead dozo's non-dozo son from catastrophe. The dozo in question had reportedly shot himself in the mouth with a rifle after raping his daughter, an event that could have harmful consequences (*namara*) for his son. When dozos heard the news, they recognized the suicide as that of a dozo who once lived near Odienné's rice-packing plant. Adama Fofana and his brother Dramane said that Manimory had sent the dream to a Malian to make the message more compelling. If an Odiennéka had dreamt it, Adama said, it would have seemed less credible.

On the appointed morning, dozos gathered in Odienné's *dangun* next to a dirt path that led west of town through grassy, forested savanna. The *dangun* centered on a tall, abandoned termite mound (*bagabagaton*) anchored to the trunks of two mango trees. Chief Soumaïla, sitting on the base of the mound, asked Manimory to protect dozos while hunting and to hasten the start of Benkadi patrols in Odienné, pairing hunting and Benkadi-related intentions with no contradiction. Then he poured a small amount of water from a small calabash onto a hump on the mound, removed a kola from the calabash, split it in two, and tossed the halves twice before Manimory made them land as Soumaïla had requested: one face up, the other face down (see fig. 11).[14] Dozos then cut the throats of twenty-five roosters—offered by as many dozos—and placed them in a cauldron of boiling water to remove the feathers. Then an influential, bearded, senior dozo, Bogodougou Brahima, approached the mound to ask Manimory to protect the son of the dozo who had killed himself. He chewed a kola nut and spat the pieces onto the mound as an offering for this intention.

Later, after the dozos had roasted and eaten the roosters, Adama Fofana summarized Soumaïla's requests to me in French. Dozos had forbidden me to tape-record them in Julakan:

> When we go into the bush (*brousse*), may dozos avoid wounding each other. May we avoid shooting each other. If someone steals, may Manimory tell us. If someone steals and tries to hide it, may Manimory expose him so that dozos can capture him. May Manimory protect us from serpents, thorns, and the sharp wood that can pierce our feet in the bush. And may Manimory show us the men who plot against [us].

Here dozos combined offerings to protect a non-dozo man from catastrophe and dozos from the risks of both hunting game and fighting crime. The rite made restitution for past acts of dozo violence and prevented new acts of non-dozo mischief. Dozos considered these intentions similar enough to address in the same sacrifice. To many observers, Benkadi was an awkward amalgam of hunting and police work, but these goals appeared in sacrifice as analogous aims linked by ethical obligations. To paraphrase Boas, dozos' "alternating" roles were "in reality alternating

11 A senior dozo tosses a halved kola nut on the *bagabagaton* termite mound in the *dangun* near Odienné.

apperceptions of one and the same" responsibility (Boas 1974, 76), to rectify violations against human reciprocity. Another case of dozo sacrifice should explain why.

Venerating Manimory

On December 5, 1996, before the hunting and forest burnings of the dry season began in earnest, dozos in Odienné performed the *Manimorisɔ*, or "Manimory veneration." *Sɔ* comes from the infinitive *ka sɔ* meaning "to make an offering" or "to water" (Bailleul 2000a, 432; Braconnier 1999; Carr 1995b, 97; Delafosse 1955, 674–676; Missionnaire de la Congrégation du Saint Esprit 1906, 162). Dramane Fofana, Adama's older brother, and I arrived at 8:30 a.m. at the *dangun* on my moped with a large plastic container of water that chief dozo Soumaïla had given us to carry. Eight young men, including dozo singer (*ngɔnunfɔcɛ*) Movaly Fofana who had brought his calabash-based harp-lute, were clearing the *dangun* of weeds that had grown since its last use. We shed our shoes before entering and helped uncover three *tiningun* termite mounds, each about a foot tall, that would serve as a cooking tripod. We then picked flexible, leafy branches from nearby trees to offer as cushions to senior dozos before they sat on the ground. Meanwhile, a dozo arrived with a stack of firewood. Another gathered more nearby. Dozos placed the wood in the tripod and lit it with gasoline taken from the tank of a parked moped. The fire would soon roast the goat now tethered to a tree stump as well as the roosters that other dozos would bring. Each dozo had been asked to donate one hundred francs CFA (about twenty cents) for the goat, which had cost ten thousand. About forty dozos arrived for the event.

At around 9:30 a.m., chief dozo Soumaïla Fofana's adjutant, Kanamankan Diarrassouba, gave two roosters and three leaf-wrapped bundles of ten red kolas each to a chief dozo from one of Odienné's neighborhoods, who conveyed them to other senior dozos seated on or near the large termite mound. They later shared them with each other and younger dozos. One dozo gave yet another rooster and several kolas to Bogodougou Brahima, who announced them to Kanamankan.

At that point, Movaly began to play his harp-lute and sing, as Abdoulaye Komara, a middle-aged dozo, crouched over a hump on the mound. Pouring water onto the hump from a small, spoon-handled calabash, he invoked Manimory and removed a kola from the calabash. He asked Manimory to protect dozos on the hunt and make the kola nut land, one half face-up, the other face-down, to indicate approval of the request. Then he broke the kola nut and tossed its halves into the air. They landed as requested. Then he moved aside as three dozos held the goat over the mound and a sacrificer slit its throat, letting the blood drip where Abdoulaye had poured the water. The sacrificer then cut the roosters' throats. Blood flowed on to the ground along with Abdoulaye's libation as several dozos fired gunpowder volleys from their muskets in appreciation. Abdoulaye then killed two roosters over the mound to initiate two new dozos. Both roosters landed favorably on their backs. Finally, Bogodougou Brahima took Abdoulaye's place, halved two kolas, and tossed the four halves into the air. One landed heads, the other three tails. Brahima then stood and, as he crushed the kolas underfoot, asked Manimory to smash the enemies of the dozos and Benkadi.

It was time to cook. Dozos used a machete to carve the sacrificed meat over a severed branch serving as a butcher's block. By 10:00 a.m., they were roasting the goat and roosters. Steam rose from the pot where onions, hot peppers, and fonio millet boiled. After roasting the goat meat, the cook (*gbakɛkuntigi*, "cooking chief") and his assistant (*gbakɛla flanan*, "second cook") distributed it. The singer took the neck (*kan*); senior dozos (*dozoba*), the chest organs and ends of the ribs (*sisi*); the sacrificer, the testicles and scrotum (*bara*); and junior dozos (*kambɛrɛn*), the stomach (*furu*), intestines (*nogo*), head (*kungɔlɔ*), and shins and forelegs (*gbɛnɛn*). To those who had prepared the meal went a portion of the abdominal organs (*kasamba* or *kɔnɔgbolo*): the liver (*byɛn*) and intestines (*nogo*). All dozos shared the haunches (*woro*) and forelegs (*kaba*). The spine (*kasamba*), peritoneum (*kɔnɔgbolo*), remaining ribs (*duangaman*), and lumbar vertebrae and kidneys (*kɔ*) appear to have been shared, no doubt due to women's absence and dozos' ubiquity. But in all other ways the goat's distribution resembled dozos' sharing of game meat after hunting. Young dozos took the head, hooves, and intestines just as children did in the case of game; senior dozos, the heart and lungs, like the father did for hunted meat; the sacrificer, the scrotum and testicles (*bara*) in a supportive role akin to the younger brother of the dozo who hunted game meat; and the musician who lauded dozos, the neck, just as an unmarried dozo's sister-in-law or married dozo's wife (if his mother still lived) took the neck of slain game—a testimony to how much dozos relied on the support of these persons.

The distribution of meat at the *Manimorisɔ* clarified the parallels that dozos discerned between hunting and Benkadi. Dozos shared sacrificed meat with other dozos in the *dangun* according to the same pattern that dictated the distribution of game meat to non-dozos in compounds. Reciprocal ties between dozos and non-dozos structured dozos' sacrificial relations with other dozos and vice versa, revealing that the boundary that distinguished dozos' forest pursuits from their protective roles beyond the forest was a highly porous one. Benkadi was therefore no historical accident. Gifts of domestic animals in the *dangun* created protective ties to Manimory that extended to noninitiated hunters through the *kalanvaŋ* and to all non-dozos through gifts of game meat. Wherever dozos lived in Côte d'Ivoire, their watchfulness over non-dozos pervaded their work just as Manimory's presence filled the forest. Game depletion, political instability, and economic decline fostered crime and shaped dozos' response to it, but dozos apperceived these problems through the ethical lens of sacrifice, giving them ample reason to protect their communities from these threats, as their funeral sacrifices demonstrate.

Managing the Dead

Muslim burials immediately followed the deaths of most dozos in Denguélé, but their families and fellow dozos usually waited to perform specifically dozo rites until the dry season in that or a subsequent year when Odiennéka were farming less intensively, after harvests had supplied surpluses of food and cash, and when travel was easier over dirt roads. Holding a dozo funeral depended on whether a family could meet the logistical and budgetary challenges of inviting, feeding, and hosting relatives, friends, and dozos for the event. As a result, months or years might pass between a dozo's death and the conclusion of his dozo funeral rites (cf. Cashion 1984, 1: 228–229).

A pair of funeral rites, the *yaladon* and *kozi*, assured that the dead man's spirit (*ya*) moved peacefully from this world (*duniya*) to the next (*kiyama*). Each rite constituted an offering to prove the living's esteem for the dead by fostering good will (*bɛn*) among the participants. Dozo musicians, called *dozongɔnunfɔcɛ*—or *ngɔnunfɔcɛ* for short—emceed both events. They took their title from the instrument they played, the *dozongɔnun*, often abbreviated as *ngɔnun*.[15] In Julakan, the verb *ka fɔ* means "to play," and *cɛ* means "man."[16] *Ngɔnunfɔcɛ* thus translates as "*ngɔnun*-playing man."[17] The *ngɔnun* resembled a kora but with six strings made of fishing line.[18] It sprouted a long wooden neck to which the strings were attached after stretching from a wooden toggle held in place by a bamboo-reinforced piece of goat skin that covered a large hole atop a round calabash gourd.[19] A small hole in the gourd's side allowed the music to resonate. Dozo musicianship and *ngɔnun* playing went hand in hand (see fig. 12).[20] But unlike *jeli*s ("griots") who were born into their family's musical profession (Camara 1992, 78–81; Hale 1998, 172–177; Toungara 1980, 15–17), the *ngɔnunfɔcɛ* pursued music due to a personal affinity for it (Cashion 1984, 1: 286, 290–291).

At dozo funerals, *ngɔnunfɔcɛ*s led dozos in counterclockwise dance circles around a central fire or fires in the dead dozo's compound. They sang and danced to put the living and the dead at ease. In return, the family offered kola nuts to the dozos. For the nightlong *kozi*, the dead man's family prepared dinner and the next day's breakfast with the help of local dozos' wives. Some dozos' wives and the sisters and daughters of the dead man later gathered in the dead man's home. Musicians stopped here during the *yaladon* and *kozi* to sing and provoke these women—and sometimes the men listening as well—to tears with songs about the deceased.

Dozo singers played a key role in dozo funerals. In the dead dozo's compound, the longstanding relationship of delayed generalized exchange—of giving meat to kin in recognition for their help and kinship—imploded after a dozo's death. The relationship suddenly became one of balanced reciprocity. The dead dozo demanded an immediate return gift for his

12 Dozo singer Movaly Fofana (*center*). His two apprentices flank him in front of Odienné's *dangun*. Fofana wears an amulet-laden *dozodɛrɛkɛ*. The apprentice to his right holds a dozo's harp-lute or *ngɔnun*. The apprentice to his left wears a *namaturu* hat and, like Movaly, carries a *lɛnyigin*, a fly whisk made from the bristles of a wild boar.

past gifts of game meat, in the form of funeral rites and sacrifices of domestic animals. Without some sort of immediate reciprocity, the dead man would sicken his family's livestock and ruin their crops and spoil the hunt for the entire village. In death each dozo became as potent a threat to the living as the *nyama* he once repelled from the game he killed. Dozo singers led elaborate rites to repel this danger.

I now discuss each funeral rite in turn to show how dozos sustained their ethos of generalized reciprocity after a dozo's death by coming to the aid of the dead dozo's family.

Farewell to the Shadow

In Julakan, *yaladon* means "making the shadow enter." *Ya* is a cognate of the Bamanankan word *ja* (or *dya*), variously meaning one's shadow, one's reflection in a mirror or on water, or one's intangible, intelligent self or "double" (Y. Cissé 1973, 151). The *ya*'s presence in a person is vital to one's physical existence but detachable from the body, which it leaves in dreams or, in the case of witches (*subaga*), to devour the *ya* of others. As opposed to the soul (*ni*), it remains on earth after death. Dramane Coulibaly and other Odiennéka equated it with one's shadow. The verb *ka don* means "to enter," and the prefix *la-* makes this intransitive verb a transitive one: "to *make* enter." A successful *yaladon* ushers the dozo's spirit into the afterlife so that he neither disturbs nor is disturbed by the living due to unresolved grudges.

Before every *yaladon*, dozos prepared to divine the deceased's feelings toward them through the *dagalabirin*, or "pot overturning." *Daga* means "clay pot," and *ka birin* means "to turn over" or "turn upside down" (Braconnier 1999, 1965), the prefix *la-* making the verb unambiguously transitive.[21]

Dozos met privately at the dead dozo's home to overturn a clay pot onto various food items, as the chief dozo of Somokoro explained in Julakan on May 8, 1997:

> You get fonio grains and fill a small piece of calabash with them. There is a tree here called *bureŋ* [or *bleŋ*]. You take one of its fruits and place it on top of the fonio seeds. Then you take an onion and lay it on the fonio. You take some dried meat and lay it on the fonio. When all of this is on the fonio, you enclose it under an overturned pot.

These items, like dozos' offerings of kolas, roosters, and goats, indexed the place of dozos in the wider social order. Each item represented a means of sustenance: fonio, farming; the *bureŋ* fruit, forest gathering; dried meat, hunting; and onions, market exchange. Although women in Denguélé grew onions, just as many, if not more, acquired them through barter or cash at village markets or through purchase at Odienné's permanent market to which women arrived en masse by vans from throughout the prefecture every Sunday.

Dozo Kanamankan Diarrassouba made no mention of putting fonio, onions, or meat under the clay pot but said that dozos may leave rice (*malo*), millet (*nyɔ*), maize (*kaba*), yams (*ku*), and peanuts (*ciga*) under the pot with *bureŋ* and wild yam (*nyami*), items that also indexed a range of domesticated (rice, millet, maize, yams, and peanuts) and undomesticated foods (*bureŋ* fruit and wild yams).

Although I never witnessed a *dagalabirin*, Drissa Koné told me that dozos sealed the pot to the floor of the deceased's home with a band of clay drawn from the soil, from a stream, or from recycled housing material. They sacrificed a rooster over the pot in the dead man's name and left the pot in place until the second rite of the funeral sequence, the *kozi*, occurred, when dozos sacrificed another rooster over the pot. If on unsealing the pot at the *kozi*, they found the food intact, untouched by ants or other insects, dozos knew that the offerings had resolved any problems (*namara*) with the deceased. Once more, intending the potential destruction of metonyms of dozos' relations to their communities and to dozo spirits resulted in protective agreement among the parties concerned. But if dozos discovered that insects had nibbled on or devoured the pot's contents, they performed further sacrifices to placate the deceased and to prevent him from ruining the hunt, spoiling crops, and making livestock ill.

The *yaladon* proper began on the appointed day after dozos finished their evening meal, which began shortly after dusk. In Denguélé, dusk fell roughly between 6:00 and 7:00 p.m. all year long. This meant that the *yaladon* typically began between 8:00 and 10:00 p.m. and lasted until about 2:00 or 3:00 a.m. It took place in the dead dozo's compound and centered on musicians' songs to his widow(s) and dozo colleagues. Dozos danced to most of the songs intended for them; widows did not. Many dozos brought gifts of smoked game meat or freshly hunted game to the event for the dead dozo's family. Together, the songs, dances, and hunting done at and for the *dagalabirin* and *yaladon* amounted to a sacrifice. Chief dozo Sylla of Niamasso explained:

> The *yaladon* is a sacrifice [*sarakabɔ*[22]] [that we perform by] pleasing each other with music and dance. We offer a rooster to the deceased to give him strength [at the *dagalabirin*]. The young dozos go into the bush. If they kill game, they give it to the family of the deceased, to his kin. All this gives him strength. It's a sacrifice. As for the family, they will call on the dozos again when they have found the money to have the *kozi*. The dozos coming from other villages for the *kozi* will offer the shoulders (*kaba*) of the game they kill to the family.
>
> When a dozo dies, he goes to Manimory, to Allah.

In calling the *yaladon* and *dagalabirin* a sacrifice, Sylla defined sacrifice as more than consuming meat and kolas. Singing, dancing, and hunting also expressed dozos' amicable intentions toward the dead dozo.

At the *yaladon* held for chief dozo Soumaïla Fofana in Odienné, Moussa Fofana, the president of Benkadi's office in Odienné, explained in French that dozos' singing and dancing reinforced the good feelings needed to put Soumaïla's spirit (*ya*) to rest. Kanamankan Diarrassouba listed further means to achieve this:

> If you have a lot of money, you give the singer five thousand francs to pay him,[23] but if you don't have a lot of money, you give him what you can. There is no fixed price . . . You get lots of kola nuts to thank the dozos and their wives. The meal that you prepare—if there is a lot, yes, everyone there can eat something. No one will go hungry.

As a result, Kanamankan concluded, "the [deceased's] compound will be strong [*a bɛ baraka*]."[24] But if participants failed to cooperate, they might displease the dead and suffer the consequences.

For this reason, dozos tried to resolve any disagreements among themselves before dozo funeral rites began. For example, on June 25, 1996, I drove Abou Touré, Dramane Coulibaly's principle accompanist, on my moped to the village of Fèrèfougoula for a *yaladon*. At about 6:00 p.m., he began singing for nine or ten dozos who had just returned to the village after hunting. When Dramane arrived about fifteen minutes later, two dozos visiting from the village of Bojubala, arrived at the chief dozo's house where Dramane was staying. They had come to talk to him. They said that Abou had been quarreling with dozos in Bojubala. They sought Dramane as a *sababu* ("intermediary") to settle the matter. Dramane insisted that the fighting stop and said that he had already spoken with Fèrèfougoula's chief dozo about the problem. By the end of the discussion, he and the dozos from Bojubala were laughing together. They had resolved the problem.

Dozo singers like Dramane cultivated *bɛn* or "agreement" at dozo funerals in other ways as well. When unaffiliated singers met at a *yaladon* or a *kozi*, they worked as a team, taking turns as lead singer. At one *yaladon* in Odienné, for instance, Dramane Coulibaly bowed to a singer much younger and less experienced than himself before performing. As he bowed, he crossed his wrists behind his back in the position of an enslaved captive, a remarkable sign of deference to a junior. Such acts, together with the *yaladon*'s offerings of game meat, ensured harmony among dozos and non-dozos and between the living and the dead.

Night of the Dozo

The final dozo funeral rite, the *kozi*, had the same aim as the *yaladon*. The term appears to be a cognate of the Bamanankan word *konsi*, which combines the word *konko*, meaning "fields" (*kɔŋ* or *kɔŋɔ* in Wojɛnɛkakan) or "master hunter" (Cashion 1984, 1: 228), and *si*, the Bamanankan word either for "night" (also *su* in both languages) or "to spend the night" (Bailleul 2000a, 416). Together, they give "night of the master hunter" (Cashion 1984, 1: 228) or "spending the night with the master hunter." Dozos sang, danced, ate, and sacrificed a rooster before freeing the dead dozo's spirit the next morning. Like the *yaladon*, the *kozi* began after the evening meal but ended at around noon the next day. Early the next morning, dozos said the day's first Muslim prayers and retreated to the *dangun* to sacrifice and consume a goat. Then they returned home, sometimes over tens of kilometers by foot, bicycle, or moped and after little or no sleep.

As at the *yaladon*, singing and dancing evoked tears from the dead dozo's widow(s), female relatives, and male friends, too. Because *kozi*s lasted all night, dozos prepared a meal after midnight that included game hunted on previous nights or on the way to the *kozi* and peanuts and yams provided by the deceased's family and roasted over hot coals in the dead man's compound.

Well before dawn, senior dozos, the dead man's eldest son, and dozos close to him entered his house to complete the divination begun at the *dagalabirin*. This time they turned the pot upright in a procedure called the *dagalawuli*. The verb *ka lawuli* means "to stand something up," so *dagalawuli* translates as "standing up the pot." But before dozos did so, they sacrificed a rooster over it in the dead dozo's memory to help assure a favorable outcome. Somokoro's chief dozo explained:

> On the day you remove the pot, if the fonio [and everything else beneath it] is in place, people will say that your pot is good . . . Your problems [*namara*] are over. Everyone will be at peace . . . If the fonio is partially eaten, [however,] there is a problem. If the fonio is completely gone from inside the pot, and nothing is left, there is a . . . big problem. If you fail to make a sacrifice [*fangadegi*], there will be trouble. That's what [the *dagalawuli*] is all about. If things are as you placed them, everyone is happy . . . They'll have good harvests. They'll do good business. They'll hunt and find game.

As at the *yaladon*, risking things that symbolized the dead dozos' relations with his non-dozo family, other dozos, and non-dozo hunters ensured everyone's safety.

The word that the chief dozo used for sacrifice, *fangadegi*, denotes a "sacrifice of which the precise nature is left to the free choice of the one who offers it" (Braconnier 1999, 188). Braconnier translates the related phrase *ka a fangadegi kɛ* as "to do something, intervene, not stand around with your arms crossed" (188). The word *fanga* connotes such intervention. It is the root of the Julakan words for "sovereign," "king," or "one in power," *fangama*, and for "police officer," "gendarme," "prefect," or any other state functionary who enforces the law, *fangamamɔgɔ* (188). Each *kozi* asserted dozo jurisdiction over the dead dozo's compound and fields when the entente that normally governed them disintegrated with his death. The forest also fell under their oversight. In the state of crisis following the death of a dozo *lutigi*, his dozo colleagues assumed collective responsibility for assuring his compound's domestic welfare in collaboration with the other *kozi* participants. The compound and, through it, the village—to the extent that it depended on continued good hunting—fell under temporary dozo management, as did Côte d'Ivoire as a whole in the 1990s.

Dozos enacted their sovereignty by putting it at risk. "If you leave neither rice, nor fonio, nor yam, nor millet, if you set the pot up empty," Kanamankan Diarrassouba told me, "you will starve to death. You try to farm; it will spoil. You'll find nothing to eat . . . It's the same for sheep and goats. Everything in the compound [will be] spoiled." Overturning the pot symbolized the degree of the compound's vulnerability to harm so that dozos could avert it. If dozos found the food under the pot consumed, they named possible reasons for this and, after each one, tossed a split kola nut to divine the cause. When the kola pieces fell as called, dozos knew they had identified the problem: lingering disagreements between the dead dozo and the living, disputes in the dead dozo's family or among dozos, or some other problem that dozos could settle before making a final offering to resolve the situation. Drissa Koné called this process *matɛgɛli*, the "cutting away," of false explanations for the problem, as when dozos cleared grass with machetes to make a path through the forest (Braconnier 1999, 533–534).[25] On the night of May 12, 1997, I attended a *dagalawuli* in the village of Kouroukoro-Mafèlè that required no such measures,[26] but it showed how centrally the welfare of non-dozos figured in dozo sacrifices.

Dagalawuli

Rain had delayed the start of the *kozi* for Diakité Madou in Kouroukoro-Mafèlè until about 10:00 p.m. Such was the risk of scheduling a *kozi* so late in the dry season, on the eve of the rains. When the rain finally stopped, women, children, and non-dozo men crowded around the edge of Diakité's compound to watch as dozos from other villages entered in separate delegations led, one at a time, by Dramane Coulibaly who sang to welcome them as they danced slowly around the compound, bearing gifts of game meat. After a single loop around the compound, the visitors presented the meat to local dozos, who accepted it on behalf of the dead man's family. In return, dozos from Kouroukoro-Mafèlè distributed one leaf-wrapped bundle of kola nuts from the family to each delegation. Dancing, singing, and a midnight snack of yams and peanuts for dozos followed. Then, at about 3:00 a.m., dozos entered the dead dozo's home for the *dagalawuli*.

Before the *kozi* began, I had asked Madou's son, Lansiné, a friend of Drissa Koné's with whom we had once gone hunting, for permission to join him and other dozos in his father's house for the event. He then went to ask the senior dozos. When he returned he told me that they had granted my request. But later, when I stepped into the line of dozos entering Madou's mud-brick house, a dozo my age from Odienné told me that I should stay outside.[27] I told him that I had received permission, but he protested. Given the event's restricted nature, few dozos my age witnessed it, making it a controversial privilege.

Dozo Offerings, Domestic Sacrifices

After dozos filled the deceased's small, circular house, having entered it backwards, the door was shut. A dozo visiting from Guinea, whom I knew from other dozo events, directed me to the back of the house to sit on a stack of woven plastic rice bags across from where Diakité Madou's pot stood. Before I took a seat, I asked the dozos, against all odds, if I could tape-record the event. They politely refused, and I placed my unused equipment in full view of the dozos next to me.

Some thirty of us sat closely packed inside the house, lit by a single kerosene lamp. A sacrificer whom I had never seen squatted before the clay pot and placed a rooster with its legs tied along with a calabash of water containing a kola nut next to the pot on the earthen floor. The sacrificer spat lightly onto the pot three times, repeatedly addressed the dead dozo by his personal name, and offered him the water, kola nut, and rooster. In the quiet darkness of his house, under multiple invocations of his name, Madou's presence became as tangible as Manimory's in the *dangun*.

As the sacrificer spoke, Brahima and a few senior dozos corrected some of his phrases and added others to show respect to Madou. The sacrificer quickly repeated their corrections. He then sipped water from the calabash, spat it in a stream on to the still overturned pot, removed the kola nut from the water, split it, and threw its halves into the air. He did so three times, each time rephrasing his address to the dead before they finally landed, as I understood it, one side face up, the other face down. Dozos now saw that Madou bore no grudge against the living. They blew their hunting whistles to share the good news with everyone waiting outside.

The sacrificer then slit the rooster's throat and let its blood drip onto the pot, as onto the termite mound in the *dangun*.[28] Then, setting aside the rooster, he removed the band of clay securing the pot to the mud floor. Lifting the pot, he revealed a small calabash filled with millet on top of which sat a small onion and some other fruit or vegetable-like substance that I could barely see and failed to identify. It may have been *bureŋ* fruit. The items were undisturbed, a good omen, as Kanamankan Diarrassouba told me: "If you fill the calabash . . . and lift the pot to find everything in place, you will avoid hunger until the end of the world. You will always eat."

Dozos then stood and began to exit, walking backward out the door. Madou's son Lansiné left first, holding his dead father's pot upright on his head with both hands. Dramane began to sing as his accompanists played their harp-lutes. Other dozos fired gunpowder volleys from their muskets. Outside, Lansiné danced backward into the compound, stepping slowly with his right foot to the right, then his left foot to the right and repeating these steps, inching his way gradually behind him with each movement, before stepping with his left foot to the left, then his right foot to the left, and then repeating these steps, continually performing this oscillating sequence. The other dozos in the house and I followed in the backward-dancing line. As the last dozo exited, he closed the door, reversing the process whereby the deceased had entered his home each day, bearing his soul away with music. The dozos waiting outside joined the train as we moved counterclockwise, still backward, into and around the deceased's compound, circling the fires burning there three times, after which the music and dancing stopped, and Lanciné placed the clay pot next to one of the fires. Dozos then socialized and danced until before dawn, moving forward this time with their shuffling movements when not breaking apart from the circle in a faster step. Before dawn, most laymen and children had gone home to sleep, and women were preparing breakfast while dozos were praying.

At around 6:50 a.m., the dozos exited the village, heading westward single file on a dirt path leading through the forest to the *dangun*. Lanciné led the way, holding his father's clay pot on his head and wearing his father's musket slung over his shoulder. The dozo behind him carried a smoldering piece of wood from one of the fires in his father's compound. Two more dozos followed him, then Dramane and his three accompanists, who sang as we walked. I followed them. Behind me, a dozo carried a bleating goat upside down by its hooves. A hundred or so more dozos followed until we stopped at the *dangun* located on the path's northern side. It was a small clearing, already cleared of underbrush and debris, with a single slim tree standing at its center. Those wearing shoes removed them before entering and lay small leafy branches next to the tree for Manimory, as if he sat among us. The dozo who had brought the goat hitched it to the tree with a cord. Then several dozos, I among them, danced briefly to the musicians' accompaniment in a counterclockwise, forward-facing circle at the *dangun*'s edge. Afterward, all the dozos sat in and around the *dangun*, spilling onto the path. Senior dozos sat on piles of leaves that younger dozos and I had placed as cushions on the ground for them before we picked our own. In the meantime, Lanciné had set his father's clay pot upright on the *dangun*'s westernmost edge.

All now turned their attention to the center of the *dangun*, where a dozo came forward with a calabash of water and two kola nuts. Squatting before the tree and speaking to the Madou, he said, "This is your water," and dripped some of it onto the ground before spitting twice at the base of the tree. He then split one of the kolas and tossed it. One half landed face up, the other face down. Madou's spirit, still in our midst, had accepted the offering of the goat, and dozos blew their whistles. The goat now seemed confused, as if suddenly startled by the absence of other goats. It breathed loudly, roughly, and anxiously as a few dozos came forward to untie it and hold it still while the sacrificer cut its throat, spilling its blood onto the pile of leaves next to the tree.

Then another dozo came forth with a rooster for which the sacrificer repeated the same steps as for the goat, this time presenting the animal to Manimory on behalf of Madou's son Lanciné. Now that Madou had died, the dozos were initiating Lanciné in his place. While Lanciné was uninitiated he had attended dozo events with his father or as his father's *sababu* or "stand-in." To continue to attend dozo events after his father's death required initiation.[29]

After the sacrificer cut the rooster's throat and dropped it onto the ground, it stood for a moment then fell on to its back. The sacrificer ordered two dozos to hold it in place to show Manimory's approval. Dozos then left the *dangun* as Laciné approached with his father's gun. He placed the muzzle next to the pot and fired a round of gunpowder to shatter it.

Eleven more dozos fired in the same direction to disperse any problems (*namara*) that might have remained in the pot after the sacrifices.

As the smoke cleared, and while the dozos were still seated, a senior dozo raised a controversy that had been simmering in Kouroukoro-Mafèlè for some time. A month before, Kouroukoro's dozos had begun Benkadi patrols in their village. During one nighttime patrol, a dozo had blown his whistle to try to locate his companions who were patrolling at a distance. In reply, a group of uninitiated youths responded by blowing whistles of their own, making the dozo think that his fellow dozos had replied. Dozos took offense at this but had not yet decided how or even whether to punish the culprits. The issue remained a bone of contention that dozos hoped to settle before the *kozi*'s end. Dramane Coulibaly moderated the discussion while younger dozos skinned the slain goat, plucked the rooster's feathers, and used the smoldering wood they had brought to start a fire. Other dozos arrived with cooking pots, fonio millet, and a basin of water for cooking it. The rest of the dozos adjourned to the village for a morning meal of rice. There they decided to fine the whistle-blowing dozo imposters 1,000 francs each before returning to the *dangun* after 9:00 a.m. to eat the goat, rooster, and fonio together, concluding the *kozi*.

Ritual Sovereignty and Social Action

In a single ritual event, dozos safeguarded a dead dozo's family, assured continued hunting for his village, and protected his village from crime. Their gifts of game meat, kola nuts, roosters, songs, and dances reestablished the cycle of generalized reciprocity with Madou's family that Madou's death had interrupted. By initiating his son, they replaced his missing father. And by punishing nighttime pranksters, they analogized the threat of crime to Madou's death, stigmatizing behavior that, in however small a way, threatened the agreement between dozos and non-dozos that enabled Benkadi to prevent crime and dozos to protect non-dozos from Madou's spirit.

Dozos sustained the agreement vital to moral reciprocity through sacrifice. They immolated and consumed animal victims and other gifts as metonyms of their ties to non-dozos and dead dozos in order to fashion themselves as intermediaries (*sababu*) between them. If the dead dozo's family accepted these gifts, if dozos accepted the meal that local dozos' wives prepared, and if dozos enjoyed each other's company without rancor or regret, then the dead dozo retreated, and his potential to undo *dozoya*'s foundational role in domestic life ended, transforming the negative reciprocity of his death into regenerative exchange, just as Manimory's sacrifice of his family and his own disappearance resulted in safe hunting for dozos.

At *kozi*s, dozos enacted a ritual sovereignty (*fanga*) to sustain a long-term cycle of transformative exchange between forests and human settlements, often in domains that may at first seem beyond a hunter's purview. Dozos distributed game meat in their own and neighboring compounds, but they also worked beyond the forest, and beyond hunting per se, to guard fields from vermin and protect people and livestock from shape-shifting sorcerers and dead dozos. In *kozi*s, they presented themselves as the ultimate guarantors of social order. Through time, as threats against this order shifted shape, from *nyama* and other occult powers to crime and criminals, dozos adapted to these new offenses in the same sacrificial terms by which they repulsed affronts to domestic reciprocity and village concord. The appearance of Benkadi-related intentions and discussions in their *dangun* and *kozi* sacrifices indicated as much. Just as dozos used *dozoya* to secure the void left by absent compound heads, they marshaled it to confront the virtual absence of state security agents from poor and working-class neighborhoods. Their hunting aesthetic had long focused their attention on just such gaps, as we shall now see.

FIVE

Disappearance as Power: Islam and the Secret History of Manimory

Manimory and Mimetic Aesthetics

By the 1990s, the political economy of Côte d'Ivoire had left a hazardous void in public security. Dozos entered the breach in response to obligations encoded in their sacrifices. The aesthetics inherent in their hunting lore and rituals made them attentive to such gaps. If dozos pursued security work so readily, it was in part because a vacuum similar to the state's absence from public security figured centrally in their ritual ethos: that of Manimory's disappearance along with that of his wife and son in the forest. Through sacrifice, dozos replicated and participated in this assimilation to the forest. When they realized that the state could no longer guarantee public security, they adopted its security roles as their own. They were familiar enough with the state from a history of migration and immigration that they too wanted to benefit from the prosperity that they had helped create through their labor and that now increasingly eluded them. Uncertain of the state's ability to provide public safety, dozos imitated police duties just as Bédié, uncertain of his regime's standing, tried to reinforce and

The chapter draws extensively on Joseph Hellweg, "Manimory and the Aesthetics of Mimesis: Forest, Islam, and State in Ivoirian *Dozoya*." *Africa* 76, no. 4 (2006).

transcend Houphouët-Boigny's authority. Mimetic transformation became a shared means of adapting to life in post-Houphouët-Boigny Côte d'Ivoire. Far from proving an exception to Ivoirian statecraft, dozos' mimetic aesthetic was a variation on this theme. If a dangerous void stood at the center of *dozoya*, then Manimory's sacrifice, which enabled him to imitate the forest, offered a ready inspiration for filling the void at the center of state security. Dozos' assumption of security roles resulted as much from ritual design as from historical contingency.

This chapter analyzes dozo stories of Manimory, other dozo epics, and dozos' hunting aesthetics as components of a dozo "historicity" (Trouillot 1997, 4, 26) of Benkadi that is crucial to understanding Benkadi's place in Ivoirian politics. I begin by exploring the tropes that framed dozos' approach to hunting and that illuminate Manimory's relationship to the forest. I then examine tales about Manimory, stories about other dozo heroes, hunting songs, and incantations to show how Manimory's forest mimesis served as a trope by which dozos organized their relationships with Islam and, by extension, the Ivoirian state.

For dozos, Manimory's disappearance in the forest was an original act of mimesis that dozos copied. Taussig (1993, 47–48) has defined mimesis primarily as the process by which a copy affects "*the original to such a degree that the representation shares in or acquires the properties of the represented*" (emphasis in the original). But Taussig has also noted that, while the ethnography of the Cuna of Panama "describes the Cuna world as made up of spirit doubles, it later on proceeds to inform us . . . that the spirits of plants and animals and so forth exist in human form" (115). What the Cuna copied, copied the Cuna, undermining any strict chronological order between originality and imitation. Cuna hunters lured sea turtles with wooden sea turtle decoys (11), while sea turtle spirits allegedly impregnated women by assuming the shape of men in women's dreams (126–127).[1] People copied turtles, who in turn copied them. Power depended on one's ability to double oneself: "The healer's capacity to diagnose and cure, to restore souls (read double, read image) depends on out-doubling doubling" (128). In an Ivoirian state doubled by Bédié's imitation of Houphouët-Boigny—to the disadvantage of northern-descended, Muslim populations—dozos doubled themselves to heal a nation weakened by crime and fractured by ethnic, regional, and religious cleavages. As hunters, they had precedent for doing so.

Bamori and Kowulen

The Denguélé epic of the dozo Bamori, as sung by Amara Fofana (M.-J. Derive 1978),[2] illustrates the double nature of the hunt. Bamori's story begins at night at a dozo's funeral (*kozi*). Among the dozos present stands Kowulen, a shape-shifting elephant-sorcerer responsible for the deaths of 280 dozos. He has taken dozo form and offered a chicken and two kola nuts as a sacrifice for the occasion, outmiming dozos' miming of the forest. He is present when dozo singer Yiran challenges Bamori in song to kill game in the dead dozo's memory:

If you have become a dozo
If you are not a homebody . . .
Then give me Kowulen's tail.
(M.-J. DERIVE 1978, 20–21, LINES 138–144)

Yiran compares Bamori to the vultures that dozos emulate (M.-J. Derive 1978, 53, n. 16):

Empty-handed . . .
The vulture has no bow
The vulture has no trap
But the vulture's beak is never empty.
(M.-J. DERIVE 1978, 14–15, LINES 75–78)

Like a vulture, Bamori hopes to return with meat from the forest to fill the stomachs of those who depend on him for food. Then Bamori vows to kill Kowulen, who overhears him, having now assumed a woman's form.

The next morning, after a quick breakfast, Bamori leaves his village in search of Kowulen despite the fact that oracles have foretold his death. When he finds Kowulen, the battle begins. The two chase and elude each other through sorcery. When Bamori shifts shape to become a ditch, Kowulen becomes a rushing stream. Bamori becomes a fly, Kowulen a bee. Bamori becomes a monkey, Kowulen a dog, all in rapid succession, until, at last, Bamori throws his gun's stock—what is left of it—into the air and leaps upon it, high above Kowulen. But Kowulen becomes a swallow, flies skyward and, with un-swallow-like power, dismembers Bamori, strewing his remains across the forest floor.

Sometime later, Bamori's dozo colleagues find and collect his remains in a blanket and return them to his widow for burial:

[The dozos] saw Bamori's footprints
They saw Bamori's axe and satchel
They saw his old pants
They saw his old shirt . . .
They saw one of Bamori's feet . . .
They saw Bamori's head
And put [them] in the blanket.
(M.-J. DERIVE 1978, 46–47, LINES 395–402)

The scene recalls Manimory's disappearance in the forest, along with his hunting clothes and equipment, illustrating dozos' potential to replicate Manimory's undoing themselves.

As Bamori's colleagues return to the village, Yiran sings of the dangers that dozos face:

What then can I say to dozos' wives?
Speed the dozos' breakfast
It is my men's food for the afterlife.
(M.-J. DERIVE 1978, 46–47, LINES 415–417)

The word for "afterlife" here is *kiyama,* from the Arabic *al-qiyamah,* or "resurrection," linking hunting and Muslim salvation. The word anticipates the Muslim tone of the epic's final refrain: "A good person's death . . . is the mark of Allah" (M.-J. Derive 1978, 50–51, line 453), a refrain that Dramane Coulibaly sang at every dozo funeral (*kozi*) I attended: *Mɔgɔ bɛrɛ sa Ala le nɔ.*

In Bamori's epic, Yiran called Bamori to hunt, Bamori shifted shape to fulfill Yiran's expectations, and Bamori's death won him favor with Allah. Like Manimory, Bamori disintegrated into the forest and attained paradise. He demonstrated dozos' ability to adapt to a plural world—in both the forest and Islam—without contradiction. He died a Muslim's death due to his hunting and sorcery, moving so adroitly across both worlds that he gained power in each.

For dozos like Bamori, the use of mimesis as a hunting strategy flowed from an original doubling of the world. But this original/copy relation existed less between dozos and Manimory per se than between dozos' relation to their world and Manimory's relation to his, both within and beyond the hunt, in both the forest and Islam. I suggest that mimesis works the way totemism does for Lévi-Strauss (1971) and the way signs do for Saussure (1983). In each case, significant relations lie less between individual elements—such as between totems and clans, signifiers and signifieds, copies and originals—than between parallel chains of totems as related to clans, signifiers as related to signifieds, and copies as related to originals. The one-to-one mimetic relationship between dozos and Manimory apparent in their respective sacrifices (see chap. 4) was overshadowed by the symmetry between Manimory's assimilation to multiple realms in the past, to the forest and Islam, on one hand, and dozos' ability to transpose Manimory's mimetic perspective onto other domains, including the state, in their own time and place, on the other. Just as dozos shifted between their compounds and the *dangun* as hunters (see chap. 2)—and between the village and forest like Bamori—their stories of Manimory revealed a capacity to oscillate between *dozoya* and Islam and between *dozoya* and the state.[3]

Dozos looked to Manimory's cohabitation in diverse realms to model, without dictating, how they might coexist similarly within the colonial and postcolonial states into which they transferred the *dangun*. But to understand dozos' flexibility before the state, one must first understand their adaptability to Islam. Their stories of Manimory are indispensable in this task.

Manimory as Dozo Exemplar

Long ago, dozos claimed, Manimory vanished in the forest (*tu*) to protect dozos while they hunt in it. Some dozos believed that his disappearance made him a Muslim saint (*wali*) and that he had descended from Ibrahima—Abraham—who, in Islam, was the first person to worship Allah.[4] But given the sacrifices that dozos made to Manimory and the Muslim tenet against adoring anyone but Allah, dozos' identities as Muslims and followers of Manimory were no mean feat to maintain. Many Ivoirian Muslims, including the self-styled "followers of the Sunna," the so-called "Wahhabis" (Amselle 1985; Kaba 1974; Launay 1992, 86–90),[5] drew on the Qur'an and Hadiths to accuse dozos of *shirk*, or "idolatry" (Ibn 'Abd al Wahhāb 1992, 53–67 passim) for a variety of sins, from making sacrifices to Manimory to using sorcery, talismans, amulets, power objects, and divination, to consuming *haram* meat (see Miran 2006a, 10–16; 2006b).[6] Dozos sometimes felt the brunt of public condemnation for such behavior, responding with violence.

In 1996, in the southwestern city of Gagnoa, dozos bound and beat an imam who had reportedly preached that if "a dozo dies here in Gagnoa, it is out of the question that a believer approach his corpse, for he is not a Muslim" (Mambé Fofana 1997). Although dozos and their Muslim critics rarely came to blows, many Muslims accused dozos of impeding the purification of "folk" Islam (see Brenner 1993, 62, 65–67).

Dozos, in contrast, played on the plurality inherent in their roles (see Jackson 1990, 63–65; Piot 1999, 22–24), approaching Islam as a hybrid enterprise symbolized by Manimory's multiplex self (see Nyamnjoh 2002, 112–13; cf. Comaroff and Comaroff 1997, 34; 1999, 20; Ferme 2001b, 220). Dozos' fractal hunting aesthetic enabled, encompassed, and foreshadowed their mediation of the forest, Islam, and the state, respectively (see Mosko 2005).[7]

I define aesthetics as a hierarchy of preferences for satisfying sensual expectations or, in other words, as the inventive deployment of signs and symbols derived from sensuous experience (see Morphy 1996, 255, 258–259; Stoller 1989b, 8–9). Dozos described the hunt and related to Manimory, the forest, Islam, and the state with images for how things tasted, satisfied hunger, and appeared. They created an aesthetic formal enough to span different areas of experience—like taste, hunting, Islam, and policing—but grounded enough in specific metaphors to resist a rigid formality. An aesthetic approach to *dozoya* and Benkadi can therefore aid in comparing the various pursuits that dozos analogized through sensual metaphors without essentializing aesthetics as a cross-cultural category (see Coote 1996; Gow 1996; Overing 1996). An aesthetic focus, as I define it, challenges universalizing statements about experience (see Stoller 1989b, 37–39), emphasizing the relativity of all systems of classification (Boas 1974), and justifying the exploration of embodiment as a template for sociopolitical life (Boddy 1989; Ferme 2001b, 159–186; Geurts 2002; Hardin 1993; Taylor 2004).

Mbembe (2001, 102–141), for instance, has observed an aesthetic of "vulgarity" shaping politics in many African states. Autocrats have sustained "obscene and grotesque" discourses centered on bodily idioms of consumption, reproduction, defecation, and death to create easily controlled worlds of personal accumulation centered on themselves. The public has participated by seeking similar excess while ridiculing autocrats for theirs in the same vulgar idioms (105–110). This complicity between rulers and ruled has undermined "the binary categories used in standard interpretations of domination, such as resistance vs. passivity, autonomy vs. subjection, state vs. civil society" (103). Mbembe's remarks apply equally to dozos who premised their mimesis of police roles on

Manimory's violent assimilation to the forest and who sometimes resorted to violence as unofficial police. Dozos participated in the same mutually exploitative collusion between president and populace that Mbembe described (104). But to understand the aesthetic link between Manimory's sacrifices and the state, one must first understand the aesthetic relation of these sacrifices to hunting.

Hunting Aesthetics

Denguélé *dozo*s described the hunt in Julakan in ways that may at first seem contradictory. They depicted it as difficult (*dozoya a gbɛlɛn*), much as someone's words might be difficult to hear, tolerate, or understand (*a kumakan a gbɛlɛn*), or as a job might be "really hard" to do (*bagala a gbɛlɛn dɛ*). They also considered it "sweet" (*dozoya a di*) in the way that one might say that honey, tea, or even meat or money are "sweet" or "satisfying"—that is, delectable without being sugary (*timin*). In Julakan, one uses the verb phrase, *a a ja ni ye* ("is sweet to me") to say, "It pleases me" or "It is sweet to me." I heard Odiennéka translate this expression into French as *Ça c'est doux moi*, "It is sweet [to] me." The French word *doux* translates into English as "soft," "mild," "gentle," "sweet," "good," "agreeable," or "pleasant," depending on the context. Benkadi dozos saw the "agreeable" result of curbing crime as "sweet" enough to name their movement "Agreement is sweet," or *bɛn ka di*. To express satisfaction with a particular hunt, dozos said that the "fields were sweet," *koŋ janin*, an expression my friend Drissa Koné once translated into French as *La chasse a été belle*, "The hunt was beautiful,"[8] equating the francophone idea of beauty with the Julakan notion of sweetness,[9] evidence enough that aesthetics is a relevant category.

If you were to ask a dozo why hunting is sweet, he might say that he learns many things as a hunter: how to heal or do sorcery with the plants and incantations he discovers when dozos, animals, or spirits (*jina*) reveal them,[10] and how to stalk game, use guns, and navigate the forest. These skills enabled dozos to protect and heal others, combat sorcerers, and provide meat to family and friends. Dozos learned these skills by fraternizing with each other while hunting, at dozo funerals, or during casual conversation. In the company of colleagues, a dozo strived to "cool his heart" (*k'a jusu suma*) to build trust by humbling himself (*k'a yɛrɛma jigi*) and respecting (*ka bonya*) those whose trust he hoped to gain.

Now, if hunting went poorly, a dozo might say, *koŋ ma ja*, "The fields weren't sweet." The verb *ka ja*, "to be sweet," is a verbal form of the adjective *di* ("sweet"). Dozo musicians often sang the words *koŋ ma ja* at dozo funerals to greet arriving dozos:

Hunting master, oh
His fields weren't sweet
Night fell on the hunters
His fields weren't sweet.
[*Karanmɔgɔ we*
A koŋ ma ja
Su kola dozoy la
A koŋ ma ja]

Just as dozos returned at night empty-handed and saddened from unsuccessful hunts, sad dozos arrived in a dead dozo's compound at night to mourn him. Losing a colleague and failing to kill game were not sweet.

On the other hand, leaving one's village in the morning, killing game, and returning before nightfall *was* sweet. Eating honey or meat was sweet. Learning incantations and the medicinal powers of plants was sweet. All that was sweet satisfied one's hunger for food, knowledge, or camaraderie. That which was sweet filled one up. When a host offered more rice at the end of a meal, one might say, *n'bara fa*, "I am full"—or, *n'bara fa kinin la*, "I'm full of rice." One denoted a powerful sorcerer by saying, *a fanin*, "She or he is full," as opposed to "empty" (*lokolon*), lacking in occult knowledge. Like food, sorcery filled one's empty "stomach," or "insides" (*kɔnɔ*). The phrase *a kɔnɔ fanin*, "His or her stomach is full," could describe a sorcerer, a glutton, or both. Across this field of fullness and sweetness, dozos played vital roles. They supplied, cultivated, and safeguarded things that "filled" people in the best sense. Dozos shared meat, healing, and sorcery with others. They were "full," and their fullness allowed them to fill others with "satisfaction," *janna*, from the verb *ka ja*, "to be sweet."

But sweet satisfaction came only after hard work. Catching game and knowledge required sweat and perseverance, risking injury and death. Hunger, heat, thirst, exhaustion, game run amok, gunfire from hunters who mistook colleagues for game, and forest fires that hunters set in the dry season could weaken, wound, or even kill dozos. Like all things sweet, the meat, healing, and sorcery that dozos provided were hard to acquire. The greetings they exchanged and with which non-dozos greeted them acknowledged these perils and dozos' forbearance in confronting them: *I ni ko*, "I salute you and your exploits"; *I ni nyanin*, "You and your suffering"; *I ni sɛgɛ*, "You and your weariness." Pain and exhaustion plagued dozos due to the hazards of hunting and the impossibility of fulfilling others' desires for sweetness once and for all. Meat was eaten, medicinal plants consumed, and sorcery dispatched, requiring further meat, medicine, and sorcery. "Good sauce," Odiennéka said, "does not last long in the pot" (*Na duma tɛ myɛnla daga rɔ*). The image of a needy emptiness always followed the fullness dozos offered. Their narratives of Manimory, in which he walked a narrow path between plenitude and privation, difficulty and delectability, exhibited the same ostensible paradoxes.

Dramane's Story of Manimory

In May 1997, after dozos had gained national renown for curbing highway banditry as well as crime in Côte d'Ivoire, Ivoirian Radio and Television (RTI) invited dozos from across the country as guests to the evening talk show Appatam to explain Benkadi to viewers.[11] Inza Fanny, who led an Abidjan-based nongovernmental organization that represented dozo interests to the state, had agreed to recruit dozos for the show. He phoned Moussa Fofana, Odienné's main Benkadi organizer, and instructed him to do so. Fofana asked me if I would tell Dramane Coulibaly about the event. Fofana wanted him to come because of his knowledge of dozo lore. He also invited three other senior dozos from Denguélé: Gbaga Soungalo, Fofana Lansiné, and Odienné's chief dozo, Kanamankan Diarrassouba. Drissa Koné, along with another junior dozo and me, accompanied them.[12] Fanny also invited dozos from across Côte d'Ivoire to the event. In all, over a hundred dozos arrived.

On May 14, Fofana, his five dozo colleagues, and I took the thirteen-hour bus ride to Abidjan. The next day, before the taping of the episode of Appatam, Fofana asked the three senior dozos to share with the rest of us any stories they could tell about Manimory. He thought the stories might give the public some much-needed background about Benkadi. The six of us met that morning in a compound owned by Fofana's family in the mostly poor, working-class district of Abobo. Fofana lived in a compound nearby, where I was staying in his son's quarters. By now, the senior dozos present were used to me recording the public aspects of their funeral performances and let me tape their group conversation despite their usual reticence to let me put their individual knowledge of *dozoya* on tape. The room where we met stood on one side of a walled compound that opened onto a narrow path between the wall and a stagnant pond covered with algae. The pond and the improvised plumbing, construction, and dirt roads of the neighborhood typified the poor neighborhoods that dozos patrolled.

After a delicious lunch of golden, gelatinous cornmeal patties (*kabato*) and okra sauce, Fofana opened the discussion. Dramane was the first to speak. He explained that Manimory became important to dozos because of the sacrifices he made. As soon as Manimory married his first wife, Matènè (*Matɛnɛ* or *Matinin* in Julakan), Dramane explained, he sacrificed her in the forest. Then, after Manimory's second wife had a son, Manimory sacrificed him as well. Eventually, Dramane said, Manimory also vanished. "This is the basis (*ju*) of *dozoya*," Dramane said of Manimory. "He disappeared (*a tununin*)." Dramane implied that without Manimory's sacrifices and disappearance, there would be no *dozoya*.

Dramane portrayed Manimory as a man who sacrificed his own family for dozos' sake. Scholars have likewise portrayed dozos as capable of violating the social order to pursue a "name" or "reputation" (*tɔgɔ*) for the greater good. "They are not opposed to seriously disrupting social harmony and cohesion to achieve their ends, and they are frequently perceived as threats to social stability, in spite of their ability to save it in periods of acute duress" (McNaughton 1988, 71; see Leach 2000, 582; McNaughton 1995, 50–51). Manimory's violation of his roles as a husband and father made him an "agent of disequilibrium" (Bird and Kendall 1980, 13), a dangerous hero "operating on the fringes of 'normal' social relations" (Leach 2000, 581), less motivated by "issues of good and evil" than by the accumulation of "means and power" (McNaughton 1995, 51):

> Although the hero may bring prestige and even wealth to his people, he is not so much admired personally as he is feared. For example, one major method the hero may employ to gain occult power (*nyama*) which is used to assist him in fulfilling his destiny, is to violate the tabus of society. If the hero is strong enough—that is to say, if he is in tune with his destiny at the stage of its fulfillment—he will be able to gain control over the occult power released by the violation and become even more powerful for the next step. If, on the other hand, he has attempted too much too fast, he may become consumed by power. (J. W. Johnson 1992, 8–9; see Consentino 1989, 22, 30)

Dramane's story of Manimory apparently confirmed academic depictions of dozos as exceptions to conventional morality.[13]

At the same time, Denguélé dozos failed to conform entirely to scholarly expectations. For example, they used the word *se* or "capacity" to denote "power" rather than the word *nyama*, as John Johnson (1992) does in the above passage. For Odiennéka, *nyama* meant only the vindictive soul force released after slaying game. It was not morally ambiguous;

it was *always* "bad" (*jugu*) in the most *unambiguous* sense of the word. If dozos failed to repel it, it could make them, their wives, or their unborn children ill or worse.[14]

Dramane conveyed a more subtle message about dozo power than that which concerned its ambiguity. He claimed that after Manimory had offended human decency by killing his wife and child, he won a return gift for their demise and his own disappearance: the protection he would offer future dozos to help them supply meat, medicine, and protection from *nyama* and sorcery to their families and neighbors. Dozos' moral ambiguity ultimately coexisted with and, according to Dramane, upheld the moral reciprocity that dozos sustained.

Soungalo's Tale

When Dramane finished his story, Gbaga Soungalo, the group's eldest dozo, gave a more detailed account of Manimory's disappearance. At some point after Manimory's sacrifices, Soungalo said, the celebrated dozo took three more wives. Early one morning, he told one of them that he was going hunting and left. The day ended without his return. This prompted other hunters to look for him. Following his footprints, they came to a fork in the path he had taken next to the spot where he had sacrificed his first wife and son. There his footprints ended, and there the hunters found his rifle and hunting shirt in a tree but found no trace of his body. He had vanished. At that spot, they made sacrifices in his name, inaugurating the first *dangun*. Ever since, Soungalo said, dozos have made sacrifices to Manimory in *danguns*.[15] Although neither Dramane nor Soungalo explained to whom or what Manimory had sacrificed his wife and son or why Manimory disappeared, both portrayed him as inventing the *dangun* and *dozoya* through sacrifice.

I infer three things from their stories. First, he sacrificed his family to protect dozos and their families. The death of his wife and son assured his immortality and his ability to protect future hunters in the forest. Second, he invented *dozoya* by disappearing at the same spot where his wife and son had died. He sacrificed his family and abandoned his hunting clothes and accoutrements before vanishing to make his disappearance, like theirs, a kind of sacrifice. Finally, subsequent dozos stood in (see Wilshire 1982, 44) for Manimory by making sacrifices in the same virtual location, the *dangun*, where he had made his. Dozos mimed Manimory's mimesis of the forest, which in turn depended on his family's metamorphosis into it. The template of his wife and son's sacrifice became a repeatable event, capable of encompassing new circumstances wherever dozos performed it.

The sacrifices of Manimory's wife, son, and Manimory became the source and cause (*sababu*) of dozo power (*se*) or sovereignty (*fanga*).[16] His sacrifices identified the sacrificer with his victims and the first dozo with non-dozos in a substitutive, mimetic relationship with reciprocal moral implications. If dozos' origin stories claimed that *dozoya* stemmed from a dozo's sacrifice of non-dozos, then dozos owed non-dozos a share in that power. As both antihero and hero, Manimory violated the principles of marriage and kinship to enable dozos to reaffirm them, transforming arboreal deaths into domestic opportunities through his violent assimilation to the forest.

Dozos as Chameleons

Dozos blended into their forest surroundings with similar occult power. Drissa Koné once related an incantation to me for just this purpose:

To whom did Allah give the power to change shape?
The chameleon says something,
The chameleon becomes it.
That which sees the chameleon,
The chameleon becomes.
[*Ala tagana yɛlɛmali bisi jɛnin bolo?*
O nɔziŋ k'a fɔ min ye,
Nɔziŋ i kɛ we
Fon min ka nɔziŋ ye,
Nɔziŋ i kɛ we.]

Drissa said that if a dozo uttered these words and made the correct gestures, his prey would see the dozo as one of its own kind, oblivious to the peril in store for it.[17] Such mimesis epitomized *dozoya*.[18]

The Dozo Who Said "Nee—"

After Drissa recited this incantation to me, he told me a story to clarify his point. Once, he said, the animals learned that a renowned dozo was seeking a wife, so they became women to become intimate with him to acquire his hunting secrets. Soon enough, he began to share his knowledge with them. One day, he was in the middle of telling the ersatz women that he could turn himself into a rock, a leaf, or a "nee—" (*mɛ—*), but his mother shushed him before he could finish that last word, warning him not to share his secrets.

Eventually, the dozo married one of the shape-shifting creatures who was in fact a hyena.[19] One day she invited him into the woods, supposedly to meet her family, insisting that he leave his gun behind. While they were walking through the forest, the other animals ambushed him, but he vanished before they could seize him. The animals, knowing that he could become a rock, overturned every rock in sight. But as they neared the rock he had become, he vanished once more. Then they remembered that he could become a leaf, so they scrutinized every leaf they saw. But as they neared the leaf he had become, he vanished again. Then the animals recalled that he could become a "nee—," but, not knowing what a "nee—" was, they searched for one in vain, never finding the *needle* (*mɛsɛni*) he had become. In this tale and in Drissa's incantation, dozos sought an occult fullness that emptied them of their human appearance, sweetening their forays into the forest. Further stories showed that Manimory protected dozos in other domains as well.

A Hunter's Hagiography

Seven months before Dramane and Soungalo told me their stories about Manimory, dozo Mory Diakité told Drissa Koné and me other stories about Manimory in his village of Kiémou in the Korhogo prefecture, two hundred kilometers east of Odienné. Drissa and I had come to the region to attend a Benkadi meeting and visited Kiémou at the invitation of a dozo friend of ours, Tiécoura Ouattara, who had grown up there but who was living in the southern city of San-Pédro at the time (see chaps. 6 and 7).

Years before, Diakité said, he had left his natal village in Denguélé to settle in Kiémou. He now spoke a form of Julakan more typical of the Korhogo region, but he attributed the story he told to his dozo mentor (*karanmɔgɔcɛ*) who, he said, still lived in Denguélé. Then Diakité told us the following:

One day, Manimory of Wassolon and Asanènè of Guinea met each other in the bush. "Good day, Master," they said to each other.[20]

At the time, due to constant warfare, each was wary of the other, but since they met repeatedly at the same spot, they agreed to work together.[21]

"Master, we run into each other all the time," said one, "so let's look for a place where there's water, where we can set up camp to work together. We can hunt together since there are two of us, and we can talk [together] to relax." That's how it went.

"So," said one, "when we hunt, we'll have a place where we can prepare for hunting and also talk. If one of us betrays the other, he shall die."

You'll see that if people fear hunters, it's because of this oath.

"You will hunt in that direction," said one, "and I'll go in the other. When we come back, we'll build a shelter. [Then] we'll sleep. In the morning, we'll move out again, and if we catch something, we'll sell it and return here."

It is this agreement that we call "Manimory and Asanènè." [22] It was Allah who decided that Manimory should be like a hunters' chief or saint [*waliju*].

Eventually, Manimory and Asanènè's place became like a village. They stayed.

When they were old, Manimory said to his friend, "Nènè, I'm going to hunt today . . . If I don't return, so be it. If you don't see me again, take care."

Then he left and went into the bush. Where the path splits, he took off his shirt and put it on the ground. He did the same with his knife and gun. He took off all of his hunting tools and equipment and laid them together at the fork in the road. Then he vanished.

They tried in vain to find him.

Asanènè said, "You don't know what has just happened, [but] I know [my] master," he said. "He wasn't just anybody. From the way he worked and the way he disappeared, he was a saint [*waliju*]."

Asanènè said, "Let's go," and all the hunters followed. They found one or two kola nuts and made a sacrifice where Manimory had left his things. [Then] they took his things back to the village and fired [several] shots. If you see today that we speak of the *dangun*, this is how it began.

Like Dramane and Soungalo, Diakité spoke of events from Manimory's life to explain the origins of *dozoya*. When Manimory befriended Asanènè, the two promised not to betray each other, giving dozos a model for their initiatory vows. When Manimory disappeared, Asanènè made a sacrifice, inaugurating the first *dangun*. Although Diakité made no reference to Manimory's wife or son in this context, he treated the same themes of disappearance, power, and sacrifice that Dramane and Soungalo placed at the heart of their stories.

Diakité also went a step further. He called Manimory a *waliju*, from the Arabic *wali* or "friend of God" (Soares 1996, 741–742). A *wali* is a "saint and wise man of God, living by and for the love of God" (Bâ 1972, 52; Delafosse 1955, 808). Diakité thus attributed a Muslim title to Manimory (cf. Y. Cissé 1994, 17–29 passim), describing the hunt as a means of assuring dozos' salvation:

Without hunting . . . the things of the bush would have snuffed out human beings altogether . . . When you go into the bush to hunt, you expiate your sins . . . [The hunt] takes sins away from your body as if you had washed yourself of them. All your sins are removed . . . Hunting is a . . . good thing because Allah loves people more than anything else. Without dozos, the things of the bush would have exterminated humanity. (cf. Hellweg 2004, 11; 2006)

In other words, if dozos had not protected human beings from predators, then humans would have become extinct, depriving Allah of His most precious creations. Allah rewarded dozos for this protection by forgiving their sins.

When Diakité explained this to me, he did so as if he were talking to his own hunting apprentice—as if I had "killed my chicken with him," he said. "You will say that you killed your chicken with me," he continued. "I will say that I killed mine [with my master], and so on, back to . . . the great hunters of the past [and], we will all be at peace" (see Hellweg 2004, 11; 2006). The virtuous acts of dead dozos, he implied, would win paradise for their apprentices through a long line of initiations, defining *dozoya* as much in terms of Islam as hunting. For this reason, dozos invoked Manimory and Allah in the same breath in benedictions (*duan*) that they recited for each other: *Ala Manimory duan ye*, "May Allah grant Manimory's blessing," or *Ka koŋ ja ka faran Manimory ya, Ala o kɛ*, "May Allah make the fields sweet by Manimory's intercession." Dozos kept one foot in the forest, the other in paradise, one in *dozoya*, the other in Islam. Diakité read Manimory's assimilation to the forest as proof of dozos' Muslim pedigree. Despite the assumption by some scholars that *dozoya* developed before Islam arrived in West Africa (Y. Cissé 1994; Thoyer 1995; cf. Amselle 1998, 120), Diakité saw *dozoya* and Islam as inseparable.[23] He canonized Manimory.

Esau, Ishmael, and Abraham

Back in Abobo, Lanciné Fofana did the same. He was the first among his colleagues to mention Islam in relation to *dozoya* in a story he told about Manimory's ancestor, "Inzu."

"There were twelve boys," he began:

Their father said [to one], "Go to the bush (*koŋ*) today and come back so that I can give you my blessing."

[Inzu's] mother's cowife was standing by the door at that moment. Then she went and found her son, Ismaïla, and said, "Things are falling into place. Your father just called Inzu and told him to come back for a blessing since his father's days are numbered. Go catch a sheep and come back."

They went to do so. They killed it, skinned it, and put the fleece around Ismaïla's waist [to make him seem hairier like Inzu].

[Their father] could no longer see, but he could distinguish people by their odors. He put his hand on Ismaïla.

"Hunh! Is that you, Inzu?" he asked.

His wife said, "Really! Are you so old you no longer recognize your son?"

The old man then blessed his son, doubting nonetheless. Who was it? It was Ismaïla.

No sooner had Ismaïla left than Inzu entered with game.

"Father, I have come," he said.

"Hey! Where have you been?"

"I've been looking for game."

"So who came with meat today? . . . Until the world ends, God willing, your name [Lanciné was referring to Inzu] will not fade. All your disciples will honor you."

This is how Manimory came to be.

Lanciné's story echoed the account in Genesis 27 of Abraham's son Isaac and Isaac's two sons, the hunter Esau and his younger, homebody brother Jacob.[24] In that story, Jacob disguised himself as Esau to steal Esau's inheritance. But Lanciné called Esau Inzu, and Ismaïla (Ishmael) takes Jacob's role. The boys had different mothers whose competitive relationship resembled that of Hagar and Sarah, the Biblical mothers of Ishmael and Isaac, respectively. Inzu lost his inheritance, as in Genesis, but he won dozos' future reverence.

Beyond the story, Lanciné referred to Inzu as a *nabi*, an Arabic word for "prophet." Bâ (1972, 50–51) described *nabi*s as "holy men [who have] received a divine revelation of which they make themselves its humble servants, but . . . their message is destined in general to only a small group of men, and sometimes they must . . . keep it almost a secret." The title of *nabi* differentiated Inzu from prophets like Muhammad or Ibrahima who were called *rasul* in Arabic, "the instrument[s] of a major revelation on God's part, destined either to a vast people or to all of humanity" (50). Although scriptural scholars would quibble with the details of Lanciné's story, they should at least appreciate the restricted scale of renown he attributed to Inzu, Inzu's message being intended only for dozos. The moral of the story seems to be this: dozos have a place in Islam because Manimory followed in the footsteps of Nabi Inzu.

After Lanciné finished his story, Dramane corrected him: "When Ismaïla's mother was pregnant," Dramane explained, "his father, Ibrahima, sent her into the bush (*biŋ*), where she gave birth." Dramane asked, "How could the son of one born in the bush know fear?" Then Dramane concluded: "Inzu is the son of Ismaïla, who was born in the bush . . . Manimory descended from Inzu." For Dramane, Ismaïla was Inzu's father rather than his sibling. Manimory descended from Inzu, Inzu from Ismaïla, and Ismaïla from Ibrahima. Lanciné deferred to Dramane. Both men had found shared roots for *dozoya* and Islam in events involving Abraham and his progeny.[25] Dozos inhabited the forest as followers of Allah and Manimory, disciples of proto-Muslim holy men. They had *sababu*s in high places.

Dozo Prophets

Not surprisingly, most dozos in Denguélé prayed as Muslims (*ka seli kɛ*), attended Friday prayer (*seli*) at mosques, celebrated Muslim holy days (*ka seli ba kɛ*), gave alms (*ka yaga bɔ*), fasted during Ramadan (*ka sun tɛgɛ*), and hoped one day to make the pilgrimage to Mecca (*ka heji kɛ*). Only a minority did not, but they retained their place as dozos.

For example, when rain threatened on the night of May 4–5, 1995, at a dozo funeral (*kozi*) in the village of Zongogoba, I heard a young dozo declare that not even Allah could prevent his power object (*jo*) from stopping the rain. Other dozos expressed audible disapproval at his blasphemy, but no one punished or censured him. Shortly thereafter, the dozo disappeared into the forest, presumably to do his sorcery, reappearing later to participate in the *kozi*. For the rest of the night, although I saw lightning all around us in the distance, a cookie-cutter-like circular hole stayed open directly above Zongogoba all night long through which I could see the stars of the night sky.

On another occasion at a Benkadi meeting in Denguélé on the night of July 17–18, 1995, I met a young dozo who belonged to the occult *kɔma* society (see Zobel 1996; also called *kɔmɔ* in Mali) and claimed not to practice Islam. Such dozos were rare in Denguélé, but their differences caused few tensions because all dozos shared a reliance on Manimory.[26] Dozos pragmatically demarcated their dozo lives from their lives as Muslims without ever entirely separating them. At *kozi*s, they said their Muslim prayers after putting aside their dozo accoutrements and completing the nighttime portions of their *kozi*s. Dozos offered goats or roosters for their own sacrifices but reserved cattle and sheep for sacrifices on the Muslim holy days of Tabaski and Ramadan. And every *dangun* I visited in Côte d'Ivoire lay to the west of the village, town, or city next to which it stood, opposite the eastward orientation of the mosques.

Dozos' stories of Manimory reflected this compartmentalized religious pluralism. Gbaga Soungalo and Dramane Coulibaly in his first story depicted *dozoya* without reference to Islam, whereas Mory Diakité, Lanciné Fofana, and Dramane in his second story put Islam at the center of *dozoya*. But all five dozos depicted dozos as gaining power in dangerous surroundings—the forest, final judgment, and a disputed inheritance—by making themselves vulnerable within them. In Diakité's tale and Dramane's first story, Manimory vanished in the forest. In Diakité's stories, dozos risked their lives on the hunt to protect non-dozos and win paradise. In Lanciné's story, Inzu won future renown by losing his inheritance. And in Dramane's second story, Inzu became a powerful hunter after being born in the bush. But from disappearance, altruism, and disinheritance emerged a prophetic line that tied *dozoya* to Islam—at least from dozos' point of view—even as dozos engaged in practices that some Muslims condemned.

Genealogies of Islam

Dozos followed a well-established strategy for reconciling *dozoya* and Islam (Robinson 2004, 49–55). From the eighth century onward, West Africans encountered Islam through the trans-Saharan trade (Robinson 2004, 38–40; Trimingham 1962, 25–33). Rulers sought to control the trade and practiced aspects of Islam alongside other ritual practices to gain influence with Muslim traders (Trimingham 1962, 37; see Robinson 2004, 28). El-Bekri (1965, 328–330), for instance, describes the eleventh-century ruler of Ghana as nominally Muslim. He lived next to the residences of local ritual experts, but within his royal residence, he had constructed a mosque.

Court praise singers (*jeli*) traced such rulers' genealogies to members of the prophet Muhammad's family or to his close associates (J. W. Johnson 1992, 25–27). In retelling the epic of Sunjata, for example, Mamadou Kouyaté and Fa-Digi Sisòkò traced Sunjata's ancestry to Bilali Bounama, "the first muezzin and the Companion of the Prophet Muhammad" (Niane 1989, 2, 85–86, n. 4; J. W. Johnson 1992, 25–27). Askia Muhammad Touré of Songhay reportedly sought and received from the ruler of Egypt the title caliph of the Sudan (Hunwick 1976, 292; Trimingham 1962, 98), signifying political succession from Muhammad. And bards, both *jeli* or *fune*, traced their descent from Muhammad's associates (Conrad 1995, 88–89; Hale 1998, 64–67; Makarius 1969; Zemp 1968). These genealogies gave their claimants access to diverse forms of power while reconciling, or at least deferring through kinship idioms, the potential contradictions among them.

In Côte d'Ivoire, Suwarian Muslim scholars have shown a similar penchant dating back to the fifteenth century for tracing their scholarly genealogies (*isnads*) back to the Middle East to establish academic credibility (Launay 1992, 79). Such histories have long justified the coexistence of literate and local forms of Islam (81).[27] Like Sufis, Suwarian scholars considered "the tombs of certain founders of scholarly lines" as "legitimate objects of veneration" (87). Dozos likely began to perceive Manimory as a *wali*, or perhaps even to revere him altogether following contact with Muslim notions of Sufi or Suwarian sainthood. According to Amselle (1998, xi–xii), "Ancestor cults and [Muslim] saint cults are similar, if not identical." The same could be said for *dozoya* and the Muslim reverence for saints.[28] It is impossible, then, to understand *dozoya* without understanding its relationship to Islam, one that preceded and framed dozos' interactions with the Ivoirian state.

How the Northwest Was Won

Historians surmise that dozos and other Mande migrants were founding or taking over existing villages in northwestern Côte d'Ivoire by the fifteenth century (O'Sullivan 1976, 66–68, citing Person 1968, 74). These villages, many of which were allegedly founded by dozos, grew when Muslim Jula traders (*jula*) and religious experts (*mori*) began to settle in this non-Muslim, Syenara-speaking area prior to the eighteenth century (O'Sullivan 1976, vi, 73–77, 81; see Launay and Soares 1999, 500). I interpret Manimory as a trope that personified dozos' ability to inhabit the realms of hunting, Islam, and merchant exchange which featured prominently in the Mande diaspora to Denguélé. An attenuated form of the word "Mande"—"Mani"—appears to supply the first half of Manimory's name, echoing the name of the nearly identical hero of Malian *donsos*, "Mande Mori," whose earthly life also ended in the forest (Cashion 1984, 2: app. 2; Thoyer 1995, 131–175).

The title *mori*, which forms the second half of Manimory's name, is usually applied to Muslim scholars (Launay and Miran 2000, 3–4). In popular parlance, it denotes Muslim diviners (*marabouts*; Braconnier 1999, 547; Coulibaly and Haraguchi 1993, 108; Delafosse 1955, 512–513) and is used as a name for boys named after men who are or were diviners.[29]

Historically, dozos had good reason to cultivate Muslim reputations. The process of precolonial West African state formation ran from roughly the eighth to the nineteenth centuries, following the initiatives of rulers, aristocrats, and traders who justified the enslavement of ostensibly non-Muslim populations by cultivating Muslim identities for themselves (see Meillassoux 1991, 43–64). Because Islam forbade the enslavement of Muslim-born captives, the cultivation of Muslim identity provided a potential if uncertain hedge against enslavement (Robinson 2004, 65–68).[30] Although Muslim scholars such as al-Maghili (Hunwick 1985: 77–79, 122) proposed criteria by which to emancipate freeborn Muslims, Muslim rulers most often neglected to enforce them.[31]

Denguélé underwent these same dynamics of state building and enslavement in the nineteenth century. The non-Muslim dozo Ngolojan Koné, for example, reportedly founded the village of Samatiguila as a hunting camp.[32] But when the Muslim Diaby family arrived from a Malian town near Djenné, they usurped the Konés' rights as town founders and owners (*dugutigi*). The Konés left for Bougoussa in the late nineteenth century as a result (O'Sullivan 1976, 80). Later, the Diabys allegedly enslaved the Konés (197–198) during a series of conflicts that elevated war and enslavement to modes of production and state building. These conflicts followed from the emergence of the Muslim polity of Kabadougou, centered on Odienné, and its eventual conquest by Samory Touré (vii, 26, 46–48, 55–59, 122, 160–161).

Given the high stakes involved in possessing a Muslim pedigree or lack thereof, one can understand why dozos' stories of Manimory incorporated Muslim elements. The rise of Islamism under French colonialism gave dozos similar cause for concern. Islam's challenge to *dozoya* came, in this case, not from predatory states but from internal dissension. "Clashes between Wahhabis and their opponents were not just about leadership over the Islamic community, but about the very nature of that community itself" (Launay and Soares 1999, 512):

> ["Wahhabis"] denounced all forms of Sufism as an illegitimate attempt to introduce intermediaries between God and the believer; by the same token, they rejected all forms of veneration of holy men, alive or dead. They opposed any production or use of magic, for example the manufacture and sale of amulets; in fact, such goods and services constituted an important source of income for clerics. They decried a host of practices—for example, the ostentatious distribution of 'alms' (*sadaqa* in Arabic) during life-crisis ceremonies—characteristic of the 'old' commercial/clerical elite. They also denounced all ostentation in dress, adopting plain white (or sometimes, for women, plain indigo) robes . . . (511)

Given dozos' reverence for Manimory, their reliance on sorcery, fondness for amulets and power objects, predilection for almsgiving, and "ostentatious" costumes, it is easy to see why dozos would have perceived Muslim critics as a threat both to themselves and to their communities.[33]

It is also easy to understand why some Muslims would have ridiculed dozos' origin stories, which to them failed to resolve the contradictions they saw between *dozoya* and Islam. And yet, to see these stories "as just folktales . . . would be to misunderstand their true meaning . . . [Their tellers] were not presenting these actions as literally true [or] as verifiable in the eyes of Islam . . . They meant that their mythico-ritualistic practices were indissolubly linked to the religion of the Prophet" (Amselle 1998, 119–120). Historical situations of potential enslavement and the more recent threat of stigma in certain Muslim communities made written theology a practical concern for dozos, whether they could read it or not:

> Rustic illiteracy could hardly be expected to be the necessary precondition for developing a Sufistic interpretation of Islam; indeed, rather the contrary. . . . phenomena characterized as "fringe" or "marginal" Islam are, on closer inspection, sometimes so intimately connected with "core" Islam that they seem part of a single complex. Moreover, that which in a specific context is regularly categorized as 'pre-Islamic survival' is in many cases nothing of the sort. (I. Lewis 1996, 96)

Dozos' stories of Manimory as a Muslim saint made sense in a historical context in which dozos felt the need to stress the Muslim aspects of their ideas and practices.

Consequently, dozos in Denguélé focused as much on Islam as they did on hunting:

> In its most basic terms, what is really at stake here is a broader issue: the fierce and constantly recharged theological debate concerning the interpretation of the Prophet's message. Here attention focuses on the meaning and importance of such famous revelatory passages in the Koran as the injunction to believers to "seek the means to come to Him" (v. 39),[34] traditionally taken by Sufis to signal the mediatory power of saints. (I. Lewis 1996, 95–96)

Dozos' stories of Manimory created the same relationship between *dozoya* and Islam that dozo sacrifice created between *dozoya* and domestic life: a retromimetic one. So closely did dozos associate the two poles of these respective contrasts that it was no longer possible to tell which came first—which was the original and which the copy (see Amselle 1998, 120). Manimory's assimilation to the forest and Islam joined the two realms as contrasting aspects of one and the same reality, legitimizing *dozoya* as licit for Muslims while reaffirming *dozoya*'s autonomy from Islam for those who eschewed it.

Of Credos and NGOs

As forms of religious apologetics, dozos' stories of Manimory were as political as they were religious and as relevant to twentieth-century Côte d'Ivoire as to precolonial and colonial Côte d'Ivoire. After 1993, the state's covertly anti-Muslim rhetoric of *ivoirité* and Alassane Ouattara's exclusion from presidential elections gave dozos new reasons for vigilance, although this time it was dangerous *to be* Muslim. Once again, dozos transformed themselves in response, becoming ersatz police to create, at least for the moment, a privileged relationship with the state.

In this sense, dozos shared something in common with Wahhabi and Reformist Muslims who, in the early 1990s, were trying to engage fellow Ivoirians in a national conversation about Islam. In contrast to dozos, these "two groups share[d] a more normative interpretation of religion, a concern for reforming and democratizing Islamic education, the use of local languages for this purpose and a pro-active promotion of a new kind of Muslim identity" (Miran 2006a, 12). Wahhabis established madrasas and built mosques to preach "a return to . . . pristine Islam" (11–12), feeling "ill at ease with the traditional Islamic heritage that their parents had transmitted to them." Reformists, on the other hand, tried to "reconcile spirituality and modernity":

> [They] advocated the community's unity within absolute respect for the pluralism of Islamic expressions . . . unflinching tolerance for other religions, including African traditional religions, a strict separation between Islam and issues of ethnicity and nationality, and a liberal approach towards Muslim women and gender relations. (14)

Regardless of their differences in approach, Wahhabis, Reformists, and dozos were making self-conscious attempts to engage audiences with viewpoints different from their own.

All three groups formed state-approved bureaucratic organizations to do so. "Wahhabis created the Association des Musulmans Orthodoxes de Côte d'Ivoire (Association of Orthodox Muslims of Côte d'Ivoire or AMOCI) in 1976." It "reconstituted itself as the AMSCI" in 1994, "changing the epithet 'Orthodox' for 'Sunni'" (Miran 2006a, 12). Reformists founded the Association des Élèves et Étudiants Musulmans de Côte d'Ivoire (Muslim Students Association of Côte d'Ivoire or AEEMCI)" in 1972 and, in 1982, the "Communauté Musulmane de la Riviera (Riviera Muslim Community [CMR]) (14). Between 1991 and 1993, they founded no less than six more organizations, culminating in the Conseil National Islamique (National Islamic Council [CNI]) in 1993. The CNI, in turn, won backing from "all reformist associations, the Wahhabi national organ and 45 local Muslim associations and communities (500 in 2005)" (15).

At the same moment, in 1992, a dozo diplomat and businessman, Inza Fanny, founded the NGO Afrique Environnementale to represent Benkadi's interests to the state. I examine Afrique Environnementale in depth in chapter 6. For now, I mean only to place this dozo NGO and Benkadi in the broader context of an emerging collaboration between religious organizations and the state.

Shortly after the start of multiparty democracy in Côte d'Ivoire, Muslims were forming state-recognized NGOs at the same moment that dozos were organizing Benkadi and Afrique Environnementale. Dozos and mainstream Muslims alike were looking to play new roles on a rapidly changing political landscape. They had different goals in mind but the same institutional savvy in pursuing them. Dozos were more than country bumpkins or urban ne'er-do-wells facing the challenges of modernity, cultural diversity, and religious pluralism for the first time. They had been doing so for at least a century.

Muslims in the *Dangun*, Dozos on Appatam

Against the changing religious contexts of colonialism and independence, dozos had articulated a Muslim apologetics for their ritual and hunting practices. They had integrated a local approach to Islam into Islam's increasingly global presence through an aesthetic that linked their hunting-related pursuits to Islam's universal concerns (see Mudimbe 1988, 196, 199–200). Before Benkadi, then, dozo mimesis was already an "engaged universal" (Tsing 2005, 8, 10). Dozos structured their hunting practices with tropes of sweetness and difficulty, fullness and emptiness, and the process of mimetic transformation that mediated these contrasts. They shifted shape in the forest to bring the sweetness of food, medicine, divine grace, and salvation to their families, neighbors, and apprentices, moving as easily between Islam and *dozoya* in the footsteps of their proto-Muslim heroes as they did between their compounds and the forest.

Dozos linked themselves to prophetic figures who predated Muhammad but revered Allah: Inzu, Ismaïla, and, through them, Ibrahima. Dozos' approach to Islam therefore stood at some remove from the Qur'an and the Hadiths. Nowhere in the Qur'an does Esau appear or his father make a favorable prediction for him—the latter not even in Genesis. Nor does Manimory descend from Ismaïla or Inzu, or hunting expiate sins. But dozos associated *dozoya* and Islam without confusing them. Their power lay in their ability to fluctuate between the two. Their Muslim pedigree was intertextual, provisional, and contested rather than Qur'anic, definitive, and hegemonic. It referenced the Torah, the Qur'an, and dozo orature, alluding to Muslim scriptures while reinterpreting them as dozo epic narratives. In Ricœur's terms (1981, 110–114, 131–144), dozos "distanciated" rather than violated scriptural meanings. In that spirit, Dramane Coulibaly called his harp-lute the "dozos' Qur'an" (*dozo ya kurana*). The songs and epics it accompanied, like that of Bamori and Kowulen, paralleled the Qur'an as sources of dozo revelation.

Following Ioan Lewis (1996), one need not oppose *dozoya* to Islam because *dozoya* relied on local ritual practices. Dozos who recited the Muslim credo, prayed, fasted, gave alms, and made or contemplated the hajj were Muslim dozos. They told *dozoya*'s origin stories to reflect this. Islam and *dozoya* worked toward the same ends in these stories: the salvation of dozos and their communities. "It is a truism," as Lambek (1990, 23) has written, "to say that Islam is a text-based religion." But without examining the "local hermeneutics" of religious practice (23–24), one assumes at one's peril that Muslim texts are primarily or uniquely literate. By reinterpreting and combining Muslim texts and practices, a Biblical story, dozo oral epics, and hunting, dozos invented *dozoya* not only as a legitimate Muslim pursuit—if only in their eyes—but as a cross-cultural form of ethical practice. Muslim dozos faced state power in the twentieth-century, as in the nineteenth, under conditions of sociopolitical uncertainty. Like the more formally Muslim NGOs that appeared in the 1990s, Benkadi pursued a strategy of bureaucratic "accommodation" with the Ivoirian state (see Miran 2006a, 16).

None of this was apparent on the television show Appatam. The preparations that the Denguélé dozos had made to explain the relationship between Manimory and Benkadi bore no fruit. Moussa Fofana told the story of Nabi Inzu in French, but accidentally substituted the name of another Abrahamic prophet, Youssouf (Joseph), for Inzu.[35] Dramane and a group of Senufo dozo musicians sang, but with no one to translate their lyrics into French. The Ivoirian dance company Djolèm performed a dozo dance—by non-dozos. And non-dozo "experts" commented on Benkadi. The show's host sat against a painted backdrop depicting the open-air, thatch-roofed patio intended for conversations with guests but managed little interaction with the over fifty dozos in uniform—I among them—who sat on either side of the studio along with the RTI crew and other guests, all sweating from lack of sufficient air conditioning. The state's mimesis of dozos, with its television host and experts, had outflanked dozos' mimesis of the state. It was a portent of things to come.

The next chapter examines Benkadi's troubled, six-year existence as a form of "constructive engagement towards the state" (Miran 2006a, 16).

SIX

Organizing Benkadi

Changed Men

Because dozos aimed to win the state's approval for their Benkadi activities, they allied themselves with two bureaucratically organized national dozo associations, and they developed a legal framework with which to define and punish crimes through a form of restorative justice. Since dozos approached crime through the mimetic lens of their hunting aesthetics, they readily adapted to the bureaucratic structure of the state they were trying to imitate. True to their chameleon-like nature, the more they changed, the more they stayed the same. But in the increasingly unstable environment of fin de siècle Côte d'Ivoire, their new security roles assumed a controversial political aura.

The Benkadi movement first arrived in northwestern Côte d'Ivoire from Mali as a dozo-centered, community-based self-help movement. It aimed to resolve long-standing conflicts between subsistence hunters and state hunting laws. Ivoirian hunting laws, first codified under colonialism and modified under independence, regulated a domain that dozos had long managed through ritual. Benkadi dozos thus found themselves astride two contrasting legal systems: one, a routinized set of laws alienated from everyday life; the other, a reciprocal ethic of virtue grounded in ritual practice.[1] The discrepancy did not prevent local officials from collaborating with dozos. But as Benkadi patrols began surfacing in major Ivoirian cities and as dozos began to air their grievances, national officials sought to check dozos' advances. They did so by engaging the same national dozo organizations that dozos hoped would resolve their differences with the state.

This chapter shows how the tenuous alliance between dozo organizations and the state began, developed, and disintegrated. I begin by describing Benkadi's arrival in Denguélé, its early collaborations with local officials in Denguélé's northernmost reaches, and the legal context in which these collaborations occurred. I then detail the laws that Benkadi dozos proposed for regulating crime in areas that lacked a regular police presence, and I describe the network of meetings dozos held to spread Benkadi in the Odienné prefecture. Finally, I examine the two national organizations that claimed to represent dozo interests to the state and whom the state managed to turn against each other to its own advantage.

Transnational Origins

In the 1980s, Malian *donsos* created the National Hunters' Association of Mali (Association Nationale des Chasseurs du Mali) to manage a social security fund for its members (Cashion 1984, 1: 103). *Donsos* paid 1,500 francs per year for a membership card. A president (*président*), secretary general (*secrétaire générale*), and treasurer (*trésorier*) distributed the funds to ill or injured members (103), taking their titles from the bureaucracy with which French officials had ruled West Africa and that African leaders used to structure their postcolonial states (see W. Cohen 1971, 61–62; République de Côte d'Ivoire n.d.). *Donsos* named the movement "Benkadi." They justified their entry into national affairs on claims that past *donsos* had founded a majority of Mali's villages and contributed to national well-being by healing illnesses, defending villages from attack, identifying fertile fields for farmers, blazing trails over which the state later built roads, and protecting livestock by killing carnivores.[2] They consequently requested hunting rights over and against the Malian laws that restricted their hunting.

Mali's colonial and independence regimes had discouraged peasants from killing game, ostensibly to protect the environment. Mali's Water and Forest police (Les Eaux et Forêts) routinely confiscated *donsos*' game and weapons when they caught them hunting. *Donsos* claimed that the state, in contrast, ignored wealthy elites who hired poachers to kill game on a more massive scale, which harmed the environment far more than *donsos* did. But when *donsos* tried to bring such discrepancies to the state's attention, officials reportedly ignored them. Benkadi thus called for an end to police harassment, a 50 percent reduction in the Malian gun tax followed by its eventual abolishment, and official papers to authorize *donsos* to carry guns. In exchange, *donsos* pledged to cooperate with the Water and Forest police in overseeing national parks, as dozos were already doing in Guinea (M. Diarra n.d.; Leach 2000, 580).[3]

Benkadi Comes to Côte d'Ivoire

Ivoirian dozos embraced Benkadi's goals. Côte d'Ivoire imposed similar restrictions on hunting and gun ownership. Ivoirian dozos saw in Benkadi a strategy for overturning these restrictions and reasserting their ritual sovereignty over the forest. They challenged Ivoirian law in doing so.

In Côte d'Ivoire, French colonial law had allowed for "each member of a local ethnic group to hunt individually—and for his subsistence—nonprotected animals with customary, authorized weapons of local manufacture." These included certain kinds of firearms, namely, "trade arms limited to flint lock and piston guns" (Roure 1956, 154). But after independence, Côte d'Ivoire as a rule forbade the use of *all* firearms for either "customary" (*coutumier*) or "traditional" (*traditionnel*) hunting (Ministère de la Protection de l a Nature 1968, 7, art. 11). And, following the colonial precedent of restricting populations to their administrative units (*cantons*) for hunting purposes (Roure 1956, 154–155), postindependence law confined "traditional" hunters to their prefectures to hunt as long as they did so mostly without firearms (Ministère de la Protection de la Nature 1968, 7, art. 12). The only exceptions applied to "customary" hunters using locally manufactured muskets. They could only hunt animals that were either listed as "nonprotected" or were absent from lists of fully or partially protected animals (Ministère de la Protection de la Nature 1968, 6–14, art. 9; Roure 1956, 155–156; see République de Côte d'Ivoire 1994). But in a nation lacking the means to enforce its laws, many citizens and residents owned and hunted with industrially manufactured firearms without applying for permits and without regard for protected species. Similar laws regulated "classified forests" (*forêts classifiées*), forbidding hunting, burning, and even the commercial exploitation of medicinal plants within them (Ministère de l'Agriculture 1968, 6–7, 8, 39).

The state's oversight of forests contradicted, point for point, dozos' stewardship of them. State law forbade dozos from exploiting the forest in ways that sustained the reciprocal exchanges with non-dozos that defined their roles. Whether dozos and the state intended it or not, the exercise of *dozoya* was an inherently political act. Since 1965, when Côte d'Ivoire adopted most of its hunting code, forest rangers (*agents des Eaux et Forêts*) and other security agents had ample precedent for confronting dozos and other hunters when they returned home from hunting with firearms and/or game or from setting brush and forest fires. Such confrontations usually ended with the confiscation of hunters' guns and/or game or with an "arrangement" (*arrangement*) in which hunters offered money or game in exchange for permission to keep their guns. But three decades after the hunting code's original promulgation, one Ivoirian journalist wrote that "traditional hunters of the villages of the northwest, both peasants and herders, [still did] not understand the behavior of security forces toward them as soon as they [were] in possession of a firearm" (L. Kouassi 1993a). Whereas dozos took a decentralized approach to managing forests and the state, a centralized one, Benkadi sought a compromise. This alone assured widespread interest in Benkadi among dozos, noninitiatied hunters, and the many non-hunters who benefited from hunting. Whereas state laws treated dozos and other hunters as traditionalists whose illegal practices placed them outside the law as subjects, Benkadi reframed dozos as modernists, justifying their assumption of a position as full citizens within the nation. The transformation began in one of Côte d'Ivoire's remotest areas.

Benkadi Networks

Close to the Malian border in a Denguélé village that I will call Borosso, dozo Inza Konaté told me about the role that senior dozo Yaya Cissé had played in bringing Benkadi to Côte d'Ivoire.[4] Yaya first heard about Benkadi by word of mouth from other dozos. He then sent two Ivoirian colleagues to Mali, Inza Konaté from Borosso and Kemba Koné from the village of Yorojan,[5] to learn more.[6] After Inza and Kemba returned, Yaya sent another dozo, Yacou Cissé, to Mali to confirm what Inza and Kemba had said about Benkadi. Then in late 1990, Kemba and Yacou Cissé attended a Benkadi meeting in the Ivoirian village of Gbèya,[7] where Malian dozos had arrived to explain Benkadi's principles.[8] Kemba Koné claimed that when he first heard Malian dozos preaching vigilance against livestock theft, he said to himself, "I like this," and told his father about it.[9] "I have gone to [meet] the dozos," he reportedly told his father. "They told me something I liked: 'If you agree [*ka bɛn*], then together we can find a solution'"—to Côte d'Ivoire's problems with theft and crime.

Inza Konaté said that by the early 1990s, criminals were running rampant in Côte d'Ivoire. In rural areas, he claimed, criminal Fulbe cattle

13 Women prepare a meal for dozos before the *tonisigi* in the village capital of the subprefecture of Bako. The scene was roughly identical when women cooked in anticipation of a dozo funeral (*kozi*).

herders were beating people and stealing their crops, livestock, and cash, while police and gendarmes gave preference to Fulbe suspects in disputes with Julakan-speaking farmers. The herders' cash revenues from cattle sales allegedly enabled them to pay large sums to resolve their legal problems with authorities. Because Benkadi threatened to put an end to such corruption, Yaya Cissé had little difficulty rallying dozos to Benkadi's cause throughout the Toudougou area in the Goulia subprefecture where he lived.[10] On June 11, 1991, about a year after Yaya sent Kemba and Inza to Mali, dozos in Goulia founded an Ivoirian branch of Benkadi, naming Yaya Cissé as its head.[11]

Benkadi spread to other northern Denguélé villages in the following way: Proponents in a given village asked permission from village notables—the chief (*dugutigi*), imam (*almami*), women's chief (*mosokuntigi*), and young men's chief (*kambɛrɛnkuntigi*)—to invite Benkadi dozos from another village to come and explain Benkadi's principles to them. In Borosso, for example, Kemba said, pro-Benkadi dozos addressed 125 people in addition to village notables to win approval to call on Benkadi dozos to explain Benkadi procedures to them. A search for agreement (*bɛn*), then, guided the establishment of Benkadi from the start. Once villagers agreed to allow Benkadi to operate in their village, local dozos told Benkadi representatives to arrive on a given day, and women prepared food for the guests (see fig. 13). When the visitors arrived, according to Inza, they first thanked the women for the meal. Then they explained Benkadi's principles. Dozos called these subprefectural or village-level meetings *dozotonsigis*, or "association inaugurations"—*tonsigis* for short—from the Julakan word *ton*, "association,"[12] and *sigi*, "to be seated," "set up," "found," or "establish." Dozos commonly referred to Benkadi as the *dozoton* or "dozo association."[13]

Tonsigis

I attended four subprefectural *tonsigis* between 1994 and 1997. Each drew hundreds of dozos from across Denguélé. Festivities occurred in an open area used for public gatherings. But in most other ways, dozos organized *tonsigis* in much the same way that they did dozo funerals. Meetings occurred mostly in the dry season, began after the evening meal, and lasted until early afternoon the next day. As at dozo funerals, dozos listened to songs sung by dozo musicians and danced in counterclockwise circles while women and children clapped to the music and sang the songs' refrains from the edge of the dance grounds. Uninitiated men watched. When dozos who were ironsmiths (*numu*) danced, they brandished burning pieces of wood and red-hot coals, piercing or slashing themselves with sharp objects without bleeding, blowing sparks out of their mouths (see McNaughton 1988, 44–46), and performing other magical feats, just as they did at *kozis*.

At some point after midnight, dozos prepared a meal of roasted peanuts, yams, and game meat for each other on the open fire or fires in the center of the dance grounds. Shortly thereafter, a visiting Benkadi representative, usually from the northern village of Yorojan, publicly recited Benkadi procedures for fining criminals. Then dancing and singing began again and lasted until morning. By that time, most spectators had returned home, and activities paused with the first 4:30 a.m. call to prayer, at which point dozos left the dance grounds to pray. Just before daylight, they walked to the *dangun* to discuss Benkadi affairs in private. These discussions often involved more than crime. In one dozo conclave I attended, dozos suggested remedies for illnesses from which local people were suffering. One dozo conveyed the symptoms that various sick persons were suffering, and his colleagues proposed treatments that might help.[14] The same dozo relayed these suggestions to the persons in question. At the same conclave, dozos discussed what to do about a series of sorcery attacks in a village on the Guinean border whose dozos had asked for help. They strategized about how to respond to the attacks with sorcery of their own.[15] At similar conclaves I attended, dozos also initiated new members.

The lack of blood sacrifices at *tonsigi*s, apart from dozo initiations, seemed to be the only exception to usual dozo practice. I once saw dozos crush a red kola nut in the *dangun* at a *tonsigi* I attended in Duékoué. But if Benkadi had been inconsistent with *dozoya*, it is unlikely that dozos would have adopted it so readily, over such a broad territory, or with the approval of its initial, rural constituency. Once Malians introduced it to Borosso, and Borosso adopted it, nearby villages in turn asked Borosso dozos to explain Benkadi to them. These villages introduced it to others, and so on. In this way, Benkadi spread far and wide across Denguélé and Côte d'Ivoire, establishing a national, indeed transnational, network parallel to, though vaster than, the ones dozos maintained by attending colleagues' funerals. As Kemba Koné implied, dozos could in principle identify the village by which Benkadi came to them. They could also identify those villages to which they introduced it. Such relationships created a hierarchy visible in the way that Odienné's dozos deferred to Yorojan's in all matters Benkadi. Yorojan dozos explained Benkadi at most of the *tonsigi*s at which dozos established new Benkadi branches in Denguélé.[16]

Given Benkadi's transnational origins and immigrant members, it challenged Côte d'Ivoire's territorial integrity as a nation-state (see Anderson 1991, 7; Handler 1988, 32, 39–43) as well as the state's monopoly on law enforcement and firepower. But dozos saw little contradiction between their historical responsibilities and their new security efforts. Indeed, they saw Benkadi as contributing to national stability by policing rural areas neglected by official police. In northern villages such as Yorojan, they undertook their first Benkadi patrols. These early initiatives stand as models against which to compare subsequent iterations of Benkadi.

Benkadi in Yorojan

Kemba said that dozos began their Benkadi patrols in Yorojan at midnight. Villagers knew to be indoors by then to respect the curfew. Between midnight and the 4:30 a.m. call to prayer, dozos questioned anyone they found outside. If curfew breakers offered good reasons to be out—work, travel, or an emergency—dozos left them in peace. Otherwise they would detain them until morning. Dozos also manned a roadblock on the dirt road at the entrance to Yorojan, just as police or gendarmes did at the entrances and exits of less remote villages, subprefectural capitals, towns, and cities. Dozos did so to prevent criminals from traveling unnoticed between Yorojan and the subprefectural capital, Goulia. When nighttime travelers could offer no convincing explanation for their late presence on the road, dozos seized and questioned them. Depending on suspects' answers and demeanor, dozos might release, fine, or punish them or hand them over to the authorities.

Kemba gave two examples of how dozos punished alleged local criminals. Once, he said, a Yorojan ironsmith learned that a young man had stolen a piece of iron from him. The young man had reportedly tried and failed to sell it to another smith. When the first smith questioned the thief about the matter, the thief confessed to the crime, and the smith alerted dozos. The dozos then punished the thief by making him greet Yorojan's elders while wearing the stolen piece of iron on his head. Similarly, after a father told dozos that his son was stealing yams from his fields, dozos caught the son and had him greet villagers wearing a yam on his head. Whenever possible, Kemba said, dozos preferred to avoid imposing fines or physical punishment in favor of shaming, especially for thieves from their own villages. According to Kemba, this strategy worked. He claimed that Yorojan had had no further thefts since the incidents narrated here.

Kemba described less agreeable procedures for dealing with criminal suspects from beyond Yorojan. He said that dozos bound them hand and foot and waited for anyone who might be pursuing them to arrive. While interrogating such suspects, Kemba said, dozos sometimes administered hot pepper to their bodies. I failed to ask Kemba how, but I presumed by introducing it into the victim's eyes, nose, mouth, genitals, or anus, as I learned dozos did in the western Ivoirian town of Duékoué some 450 kilometers south of Yorojan. While in the compound of Duékoué's chief dozo, I was told that dozos had used pepper in this way on a robbery suspect whose swollen eyelids immediately caught my attention. Dozos had bound the albino man's hands together with a long wire that they had anchored to a tree shorn of its branches. Intentionally or not, they left the light-skinned man to burn in the sun.

Kemba distinguished such measures—rather dubiously, I thought—from brute force, of which he said he disapproved. It may be that the use of pepper had domestic correlates in Denguélé. Galy (2004, 123) reports pepper being used in this way before 1990 by families against delinquent adolescent children, particularly among Guéré-speaking populations (123, n. 15).[17] What appeared to outsiders as vigilante justice may have seemed to dozos and other Ivoirians as a resort to domestic punishment to deter crime given the lack of police. I found it disturbing nonetheless.

Kemba and other dozos walked a fine line between justice and excess, as did Ivoirian police, whose reputations for mistreatment of suspects, arbitrary arrests, extrajudicial killings, inhumane prison conditions, and torture were well documented (Amnesty International 1994, 1995, 1997; U.S. Department of State 1997, 1998, 1999). At roadblocks across Côte d'Ivoire, police, gendarmes, and customs agents decided the applicability of laws over and against the texts that specified their application. If travelers lacked identity papers, if drivers' vehicles violated the code of the road, or if merchants were transporting goods without proper authorization, they could pay a few thousand francs, and agents would let them continue (see Galy 2004). The symbolic violence alone perpetrated by such fines made state security agents a law unto themselves, for these transactions occurred undocumented, unregulated, and unpunished by state authorities who were fully aware of them.

In a country where state security agents enforced laws as they pleased, Benkadi dozos, imitating them, did the same.[18] Whether through physical force or symbolic shaming, they resorted to "lawmaking" violence (Benjamin 1978, 283–284, 287) to counter crime, in the absence of any reliable check on their authority. Dozos nonetheless adapted to this permissive environment in original ways. They adopted the state's penchant for charging fines for various infractions but in such a way as to avoid any overt challenge to the authority of local officials.

In Yorojan, dozos developed a thematically consistent but locally variable approach for fining thieves for their misdeeds. Long before I ever spoke with Kemba Koné, I had seen him explaining Benkadi's fining procedures at various *tonsigi*s in Denguélé. During my conversation with him in Yorojan, he outlined these principles. He began by describing the conditions under which Yorojan dozos investigated crimes. A victim, he said, first had to decide whether to approach local authorities or dozos. Since the authority of police and gendarmes trumped that of dozos, dozos deferred to them. If a crime victim opted for dozos, and dozos failed to solve it, Kemba said, the victim could turn to police, and dozos would desist. But if a victim turned to local authorities first, dozos would only intervene if the complainant abandoned his call to the police and turned to the dozos within three days.

Yorojan dozos likewise informed local officials of their work. Once dozos had established Benkadi in Yorojan in 1991, they explained its objectives to the subprefect in nearby Goulia and to the local secretary of the then ruling PDCI party. "Nothing can work well today if you don't have papers," Inza Konaté explained. In response, the subprefect collaborated with dozos, reinventing the law, like them, as he went along. He charged dozos 1,000 francs apiece for the makeshift gun permits that he sold them, even as the Water and Forest police continued to confiscate dozos' weapons when they could. Kemba did not remember how much money the subprefect made by selling these unofficial permits, but Kemba implied that it was a large sum. More sophisticated attempts to negotiate official approval for Benkadi emerged later, but in the meantime, Benkadi's fining system offered a viable means for punishing criminals, reimbursing victims, and rewarding dozos for their work without provoking the ire of local officials.

According to Kemba, dozos imposed two kinds of fines on alleged criminals: one to reimburse victims, the other to reimburse dozos' time and expenses involved in solving crimes. An egg thief paid 1,000 francs to the dozos who captured him, for example, and as much as 1,500 to 2,000 francs to reimburse the victim for her or his trouble. Theft of oranges or mangoes also netted dozos 1,000 francs. I infer that victims of thefts of fruit received an amount comparable to that for thefts of eggs since Kemba said that dozos collected the same amount for themselves for both crimes. In each case, Kemba claimed, dozos collected less than the victims.

The more serious the crime, the costlier the fine, with sums paid to victims growing out of proportion to those received by dozos. A goat theft brought 2,500 francs to dozos and 25,000 to the owner, the theft of an ox or cow, 25,000 francs to dozos and 50,000 to the owner. At the time, a goat would have cost 40,000 francs and an ox, 300,000 or more. With regard to these cases, Kemba had in mind thefts in which dozos had recovered the stolen livestock. In contrast, in the Denguélé village of Bako, a Fulbe man had secretly sold one of the cattle that a local farmer had entrusted to him. Since the thief could no longer recover the animal, dozos had him reimburse the owner for its entire price (see chap. 7).

Kemba also detailed fines for thefts of nonfood items. Thieves had to pay combined fines of 2,500 francs for a stolen bicycle and 25,000 for a stolen moped to dozos and the owners of the stolen items if dozos recovered the objects. Each one cost much more than its fine. As for cash thefts, Kemba said that dozos were still deciding how to fine perpetrators. Although I never received a comprehensive list of Benkadi fines from Kemba Koné or Inza Konaté during my visit to Yorojan, they showed the extent to which dozos tried to systematize Benkadi's approach to crime and reimburse victims rather than merely enrich themselves. They shared the profits of their policing just as they shared portions of the game they killed, enacting as unofficial police the same kind of moral reciprocity they did as hunters.

Public Health and Restorative Justice

To focus exclusively on dozos' theft-related fines, though, is to overlook Benkadi's other concerns. Dozos tried to regulate gender relations, hygiene, sanitation, and intergenerational conflicts, too. Kemba told me, for instance, that dozos took extensive measures to maintain public health. He claimed that dozos tried to prevent the spread of a urinary tract infection he called *sobisi*, or "warm piss," from the French term *chaude pisse*.[19] He blamed the infection on the consumption of food prepared and/or served in mortars or bowls licked by infected dogs. He also said that dozos tried to prevent a cough spread to humans when goats coughed into unattended mortars and bowls and that, when women left sliced okra out to dry under the sun on the ground in the afternoon and forgot to bring it in before nightfall, they risked letting a beetle bore into it at night that could sicken any children who consumed it.[20] To prevent such problems, dozos fined the women responsible. While on patrol, they confiscated cooking pots and implements left outside or uncovered in compounds. The next day, they returned the objects to those who paid a fine to retrieve them. They kept the objects of those who did not. Like crime, illness was a form of negative reciprocity. Here, too, dozos managed conduct in the compound to the extent that it impinged on the kind of community agreement characteristic of moral reciprocity.

Kemba claimed—somewhat unconvincingly, to my mind—that Benkadi had no intention to coerce women into changing their cooking habits. The choice to change, he said, was theirs. Along similar lines, dozos refused to ban young people's parties in Yorojan and instead chaperoned youth to prevent teen pregnancies. According to Kemba, dozos aimed through their punishments to exhort non-dozos to be better persons rather than to punish them per se. But even dozos recognized the limits of their own moralizing. Kemba told me, for instance, that Benkadi had initially intervened to settle marriage disputes—as when a younger man eloped with an older man's bride. Given dozos' claims to authority over compound life, this is not surprising. But such disputes proved so complicated, Kemba said, that dozos in Yorojan eventually refused to intervene in them. They saw that some domestic decisions remained beyond Benkadi's purview. "Today not even the government can solve them," Kemba said, indicating that contemporary problems challenged local morality and *dozoya* in new ways.

Although Kemba said he believed that population growth, dwindling resources, and desperation to provide for one's family and oneself had fueled crime, he claimed an additional cause. In the past, he said, people knew shame (*malo*). "But today," he said, "one eats yam futu without owning yams. One eats chicken without owning chickens."[21] People, he said, now took what belonged to others out of "laziness" (*salabagatɔya*). So when I asked him whether crime might stem from poverty, he disagreed. "There's money," he said, "[but] the thief doesn't want to work. If a person has no shame, everything sounds good to him. He'll still eat even if he doesn't work. But a person must know shame to work. This is why people are spoiled: they have no shame." Crime, for Kemba, resulted from a shamelessness (*malobɛliya*) that violated the morality of exchange.

Benkadi dozos tried to inculcate virtue as much as they tried to enforce laws. They intended their fines, physical punishments, and public shamings to incite the same sort of moral reflection on shameful behavior that dozos undertook by making their vows at their initiatory sacrifices. In contrast to state police, which exercised punitive justice over infractions they interpreted as committed above all against the state, dozos enacted a kind of restorative justice for acts they viewed as committed primarily against the reciprocal relations that regulated exchange (see Zehr 2003; Howley 2003). They consequently tried to repair rifts between criminal suspects and victims by sharing payments extracted from the former with the latter.

If crime arose primarily as a result of immorality, Kemba implied, then dozos needed to reinvigorate an entire moral community to combat crime and not merely punish criminals. Since dozos had historically done this through their hunting and sacrifices, Benkadi based its legal framework on the same kind of gifting to non-dozos that already shaped dozos' hunting practices, initiatory vows, and sacrifices to Manimory (see chap. 3). Dozos may have expressed their juridical principles in a code of fines unrecognized by state law, but Benkadi fines were far less arbitrary and onerous, and potentially far more productive, than those assessed by police at roadblocks across the country.

This is not to say that Benkadi's appeal was universal. Those who felt most comfortable with dozos were the Julakan- and Syenara-speaking populations across the country who already recognized dozos' authority.

This made Benkadi an exercise in "moral ethnicity" (Lonsdale 1992, 1994). In a country that had for so long favored nationalism over ethnicity as a form of identity (Badmus 2009, 50), a mostly Muslim and almost exclusively northern-descended group of men momentarily emerged as quasi-state agents, suggesting, for their part, that ethnic and national identities might be compatible.[22] Meanwhile, attentive entrepreneurs in Abidjan and Korhogo realized the awkwardness of the situation. They were watching Benkadi's development with interest, preparing to help dozos engage the state beyond the movement's ethnic and regional limitations.

Afrique Environnementale

Inza Fanny, an Abidjan landlord and inspector of diplomatic posts in the Ivoirian Ministry of Foreign Affairs, was one of these entrepreneurs (cf. Woods 1994, 471).[23] In the early 1990s, he was visiting his natal village of Kaniasso in Denguélé when, he told me, he encountered two dozos tracking stolen cattle. "Why not involve dozos from surrounding villages instead of working alone?" he reportedly asked them. The dozos said that they had recently been to Mali and learned that Malian *donso*s had begun working together in a similar way to recover stolen cattle.[24]

Fanny claimed that this chance meeting inspired him to found an Ivoirian NGO to focus dozo and public attention on environmental issues. He named the organization Afrique Environnementale (AE). He then broadened AE's mission to organize dozos as a national security force and lobby the government for their right to hunt and bear arms. Fanny assumed Benkadi's agenda as his own and managed dozo business from his Abidjan office in the Ivoirian Ministry of Foreign Affairs. Given his position as a state bureaucrat, his familiarity with Ivoirian law, and his claim to have been initiated as a dozo as a young man, he presented himself as an effective advocate for dozos from within the state, and dozos took him as such. Fanny capitalized on the opportunity by seeking official approval for AE as an NGO.[25]

On March 27, 1992, the Ivoirian Ministry of the Interior granted Fanny a "receipt" (*récépissé*) conferring the state's recognition of AE as an independent association (République de Côte d'Ivoire 1992a).[26] The receipt's text described AE's goals as follows:

> To find and enumerate the environmental protection assistance needs of populations in distress; to assure the identification, coordination, and follow-up evaluation of all activities aiming to fight deforestation, desertification, and the impoverishment of soils

> in Africa; to educate rural and urban populations and to raise the consciousness of policy makers on the risks of environmental degradation [caused] by the anarchic development of agriculture, industry, and urbanism; to help elaborate strategies and policies for protecting endangered animal, plant, and aquatic species; [and] to fight the proliferation of toxic waste by industries, agriculture, or households.

Nowhere did the text mention dozos.[27]

An undated, unattributed, typewritten prospectus (*présentation*) details AE's focus on the environment in similar terms. It claims that environmental problems had resulted from the impact of growing populations on scarce resources (Afrique Environnementale n.d.a, 2): "The anarchic options for man's development, which no longer obey natural laws of vital ecological equilibrium, have led to a catastrophic weakening of flora, with perverse effects that many African countries assume are inevitable: soil impoverishment, drying waterways, [and] inexorable desert advance with its consequent loss of human, animal, and plant life" (2). The prospectus presented AE as an advocacy, fund-raising, and mediation organization intended to solve these problems (5). It proposed consciousness raising, conservation, legislative lobbying, research, and an audacious agenda of building projects as strategies for safeguarding Africa's natural and cultural resources. Proposed initiatives included inventorying aquatic- and birdlife; protecting classified forests; reforesting deforested areas; teaching villagers to use less firewood for cooking and heating; and instructing farmers to preserve and improve soil fertility, minimize forest burning, use natural fertilizers, and better manage pastures.

According to the text, AE planned to preserve "at least ten . . . endangered animal species" in each African country and either protect or commercialize various species of fish. It aimed to reduce toxic emissions and promote solar power, planned public education about hygiene and sanitation, and hoped to monitor air and water quality and levels of noise, water, and park pollution. The project aimed to find more efficient means for organizing transportation and home building and planned cultural centers across the continent to house the fine arts, libraries, performing arts, vocational training, and technology transfers (Afrique Environnementale n.d.a, 7–9). AE proposed community programs to provide training to women, youth, and men suffering from wars and famines to make them healthier and more economically self-sufficient. The NGO also proposed literacy programs and the integration of African languages into national public life and planned to transfer surpluses of essential items to refugees and other homeless, catastrophe-ridden populations in Africa (9–11).[28]

For AE, the key to providing these services was a continent-wide bureaucracy. Fanny foresaw a network of regional offices in central, eastern, northern, southern, and western Africa and country offices in each African state (Afrique Environnementale n.d.a, 13). AE would keep its headquarters in Abidjan, where "dynamic and productive" committees of specialists and experts would research and propose solutions for Africa's problems (Afrique Environnementale n.d.c). To "affirm [AE's] continent-wide mission," Fanny proposed inviting all African heads of state to sign an "Environmental Protection Charter" (Afrique Environnementale n.d.a). Then, in each host country, AE would organize "development legions" from the ranks of unemployed youth aged eighteen to thirty-five—an "enormous human resource"—to pursue development projects. Eventually, each country's legion would stand as "a civic service in place of military service or as a civic contribution to national progress" (Afrique Environnementale n.d.a, 13). AE indicated two sources for the funds for its projects: membership fees from individual, organizational, and state participants and contributions from national and international organizations (14). As utopian as Fanny's vision was, it attracted enough attention to win state approval for AE and a platform for presenting what seemed to be Fanny's real interest: dozos' security concerns.[29]

Although AE never named dozos in its prospectus, Fanny organized a conference for them in his natal village of Kaniasso on April 4–8, 1993. Between 1,500 (M.-F. Touré 1993; Krassault 1993) and 3,000 dozos (L. Kouassi 1993a) from Côte d'Ivoire, Burkina Faso, Guinea, and Mali attended. At the conference, Ivoirian intellectuals and authorities took part in a colloquium and discussions with dozos that focused on the theme "Hunters' Contributions to the Protection of Flora and Fauna." At the conference, Fanny's spokesman, Moussa Fofana, told journalists that AE would turn dozos into environmentalists (M.-F. Touré 1993), offering the state a kind of quid pro quo. Fofana suggested that the state modify its current hunting restrictions by delineating specific hunting and nonhunting seasons in designated hunting preserves. In return, dozos would agree to adopt new ecosensitive hunting practices in addition to those they already practiced, such as refraining from killing pregnant or nursing animals (L. Kouassi 1993a). If the state were to grant dozos the right to hunt with modern firearms in these preserves, then AE would organize dozos to guard against poaching within them. Although dozos had embraced Benkadi for security reasons, AE tried to market it to the state for ecological ones. Dozos offered the state a money-saving conservation service in exchange for concessions on hunting and guns (L. Kouassi 1993a).

Fanny and Fofana played on the state's neoliberalism and ostensible interest in environmentalism to argue for a place for dozos within it.

In the same interview, Fofana proposed that dozos "assist in maintaining peace and security for Ivoirian citizens," which he called "a matter of backing up the forces of law and order and not of substituting . . . for them" (M.-F. Touré 1993). Journalist Mory-Frey Touré (1993) then suggested that dozos might use this situation as a pretext for establishing armed vigilante groups. Fofana replied, "It is exactly to avoid the excesses about which you are speaking that Afrique Environnementale has begun to educate hunters about the role that they must play in our changing societies . . . The hunters exist as an association. One must deal with them." In fact, dozos already constituted just the kind of armed groups that Touré had in mind.

AE used its conference in Kaniasso as a national forum for mediating between dozos and the state.[30] Fanny had arranged for Ivoirian academics and security officials to attend, inviting them to consider the conditions in which dozos might work hand in hand with national authorities. Anthropologist Memel Fotê Harris discussed the rupture of dozos' relations with the environment in the wake of Islam's arrival and colonialism. Geographer Dian Boni and oceanographer Etienne N'Da spoke of the environmental risks of slash-and-burn agriculture when combined with hunting and the pollution of water routes by fishing poisons (L. Kouassi 1993b). And police and customs officials urged dozos to identify themselves to authorities so that police could distinguish them from poachers, to register their guns with authorities in exchange for legal gun permits, and to bring poachers and other criminals to justice (L. Kouassi 1993c).

The dialogue had begun. AE had positioned itself between the state and Benkadi as a privileged intermediary by speaking the state's neoliberal language of national problems, global partnerships, and international solutions. It found an "*axiom of unity*" between dozo and state interests in the form of ecology and security (Tsing 2005, 89, emphasis in original). These interests bridged the otherwise "incompatible differences" that separated dozos and the state (89). Whether dozos originally had ecological goals in mind or not, they were now ersatz environmentalists as well as unofficial police. Benkadi's collaboration with AE, and AE's attempts to collaborate with the state, created a set of "convincingly agreed upon observations and facts that then appear[ed] to support generalization *directly*, that is, without the prior mediation of the collaboration" (89, emphasis in original). Dozos appeared "naturally" useful to the state for environmental and security reasons. "The contingency of collaboration, and its exclusions, no longer seem[ed] relevant because the facts [had] come to 'speak for themselves'" (89). Absent was any mention of dozos' long involvement with the colonial and postcolonial state, the complex analogies they drew between hunting and policing, healing and public health, or their own management of Benkadi apart from AE. From the state's point of view, AE *was* Benkadi, and dozos shared its strategy of dissembling their true intentions behind the disingenuous veil of environmentalism.

Not surprisingly, Fanny's 1993 Kaniasso conference closed, as so many conferences do, with mere resolutions: to establish demarcated pastures in order to lessen conflicts between Fulbe herders and Jula and Senufo farmers, encourage collaboration between state security forces and dozos, establish reserves for fauna and flora (including medicinal and commercial plants and trees), promote water sanitation by creating reservoirs and wells, conduct a census of locally made guns owned by dozos, hold bimonthly dozo meetings and an annual dozo conference at rotating locations as well as in Kaniasso, and hold periodic meetings for youth in Kaniasso (Afrique Environnementale n.d.c; Krassault 1993). Odienné's prefect, Gonnet Zando, responded with "great uneasiness concerning the hunters' wish to see their request to bear arms granted." He nonetheless "affirmed that this grievance would be submitted to the Ministers of the Interior and Internal Security for examination" (Krassault 1993).[31]

Three years later, in 1996, AE held its second dozo conference in Kaniasso, which I attended. By then, AE had realized none of its 1993 Kaniasso resolutions. To my knowledge, its committees existed in name only and without working budgets. "Development legions" had never been formed. No plant reserves, literacy projects, or initiatives to integrate women and young people into national life had taken shape. Only dozos continued to show interest in AE, which had recruited hundreds of them across the country as new members. They joined en masse, pleased by AE's apparent efforts to win official approval for Benkadi. This growing membership proved increasingly lucrative for AE. Inza Konaté reported that Borosso dozos who attended Fanny's conferences paid 500 francs apiece for initial membership cards and 2,600 francs for subsequent membership documents. How much of this money made its way back to local AE offices—as opposed to Inza Fanny's office in Abidjan—I do not know. I do know from my visits to Fanny's office at the Ivoirian Foreign Ministry that AE members came from across Côte d'Ivoire to visit him there and that they returned the stubs of sold membership cards to him. To my knowledge, AE made no public accounting of its finances.

14 The Benkadi and Afrique Environnementale headquarters of the "Northwest Zone" (Zone Nord-Ouest) in Odienné.

Afrique Environnementale at Work

Far from its Abidjan headquarters and beyond the spotlight of its conferences, AE's most important accomplishments occurred through the efforts of Fanny's Denguélé representative, Moussa Fofana. Fofana originally hailed from the village of Kimbirila Sud, located to the north of Odienné. After a career as a guidance counselor (*éducateur*) in the Ivoirian school system, he returned to Odienné to retire. There, his education, professional background, fluency in French, and connections in the region attracted Fanny's attention when Fanny was looking for someone to serve as president of the AE office in Denguélé. Fofana at first managed AE from his home and then from a former house that AE rented along the road running eastward from Odienné to Boundiali (see fig. 14).

On Fanny's behalf, Fofana organized a series of *tonsigi*s modeled on those initiated years earlier by Denguélé dozos along the Malian border. Fofana hoped to recruit new AE members at these meetings, planning one *tonsigi* for each of Odienné's subprefectures. I attended those *tonsigi*s

15 Moussa Fofana (*standing*) discusses Benkadi business with dozos in Odienné's *dangun,* 1994

held in the Bako, Dioulatiédougou, Odienné, and Tiémé subprefectures, as well as a preparatory meeting for one planned in Minignan. I also accompanied Fofana to the northern Denguélé village of Gbaga, where he explained AE's agenda to dozos and lay people who had invited him to visit. In this way, Benkadi and AE spread together as two parts of the same movement, just as AE had hoped they would.

Prior to each *tonsigi,* Fofana laid the necessary groundwork. He did what Benkadi's earliest representatives had done in Denguélé's northernmost reaches. He held a public discussion about AE's and Benkadi's goals for all interested parties: dozos and non-dozos, men and women, old and young. In Minignan, a *jeli* (griot) announced the meeting aloud as he walked through the village after Fofana and I had arrived from Odienné. At that meeting, Fofana summarized Benkadi's procedures for fines, outlined AE's and Benkadi's goals, and encouraged those interested to set a date for a *tonsigi* so they could begin preparations.

What Yorojan dozos had begun by implanting Benkadi in northern Denguélé, Fofana extended throughout the prefecture (see fig. 15). He almost always traveled alone to his destinations on a used motorcycle. When planning each *tonsigi,* he arranged transportation for dozos, with

Odienné as the central transit point. As Dioulatiédougou's *tonsigi* approached, for example, he rented several trucks to transport dozos from northern and central Denguélé to the *tonsigi*'s remote southern location. He arranged for at least one Benkadi representative, usually from Yorojan, to travel to each *tonsigi* to explain Benkadi law. And he attended each *tonsigi*, selling AE memberships to interested dozos and keeping records of new members.

What Fanny conceived, Fofana achieved. He helped dozos establish local AE offices across Denguélé, each with its own minibureaucracy of president, treasurer, and assistants. These offices paralleled dozos' preexisting hierarchy based on ritual initiation. Francophone men like Fofana, many of whom with little to no hunting experience, manned this bureaucracy. They sought dozo initiation to join Benkadi, not to hunt, gaining influence because of their literacy and fluency in French. Still, chief dozos known for their hunting expertise and ritual knowledge retained their authority. Fofana served as their liaison to the local authorities.

In other cities where AE flourished, younger francophone men who had at least minor careers in business or industry became AE leaders alongside dozo chiefs. Tiécoura Ouattara, for instance, the president of San-Pédro's AE office, once worked as a computer operator in a Duékoué sawmill, while a senior dozo hunter served as the city's dozo chief. Similarly, in Abidjan, Bangaly Doumbia, a clerical worker at a government research institute, was AE's president, while senior Malian dozo Béma Koné served as Abidjan's chief dozo. Bangaly spoke and wrote French fluently; Béma communicated entirely in spoken Mandenkan. And in Denguélé the collaboration between Inza Fanny of AE and chief dozo Yaya Cissé of Benkadi in likewise enabled dozos to shift with greater ease between *dozoya* and their new quasi-state roles.

Both sides saw their collaboration as profitable. Fanny hoped to gain state approval to organize dozos as a private security force that he planned to call *Manimoriton*, the "Manimory Association." Those dozos familiar with the plan hoped to find employment as security guards. But Fanny was not alone in trying to mediate between dozos and the state. He faced competition from Korhogo-based businessman Édouard Coulibaly.

The Ivoirian National Hunters' Association

On October 10, 1996, Drissa Koné and I traveled to the north-central Ivoirian city of Korhogo, hoping to attend a dozo meeting in the village of Katogo where dozos were going to plan a subsequent meeting between government ministers and dozo representatives scheduled for December 5, 1996, in the village of Kombolokoro. Édouard Coulibaly, who was organizing the meetings, was president of the Ivoirian National Hunters' Association (L'Association Nationale des Chasseurs de Côte d'Ivoire [INHA]). Like AE, the INHA was trying to negotiate a collaborative relationship with the state on Benkadi's behalf.

At the time, Ivoirian security minister Marcel Dibonan Koné was waging a national campaign against Benkadi. While touring the cities of Toumodi, Yamoussoukro, Daloa, Danané, Odienné, Man, Korhogo, Bouaké, and Abidjan (Coulibaly 1996; Lébry 1996), he called dozos an illegal "parallel police force" (Bouabré 1996; *Le Jour* 1996) estimated by AE to number 22,000 men (L. Kouassi 1996b), who included many foreigners (Bouabré 1996). Minister Koné warned that dozos could destabilize Côte d'Ivoire (N'Dri 1996) and called on them to lay down their arms, end their surveillance activities (Bouabré 1996; A. Dembélé 1996; L. Kouassi 1996a), and return to their "fields" (N'Dri 1996). He overlooked the fact that many dozos—and the ones with whom he was most preoccupied—were urban dwellers. Even in the western city of Man, where the population wanted dozos to continue their work, Minister Koné called for Benkadi's dissolution (L. Kouassi 1996b).

Édouard Coulibaly made the following remarks to the press in response:

> No one can obscure the voluntary, efficient work of dozos in this country. We receive no funding. We save money to put ourselves at the community's service, for our motto is "Serve." We consider ourselves auxiliaries to the police and intend to remain so. We are not a parallel force. One must recognize what we do for the country. (Agence Ivoirienne de Presse 1996b)

Coulibaly echoed Houphouët-Boigny's unfulfilled promise that work on the nation's behalf entitled one to rights as a citizen or resident within it (Amondji 1984, 278).

The secretary general of the ruling PDCI party, Laurent Dona Fologo, a native of the Korhogo region, sympathized with Coulibaly.[32] He did so publicly while addressing a group of dozos gathered in Korhogo, assuring them, "In the name of President Bédié," that they had "nothing to worry about" (Bah 1996). The now public differences between Minister Koné and Secretary Fologo with regard to Benkadi, along with President Bédié's reluctance to speak publicly about the issue, indicated that the state remained undecided about the stance it should take toward Benkadi. Meanwhile, dozos recognized and exploited this situation. They tried to win support from those officials who were well disposed toward them. Édouard Coulibaly took the lead in this effort.

After Drissa and I had arrived at Coulibaly's house in Korhogo, we traveled with several other dozos over some eighty kilometers of dirt roads in the back of a covered pickup truck (*bâché*) to the village of Katogo. Édouard Coulibaly rode in the front passenger seat. At the meeting, he portrayed the INHA as working to legitimize Benkadi in the eyes of Ivoirian officials and expressed grave doubts about AE's commitment to securing dozo interests. At the end of the meeting the next morning, he announced a further preparatory meeting for the Kombolokoro conference in Nènèkiri on October 25.

The stakes were high. Coulibaly and Fanny were competing for the same position as Benkadi's liaison to the state. Each wanted to be the first to speak with state ministers, ingratiate himself to thousands of dozos, and gain more as a result. At Katogo, I met INHA dozos from Bouaké, Gagnoa, Issia, San-Pédro, Soubré, from villages throughout the Korhogo prefecture, and from Denguélé's subprefecture of Madinani. Like AE, the INHA drew on a national dozo network in which many dozos belonged simultaneously to Benkadi, AE, and the INHA. But no matter how well-organized, influential, or popular the INHA or AE had become, they remained at the state's mercy. Dozos could propose as many meetings as they wished; the state could refuse the invitation.

Édouard Coulibaly was particularly adept at negotiating the perils of this delicate situation. He offered me a glass of honey wine (*lidolo*) after my arrival in Katogo, where I had hoped to interview him, but he said that he had no time to speak with me about the INHA agenda. On a cloudy afternoon two days later, back in Korhogo, I caught up with him at the three-story hotel he was building, the Hôtel Pacifique. His clean, blue Mercedes was parked outside. Like AE's Inza Fanny, Coulibaly was an affluent, francophone entrepreneur whose interests and influence reached far beyond those of most dozos. When I arrived at the hotel, he was talking with two construction workers in the hotel's interior courtyard that opened to the sky. He wore an ankle-length *boubou* and dark sunglasses.

After the dozo who had led me to the hotel explained why I had come, Coulibaly greeted me, and we began to talk. He told me he would be in Yamoussoukro the next day on family business. He said he would return to Korhogo the following evening or the day after and be off again to Abidjan for a television interview on the popular noon talk show Midi-Première, perhaps to announce the dozo meeting scheduled for Nènèkiri or Kombolokoro. Given his schedule, I took the only chance I saw to ask what he thought of Minister Koné's anti-dozo campaign.

He said that Houphouët-Boigny, while still alive, had agreed that dozos could help provide public security, adding that Houphouët-Boigny's successor, Henri Konan Bédié, had said that he "could not forbid dozos" from doing so, no doubt referring to Bédié's call to dozos to help guard polling places in the Korhogo region during the presidential elections of 1995. He concluded that he had nothing to say to Minister Koné, implying that the minister had failed to represent accurately the president's stance toward Benkadi.

I then asked Mr. Coulibaly how he judged the media attention dozos had received since the early 1990s. He cited dozos' successes against bus robberies near the cities of Ferkessédougou and Tafiré along the Abidjan-Korhogo highway as reasons for the interest but refused to elaborate, he said, because circumstances made any additional "declaration" unwise. "We now work unofficially, but we are also looking for contacts . . . to develop our organization. But at present we have not been officially recognized; therefore, if we talk about our activities now, we could easily be misinterpreted. You know, Ivoirian journalists are very political. We [dozos] are apolitical."[33] He then affirmed his loyalty to the state, referring to President Bédié as Côte d'Ivoire's "supreme leader," and stated that Benkadi could only continue its work with the president's approval. Coulibaly added that if dozos had begun their security work without state approval, they had done so out of necessity. He portrayed Benkadi the same way that dozos in AE and Denguélé had, as a response to a problem so severe that it overrode, at least temporarily, any concern for official legality. Now that Benkadi had proven its worth, he suggested, dozos were seeking state approval for their work. They hoped that authorities would oblige. As our discussion was ending, I asked Coulibaly if he might grant me an interview were the INHA to receive approval for its work. He agreed.

But the meetings he had scheduled with government ministers never occurred. The meeting at Nènèkiri was canceled at the last minute, as were all subsequent ones. While Fanny and Coulibaly were competing with each other for state favor, the state outmaneuvered them both. Each had offered dozos the promise of legitimacy in spite of the illegality of their hunting and security work. But in pursuing their common goal, rivalries had emerged. Within nine months of my visit to Korhogo, Édouard Coulibaly sent a letter to his associates in and around Korhogo and, I suspect, to other INHA offices across the country warning dozos to avoid all contact with Inza Fanny. Meanwhile, Fanny, under pressure from the state, had agreed to embark on a national tour to tell dozos to cease their Benkadi activities. In response, Coulibaly denounced AE. But the state had already won. It had turned INHA and AE against each other, by courting the INHA and then strong-arming Fanny to call dozos back from their security work, defeating Benkadi's attempt to gain official recognition for its work.

Benkadi Is Dead, Long Live Benkadi

The same mimetic strategy that had brought Benkadi national success also contributed to its downfall, creating "unsavory collaborations" with "government bureaucracies and commercial and policy elites" that resulted in dozos' "co-optation" (Tsing 2005, 264) by the state. By imitating state officials, dozos risked making themselves agents and/or victims of state interests. From the spread of "agreement" in Odienné to the eruption of disagreement in Korhogo, Benkadi had come full circle. By mid-1997, the state was playing the country's two most important dozo organizations against each other, canceling a meeting with one and encouraging the leader of the other to betray Benkadi members. Like Manimory, dozos appeared vanquished in their own domain. But AE and the INHA had spread awareness of Benkadi across Côte d'Ivoire along with the bureaucratic savoir faire needed to acquire at least informal consent from local authorities for their work. Like Manimory, dozos seemed only to benefit from their apparent defeat. Despite the downfall of AE and the INHA, Benkadi survived intact.

AE and the INHA had succeeded so well in their efforts on Benkadi's behalf that Benkadi no longer needed them. On July 7, 1997, Moussa Fofana, Kanamankan Diarrassouba, and a host of senior dozos sent a letter to Fanny from Odienné ending their association with him and protesting his request to discontinue their armed security patrols (Moussa Fofana 1997). Fanny claimed that he had made the decision under government duress,[34] but this mattered little to dozos in Odienné, who renamed their AE office *Binkadi*, using what Fofana claimed was the original Malian spelling of the word in order to distance themselves from Fanny's appropriation of Benkadi through AE.

Ultimately, Benkadi's efforts to assimilate to the state bore fruit. Benkadi had enhanced its national prominence thanks to AE and the INHA. The collaboration compelled even government officials to take note of dozos' grievances. But by adapting Benkadi to Côte d'Ivoire's divisive state politics, dozos forfeited the single voice that Benkadi had once given them. Now only a fractured Benkadi endured, pursuing its goals locally if not nationally after 1997. In Odienné, dozos reorganized themselves to work independently of AE. Across Côte d'Ivoire, local authorities let dozos continue their police work despite Minister Koné's anti-Benkadi crusade. If Benkadi had endured inter-dozo rivalries, state repression, and the manipulation and implosion of its national, bureaucratic, francophone organizations, then its success depended on something more than guns and diplomacy for its coherence, and that was *dozoya*.

SEVEN

Stalking Crime

Waiting for Dozos

This chapter details the ways in which Benkadi dozos used and misused *dozoya* to confront and resolve but also commit crimes. Despite dozos' ostensibly rural "traditional" roots, Benkadi introduced *dozoya* into urban national life as part of a growing trend: a shift toward reliance on privatized, as opposed to state-sponsored, security in Africa (see Gumedze 2007a, 2007b, 2008). But dozos' privatized use of violence occurred in collaboration with the state. A silent partnership between the two emerged in which dozos fought crime with the tacit approval of local officials in spite of opposition from the national level. Their alliance exemplified the novelty of dozos' relationship to the state. Benkadi's form of privatized violence did not correspond as a whole to the four commonly conceived "ideal types": criminal, terrorist, warlord, or rebel (Mair 2005, 48), at least not before 2002. In contrast to "social bandits" who steal from the powerful to protest state authority (Hobsbawm 1959, 20–21), dozos tried to protect Ivoirian citizens and residents from crime so as to affirm the state's legitimacy.

Granted, dozos challenged state hunting laws and illegally replicated state police roles, but the regimes of Houphouët-Boigny, Ouattara, and Bédié also acted at the margins of constitutional law. Such an impulse did not distinguish dozos from the state. Nor were dozos mere "shadows" or "doubles" of state authorities (see Ferguson 2006, 15–17), although they both doubled and shadowed them.

They doubled the state to assert, as Houphouët-Boigny had once promised, that those who worked for it would have rights within it. And they shadowed the state to the extent that they had become not just "a copy" of it "but an attached twin" (17). Benkadi's mimetic strategies were variations on the state's and vice versa:

> In this optic, it might make sense to think of the new organizations that have sprung up in recent years not as challengers pressing up against the state from below but as horizontal contemporaries of the organs of the state—sometimes rivals, sometimes servants, sometimes watchdogs, sometimes parasites, but in every case operating on the same level and in the same global space. (103)

Indeed, state authorities also shadowed Benkadi. Those officials working in proximity to dozos in prefectures, subprefectures, cities, and villages at some remove from Ivoirian centers of power tacitly approved Benkadi's activities, overlooking the illegalities involved. They enabled Benkadi to spread across the country—first with, then without, the help of an NGO anchored in the Ivoirian Ministry of Foreign Affairs. Ultimately, dozos were working beyond the limits of the so-called state/civil society divide (98–99), as were state officials. Their story is one of cooperation.

To tell it, I offer a series of ethnographic vignettes of Benkadi security work from four major Ivoirian cities. I start by recounting a case of burglary in Yamoussoukro and how victims resorted to dozos as a preemptive measure against future break-ins. I then describe my tour of dozos' urban security measures in San-Pédro, including the tactics by which they caught and detained criminal suspects. I end by detailing similar procedures for detaining and trying suspects in both Odienné and Abidjan, focusing on how dozos, police, and other local officials worked together against crime.

Breaking and Entering in Yamoussoukro

On the night of Friday June 13, 1997, I arrived in Yamoussoukro by bus from Odienné on my way to visit dozos in Abidjan. Instead of disembarking in Abidjan's Adjamé bus station at 3:00 a.m. and sleeping in the bus until dawn, as travelers usually did for fear of being mugged, I left the bus in Yamoussoukro at midnight and took a taxi to the compound of a Malian family that had befriended me and with whom I stayed from time to time while en route to and from Abidjan. I first met them while recovering from malaria and food poisoning in early 1994 at the home of an American friend of mine who was teaching English at two of Yamoussoukro's universities (*grandes écoles*).

The couple who hosted me spoke Soninké and Bamanankan, but their younger children favored Julakan after having lived in Côte d'Ivoire for over a decade. The family typified the kinds of immigrant families who had moved to Côte d'Ivoire for economic opportunities after independence. Like so many such families in Yamoussoukro, they lived in the poor, mostly Muslim, Julakan-speaking, immigrant neighborhood of Dioulabougou, the "Jula Quarter."

Dioulabougou sat behind and diagonally across from the Félix Houphouët-Boigny Foundation for Peace, a stunning concrete-and-glass edifice named after Côte d'Ivoire's first president. The marble floors, chandeliers, and panoramic view of its ballroom once symbolized Côte d'Ivoire's wealth and promise. In the other direction from the Foundation, one could see the dome of the Basilica of Our Lady of Peace in the distance, one of the largest Christian churches in the world, which towered over the city. Houphouët-Boigny had built it in his birthplace and offered it to Pope John Paul II as a gift to the Vatican when the pope came to consecrate it in 1990. It was the stage for Houphouët-Boigny's funeral in 1994, which French Presidents François Mitterrand, Valéry Giscard d'Estaing, and other world leaders attended. Since then, few people came to its Sunday masses. Dioulabougou's mosque was wanting in comparison.

After I spent Saturday with my hosts, I planned to leave for Abidjan the next morning. That night, rain poured in torrents onto the corrugated metal roof of my hosts' cinder block house, its soft roar lulling me to sleep. Then, between 1:00 and 2:00 a.m., I woke to a woman's screams and to what sounded like a door being battered down in the adjacent compound. I was sharing a room with Mamadou, the family's third oldest son, in his late twenties, who was still dozing. Frightened but curious, I went to the window and slowly opened the translucent glass louver shutters by moving the lever located to the right of the windowsill. Through the window I saw a grim man standing in a raincoat and brimless hat surveying the area. The rain and screaming had stopped. I felt strangely relieved to see someone outside.

I closed the shutters and woke Mamadou to tell him what I had seen. He walked drowsily to the window. No sooner had he reopened the shutters, though, than he swiftly closed them. "That man's a thief," he whispered to me in French. "He has a gun. Didn't you see it?"

I had not.

Again Mamadou opened the shutters—very slowly—more fully than I had. I looked once more at the man. This time I could see that he held a rifle with both hands, just below his waist, out of my previous line of vision. As Mamadou closed the window, I worried that the man had seen us. While we stood in the dark wondering what to do next, I heard the locked handle of the front door in the adjacent room turn. Mamadou and I went to investigate and found Mamadou's sister, Adja, standing in the hall. She whispered that she had just heard the handle of the front door turn, too. We stood fixed in place, facing the door as Mamadou's mother, brothers, and sisters joined us, fearing that we would be the bandits' next victims.

But no one turned the door handle again, sparing us from the neighbors' fate.

At sunrise, young men from the neighborhood including Mamadou's older brother, Daouda, rented a taxi to go report the crime to the police. When they returned they said that the police had refused to investigate without being paid, which, for the neighborhood's poor, working-class inhabitants, was impossible.

This kind of behavior was typical of Ivoirian police. In 1995, the wife of my friend Drissa Koné's high school English teacher had lost their toddler-aged daughter while selling refreshments at a political rally at the local soccer stadium in Odienné. I drove her husband on my moped to the police station seeking help finding their child. When we arrived, an officer was sitting on the front porch wearing a sullen expression on his face. He told us nonchalantly to keep looking for the girl and to return when we had more news. We eventually found the child on our own with no help or interest from the police.

On another occasion, the hostel maintained by Odienné's Peace Corps volunteers was robbed while my friend Drissa Koné was working there as a night watchman. The police jailed Drissa immediately with no evidence or accusations against him. They released him that evening on the commissioner's orders. Several weeks later, neighborhood children, not the police, discovered the thief's identity by noticing in his possession objects that they recognized as belonging to the Peace Corps volunteers. Like Yamoussoukro's police, Odienné police had also refused to investigate without remuneration from the volunteers.

Under such circumstances, poor and working-class people had little choice but to look beyond the police to assure their own security. The irony was that state agents had effectively privatized themselves, refusing to act without payment from crime victims.[1] Dozos merely followed the lead of state police when they began collecting fees for their services, initially from the criminals they captured, as noted in chapter 6, and later from the neighborhoods they patrolled. Security was already a commodity in Côte d'Ivoire.

Back in Yamoussoukro, on Wednesday, June 18, four days after police had refused to investigate the robbery in Dioulabougou, the landlord of my hosts' compound and of several adjacent compounds, who happened to be Odiennéka, held a meeting. He proposed in Julakan to twenty of his renters that they hire two Malian dozos to guard their homes at night. Each of the five compounds that he owned would pay 12,000 francs CFA per month for a grand total of 60,000 francs, giving each of the dozos a monthly salary of 30,000 francs. After a brief discussion, the residents agreed to the idea. They had no alternative. Security had become a lucrative pursuit for dozos working as private security guards (see Bassett 2003), whether they collected fees directly from home or business owners or charged fines for various infractions. Some 300 kilometers to the southwest of Yamoussoukro in the port city of San-Pédro, dozos did so on a grand scale, across the entire city.

Security at a Crossroads

In August 1996, I visited San-Pédro at the invitation of its Benkadi president, Tiécoura Ouattara, whom I had first met at Inza Fanny's 1996 Kaniasso conference and who had invited Drissa Koné and me to his home in the village of Kiémou (see chap. 5). At the time, San-Pédro had an official population of about 60,000 but counted many more residents in its burgeoning working-class neighborhoods, which had little access to police protection. These were the neighborhoods that dozos patrolled to greatest effect. When Tiécoura suggested that I accompany one of the dozos' nighttime patrols through these neighborhoods, I agreed. But first, he insisted that I accompany him to greet San-Pédro's prefect at his residence. There, the prefect made clear to both Tiécoura and me that he approved of Benkadi's work in the city. It showed me the extent to which local representatives of the state gave Benkadi tacit permission to work, collaborating with dozos well beyond any legal precedent.

Late on the night of August 8, I joined five dozos as they began their rounds from their headquarters, Camp Dynamique, which was located in the working-class Bardo neighborhood. The camp was one of two Benkadi offices in the city. Dozos called the other Terre Rouge ("Red Earth") because of its location on an expanse of red laterite soil. As we left to begin the patrol, we took a dirt road that ended at a paved thoroughfare.

We stopped there briefly as a young dozo from Mali removed from his shirt pocket a power object (*jo*) made from a sheep horn. He called the object *dibi*, or "darkness" in Bamanankan. He said it would immobilize any criminals we would encounter that night at the scenes of their crimes.[2] While squatting on the pavement, he wrapped a string attached to the object around its length while spitting lightly onto it. Then he touched the object to the road before standing up and putting the object back into his pocket.

The power object resembled those that dozos used to ambush game in forests. Such devices proliferated at the outdoor bazaars that accompanied Benkadi meetings, particularly in the more affluent southern half of the country. Here dozos sold power objects, dozo hats, clothing, guns, and ammunition to other dozos for hunting and patrolling. My friend Drissa once bought me a power object at a Benkadi meeting that I was too ill to attend. It appeared to be half a sheep's hoof hollowed out, filled with plant material, and sealed with a dark, waxy substance. Two short strings, each ending in a single knot, protruded from its wax-capped head. Drissa said that if a dozo were to place the object on the trail of an animal he wished to kill, it would compel the animal to return to that spot. The dozo, having hidden himself, could then ambush his prey. The power object of the Malian dozo in San-Pédro regulated human movement just as the object that Drissa gave me controlled animal circulation in the forest. Similar parallels between hunting and policing pervaded Benkadi.

Earlier that night, the dozo coordinator of Camp Dynamique, Ibrahima Kamagaté, had taken me by moped on a tour of dozo roadside checkpoints in San-Pédro. These checkpoints, modeled after those of police and gendarmes, took the form of roadblocks (*barrages*) at each of the city's three main entrances, to the west, north, and east, where paved highways carried large trucks hauling freight into or through the city on an hourly basis from Tabou, Daloa, and Abidjan, respectively. Dozos manned another checkpoint at the main entrance of the Bardo neighborhood where their two headquarters were located. At each checkpoint, dozos blocked the road with benches, chairs, poles, rocks, or other sturdy, movable objects. They let vehicles pass only after inspecting them, stopping drivers and asking them and their passengers to show vehicle registration papers and identity cards, and opening trunks, bags, and containers to examine their contents.

At one of the city's three main checkpoints, I met a dozo originally from Mali holding an oblong power object from which a tuft of animal hair protruded. He explained that when a vehicle tried to pass the checkpoint without stopping, he would describe the vehicle's make and driver

16 The interior of the Terre Rouge Benkadi office in San-Pédro. San-Pédro's dozo president, Tiécoura Ouattara, stands to the far left.

to the object while tightening a string around it. He would then place the object on the vehicle's tracks. Before long, he said, the vehicle's motor would stall so that the dozos pursuing it could capture its occupant(s). As we spoke, an Odiennéka dozo overheard us and showed us a baton that he held made of green bamboo. He said that he could fire the baton like a rifle or point it at people to make them freeze in place—up to forty criminals at once, he claimed. Dozos used such objects at roadblocks, much as they did in the forest, to regulate movement of the beings they pursued.

The practicality of dozos' approach became apparent when Kamagaté and I arrived at the checkpoint near the dozos' Terre Rouge office in the Bardo neighborhood (see fig. 16). Shortly after our arrival, a young man approached the checkpoint with a friend to report the theft of a sewing machine. Tiécoura Ouattara, whom we happened to meet there, told the dozos stationed at the roadblock to alert their colleagues at the other checkpoints to watch for the machine. Dozos had established their Bardo checkpoint to make themselves accessible to the local population as much as to oversee their movement, in marked contrast to the unavailability of police even at their headquarters.

Along my route that night, I saw several dozos carrying twelve-gauge shotguns and as many others carrying handmade muskets as well as machetes, knives, and the occasional bow and arrow or lightweight, crescent-bladed axe. Such weapons seemed ill fit for the realities of urban crime, but dozos' diverse arsenal of occult techniques and weapons was precisely what made Benkadi modern. They gave dozos an affordable, sustainable repertoire of tools to do the state's security work in the impoverished neighborhoods where they lived.

Infiltrating Urban Jungles in San-Pédro

Their closeness to the working-class populations they protected also gave Benkadi an intimate knowledge of their neighborhoods. Dozos knew their cities and towns as well as rural dozos knew their forests and fields. As the dozo party I accompanied passed through the empty Bardo marketplace, they lit its concrete tables and wooden stalls with their flashlights. By day, they said, the market had become the center of the city's once-flourishing drug trade.[3] By night, bandits hid here to ambush nighttime pedestrians. But no more: one could now walk through the market safely, day or night, because dozos had chased away its bandits. Dozos had used their familiarity with the area to master it. Tiécoura likewise told me that dozos had used their knowledge of the Bardo neighborhood to corner and capture a pair of thieves in a cul-de-sac by maneuvering them into it.

Dozos employed a similar strategy when the Benkadi foot patrol I was accompanying neared a bus station (see fig. 17). The dozos stopped at a distance to study the crowd gathered at the open-air food kiosk at the station. When I asked why the crowd interested them, they explained that thieves often lurked at bus stations at night to rob tired, inattentive passengers after they disembarked. Anyone present at the station without a bus ticket, they said, was up to no good. This seemed to me like an overgeneralization, but I was in no position to argue.

Rather than approach the station directly and lose the advantage of surprise, the dozos split into two groups. They planned to surround potential suspects, following the tactic I had seen dozos use in Denguélé for burning the forest from one end and bagging the game flushed out by the flames at the other (see chap. 3). In San-Pédro, one of the dozos approached the station from behind. I followed the others as they approached from the road.[4] We converged at the food kiosk where most of the crowd was sitting on stools or standing near the counter. I waited next to the kiosk while dozos culled the crowd. They soon emerged with

17 Two dozos guard a bus station by day in the coastal city of San-Pédro, August 5, 1996.

a woman and half a dozen young men in tow who had failed, according to dozos, to produce bus tickets or convincing explanations for their presence at the station at such a late hour. They credited the raid's success to the power object their Malian colleague had placed on the road.

The young people protested their innocence. They individually claimed that they had been waiting for relatives to arrive by bus, that they had just greeted previous arrivals, or that they had come for a midnight snack at the kiosk. The dozos then reminded them of Benkadi's midnight curfew, asserting that too much time had elapsed since the last bus's arrival and that too much time remained before the next one's. One of the male suspects openly sympathized with the dozos, saying that they were unable to tell the innocent from the guilty and that those without tickets were blameworthy because they were out after curfew. As he spoke, dozos tied his and the other suspects' hands behind their backs with a long rope that linked them together like members of a chain gang. The dozos then led them to Camp Dynamique. Here they left them in the custody of the dozo on guard duty. In the morning, the loiterers would either pay a fine, or family members or friends would have to do so for them to be released. The potential to abuse this arrangement by arresting suspects without any credible reason to hold them for ransom seemed evident. The dozos said that people were knowledgeable enough of Benkadi's policies now that those who noticed family or friends missing at dawn would go looking for them at dozo headquarters.

I found the situation even more disturbing when we arrived at the Camp Dynamique headquarters. There we entered a building made of wooden planks that contained two rooms with no amenities. In one, dozos stored confiscated contraband of undetermined ownership. In the other, dozos held meetings and held detained suspects. Once the dozos had locked their suspects into the holding room and were ready to resume their patrol, I asked one of them about the wisdom of leaving a woman in a room full of men who were overseen, in turn, by another man. He assured me—naively, I thought—that all would be well.

But I had reason to worry. Dozos had begun to exhibit the same sense of impunity that police and gendarmes affected. In Bouaké, they intervened in a nighttime argument between a young engaged couple. When the man told dozos to mind their own business, they reportedly shot and killed him in front of his fiancée (E. Kouassi 1996; S. Coulibaly 1997). The following year, gendarmes in Divo arrested a Malian dozo for highway banditry (C. Ibo 1997), the very crime against which dozos won national attention.

In San-Pédro, several months before my visit, police had interrogated Tiécoura Ouattara on the suspicion that dozos under his command had killed four young men—thieves by reputation—whose bodies had been found floating in the San-Pédro River (Detchi 1996). Police released Tiécoura Ouattara after questioning, but the incident revealed the extent to which authorities had come to associate dozos with violence even as they cooperated with them.

Elsewhere, in the village of Guèyo, dozos beat a young Burkinabe man so badly that his compatriots vandalized dozos' headquarters in protest. Dozos then took revenge by murdering the man, his father, mother, two girls, and a baby in their compound before burglarizing it (F. Bailly 1997;

Debali and Tagba 1997). In Daloa, dozos reportedly killed a gendarme and executed a thief (Deh 1996, 1997, 7). In Kolia and Bongouanou they wounded four women with bullets by carelessly firing guns into the air at dozo funerals (I. Bamba 1997; *Le Populaire* 1997a, 5; 1997d, 2). In Korhogo they beat two criminal suspects until they bled profusely (Agence Ivoirienne de Presse 1996a, 2). And in Guiglo, they manhandled, bound, and paraded a gendarme about town (Bledson 1997).

Dozos also committed fraud, extortion, and theft. In Tiassalé, a dozo was condemned for promising to reveal the identity of a man's murderer through occult means in exchange for 140,000 francs (B. Traoré 1997, 12). In Dabou and Divo, dozos imposed an excessive fine of 5,000 francs on those who broke curfew (*Le Populaire* 1997b; B. Cissé 1997, 3). And in Duékoué's market, they extorted fines of between 1,000 and 2,000 francs every week from merchants (*SoirINFO* 1997, 9) as protection money. And in Issia, they committed petty thefts (*Le Populaire* 1997c, 5).

Despite such abuses, Benkadi continued to operate in cities like San-Pédro, Abidjan, Korhogo, and Duékoué because their neighborhoods proved too vast for police to oversee. When the chief of the Water and Forest police in Séguéla banned dozo patrols, crime there soared (*Le Républicain Ivoirien* 1997, 12). To say so is not to justify dozo violence but to put it in the context of a country in which violence and lawlessness, through omission or commission—whether physical or symbolic, as at police checkpoints—had literally become the currency of state security forces. Dozos were as capable as anyone else of breaking the law.

But dozos relied on more than violence or the threat thereof to establish themselves as a viable security force in Côte d'Ivoire. In Odienné, they cultivated a peaceful working relationship with municipal authorities to gain approval for their patrols just as they did along Denguélé's border with Mali.

I learned of dozos' plans to begin Benkadi patrols in Odienné at a *tonsigi* there in mid-March 1995. Dozos came from across Denguélé to celebrate, and dozos from Yorojan explained Benkadi law even though officials had yet to authorize dozo patrols. It took two years of persistent lobbying, bureaucratic savoir faire, and *dangun* sacrifices before they would. I now turn to the sequence of events that led to that outcome.

Hunting Agreement in Odienné

In late July 1995, Moussa Fofana, Odienné's Afrique Environnementale (AE) president, organized a *tonsigi* in the subprefecture of Dioulatiédougou and began planning one for the subprefecture of Minignan. He estimated that four hundred dozos had come to Dioulatiédougou to hear Benkadi's message. There he told me that authorities thought that dozos were "up to no good [and] that they just [did] as they please[d]. They [did]n't understand that out of every hundred villages, eighty to eighty-five were founded by dozos. How could ne'er-do-wells or troublemakers or murderers found a village?" he asked. "No one would want to live there!" He implied that non-dozos were rallying to Benkadi as a reliable alternative to official police.

Six months later, at a *tonsigi* in the subprefecture of Tiémé, I watched one evening as an assistant to the village's Benkadi president sold AE membership cards and forms to interested dozos outdoors at a wooden table illuminated by a kerosene lamp. Next to the table stood a large metal basin filled with coffee that dozos purchased for a few francs a cup. The dozo at the table sold Benkadi memberships for 1,000 francs apiece (see fig. 18). He used a ballpoint pen to assign and write a membership number for each new member on a small yellow form. On the form he recorded the current year, the dozo's name, date of birth (to the extent possible), village, and occupation. Then he recorded the date, number, issuing authority, and place of establishment of the dozo's Ivoirian national identity card. In a curious reversal of roles, a nonstate bureaucrat meticulously recorded state-allocated information—the apogee of dozos' bureaucratic mimesis.

Both the assistant and Benkadi's local treasurer stamped and signed the sheet, along with Moussa Fofana, making the membership official. Finally, the assistant detached the member's portion of the form and gave it to him after having copied the same information onto a stub that would go to Moussa Fofana and then Inza Fanny, AE's national president, in Abidjan. The assistant then gave the dozo a folding blue membership card for 1,000 francs, bringing total membership costs to 2,000. On the front of each card, the assistant recorded the current year and the dozo's AE membership number. Inside, he wrote the new member's family name and personal name, profession, national identity card number, address, telephone number (in the unlikely case that he had one),[5] and date. Below this information stood a small empty square to which the dozo would later affix a passport-sized identity photo. Once more, the assistant and treasurer signed and stamped the document.

As part of Benkadi's plan for local patrols, Fofana organized a *tonsigi* in the Bako subprefecture in mid-May 1996, which hundreds of dozos attended. Less than two months later, in July, dozo Amara Koné dreamt that Manimory told him and other dozos to gather and carbonize some

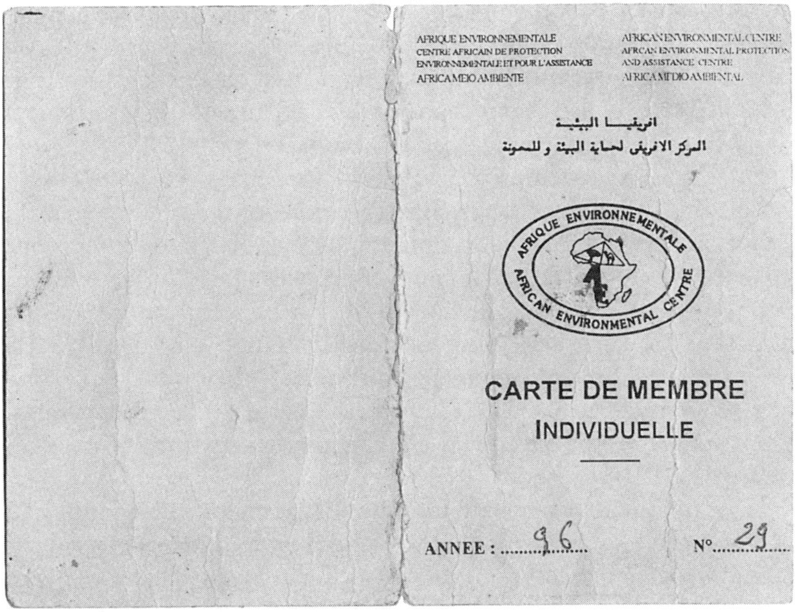

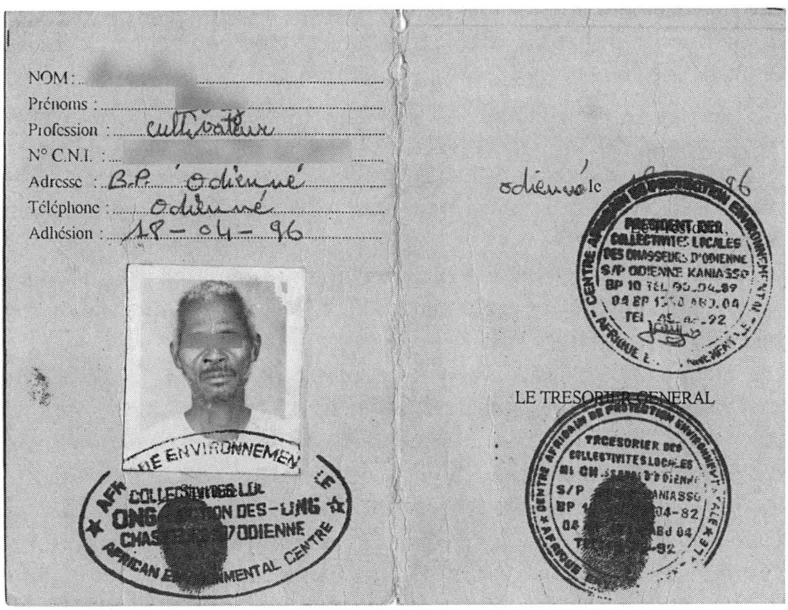

18 Dozo membership card for Afrique Environnementale.

roots to make a potion out of them with which they could wash themselves for protection while on patrol (see chap. 4). That same month, Fofana sent letters to Odienné's prefect, subprefect, chief judge, gendarme commandant, police commissioner, Water and Forest police chief, and head customs agent to request authorization for AE's security, environmental, and sanitation projects. He explained that dozos would begin their patrols at midnight and surveil the entire town, including its main points of entry. During the first month, dozos would inform the public of Benkadi's curfew without imposing fines or detaining curfew breakers. From then on, dozos would enforce the curfew, confiscating cooking utensils left outside and fining their owners if they wanted them back. Every Sunday, on Odienné's main market day, they would patrol the market from 7:00 a.m. to 4:30 p.m. against thieves. And every two weeks, they would bring to the attention of city officials any areas of the town in need of trash collection.

In early July 1996, after awaiting authorization for a little more than a month, and just a few months before security minister Dibonan Koné began his national anti-dozo campaign (see chap. 6), Fofana met with Odienné's deputy mayor and secretary general. At the meeting, Fofana presented a written request to the city council (*conseil municipal*) for permission to begin patrols in Odienné.[6] When the council met to discuss Benkadi, the chief (*dugutigi*) of Odienné attended. By hand vote, the chief and council agreed together that dozos could begin their patrols. Stories of the recent robbery of an elderly woman at 4:30 a.m. by bandits who had broken down her door helped Benkadi's case, although the deputy mayor decided to defer to the prefect and subprefect by requesting their approval before giving his.

When Fofana visited the deputy mayor for word of the council's decision, the deputy mayor explained his position and said that the prefect had asked him to have Fofana put his request for authorization in writing. Fofana did so immediately. A week later, he returned to the deputy mayor's office for a response, but the prefect had yet to reply. Another week passed before Fofana returned to city hall, only to be disappointed once again. When I spoke with him on July 31, 1996, nearly a month after he had begun his quest for authorization, he said that the prefect would soon be stepping down, leaving the council's request for his successor to decide. Fofana and the deputy mayor would have to begin the process all over again.

Undaunted, Fofana started to rent the building that would serve as dozos' AE headquarters. In August, he obtained thumbprints—in place of signatures—from ten of Odienné's sixteen neighborhood chiefs (*kab-*

latigi) as well as that of the chief (*dugutigi*) of Odienné on a document that indicated their support for Benkadi's request. In this document, dozos proposed to mount nightly patrols from half past midnight to 6:00 a m. and to patrol the market every Sunday from 7:00 a.m. to 4:00 p.m. (Moussa Fofana 1996).[7]

Finally, in early December 1996, now seven months after Fofana first asked authorities to allow Benkadi patrols and only a few months after the minister of security had begun his anti-dozo campaign, Odienné's subprefect asked Fofana to have those dozos who intended to man Benkadi patrols submit two identity photos each and a photocopy of their national identity card to his office. Odienné's chief dozo at the time, Soumaïla Fofana, and his deputies, Kanamankan Diarrassouba and Bogodougou Brahima, accompanied groups of about fifteen dozos each to the subprefectural office to submit their papers and photos. With these materials, the subprefect established a list of dozos expected to patrol Odienné. On December 5, dozos made their *Manimorisɔ* sacrifice to request Manimory's protection on their hunts and patrols (see chap. 4). But by month's end, they were still waiting for approval.

Finally, eight months later, Odienné's prefect told Fofana on Wednesday, July 30, 1997, that Benkadi could begin its patrols. He gave Fofana no signed document, only his word.[8] The prefect insisted that dozos bring no undue attention to themselves. Fofana promised that they would remain discreet. In this way local officials in Odienné began to collaborate with the same ersatz police that the minister of security had condemned the previous year. What dozos failed to achieve officially and nationally in a "state of exception" (Agamben 1998, 2005), they accomplished unofficially under an exceptional, local manifestation of the state, a notable achievement given the country's growing anti-Jula, anti-Muslim sentiment.

A Dozo Dragnet

On the night of Wednesday, August 6, 1997,[9] a week after dozos received permission to begin patrols, ten dozos arrived at Benkadi headquarters for their very first patrol. The group included seven junior and three senior dozos, including Odienné's new dozo chief, Kanamankan Diarrassouba. He cut a splendid figure in a white sport coat, purple pillbox prayer hat, and lavender pants that hugged his hips and ankles but billowed along the length of his legs. He carried a short, wrought iron javelin for the occasion, leaving with his colleagues at 12:50 a.m. on August 7 to announce that dozos would soon begin enforcing their midnight curfew.[10]

Dozos detailed their anticipated surveillance procedures to me in their office. They said that they intended to begin their real patrols on Friday, August 8, a month after they had severed ties with AE (see chap. 6). If they found a person outside at night, they would ask him or her to show them his or her house keys and identity papers. They would then escort the person home where he or she could prove occupancy by unlocking the door or confirming his or her status as a housemate with anyone who would answer it. Alternatively, they would detain anyone in their office until morning who behaved suspiciously or lacked a fixed home or papers. For a 500 franc fee—from the detainee, family, or friends—or in exchange for menial labor in or around the office, the detainee could leave the next morning. But if dozos caught someone committing a crime, they planned to hold the person overnight and take the offender to the authorities the next morning. Then at last, a month later, on August 8, 1997, one day after Ivoirian Independence Day, dozos began enforcing their curfew.[11]

At the same time, the Ivoirian government was establishing a new security agency, the National Security Council (Conseil National de Sécurité), under General Tanny Ehuéni Joseph, secretary general of the gendarmes.[12] The council would oversee and coordinate the efforts of all of Côte d'Ivoire's security forces. One of Tanny's tasks was to resolve the dozo issue after Minister Dibonan Koné's failure to do so (C. Koffi 1997; Zéguéla 1997). National officials were alarmed by dozos' potential to emulate the Kamajor hunters' militia in Sierra Leone or the warring Cobra, Ninja, and Cocoye militias in Congo-Brazzaville (Sangho 1997; C. Koffi 1997). Dozos' majority Jula and Senufo composition and Muslim religious affiliation were also cause for concern. Tanny aimed to prevent dozos from destabilizing Côte d'Ivoire as an ethnic militia that now rivaled the power of his own gendarmes.

But dozos had other things on their minds. They knew that they could use their new roles to help make a living. Many hoped to pursue surveillance as a full- or part-time job. Some dozos worked individually as private security guards for home and business owners. Others worked in groups. In a neighborhood of Abidjan's working-class Adjamé district, for instance (see fig. 19), twelve dozos regularly patrolled the streets at night. At the end of each month, they collected 500 francs from each neighborhood compound and 300 francs from each single dwelling. Each of them made approximately 35,000 francs per month, an enviable salary for the unemployed. One dozo, from Burkina Faso, worked as an electrician by day and as a dozo by night in the same entrepreneurial spirit that Houphouët-Boigny had once praised.

19 Dozo Samka Bamba (*left*) and Drissa Koné (*foreground*) in the Adjamé district of Abidjan not far from the district's bus station area. Both Samka and Drissa hold fly whisks (*lɛnyigin*) made of the bristles of wild boars. Many northern-descended migrant and immigrant families lived in this area. Samka Bamba organized and manned Benkadi patrols in Adjamé's Habitat neighborhood.

Dozos were now a "triple threat." Known for their police work and for adjudicating criminal cases from Benkadi's earliest days in northern Denguélé by imposing fees on criminals and sharing the profits with crime victims (see chap. 6), they were police, judges, and entrepreneurs, usurping the roles of several state agencies at once: the Ministry of Security and its police,[13] the Ministry of Defense and its gendarmes, and the Ivoirian judiciary and their judges. The Ministry of Security defined its responsibilities as "maintaining the State's . . . public security . . . territorial oversight, [and] oversight of the circulation of persons both within and across borders" (République de Côte d'Ivoire 1997, 9; 1991, 56). The Ministry of Defense assured "public safety, the maintenance of order, and the execution of laws for the purpose of protecting institutions, persons, and property over . . . [Ivoirian] territory" (Gendarmerie Nationale n.d., 3). And the judiciary was responsible for trying suspects according to article 60 of the Ivoirian constitution: "Any accused is presumed innocent until his culpability has been established following proceedings offering him indispensable guarantees for his defense" (Aggrey 1994, 21). Whether dozos' litigation procedures offered such guarantees was debatable, but dozos had begun to provide all of these services unofficially, not only for a perfunctory fee, but for a profit. Dozos in Odienné had not yet begun to collect fees door-to-door for their work by the time I left in 1997, but they had begun to adjudicate cases for a charge even before receiving approval for their patrols. They did so not only to support themselves but also to repair social relations ruptured by crime through a form of restorative justice.[14]

The Cattle Thief

In September 1995, nearly two years before dozos began patrols in Odienné, they settled a dispute in the village of Bako. On September 2, some thirty men including Moussa Fofana and Bako's chief dozo assembled near a mango tree at the edge of the village to deliberate a case concerning a young Fulbe cattle herder who had allegedly stolen a bull belonging to a Bako resident. The herdsman had reportedly sold the bull without telling the owner. To disguise the theft, the herdsman claimed that the bull had died and showed the owner the carcass of another bull as "proof" of its demise. The owner suspected a ruse, and villagers called on the dozos to investigate. Because roaming cattle often entered farmers' fields and damaged their crops, tensions between farmers and herdsmen ran high (see Bassett 1988; Hagberg 1998).[15]

The herdsman stood before the tribunal who sat in the shade of the mango tree. About fifteen other men, some of whom were also dozos, stood behind those seated. From 2:30 to 6:15 p.m., public deliberations took place among dozos, villagers, and the herder. An older Fulbe man represented the interests of the accused, and a *jeli* (griot) amplified the herdsman's words whenever he spoke. Moussa Fofana kept the discussion focused on the issue at hand. At a quarter past six, after all the concerned parties had spoken, and after some private consultations to which I was not privy, Fofana drafted a handwritten contract specifying that the herdsman reimburse the owner the price of the bull and pay a fine to dozos for their work in settling the matter. All parties to the dispute, including the three dozos mediating it, signed the contract, either in writing or with a thumbprint from the inkpad that Fofana had brought with him. The dispute ended quietly, in verbal and written agreements rather than in conflict. I never learned the sum to be paid. It was the first dozo trial I attended. More were to come.

The Market Squatters

Two years later, dozos took similar measures in the city of Odienné with the tacit approval of local authorities. On the night of August 10, 1997, three days after the start of Benkadi patrols, dozos reportedly found four young men sleeping in market stalls for the fourth time in a row. They said they had warned the men three times to find other places to sleep. This time, the dozos took the men to their headquarters to spend the night. The next morning, dozos gave them hand ploughs (*daba*s) and made them uproot weeds next to the office as punishment for breaking curfew. It was the kind of public shaming that dozos had also practiced in Yorojan.

The Chicken Thief

Three days after the homeless men's arrest, on the night of Wednesday, August 13, 1997, dozos found an impoverished-looking older man carrying a sack holding three chickens. Moussa Fofana recorded in handwritten French the dozo party's version of the man's capture:

> Declaration of the activities of [Benkadi] members.
>
> At 4:00 in the morning during a patrol, hunters [*les chasseurs*] arrested, in Kogobèrèla [an Odienné neighborhood], Mr. Adama . . . carrying a sack containing three chickens. After a several-question interrogation, he avows having stolen four chickens from Martine [the owner] who appears now to have left for Abidjan. He says that he has already eaten one.
>
> Asked about his origins, his name is Adama . . . born in . . . Guinea. After consultations, the hunters, under the direction of Mr. Fofana Moussa and Kanamankan Diarra[ssouba] decide to send the thief to the police . . .

Fofana noted the place and date at which dozos decided their course of action, "Odienné, 8-14-97," and wrote the name "Kanamankan Diarrassouba" on the document, under which the dozo chief attempted a signature. Fofana signed, too.

He later recounted to me the events that followed Adama's detainment.

Early on Thursday morning, August 14, Fofana sent four dozos to accompany the thief, the chickens, and Fofana's handwritten report of Adama's capture to the police. In the meantime, the police commissioner was driving to work and noticed dozos heading toward his office. He made a quick U-turn back to the Benkadi office. There, he asked Fofana to explain what was happening. After Fofana did so, the commissioner told Fofana to call back the dozos since no civilian had lodged a complaint against the thief, the dozos' accusation notwithstanding. Fofana did as instructed, and by 8:45 a.m., the dozos had returned to the office and seated Adama on a bench on the front porch where, according to Fofana, Adama drew a crowd of between 75 to 100 people.[16] Two dozos tried to locate any relatives, friends, or acquaintances of Adama's. Eventually, a matrilateral relative arrived, as did Kanamankan Diarrassouba. He allowed Adama to leave with the relative on condition that the relative return with a fine of 3,000 francs for dozos' work in capturing Adama—1,000 francs per chicken.

If the case had gone to court and the suspect had been found guilty of nighttime theft, he might have faced ten to twenty years in prison and a fine of 500,000 to 5,000,000 francs (Aggrey 1981). The likelihood of this happening was minimal due to the lack of a police presence, but the fact that a minor theft might have resulted in such severe penalties despite the lack of police interest in the case underscored the irrelevance of police to most Odiennéka's lives and the uniqueness of Benkadi's contribution to local security. The commissioner had no way of knowing whether dozos had falsely accused Adama of a crime, but instead of opening an investigation, he returned the suspect to the dozos, letting them impose their own justice. The commissioner's response mirrored the state's larger relationship with Benkadi. Dozos offered a form of justice for the poor and powerless because state police protected only those who could afford their services. "Private" agents fulfilled state functions; "state" agents pursued private ends. After Adama's case, dozos in Odienné handled all the criminal cases that came to their attention on their own without referring them to the police, which proved profitable for both dozos and crime victims.

The Sheep Theft, Part 1

In October 1997, for example, seven sheep vanished from the village of Ngoloblasso and three more from the village of Lillè. Word of the crime spread across the Madinani subprefecture east of Odienné. Early on the morning of October 23, a boy walking westward along the dirt road to Odienné noticed a lone Fulbe man leading several sheep across fields owned and rented to farmers by Côte d'Ivoire's Public Works Department (Grands Travaux).[17] Suspicious, the boy continued on his way. As the lone male suspect was walking along the same road between Odienné and the village of Samakoungolo, the subprefect of Madinani passed him in his car. He stopped and asked him, "Where are you coming from with those sheep?"

"From Lillè," the suspect reportedly said before he fled with the sheep, and the subprefect continued on to Odienné. When the subprefect arrived at Odienné's easternmost entrance, he told the gendarmes stationed there what he had seen. Uninterested, they suggested that he tell the dozos. Reportedly, the boy who had just seen the thief was nearing Odienné at the same time. After he explained what he saw, the gendarmes and subprefect told him to inform the dozos. By 8:00 a.m., Fofana had organized a dozo search party in response to these reports.

At about 9:00 a.m., two dozos left the Benkadi office on bicycles heading eastward to find the suspect. Three others followed on foot. Those on bicycles identified the sheep's tracks on the road and returned to inform the three others. The party then split again into two groups and agreed to blow their hunting whistles if either found the suspect first.

Those on bicycles rode ahead to Samakoungolo and waited at its outskirts. The three on foot followed the sheep tracks off the road and into the forested savanna. Eventually, they spied the suspect near a wet-season pond. Before they could catch him, though, he escaped, having let the sheep drift into someone's potato field to graze. The dozos blew their whistles as the man fled. They then retrieved the sheep, leaving the others to capture the suspect as he ran toward Samakoungolo. The party returned to headquarters with the man and the sheep by 4:30 p.m. where they detained him until the next day.[18] Fofana had other business to attend to in the meantime.

The Case of the Pilfered Paint

That same afternoon, Fofana and several senior dozos tried two other cases, which I observed firsthand. They began with the case of a young sign painter who was delinquent in paying back a loan of 2,500 francs to his creditor. In response, the creditor stole the painter's tools, including his buckets, brushes, and paints—most of which now sat on the floor of the Benkadi office. Fofana and the other dozos present interrogated the two men, consulted with each other, and found the creditor at fault, ironically, for taking justice into his own hands. The creditor had consulted neither Benkadi nor the police before taking the painter's equipment. Fofana said that the man should have asked dozos to intervene on his behalf. As punishment, dozos imposed a 5,000 franc fine on the creditor for their work in recovering the stolen goods, some of which the thief had lost, including several paint rollers and a small brush, valued at a total of 3,000 francs.

The painter suggested that his creditor pay the fine and reimburse him for the cost of his lost materials. Dozos agreed and raised the creditor's fine to 8,000 francs. All agreed, however, that the 2,500 francs the painter originally owed his creditor be subtracted from that sum. The dozos instructed the creditor to pay them 5,000 francs and the painter 500, resolving a matter in which police would have taken no interest but that may have led to violence had it gone unresolved.

The Curfew-Breaking Porters

Dozos then brought in two young men who worked locally as porters (*wotorotigi*). On the previous evening, a woman had sent them to carry several sacks of corn loaded into their two-wheeled wooden carts (*wotoro*) to be ground at a milling machine. When the porters arrived at the mill, they found it closed and continued on to another one. Dozos intercepted them as they were returning to the woman's house at 1:00 a.m. with the ground corn meal. Fofana fined them each 200 francs for breaking curfew and sent them away. When they returned to the dozo office that afternoon with the money, Fofana gave each of them a stamped receipt for their fines.[19]

The Sheep Theft, Part 2

With these distractions, it wasn't until 10:40 a.m. on the day after the alleged sheep thief had been caught that Fofana, seven senior dozos, and four Lillè sheep owners met to settle the sheep theft. The suspect sat in the middle of the cement floor of the AE office, his hands tied behind his back. I will call him Diallo, a common Fulbe family name.

He said he had come to work in Côte d'Ivoire from Mopti, Mali. When I first met him, late on the night of his detention, dozos had bound his hands and feet but left him able to stand or sit. He was in a small room in the dozo office where a sentry stood guard. His hair was graying. He looked to be older than fifty. In Julakan, he told me that he had stolen cattle on a previous occasion for which Odienné's gendarmes arrested him. But instead of sending him to trial, he said, they offered to release him in exchange for 350,000 francs, which Diallo paid with the help of friends. He may have told me this story to signal that friends might again be able to buy his freedom. In any case, he confirmed the kind of corruption on the gendarmes' part that Benkadi hoped to stop.

This time Diallo's situation was more complicated. It took two hours of negotiation before dozos, along with the Lillè sheep owners, Diallo, and his associates agreed that Diallo should pay 1,500 francs per sheep to the Lillè owners as reimbursement for their troubles and a fee to dozos for each of the sheep they had recovered. As best I could discern, Diallo would pay a total of 18,000 francs in fines to the sheep owners and, for breaking Benkadi law, to the dozos and 39,500 to the dozos for his capture—a total of 57,500 francs. The Fulbe tendered the money on the spot, and the dozos gave Lillè's sheep owners their portion. Fofana documented the agreement in writing, but only he among the signatories was capable of reading and signing the document (see fig. 20). Others signed with a curved pen line or a thumbprint beneath this text:

Odienné, 10-25-97

Agreement

We the undersigned hunters, members of Benkadi, [having] met on this day, Saturday, 10-25-97 at 12:45 p.m., decide, with the owners of the stolen sheep and the brothers of the thief,[20] to effect the release of the sheep and the thief . . . through a gentlemen's agreement. All unanimously agreed to settle the dispute amicably.

Then Diallo left with his comrades, and the men from Lillè left with their sheep.

But some issues remained unresolved. Diallo had left a third, pregnant sheep from Lillè in the village of Gbèrèdougou where it had reportedly since given birth to a lamb. Fofana thus wrote and sent a letter to Gbèrèdougou's chief, reporting the dozos' solution to the theft and asking the chief to let the owner of the sheep retrieve them. As for the owners of the seven sheep stolen from Ngoloblasso, they arrived only after Diallo and his comrades had left. Fofana gave them 10,000 francs, although they had a right, in theory, to 10,500 at the rate of 1,500 francs per sheep. One owner, angry with Fofana, chided him for having freed Diallo too soon. Despite the lapse in protocol, the missing 500 francs, and the fact that Fofana had charged Diallo and his colleagues far less than Yorojan dozos'

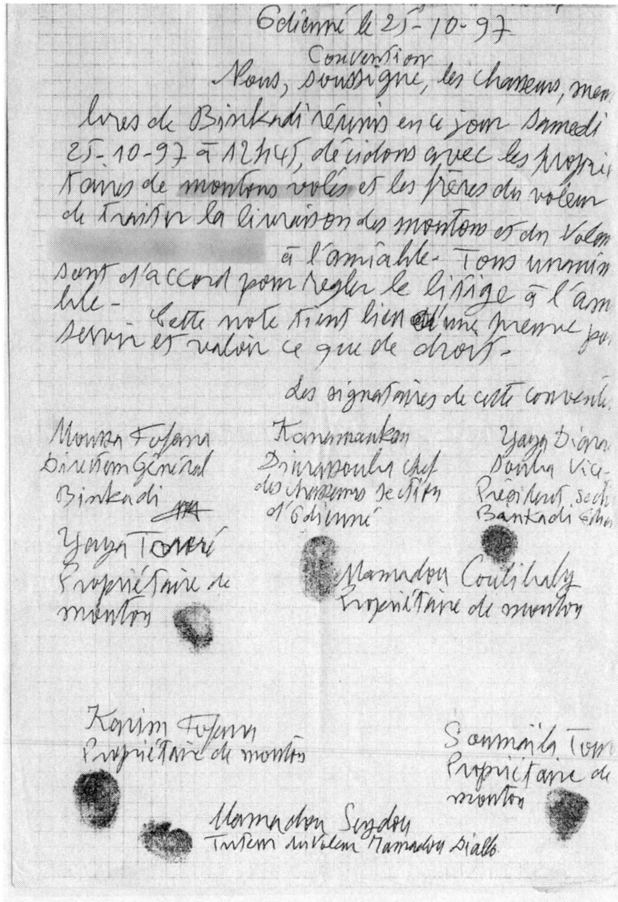
Odienné le 25-10-97
Convention
Nous, soussigné, les chasseurs, membres de Binkadi réunis en ce jour Samedi 25-10-97 à 12h45, décidons avec les propriétaires de moutons volés et les frères du voleur de traiter la livraison des moutons et du voleur [illegible] à l'amiable. Tous unanimes sont d'accord pour régler le litige à l'amiable. Cette note tient lieu d'une preuve pour servir et valoir ce que de droit.

Les signataires de cette conventi[on]

Moussa Fofana Directeur Général Binkadi

Kanmmankan Diarrassouba Chef des chasseurs section d'Odienné

Yaya Diarra Doulou Vice-Président section Binkadi Odienné

Yaya Touré Propriétaire de mouton

Mamadou Coulibaly Propriétaire de mouton

Karim Fofana Propriétaire de mouton

Samaïla Touré Propriétaire de mouton

Mamadou Sangaré Tuteur du voleur Mamadou Diallo

20 Photocopy of the handwritten agreement that Moussa Fofana wrote to conclude the matter of the alleged sheep thief, Mr. Diallo.

compensation rate of 25,000 francs per stolen sheep, Fofana and Benkadi had acted swiftly and profitably in the sheep owners' interests. Had the villagers relied on gendarmes or police, they might never have recovered their sheep, much less received any money for their trouble.

Such cases showed that dozos wanted to do more than stop crime. They also wanted to heal the tensions and disputes that arose from it in order to restore agreement to their communities. They acted where the state failed or refused to intervene, shared their profits with victims—as they shared game meat with non-dozos—and reintegrated criminals as quickly as possible into daily life. Benkadi's moralizing was not without problems, however.

A Broken Engagement

On August 19, 1997, I arrived at dozo headquarters at 9:30 a.m. to find a woman uprooting grass next to the building. Inside was another woman, Mariam, who sat near the door, looking dejected and uncomfortable. I rarely saw women at the dozo office. I greeted her and asked her why she had come. On the previous evening, she said, a number of women had gathered to celebrate the *kɔnyɔdi* or "bride giving" rite for the marriage of a friend of hers named Aminata.[21] The *kɔnyɔdi* precedes a bride's departure from her father's compound to her husband's. Aminata was to complete neither. Before her *kɔnyɔdi,* she fled to avoid an arranged marriage, embarrassing her family. And even before fleeing, she had already been protesting her engagement, which led to her older brother expelling her from his compound, where she had been living. She found refuge with her friend, Mariam, who tried to mediate the situation by asking her own older brother to speak to Aminata's brother on Aminata's behalf. Mariam's brother refused. Then Aminata disappeared altogether, provoking another of her brothers, Abou, a dozo, to go to Mariam's compound to find his sister. He reportedly arrived at Mariam's home near sunset at the same moment that Mariam was leaving to visit her boyfriend. When Abou asked Mariam where his sister was, Mariam said that she was in the compound of Mariam's younger sister. Abou told Mariam to show him the way. She did. When they arrived there, Mariam asked Abou to wait at the entrance while she greeted the family.

At this point in the conversation, Abou, who had been sitting next to Mariam and me during our conversation without having identified himself, spoke up.[22] He told me that a few minutes after Mariam entered the compound, he saw Aminata and Mariam flee together over the compound wall. He chased them with the help of some dozo friends, catching Mariam along with a woman who shared Mariam's room and who, dozos suspected, had helped Aminata escape. This second woman was the one I had seen clearing weeds outside of the dozo office. Dozos had not yet found Aminata, nor did I ever learn that they did.

Their response to the situation was revealing. Odienné dozos tried to force an arranged marriage on an unwilling fiancée, whereas Yorojan dozos had decided that intervening in such disputes did more harm than good (see chap. 6). Although most dozos privileged men's interests over women's, local Benkadi offices, like Yorojan's, might decide to do otherwise. *Dozoya* offered a flexible vision rather than a standard protocol for how dozos should police their communities. The prevailing bias for men's interests over women's did not go uncontested, at least not in Yorojan. But for the most part, dozo law reinforced the status quo, sometimes with horrendous results. In Man, for instance, dozos beat and raped a woman with objects after her father had convinced her to return home following her flight from an arranged marriage. Dozos reportedly punished her at her father's request (Gueu 1997).

Benkadi's laudable and sinister aspects were of a piece. What Laclau (1996, 60) has written of politics in general was true of Benkadi in particular: "Any concrete politics, if it is capable of bringing about social order, will be judged not only according to its merits in the abstract, independently of any circumstance, but mainly in terms of that ability to bring about that 'order.'" Benkadi flourished, in other words, not because it was the best solution to crime in Côte d'Ivoire, but because it was often the best *available* solution. When dozos went beyond the bounds of the approval that their local communities granted them, officials acted swiftly, detaining the dozo culprits or banning Benkadi, as in Guiglo and Zuénoula where dozos killed six people and beat a policeman and two gendarmes, provoking an army colonel to disarm them and end their patrols (Kouilahan 1996). Meanwhile, the largely reliable conduct of dozos enabled Benkadi to endure as a movement across the country even when some of its members violated their implicit, extralegal compact with the state.

From Agreement to Repression

Benkadi flourished for as long as it did in large part because the state allowed it to and because dozos mostly avoided offending—or in fact reaffirmed—non-dozo men's sensibilities about gender, crime, and punishment. At the same time, the largely unregulated power that local officials tacitly granted Benkadi enhanced the potential of dozos to abuse their own authority, though no more than state security forces abused theirs,[23] and certainly not without internal criticism. Dozos' atrocities defied their conventional uses of violence on the hunt and in sacrifice. Slaying a man in Bouaké, murdering an immigrant and his family in Guèyo, raping a woman in Man, and accidentally killing women at Kolia and Bongouanou violated the moral reciprocity with non-dozos that dozos affirmed. Dozos were known for using violence to restore order in times of turmoil, but these incidents exacerbated the instability they were trying to calm.

Such crimes undermined the collaborative relationship that Benkadi had worked so hard to establish with local officials. To assume that these acts flowed from the sacrificial violence of *dozoya* would be a mistake.[24] What is striking about them is the sense of impunity they displayed, as if dozos believed they were neither "*committing homicide*" nor "*celebrating a sacrifice*" and therefore free of the moral consequences or obligations of either act (Agamben 1998, 83, emphasis in original). It seems that dozos mimicked Côte d'Ivoire's state of exception so well that some analogized their authority as dozos in exceptional domestic situations as a form of the state's exceptional sovereignty, using arbitrary, extralegal violence as the basis of their authority, just as state security agents did and as Bédié had when he entered the national television station under armed escort to proclaim himself president. In such cases, dozos no longer imitated the state; they *identified* with it, vitiating the mimesis that defined their roles.

Dozos exhibited a similar sense of impunity in Odienné. To my knowledge, they never committed rape, torture, or murder, but in some cases, they flagrantly violated their initiatory vows and were punished as a result. For example, after dozos found a stolen moped in the possession of one of their junior colleagues, they reportedly discovered that the dozo in question had ties to a moped-parts smuggling ring. Dozos promptly expelled him from Benkadi, effectively defrocking him as a dozo. Similarly, when dozos allegedly learned that Bogodougou Brahima, the prominent senior dozo and dozo sacrificer, had never been initiated as a dozo, they barred him from attending all future dozo events.

Several years later, in 2002, while I was visiting Odienné, I learned that dozos had removed Moussa Fofana as Odienné's dozo president due to his allegations of financial mismanagement. A dozo who had worked closely with him told me that dozos had received no payment for their work as Benkadi agents since they began it in 1997. Dozos deduced that Fofana had been pocketing their earnings for himself. Five years after the start of such irregularities—befitting the patience (*sabari*) so highly valued in Denguélé—dozos banished him from the headquarters he had formerly managed.[25]

But no such self-correction on Benkadi's part could lull the state into accepting its abiding presence. In 1998, interior minister Émile Constant Bombet formally outlawed Benkadi in southern Côte d'Ivoire, allowing dozos to continue their security work in the country's northern half, to which he referred as dozos' "original geographic and cultural region" (Bassett 2003, 15–16; J.-R. Kouamé 1998; Y. Kouassi and Djidji 1998). He ordered that "modern" firearms be confiscated from southern dozos and allowed northern dozos to continue their patrols with only "traditional" muzzle-loading muskets. Benkadi's nationwide collaboration with state officials was over, but not without having left a lasting message.

Dozos had established a critical ethic of restorative justice with the help of state officials, including subprefects and police commissioners. Their success depended as much on these officials as on dozos. It is therefore misleading to consider Benkadi a uniquely dozo phenomenon. It was, by design, a collaboration that involved dozos, their non-dozo communities, and the state. If dozos found a place on the edge of the state apparatus, it was because citizens, residents, and local officials wanted them there. Benkadi embodied a public, though tacit, quid pro quo between dozos and the state. They did so most visibly through the songs that dozo musicians sang at dozos' *kozi* funeral rites and at the *tonsigi*s they organized for Benkadi, where they performed some of the same songs that featured at *kozi*s. The next chapter examines these songs as a dozo exegesis of the moral relations that underlay both Benkadi and *dozoya*.

EIGHT

The Power in the Nightjar's Call: Dozo Performance as Social Drama

Hunting Songs

Dozo musicians sang at dozo funerals and at Benkadi meetings to elicit action from fellow dozos. Songs evoked problems in order to resolve them, much as dozo sacrifices did. Songs were an integral part of such sacrifices. At *kozi*s and *yaladon*s, songs called to mind the danger of neglecting a dead dozo's spirit. At *tonsigi*s and at Fanny's Kaniasso conferences, they amplified the need to attend to other violations of reciprocity as well, including theft and banditry. Songs publicized *dozoya* as an antidote to these ruptures of agreement (*bɛn*) and mobilized non-dozos to support Benkadi in its work.

First among Denguélé's dozo singers was my host, Dramane Coulibaly. His work as a musician and the structure, themes, and purpose of his songs take center stage in this chapter. His attempts to provoke (*ka mabɔ*) a dozo through song to kill game at a *kozi* in the Deguélé village of Kombedougou demonstrate how Dramane reminded dozos of their moral accountability to each other as well as to non-dozos. When Dramane sang to dozos, and when they danced or hunted in response, they performed *dozoya* in a dead dozo's compound or public square in ways that premised hunting and Benkadi on the aesthetic enactment of dozos' moral obligations to non-dozos. Hunting in the forest or manning security patrols in town depended first on the musical elicitation of dozos' skills through songs.

This chapter begins with an overview of the dozo singer's role. It then explores the kinds of songs that dozo musicians sang at *kozi*s, *yaladon*s, and *tonsigi*s. Next, it turns to the confrontation between Dramane and dozo Mamadou Sylla at Kombedougou. It ends with an interpretation of Dramane's songs as a critique of Benkadi that testified to a plurality of dozo opinions about the role of dozos as unofficial police.

Dramane as *Ngɔnun* Player

When Dramane was a child, his parents discouraged him from singing. His father wanted him to focus on being a member of the occult *kɔma* association, but Dramane persisted in his pursuit of dozo songs, which he believed he was destined to learn and perform. Eventually he became an exemplary artist. When celebrities, such as the president, prime minister, or United States ambassador, visited Odienné during my stay, authorities invited Dramane to sing to mark the occasion. He was Denguélé's foremost *dozongɔnun* player. He also commanded wide respect as a singer and healer throughout Côte d'Ivoire. In the 1990s, he was training five singer-apprentices in his art. They all imitated his distinctive style. Like Dramane, they performed in Denguélé at dozo events where I observed firsthand the importance that their music had for dozos as both hunters and police.

Dozo musicians sang publicly at dozos' *kozi* and *yaladon* rites where they lauded the deceased, consoled his widow(s), lamented dozos' deaths, and serenaded dozos and non-dozos. As masters of ceremonies, they led dances, punctuated and gave continuity to events, directed dozos' movements within and beyond their dance circle (*bara*), resolved any disputes that might arise during the festivities, and provoked individual dozos to hunt. Singers also sang as dozos walked to and from the sacrifices they made in the *dangun* the next morning and on other sacrificial occasions. When dozo musicians passed through a village or town while heading to an event, inhabitants usually incited them to organize impromptu performances (*dozotɔrɔn*) unlinked to any ritual context. Wherever and whenever dozos acted in relation to non-dozos, *ngɔnun* players announced dozos' presence and roused them to action. Dozos danced in response to dozo songs, enacting the postures, movements, and attitudes of the hunt. Before stalking game, dozos hunted it symbolically through dance.

Dramane Coulibaly's performance at a *kozi* on the night of April 13 to 14, 1995, in the village of Kombedougou, Denguélé, exemplified the power of dozo songs.

Song as a Call to Action

On the afternoon of April 13, Dramane and I parked our mopeds in the compound of the chief dozo of Kombedougou. Drissa Koné had ridden with me on my moped. Dramane's apprentices had already parked their bicycles nearby. The chief dozo received us in his round, mud-brick home where we stored our things, rested, received villagers' greetings, and ate dinner. Afterward, Dramane closed the door to the house and prepared himself to perform. He was already wearing his dozo pants (*dozo kurusi jan*) that tied tightly around his waist, closely hugging his ankles and calves and expanding between the knees and waist. He opened the bag he had brought and removed a bottle, a heavy amulet-and-talisman-laden shirt (*kɔrɔdɛrɛkɛ*), a ridged, split, metal tube (*kɛŋkɛnyɛn*), and a short, thin, metal rod (*nɛgɛ*). From the bottle, he swallowed a protective potion (*flaji*) to soothe his throat and make people receptive to his words (*ka fanga kɛ a kumakan la*). He put on his heavy dozo shirt for further protection from the sorcery of jealous colleagues and donned his peaked, red-and-white hat resembling a closed bishop's miter worn sideways, fringed along its ridge with white ram's hair.

When Dramane emerged from the chief dozo's home, a striking figure, his apprentices gathered around him and began to play their *ngɔnun*s while Dramane, with his partially paralyzed right hand, ran a metal rod over the ridged tube he held by an iron ring with his left, eliciting a rhythmic, metallic rasp.[1] And he began to sing. His apprentices sang his refrains. From the crowd, a young dozo stepped forward to take up and play a pair of bell-shaped basket rattles that Dramane had brought with him. The dozo held one in each hand by their woven, oval handles. Pumping them up and down, he knocked the small pebbles inside them against the rattles' circular, calabash bottoms, producing a crisp, gravelly sound. Dramane's rasping and the young man's clacking kept a sharp, clear rhythm. The *kozi* had begun.

By then, villagers had finished eating. It was dark. Light came only from handheld flashlights and two fires burning in the deceased's compound to which Dramane and his retinue were heading. Several young men holding tape recorders in their hands or boom boxes on their shoulders followed. They paid one to two hundred francs to the chief dozo for the privilege of recording Dramane's songs. Drissa and I walked among them, my tape recorder hanging from a band over my shoulder.

Meanwhile, inside the deceased's compound, a crowd of people waited. Senior dozos sat on chairs, benches, or stools (*kolo* in Julakan, *tabourets* in French). Younger dozos stood. Beyond them, women, children, and uninitiated men squeezed into the spaces between the mud-brick homes that marked the compound's boundary. The crowd parted for Dramane and his entourage as we arrived and as Dramane sang greetings to the villagers, dozos, and especially women. His greetings acknowledged dozos' dependence on women for the evening's success. Women had prepared the evening meal and would stay awake to sing his refrains until dawn and to make the next day's breakfast. Dramane also sang about himself, vaunting his musical talents and identity as a "stranger" and "guest" (*lonan*): "Hey, a foreigner has come" (*He lonan dɔ bara na*), he sang, to which women and Dramane's apprentices responded, 'Great stranger, welcome!' (*Lonanba, i ni sɛnɛ o!*).

Dramane routinely began his performances with this song. Because *ngɔnun* players were outsiders—"foreigners"—they were well placed to settle any rifts in the community to put the deceased at ease. They gained a more receptive hearing than insiders, who might have tried to criticize their neighbors. As a guest, the singer could say or sing what he pleased when he pleased, even if he had to interrupt a chief dozo to do so. Dozos acknowledged this license by calling their singers *diden* or "sweet child,"[2] an affectionate term for a dependent—an apprentice, child, etc.—whom one loves, protects, and tolerates despite his or her eccentricities. Dozos also called their singers "little birds" (*kɔnɔnin*) because they sang so sweetly.

Once inside the compound, Dramane and his entourage slowly circled the central fires counterclockwise. Dozos then began to line up outside the compound in groups that represented the villages from which they had come. When they blew their whistles to announce their presence, Dramane reopened the corridor he had taken through the crowd and escorted them in. Many wore stern expressions as they entered, holding their rifles (*morifa*), power objects (*jo*), or fly whisks (*lɛnyigin*) made of the bristles of wild boar hair (*lɛ*) to display their power. As each party arrived, Dramane serenaded it as women called out, *I ni koŋ! I ni koŋ!* "You and the bush!" or *I ni ko!* "You and your exploits!"[3] Sometimes a few dozos removed themselves from the crowd to fire blasts of gunpowder to greet new arrivals or to show appreciation for Dramane's words. His songs elicited the performance of *dozoya* in the village before its enactment as hunting in the forest. Some dozos yelled "Su!" while firing or as others were firing, to invoke an abbreviated form of the name of Manimory's ancestor, Inzu.

As Dramane sang, the newly arrived dozos danced the dozos' slow, trademark step around the central fires: a step to the right on the right foot, then a step to the right on the left foot until the two feet nearly touched, followed by a repetition of these same two steps. Then a step to the left on the left foot and a step to the left on the right foot until the two feet nearly touched, and then a repetition of these two steps before beginning the sequence anew, advancing slightly with each step. As each arriving party completed a counterclockwise rotation around the central fires, Dramane and his musicians stood in place, or they sang while walking beside the dozos. After each new group's counterclockwise rotation in the compound, its members found places to sit or stand or stand in the compound, or they exited with Dramane to take up the rear of the line of a newly arriving group of dozos to lengthen the line. In this way a procession of dozos—a hundred or more at larger gatherings—moved in unison into and around the compound, forming a dance circle. In a faster step, which dozos danced later in the evening, dozos broke from the circle in small groups of perhaps two to four and moved toward the musicians, lifting their feet and kicking rapidly from the knee in a blur, sending up clouds of dust while holding their upper bodies still in a stylized rendition of the careful, decisive movements they made in the forest while hunting game.

From these opening moments of the *kozi*, Dramane announced himself as an *agent provocateur*:

Man! I entered Tagbana.
I made the dozos suffer.
I entered Yanfolila.[4]
I exhausted the dozos . . .
I entered Nafana.
I called the dozos . . .
Hey man, I don't lie to you . . .
Kombedougou dozos have wasted [animals'] souls.
Once fresh meat is in my dinner,
I say, I say there are dozos in Kombedougou.
[*Cɛ, ni nɔ dola Tagbana na.*
Ni nɔ dozo tɔrɔla.
Ni nɔ dola Yanfoila.
Ni nɔ dozo tɔrɔla . . .
Ni nɔ dola Nafanan.

Ni nɔ dozo kirila . . .
ɛ cɛ, n'tɛ wuya fɔ i nyɛnɛ . . .
Kombɛdugu dozo ye nɔ ni lɔnɔgɔla.
Sogo kɛnɛ kɛnun kɔ ni wulala la,
Ni ko, n'ko dozo Kombɛdugu.]

Dramane portrayed himself as a gadfly who prodded dozos to hunt through song. Only when they gave him fresh game were they true dozos. Dozos and dozo singers opened their *tonsigis* with the same sequence of events, but in a public plaza rather than a dozo's compound and with no expectation to hunt, extending dozos' domestic authority beyond the hunt and the compound with many but not all of the same songs dozos used in their hunting-related funeral rituals.[5]

Songs played a similar role in spurring non-dozos to action as well. On the morning of June 19, 1995, in Nienesso, for instance, I accompanied several Nienesso youths, including Dramane's son, Yacou, to clear a field for farming. It took nearly an hour to walk there. It was still morning, but the day was already hot. When we arrived, we spaced ourselves several paces apart from each other and began using hand ploughs (*daba*) to uproot grass that stood about a meter high. As we worked, two male drummers and a young woman serenaded us with music and song, praising our efforts by singing our names. *I ni bara, Yaku!* "You and your work, Yacou!" *I ni bara, Yusuf!* "You and you work, Joseph!," they sang, approaching each of us in turn. As they did, I noticed that the person to whom they sang began working more vigorously. When the musicians approached me, I was near exhaustion but felt a burst of energy from the music. I think I sped my work because the musicians "invited" me to "actualize all [my] capacities" (Lee 1976, 19), calling forth reserves of which I was unaware, as if my full abilities remained incomplete without their elicitation from beyond me. In Nienesso, I asked Dramane if he empowered dozos to hunt the way these singers inspired me to clear grass. He agreed that he did.

Both farmers and dozos realized their roles in response to the expectations of others, leading *dozongɔnun* players to perform for both audiences. Far from Odienné, in the village of Kiémou, a Senufo *ngɔnun* player named Silué Nabana told me that he routinely sang for friends as they farmed because he knew their "strengths and weaknesses."[6] While singing, he said, he accompanied himself on the notched, split metal tube that *ngɔnun* players used when not playing the *ngɔnun*. Odiennéka women said that they also sang to each other while damming and emptying creeks of fish. In West Africa, singers have long "prompt[ed] people to . . . action by their words" (Hale 1998, 40). The Julakan word *donkiri* (or *jonkiri*; *donkili* in Bamanankan) means "song" (from the infinitive *ka donkiri la* or *da*, meaning "to sing") and translates into English as "call to dance"—*don* meaning "dance," *kiri* meaning "call."[7] Songs incited more than dance, however. Dance embodied the ability of songs to resonate in bodily actions of various kinds. When Dramane and his apprentices inspired dozos to fire volleys and dance at *kozi*s in ways that resembled hunting, songs enacted the hunt.

When the Nightjar Calls

Dozos fittingly called *ngɔnun* players *dibididibinun* or *kulaŋkɔnɔ*, two different names for a kind of nightjar—akin to the American whippoorwill (*Caprimulgus vociferus*)—whose call, like dozos' presence, signals impending death. The plain nightjar of West Africa (*engoulevent terne, Caprimulgus inornatus*) (Serle and Morel 1993, 113) is a small bird active "in the evening when one sees it rushing up from the ground in pursuit of insects or fluttering noiselessly above the underbrush" (117).[8] It hunts at night, perfectly camouflaged, as dozos often do. Drissa Koné called it "la météo de la mort" in French, or "weather forecast of death." The bird sings, he said, before an adult or young person (babies excluded) is about to die a sudden death in the week to come, such as due to a road or hunting accident or similar tragedy. He claimed to have heard a nightjar singing in Niamasso before and after the death of the village chief, first at 4:00 a.m. while the chief was still alive, then at 8:00 a.m. after he had died. He said that dozos imitated the nightjar's call with their whistles to announce themselves to other dozos in the forest or at dozo funerals. The nightjar's song foretold human deaths just as dozos' whistles and songs foreshadowed the deaths of animals.

When dozos arrived at dozo funerals, Dramane often led them into the dance circle singing, *kulaŋ kan ye*, "Lo, the nightjar's call":

The nightjar's call is the dozos' call.
The nightjar is not empty. . .
Clear the way!
The nightjar's call is the dozos' call.
Lo, the nightjar's call!
The nightjar is not empty.
The nightjar's call is the dozos' call.
Lo, the nightjar's call!

The nightjar is not empty.
Hey! The sorcerer's call is the nightjar's call.
The nightjar is not empty.
The nightjar's call is the bad power object's call.
Lo, the nightjar's call!
The nightjar is not empty . . .
Hey! Fatally striking knife, you and the fields!
Lo, the nightjar's call!
The nightjar is not empty.
Hunh, thirst catchers!
Lo, the nightjar's call!
The nightjar is not empty.
[*Kulaŋkan ye dozoykan ye.*
Kulaŋ lɔkolon tɛ . . .
Ai ye bɔ sira la dɛ!
Kulaŋkan ye dozoykan ye.
Kulaŋkan ye!
Kulaŋ lɔkolon tɛ.
Kulaŋkan ye dozoykan ye.
Kulaŋkan ye!
Kulaŋ lɔkolon tɛ.
He! Kɔrɔtigikan ye kulaŋkan ye.
Kulaŋ lɔkolon tɛ.
Kulaŋkan ye bolifenjugukan ye.
Kulaŋkan ye!
Kulaŋ lɔkolon tɛ . . .
He! Marakɛmuru i ni koŋ!
Kulaŋkan ye!
Kulaŋ lɔkolon tɛ.
Han milɔgɔminalu!
Kulaŋkan ye!
Kulaŋ lɔkolon tɛ.]

In this song, Dramane repeatedly equates dozos with nightjars, collapsing the contrasting images of the bird's song and the dozos' whistles into a single synecdoche that underlies both images, that of language or "throat" (*kan*), which also translates as "call." Dramane meant his songs to trigger hunting and death in their wake. When he sang like a nightjar, he hunted. When dozos hunted, they sang like nightjars.

Dramane predicated dozo action on its elicitation, blurring boundaries between act and ideology, power and representation. "The nightjar is not empty," he sang, implying that it was "full," as dozos are, of occult knowledge and power. In Julakan, the verb "to be or become full," *ka fa*, may indicate that a person possesses occult expertise. One might say, *a fanin*, she or he "is full," to imply that someone is a sorcerer. Dramane likened the nightjar's call to the calls of dozos whom he praised with epithets to signal their capacities as "sorcerers," "power-objects," "fatal knives," or "thirst catchers." His serial comparisons of different aspects of *dozoya* to the nightjar's deadly work foregrounded dozos' similar capacity to sow death, dissociating it from dozos' other abilities as *dozoya*'s most definitive feature.[9] He employed multiple, layered images to evaluate dozos' protean roles in terms of a single outcome, the death of game,[10] verbalizing non-dozos' expectation that dozos hunt.

He described the purpose of his songs in such terms. "Singing gives dozos courage," he told me as we sat together on chairs on the small concrete porch of his mud-brick home. We were speaking Julakan, but he used the French word *courage*.[11] "Not all dozos are the same," he said. "Some are real dozos (*dozo yɛrɛ*).[12] Some are just gun owners (*morifatigi*)." Many men aspired to be dozos, but few truly were. He drew an analogy to illustrate:

> If you do well on an exam, that's good. Your father and you are happy. If Dra [short for Dramane] sings, dozos are happy . . . Some are good at some things, some at others. Lots of people are students, but not all pass their exams. Lots of people use guns, but not all are dozos. You become a real student by doing well on exams. It gives you courage. It pleases you. You become a real dozo by listening to songs. It gives you courage. It pleases you.[13]

Dramane called dozos to hunt for the same reason that teachers give students exams: to test their mettle. Students who shirk their exams never graduate. Dozos who shun *ngɔnun* players never become "real" (*dozo yɛrɛ*), capable of killing game. Tests evaluate students' intellectual skills. Dozo songs gauge dozos' hunting abilities. Through song, Dramane confronted dozos with a choice: to hunt or not to hunt. He made hunting a "live option" for them (as opposed to a "dead" or "trivial" one): an uncoerced choice between equally viable alternatives in light of their noticeably different and potentially "momentous" consequences (W. James 1956, 3–4). A dozo's response showed whether or not he was "the real thing."

Drissa Koné said that a real dozo responded to *ngɔnun* players by doing "what he [had] not done before . . . When a praise-singer sings to you," he said, "someone who goes beyond his abilities, that's a true hunter." Both he and Dramane defined the dozo singer as an antagonist to whom dozos responded by transcending their previous limits (see Simmel 1971, 357, 363). Dramane called dozos to hunt to give them an objective standard by which they and non-dozos alike could judge dozos' character.[14] The *kozi*'s crisis—the need to show collective recognition to the dead through a sacrifice enacted in hunting, song, dance, and ritual immolation—forced dozos to evaluate their readiness to act in response. But responding successfully meant more than killing game, it meant accurately judging one's readiness to do so.

Even by refusing to hunt, Drissa explained, dozos could vindicate themselves. In Odienné, *ngɔnun* player Movaly Fofana once cajoled Drissa to hunt during a nighttime dozo performance (*dozotɔrɔn*) independent of any ritual occasion. I had expected Drissa to leave the dance grounds to hunt when Movaly finished singing. To my surprise, he politely and publicly declined the challenge, with no apparent loss of face. The next day, I asked him why he had not hunted. He reminded me that he was working as a night guard at the Odienné Peace Corps hostel and had to spend his nights there. But he had said nothing about this to Movaly. Instead, he told him that he knew nothing about the forest or hunting, which was untrue. Drissa was a superb hunter. He demeaned his own skills, he told me, to honor the other dozos present as worthier of Movaly's challenge, which he said he "threw back" at them. He honored Movaly, too, by acting as if he were unworthy of his praises, humbling himself to honor his colleagues.

Drissa was just following Dramane's advice. He said that Dramane had once told him to avoid responding to singers' provocations. When a dozo publicly promised to kill game, Dramane said, either the singer or a rival dozo might use sorcery to prevent him from doing so in order to damage his reputation. To illustrate, Drissa cited the epic of Bamori and Kowulen in which the shape-shifting elephant-sorcerer, Kowulen, assumed a woman's appearance at a dozo funeral in the dozo Bamori's village. While in disguise, he overheard the *ngɔnun* player Yiran challenge Bamori to kill Kowulen (M.-J. Derive 1978, 16–21). Once alerted, Kowulen was better prepared to vanquish Bamori, which he did (see chap. 5).

Drissa used the story to argue that responding spontaneously to a singer's call was less important than responding thoughtfully. A dozo gained nothing by promising great feats without accomplishing them. If he committed to a task, he must complete it, die trying, or lose face. The dozo who responded to a singer's call with an accurate judgment of his own ability to do so—whether by refusing or agreeing to hunt—passed the singer's "test." Doing so repeatedly made him a real dozo. Each dozo needed to "cool his heart" (*k'a jusu suma*) while listening to singers who tried to "heat it up" (*k'a gban*) by singing. I often watched as *ngɔnun* players sang to experienced dozos who sat, stood, or danced impassively while calculating their response.

On those occasions when Dramane sang to thank me publicly for having paid for medical treatment for him and his family, I did more than observe. His public accounting of my private deeds moved me in unexpectedly powerful ways. By singing, Dramane gave me a "name," a "reputation"—or *tɔgɔ* in Julakan—as he did for the dozos he praised for their hunting. I responded stoically only because I had seen other dozos do so. Inwardly, I felt an awkward, explosive mixture of embarrassment and self-importance, which could have easily become foolish pride and given me a "big head," or *kungɔlɔba*, as Odinnéka say, had I lacked the model of real dozos. Being a dozo meant knowing when and how to respond to singers' songs, something that even an experienced dozo might miscalculate, which is precisely what happened at one of Dramane's performances.

Dramane and Mamadou at Kombedougou

At a dozo funeral (*kozi*) in the village of Kombedougou in April 1995—said by Dramane and Drissa to have been the best they had ever attended—Dramane sang at length to Mamadou Sylla, a dozo from the village of Tiémé. Dramane's performance epitomized his art, especially in the way that he pressed Mamadou to hunt. Mamadou's eyes widened in response. He breathed rapidly, staring ahead, frisking the pockets and loops on his dozo shirt for gunpowder with which to fire his musket as he stepped back and forth to the music. In his agitation, he made an astonishing promise that would have lasting consequences.

Dramane's confrontation with Mamadou exposed the stakes involved in interactions between *ngɔnun* players and dozos: the integrity of the moral agreement that linked them both to non-dozos. This agreement provided both the structure and content of Dramane's song. He alternately targeted his lyrics to the various spectators watching his performance on one hand and to Mamadou on the other, reminding Mamadou of his accountability to them.

Although Dramane pushed dozos to hunt only at *kozi*s, *yaladon*s, and *dozotɔrɔn*s, he sang hunting songs at Benkadi events to elicit non-dozos' agreement with dozos for Benkadi's police work. The same depiction of dozos "as fragile and vulnerable to destiny and . . . death" (MacIntyre 1984, 128–129) that featured in their sacrifices appeared in their songs.

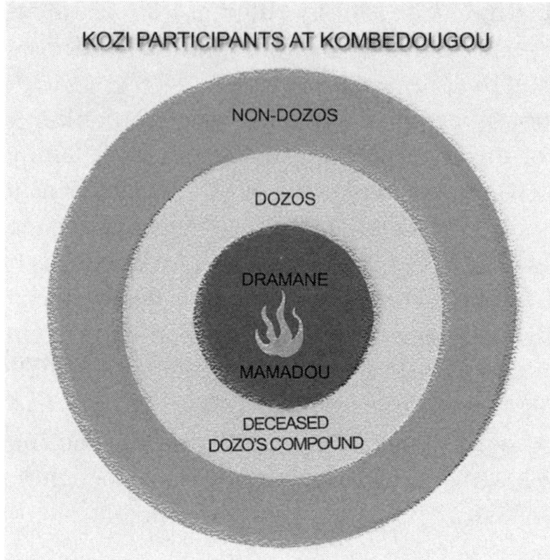

21 Layout of participants at the Kombedougou *kozi* as arranged concentrically around the central fires in the dead dozo's compound. Non-dozos stand at the edge of the compound and dozos and the dozo pair of Dramane Coulibaly and Mamadou Sylla stand inside the compound. Image by Urmilla Deshpande.

What MacIntyre has claimed for Homeric Greece and its epics, I therefore claim for dozo songs in the 1990s. For Homeric Greeks, "Heroic social structure [was] enacted epic narrative" (129). For dozos, the structure of hunting and policing was that of enacted dozo songs. Dozos' redistributive hunting ethos spurred them to hunt as a form of sacrifice and catch criminals to enforce restorative justice. But *dozoya* as performed in sacrifices alone could never assure dozos' ethical conduct, as cases of dozo violence attest. *Dozoya* required constant reinforcement. This was Dramane's job. At dozo funerals and *tonsigi*s, he and other singers dramatized and explicated the intentionality (*hakiri*), humility (*majigiya*), and patience (*sabari*) crucial to *dozoya*. Grasping the moral accountability that structured Benkadi, and that Benkadi often eluded, therefore requires grasping the form and content of dozo songs. With this end in mind, I will now analyze Dramane's song to Mamadou Sylla. Following Hymes (1981, 150–152; 1985, 393–396), I divide the text into acts, scenes, and stanzas according to the way Dramane targeted them to his multiple audiences (see fig. 21). I demarcate lines in the song, following Tedlock (1983, 55–61), according to the pronounced pauses that Dramane took as he sang.[15]

Finding Mamadou: Act 1, Scene 1

On the night of April 13, 1995, Dramane stood in the firelit compound of deceased dozo Brahima Diarrassouba in Kombedougou. The *kozi* was well under way when Dramane singled out dozo Mamadou Sylla for testing. Dramane had done his homework on Mamadou's reputation. He began his song by addressing his non-dozo spectators:[16]

Tell me, is this the Mamadou everyone's talking about? (1)[17]
[*A fɔ, Mamadu min tɔgɔ fɔla mɔgɔy bolo, ale Mamadou le ni fa?* (1)]

Then to Mamadou he sang:

Dra's not yet sure of your hunting. (2)
So don't turn us against each other. (3)
Hey, Madou [*short for Mamadou*], I'm not kidding. People push me toward you, but I have no faith. (4)
[*Dra lani t'i la dozoya la bɛrɛ bɛrɛ dɛ.* (2)
Ai don ka an nɔsu nyɔgɔn ma dɛ. (3)
He Madu, n't'i marasa. Mɔgɔlu ye ni lɔsula ile ma, ni lanako tɛ. (4)]

Dramane accused Mamadou of causing divisions over his own reputation, of making those at the *kozi* argue over whether or not Mamadou was a true dozo. Dramane wanted palpable proof of Mamadou's reputation.

So instinctive was Dramane's doubt that after his pet dog died, he raised no more dogs:

For fun I used to have a dog named "I-don't-believe-in-anything." Since it died, I no longer raise dogs. (5)
Dra really doesn't believe you. (6)
[*Ka n'masɔrɔ wulu dɔ te n'bolo ko 'N'malakola'. Ka ta o nɔ sala min kɛ, o nɔ wulublalɔgɔ bɔla n'na.* (5)
Dra ma la i la dɛ. (6)]

Dramane stood before Mamadou as the ultimate skeptic. He dismissed the game Mamadou had brought with him for the dead dozo's family as insufficient proof of his ability to hunt:

What you killed saying, "Dra the musician will come tomorrow," that's beside the point. That's not hunting. (7)

Something announced a month ago! (8)
[*Min faganin ko kɔnifo Dra natɔ sini, o ko tɛ. O tɛ dozoya ye.* (7)
Fon min lɔgɔlanin kalo kelen! (8)]

Dramane wanted greater accountability and structured his song to impose it. He organized his song's first scene as two stanzas marked by contrasts in address and content. In the first, a single line (line 1), Dramane asked non-dozos to identify Mamadou for him. In the second (lines 2–8), he questioned Mamadou's reputation. This shifting pattern of address would structure his entire song. Each scene joined two stanzas contrasting in terms of audience and message and intensifying pressure on Mamadou to hunt.

Whistles and Trouble: Act 1, Scene 2

Suddenly a senior dozo named Sy Brahima from the village of Zegbao interrupted Dramane, speaking directly to Mamadou:

Is there no whistle here? Blow your whistle. (9)
[*File tɛ yan na?*[18] *A ye file fiɛ.* (9)]

To which Dramane replied,

Why are you asking for Mamadou's whistle? (10)
[*Alugu do file manyiningala Mamadu la?* (10)]

Another senior dozo, Moussa Coulibaly, also of Zegbao, muttered something inaudible in Mamadou's defense, and Dramane scolded Moussa:

Big brother, you're coming between me and the one I'm talking to. I don't like that. (11)
If you see me with someone else, can't you take care of your own responsibilities first? (12)
[*N'kɔrɔcɛ, i do dola mɔgɔ ni kumabagalu cɛ. O tɛ jala n'nyɛ.* (11)
[*I ka ni ni mɔgɔy ye nyɔgɔn na, i t'i ta nyabɔ fɔnɔ wa?* (12)]

Moussa replied:

Come take him, don't turn your back on him. (13)
[*N'a ta i k'i ni kɔ do.* (13)]

Dramane sang that he would not:

I'm coming for sure. Just because the dog turns its back doesn't mean that the fight is over. (14)
[*N'natɔ faasi. Wulucɛ kɔ donin tɛ kɛlɛ banin ye.* (14)]

Dramane exploited the dozos' interruptions to sustain the skepticism that he introduced in scene 1. Two dozos interrupted Dramane (lines 9, 13), either to challenge or to defend Mamadou. Dramane chastised them (lines 10–12) but used their remarks (in line 14) to recall the central theme of scene 1: Mamadou's lack of credibility and the fact that Mamadou had turned Dramane and the crowd "against each other" (line 3) in a debate about his reputation.[19] This was a serious accusation given the *kozi*'s purpose of calling villagers to cooperate to propitiate the dead dozo's spirit.

The dozos' interruptions undermined the alternating pattern of address that Dramane had established in scene 1 between non-dozos (line 1) and Mamadou (lines 2–9), but Dramane swiftly and adroitly reestablished the pattern by at least indirectly returning his focus to Mamadou, promising to come back to him (line 14). Scene 1 brought tensions between non-dozos and Mamadou to light. Scene 2 revealed emerging tensions between dozos and Mamadou as dozo Moussa Coulibaly conceded, handing Mamadou over to Dramane's interrogation.

By the end of scene 2, Dramane had demarcated non-dozos and Mamadou into two opposed camps and done the same between dozos and Mamadou on the grounds that neither group could trust a dozo who inspired so much dissent. Dramane proposed himself as a mediator, arousing expectations about how Mamadou would respond to Dramane's implicit call to hunt (see Burke 1957, 124, 144, 217). Dramane also proved his skills as an improviser. He would need them again soon.

A Knifing: Act 1, Scene 3

Dramane now returned to his non-dozo audience, puzzling anew over Mamadou:

Hey, people of Kombedougou, I ask you. Women don't lie. (15)
Is Mamadou a hunter? (16)
Do you believe in him? (17)
I'm going to talk to Mamadou. (18)
Hey, Julas, good evening.[20] (19)

Hey, the animals' drum has sounded! Oh Allah! (20)
[*He, Kombɛdugukalu, n'bɛ ai nyiningala. Musoy tɛ wuya fɔla.* (15)
Ko Mamadu ye dozo ye? (16)
Alugu lanin a la fa? (17)
N'kɛtɔ do Madu makumala dɛ. (18)
He jula, i ni wula. (19)
He sogolu la dunun kan ye! O Ala! (20)]

Like one of the two senior dozos in the last scene, women were also vouching for Mamadou's reputation. Dramane purposefully doubted their claims, promising to take matters into his own hands. By "animals' drum," he meant the dozos' harp-lute, the *ngɔnun*. Like a drum, its calabash contains a resonating chamber covered with animal skin. Just as drums called people to work in the fields or attend weddings and other celebrations in compounds, the *ngɔnun* called dozos to hunt in the forest.

But Mamadou chose to reply without immediately answering that call. He unsheathed his knife and started to slide its sharp edge across the back of his forearm without bleeding, as if to affirm his skill at sorcery. Dozo ironsmiths (*numu*) typically exhaled sparks, held and licked burning wood, pierced their cheeks with large iron needles, or appeared to grow taller under sheets of cloth or black plastic at *kozi*s and *tonsigi*s when dozo musicians sang the *numu* song during which only *numu* could dance. But Mamadou was no ironsmith, and Dramane was not singing *numu*. He sang:

Mamadou, I didn't say to turn a knife on yourself. (21)
I disapprove. (22)
Mamadou, I didn't tell you to strike yourself with a knife. (23)
I don't like that. (24)
Mamadou, I didn't say to strike yourself with a knife. I don't like that. (25)
Once the animal is dead, isn't the battle over? (26)
[*A ko Mamadu, n'm'a fɔ i nyɛnɛ k'i ye muru lɔ i yɛrɛ la dɛ.* (21)
O ja tɛ n'nɔ. (22)
Mamadu, ni m'a fɔ k'i ye muru k'i yɛrɛ kan dɛ. (23)
O man di n'nyɛ. (24)
Mamadu, ni m'a fɔ k'i ye muru lɔ i yɛrɛ la dɛ. O man di n'nyɛ. (25)
Sogo ka ban faga la, kɛlɛ ma ban wa? (26)]

Dramane wanted game, not theatrics. His audience appreciated this. Dozos blew their whistles as he sang. Women punctuated pauses in his words with clapping. And non-dozo men watched captivated.

Dramane next offered an arcane syllogism to make his point, contrasting members of the secret *kɔma* society with magicians (called *soma*), and the occult mastery of forest spirits (*jinatigiya*) with hunting (*dozoya*). Each person has a particular vocation; sorcery was not Mamadou's:

Hey, Mamadou, good evening. (27)
By God, (28)
Being a member of the *kɔma* society is one thing; mastering a forest spirit is one thing.
Being a *soma* is one thing; *dozoya* is another. (29)
Kill an animal, and I will believe you. (30)
[*He Mamadu we, i ni wula.* (27)
A bɛnin Ala cɛ (28)
Kɔmatigiya ye a ta ko ye; jinatigiya y'a ta ko ye.
Somatigiya y'a ta ko ye; dozoya kɛnin a ta ko ye. (29)
Sogofagaba, ne la i la. (30)]

Dozoya was Mamadou's vocation, the only means of vindication offered him.

But Mamadou continued to slash at himself, leading Dramane to impugn his resolve:

People pushed me to you, but I don't believe you. (31)
Trying to kill game is hard. (32)
Hey, Madou, I'm going to talk to you. (33)
Madou, I don't approve of this. I don't believe it. (34)
[*Mɔgɔlu bara ni lɔsuli i ma do laninba t'i la.* (31)
Ka masɔrɔ sogo faga gboman. (32)
He Madu, n'kɛtɔ kumala i ye. (33)
Madu, ni ma lɔn min ko la fɛsɛ o fɛsɛ. Ni ma lɔn min la. (34)]

Mamadou's display was distracting from the task at hand. Dramane returned the focus to hunting:

It is for one thing that I cry in this world. (35)
I am after one thing in this world and the next. (36)
[*Kisi le kɛla ko kelen min fɛ dununya.* (35)
N'bɛ min kelen le kɔ dununya ni kiama. (36)]

In the context of the *kozi*, Dramane meant meat, to appease the dead dozo.

At this point, Dramane's words again caught the attention of dozo Sy Brahima, who insisted that Mamadou offer a dead animal's front shoulder (*kaba*) to Dramane, as was customary when singers called on dozos to hunt. Dramane acknowledged Sy Brahima's comments in the third person, maintaining the alternating pattern of address between non-dozos and Mamadou that he established in scene 1:

Sy Brahima, that pleased me. I liked that. (37)
[*Si Blama, o bara bɛn n'ma. O bara ja n'nyɛ.* (37)]

Dramane continued to address Mamadou:

One does not hunt by mouth, for the sake of talk. (38)
The animal must be killed, Mamadou. (39)
That is what I like. (40)
Your apprentices are talking you up. (41)
[*Dozoya tɛ kɛla dalɔ kuma ye.* (38)
Fo sogo le faga Mamadu. (39)
Min bara ja n'yɛ. (40)
I ya karanden kan di lɔsulanin. (41)]

For the second time, Dramane insisted that Mamadou kill game (lines 30, 39) rather than rest on his hunting reputation.

Dramane asked no more of Mamadou than he once did of the dead dozo ironsmith, Kalana Mozomba. Great dozos still lived, Dramane sang. Mozomba's home, the Wassolon region that straddles Mali, Guinea, and Côte d'Ivoire and that Dramane called the birthplace of *dozoya*, still produced great dozos. Mamadou could yet be one:

I said this to Mozomba. (42)
Kalana Mozomba should not have ended. Mozomba ended by an act of God. (43)
Mozomba was born a smith by an act of God. (44)
Wassolon is full of men. (45)
[*Ni nɔ min fɔla Mɔzon kɔ.* (42)
Kalana Mɔzonba bankun makɛ. Mɔzonba numu banin Ala bolo. (43)
Mɔsonba numu wolonin Ala bolo. (44)
Cɛw kɛnin ka Wasolon fa. (45)]

So ended Dramane's first act. He built the final scene like the first, on contrasting stanzas targeted to distinct audiences.

Opening the Gap: Reviewing Act 1

In this first act, Dramane transformed the question of whether or not Mamadou was a hunter into a moral issue on which he wagered his spectators' integrity. He composed a series of three scenes. The first and third comprised a set of paired stanzas addressed alternately to non-dozos and Mamadou. Dramane improvised the second as a dialogue between senior dozos and himself about Mamadou: non-dozos (line 1), Mamadou (lines 2–8); senior dozos, Dramane (lines 9–14); and non-dozos (lines 15–20), Mamadou (lines 21–45). Dramane ended the act after admonishing Mamadou to kill game, "The animal must be killed, Mamadou" (line 39). He doubted Mamadou throughout, accusing him of dividing Kombedougou, generating suspense by asking dozos to wonder whether Mamadou could vindicate his reputation, and admonishing senior dozos to leave the provocation to him. Dramane highlighted the double paradox of a man who called himself a dozo without proof and of non-dozos and dozos who accepted the claim on faith.

Dramane implicated Mamadou in a situation rich in dramatic irony, as an object of both praise and contempt, raising the sorts of questions crucial to dramatic performance: Could the audience trust the character they saw portrayed? And could Mamadou prove himself? Dramane identified a gap of credulity and asked whether Mamadou could fill it. By shifting back and forth between non-dozos and Mamadou, and by defending his prerogative to do so against the interruptions of senior dozos, Dramane "stood in" (Wilshire 1982, 6–7, 22–23, 43–44) for the critical perspectives of all three parties,[21] mediating among them, intertwining their fates in ways reminiscent of dozo sacrifice. He performed a social drama as well as an aesthetic one, stipulating a "public breach or non-fulfillment of [a] crucial norm regulating . . . intercourse" between his spectators and Mamadou (Turner 1957, 91). He accused Mamadou of failing to meet non-dozos' as well as dozos' expectations, refereeing between these parties on one hand and Mamadou on the other to enact *dozoya* as more than a dozo "behavioral code" or "worldview" (Cashion 1984, 1: 310–321). He portrayed it as a process of negotiation between each dozo and his wider community.

Open Season: Act 2, Scene 1

Next, Dramane directed his call to hunt to a new audience: his fellow dozos, implicating them in the challenge that both he and they had just set for Mamadou:[22]

Hey, good evening, men. (46)
If you have it in you, kill game before morning. (47a)
Then I'll let you be, Mamadou. (47b)
We've all been warned. (48)
[*He cɛ i ni wula.* (46)
Ni nya ka kɛ ai kɔnɔ, ai ye sogo faga sani dugusɛgbɛ cɛ. (47a)
Mamadu n'do fara ai la. (47b)
Min lɔgɔlanin an byɛ ye. (48)]

Dramane assured Mamadou that killing game was the only way a dozo could confirm his abilities. He thus widened the gap he opened in the first act between the credibility of non-dozos and Mamadou's veracity, expanding it to include all dozos.

Apology for the Sorcerer's Life: Act 2, Scene 2

Dramane opened the next scene by flattering dozos with an epithet full of occult implications:

Fishing nets of creeks and rivers, (49)
Spit gives magical threads their courage. (50)
[*Kɔmonjɔ ni bamonjɔ,* (49)
Daji le tafo laferinyala. (50)]

Casting dozos as nets (food-catching devices) played on an underlying trope equating people with cloth fibers. Dramane used the trope to compare dozos with *tafo*, linked strands of short, knotted, often multicolored cotton threads worn by dozos on their hunting shirts to protect them from sorcery and hunting dangers. Neither nets nor *tafo* worked, Dramane sang, without their user's spit and the appropriate incantations—metaphorically, their user's resolve.

Nor could any dozo, including Mamadou, vanquish the forest without humility:

The dance circle has filled. No one can do everything. (51)
Mamadou tried to hurry; I didn't like that. (52)
[*Baradon bara fa kɔli kɔli. Mɔgɔ kelen tɛ seya ko byɛ la dɛ.* (51)
Mamadu nɔ prɛsɛya[23] *min ma ja n'nyɛ.* (52)]

Dozos only succeeded in tandem, just as they danced. Mamdou's over-confidence was a risky pose:

Hey, dozos, good evening. Do you trust your apprentices? Are you sure of yourselves? (53)
Killing game is difficult. (54)
Hey men, if you have no incantations, don't harden your hearts against game for nothing. (55)
Men, if you have nothing to protect you, don't go after game with only your hardened hearts. (56)
They are the children of something between heaven and earth. (57)
[*He dozo i ni wula. I lanin i ya dozoden la fa? I lanin i yɛrɛ la fa?* (53)
Sogo faga gboman dɛ. (54)
He cɛ, ni dalulu tɛ i bolo, i kana i joso lagbɛlɛya sogo la te gbazan dɛ. (55)
Cɛ, n'i bolomala tɛ i la, i kana i joso lagbɛlɛya sogo la gbazan dɛ. (56)
Fen dɔ ta den le wele dununya ni lakira cɛ. (57)]

Dozos claimed that *jina* spirits herded antelope the way people tended cattle, sheep, or goats. The vindictive soul force called *nyama* marked each antelope as *jina* property, pursuing the hunter who killed it. Dozos learned sorcery to defend against such dangers. For Dramane, dozos were shamans traversing a spirit-filled landscape, the forest's invisible world, to bring meat back for the living. Dramane asked whether any of the dozos present at the *kozi* was powerful enough to do so.

Returning to Mamadou, he wielded his song like a pole that a hunter pokes into a burrow to flush out game:

Madou, good evening. (58)
Mamadou Sylla, I'm talking to you. (59)
Hey Madou, I'm not kidding. It's becoming like a poker. (60)
If I insert the pole and see no fur, I will surely put my hand inside. (61)
An animal must surely be killed. (62)
[*Madu, i ni wula.* (58)
Madu Sila, n'b'i makumala. (59)
He Madu, n't'i marasa. A kɛtɔ dugusurukɔkalanman ye dɛ. (60)
Ni n'ka kalanman do, n'ma ſye ye, n'kɛtɔ n'bolo donna dɛ. (61)
Fo sogo le faga fasi. (62)]

If Mamadou killed nothing, Dramane would have put his hand inside him to find him empty of *dozoya*. Mamadou may have seemed "full" of sorcery to others, but his true test lay in the forest:

Forest that does not die, forest that does not awaken. (63)
[*Wula saberi ni wula kununberi.* (63)]

Alive, eternal, yet never fully awake, the forest was a paradoxical realm in which hunting was the only certainty:

If the animal dies, doesn't the arguing end? (64)
It's the meat we want. (65)
Madou, I'm not kidding. (66)
It's difficult to kill game if you're not a sorcerer. Animals aren't killed without knowledge. (67)
They don't die without wizardry. (68)
[*Sogo do ka ban faga la, kiti ma ban wa?* (64)
An nɛ sogo ko le a. (65)
He Madu, n't'i marasa. (66)
Sogo faga le a gbɛlɛn dɛ ni subaga tɛ. Sogo tɛ fagala lonko kɔ. (67)
A tɛ fagala dalulu kɔ. (68)][24]

Dramane shifted his concern from hunting to sorcery, which set dozos apart from mere hunters. He upped the ante in his challenge to Mamadou and the dozos. Hunt they must, but, as true dozos, with sorcery, in order to merit Dramane's praise.

Déjà Vu: Act 2, Scene 3

Had Dramane been a formulaic composer, he might have returned his attention now to dozos, as he did in the last two scenes. Instead, he broke pattern and addressed non-dozos, act 1's primary audience, assuming the voice of a world-weary bard:

Ah, Julas, I'm talking to you. (69)
Hey, men, *ngɔnun*-playing Dra has seen many things in this world, (70)
Has traveled, has traveled, has traveled, has traveled. (71)
[*A, Jula, n'b'i makumala.* (69)
He cɛ, kɔnifɔ Dra bara ko ƒyaman ye dununya nɔ sa, (70)
Ka tagama, ka tagama, ka tagama, ka tagama. (71)]

Then he returned to Mamadou:

People have seen many things, Mamadou. (72)
An animal must be killed, Mamadou. (73)
[*Mɔgɔ bara ko ʃyaman ye dɛ, Mamadu.* (72)
Fo sogo le faga dɛ, Mamadou. (73)]

Standing in for non-dozos, Dramane ordered Mamadou for the third time—and other dozos by implication—to hunt.

Into the Breach: Reviewing Act 2

By the end of act 2, Dramane had challenged all dozos to hunt, reaffirming their collective responsibility to non-dozos and broadening the breach that he opened in act 1 between spectators and Mamadou, making it "co-extensive" with a "dominant cleavage in the widest set of relevant social relations to which the conflicting parties belong" (Turner 1957, 91): namely, the fissure between dozos as a whole, as personified by Mamadou and the other dozos to whom Dramane sang, and non-dozos.

In the first act, Dramane distanced himself from both non-dozos and dozos, questioning their credibility. In act 2, he took sides with non-dozos against Mamadou and other dozos, chiding them for their smugness, urging them to hunt. In scenes 1 and 2 of act 2, he shifted address between dozos and Mamadou: dozos (lines 46–47a), Mamadou (47b–48); dozos (49–57), Mamadou (58–68), whereas in act 1 he sang primarily to non-dozos and Mamadou. But he organized both acts in three sets of roughly paired stanzas, ending the second act with the same call to kill that closed the first (line 73). No sooner did he establish a parallel between acts 1 and 2, though, than he undermined it. In act 2's final scene, he abandoned his preoccupation with dozos and Mamadou for non-dozos and Mamadou: non-dozos (lines 69–71), Mamadou (lines 72–73). By siding with non-dozos, Dramane resolved the tensions he had created between them and himself in act 1 while heightening the tensions he created between dozos and himself in act 2's first two scenes.

Dramane performed three double movements in his first two acts. First, he shifted progressively and syntagmatically among different audiences, building suspense, while making repeated, paradigmatic attempts through parallelisms and recurrent patterns to stabilize his song's progression—most cleverly in act 1, scene 2. Second, he sustained constant pressure on Mamadou to hunt while alternating alliances with his different audiences, doubting the claims of non-dozos and dozos about Mamadou in act 1 and questioning dozos' collective competence on non-dozos' behalf in act 2. Finally, he oscillated in act 3 between praising dozos with heroic epithets and skeptically insisting that they and Mamadou live up to these praises by hunting. For Dramane, the dozo role was an ideal to be realized, not a fait accompli.

Encomium: Act 3, Scene 1

Dramane opened act 3 with a newly respectful tone:

Hey men, I salute you and the bush. (74)
You in this crowd of men, in this crowd of men here with eyes fixed. (75)
[*He cɛ, ai ni kɔŋ.* (74)
Alugu cɛkuru min nɔ ni min na cɛkuru nin nɔ ni nyakuru gbiŋbɛ. (75)]

His phrase, "you . . . with eyes fixed," imaged the expressions of powerful dozos as they looked ahead while dancing or fixed their gaze on animal tracks and trails of blood while hunting.[25]

According to Dramane, dozos required acute vision to pierce the forest's mysteries. He alluded to this in a series of oblique admonitions and outright pleas:

The house where danger lies is not the same as where it sleeps. (76)
The ashes of an incinerated, dangerous thing can't fill a duiker's horn. (77)
Fatherless forest, motherless forest. (78)
The forest with no loincloth is not the same as the shirtless forest. (79)
Give me a fresh hide, I have no bed. (80)
Give me a dry hide, I'll cover myself. (81)
[*Kojugu sibon ni kojugu labon tɛ kelen ye.* (76)
Maramafen jeninin tɛ ngoron biɛ fala. (77)
Wula fadan ni wula badan. (78)
Wula julakolon ni wula kanankolon tɛ kelen ye. (79)
Ka n'sɔ gbolo kɛnɛ la ko lafen tɛ n'bolo. (80)
Ka n'sɔ gbolo jaran na ko n'ka bringa fani. (81)]

Dramane adopted the voice of a beggar seeking alms (*saraka*), pleading for a bed and blanket and warning that the gravest dangers lurked in the smallest places. Answering his requests would be arduous. The forest withheld all clarity, solidarity, and predictability from those who entered it, shifting in aspect from moment to moment as if from sleep to wakefulness, betraying pursuers like a being without kin, lying naked in plain sight yet ever changing and impenetrable.

Dramane's new conciliatory tone toward dozos inaugurated a like change in his approach to Mamadou. He complimented him, even allied himself with him, comparing Mamadou to a sorcerer's power object and to a *kɔma* mask that kills "antisocial sorcerers" (see McNaughton 1988, 139–145 passim; Monteil 1977, 271–272; Tauxier 1927, 276–277 n. 2):

Great power object, good evening. A sweet *kɔma* mask kills no one if it lacks someone to incite it. (82)
Madou, you will be the *kɔma* mask. I will be your inspiration. (83)
[*He jo ba, i ni wula. Kɔma duman tɛ mɔgɔ faga yelemagan duman kɔ.* (82)
Madu le bɛ kɛ kɔma ye. N'bɛ kɛ i yelemagan ye. (83)]

Abandoning provocation for praise, Dramane compared himself to the man who incited the *Kɔma* mask against particular sorcerers. Dramane portrayed himself as integral to Mamadou's hunting, renewing the call to hunt, deferentially:

The day of a person's death is a nasty thing. (84)
The day of a person's death is a difficult thing. (85)
The day of a person's death is an important event, a day of consequence. (86)
[*Mɔgɔ salon kojuguba.* (84)
Mɔgɔ salon kolagbɛlɛnman ba. (85)
Mɔgɔ salon koba ye, lon ba. (86)]

Spectators had come to the *kozi* expecting dozos to hunt. Respect replaced antagonism as Dramane invited Madou to assume the greatness thrust upon him.

A Victuals Cycle: Act 3, Scene 2

Returning to the dozos, Dramane extolled them, depicting hunting as transcendent and inevitable, impervious to human alteration but open to men's participation:

Dozos, I salute you and the bush. (87)
The pregnant animal, the pregnant hunter's wife: the child of one will be food for the other. (88)

The pregnant mouse, the pregnant cat: the child of one will be food for the other. (89)
[*Dozolu, ai ni koŋ.* (87)
Sogomoso kɔnɔma, dozomuso kɔnɔma: dɔ ta den le kɛ do dɔ la balo. (88)
Kurugbeŋ kɔnɔma ye, jakuma kɔnɔma: dɔ ta den le kɛka dɔ la balo. (89)]

Dramane invoked a great chain of being in which dozos preyed on animals' offspring to feed their own while animals preyed on each other's to feed theirs. An elegant if tragic simplicity underlay hunting. Even when dozos killed no game, hunting continued among the forest's predators and prey. Dozos partook in an ongoing cycle of life and death larger than themselves, one that assured both humans' and animals' survival.

With this cycle in mind, Dramane addressed Mamadou and his apprentices:

Mamadou, dozo, I'm talking to you. (90)
You and your apprentices, I'm talking to you. (91)
Hey, Madou, good evening. (92)
[*Mamadu, dozo, n'b'i makumala.* (90)
Ile n'i ya karandenlu, n'bɛ ai makuma. (91)
He Madu, i ni wula. (92)]

As Dramane overheard shouts of praise to dozos from the crowd, he sang:

Someone said, "You and the forest! The forest!" But killing game would not make all of them happy. (93)
That is why I fear the world. (94)
That is why I say I believe in nothing, Mamadou. (95)
[*Mɔgɔ dɔ a fɔla mɔgɔ ma ko, "I ni koŋ ni koŋ!" Sogofagako man di nin byɛ ye dɛ.* (93)
Ole kɔsɔn n'bara sina ja nyɛ. (94)
Ole kɔsɔn n'ko n'ma la ko la dɛ, Mamadu. (95)]

Those cheering might instead attempt to ensnare Mamadou in sorcery to prevent him from killing game, or worse.

Dramane sang his dismay at the inevitability of death for even the greatest of dozos, recalling four:

Madou, we are all children. (96)
Mamourou of Morondo is finished, the double-edged knife. (97)
Tiécoura the elephant-killer of Djiborosso is finished. (98)

Nkosotchè of Djibrosso is finished. (99)
Benogo Dagbanan of Djiborosso is finished. (100)
Benogo Dagbanan should not have died. (101)
[*Mamadou, an byɛ lajɛ nin ye denun ye.* (96)
Mɔrɔndɔ Mamuru banin, nyaflagbɛ muru. (97)
Jibrosokai ya samafaga Cɛkura banin. (98)
Jibrosokai la Nkosocɛ banin. (99)
Jibrosokai la Benɔgɔ Dagbanan banin. (100)
Benɔgɔ Dagbanan bankun makɛ. (101)]

As surely as dozos killed animals, they, too, died (cf. MacIntyre 1984, 124).

Dramane illustrated the inevitability of this cycle with a series of tragicomic images:

The one who bursts his head open breaks his jaw. (102)
The one who bursts his face open pokes out his eyes. (103)
The one who breaks the bones in the small of his back breaks his spine. (104)
The person with diarrhea who breaks wind dirties his backside. (105)
[*Kungolobacibaga ni dabalafaranbaga.* (102)
Tindabacibaga ni nyadawɔgɔmɛ. (103)
Sorokolowaya ni kɔkolowaya. (104)
Bojicibaga ni kɔmaraka. (105)]

Dramane's humor conveyed a serious if understated message:

Everyone in Kombedougou says that you are a dozo. (106)
[*Kombɛduguka byɛ ko k'i ye dozo ye dɛ.* (106)]

Dramane reminded Mamadou that spectators expected him to hunt as surely as a flatulent diarrheic soiled his pants, and in spite of the risks.

Hunting *Ad Absurdum*: Act 3, Scene 3

In the final scene, Dramane entreated dozos one last time to hunt:

Hey, men, good evening. (107)
Tell me, was the *ngɔnun* made for anything but animals? (108)
[*He cɛ, i ni wula.*(107)
A fɔ, ngɔnun nɔ tula fon gbɛrɛ kama ni sogo fana tɛ? (108)]

He tweaked Mamadou again, prolonging the levity of scene 2, drolly suggesting that Mamadou start by killing insects the next day before moving on to bigger fare:

Madou, if you know something, (109)
Why don't you begin with ants tomorrow? (110)
The ants' little brother, Bongo Ferima—(111)
Those who did not agree in the old village won't agree in the new one—(112)
Let's kill the ants' maternal kin tomorrow. (113)
Kill the ants' paternal kin tomorrow. (114)
The mosquito and his little brother are slapping me. (115)
Let's kill the mosquitoes' maternal kin tomorrow, (116)
Kill the mosquitoes' paternal kin tomorrow. (117)
Mouse and his wife Ferima Soumbala-Spice-Stealer,[26] (118)
Let's kill the mice's maternal kin tomorrow, (119)
Kill the mice's paternal kin tomorrow. (120)
The tortoise and his wife Dry-Bark-Fire-Taker,[27] (121)
And his little brother Walking House, (122)
Let's kill the tortoises' fathers tomorrow, the tortoises' mothers. (123)
Agouti and his wife, the grass-cutter Ferima and his little brother Inza Short-Back. (124)
[*Madu ni kakɛ dɔ lon,* (109)
I y'a damina mɛnɛmɛnɛlu ma sini wa? (110)
Mɛnɛminlugu dɔgɔcɛ Bongɔ Ferima— (111)
Mɔgɔminlugu ma bɛŋ so kɔrɔ lasigi lɔ sango so kula sigi— (112)
An nɛ mɛnɛmɛnɛlugu badentanya sini. (113)
Ka mɛnɛmɛnɛlu fadentanya sini. (114)
Soso n'a dɔgɔcɛ tɛgɛdo n'dolo la. (115)
An nɛ sosolu badentanya sini, (116)
Ka sosolu fadentanya sini. (117)
Kurugbɛ na moso sumbarata Ferima, (118)
An nɛ kurugbenlu badentanya sini, (119)
Ka kurugbenlu fadentanya sini. (120)
Sulakɔgɔsɔ ni a moso Tabɔwɔmbɔ, (121)
Ani a dɔgɔcɛ Sibontagama, (122)
An nɛ sulakɔgɔsɔlu wolofatanya sini, ka sulakɔgɔsɔlu wolobatanya. (123)
Kɔnyina n'a moso gbagatɛgɛ Ferima an'a dɔgɔcɛ Inza Kɔkunini. (124)]

The song that began with provocation ended in humor. Dramane conceded Mamadou's potential to kill game—albeit *small* game—admitting that villagers might never agree about his hunting skill.

The Elephant in the Compound: Reviewing Act 3

Once more, Dramane upset the pattern he had established, defusing the tensions of the first two acts. In act 3's first scene, he lauded dozos for hunting (lines 74–81) and empathized with Mamadou (lines 82–86). In scene 2, he greeted dozos with respect (lines 87–89) and comically called Mamadou to hunt (lines 90–106). In scene 3, he greeted dozos one last time (lines 107–108) and made an amusing final appeal to Mamadou to kill game (lines 109–124). He used the "redressive mechanisms" of panegyric, empathy, and humor here to "limit the spread of breach" that he had previously instigated (Turner 1957, 91–92).

In return, Mamadou finally promised to kill an elephant, marking a pause in the drama and a provisional "reintegration of the disturbed social group" (Turner 1957, 92), reuniting non-dozos with dozos. In response, Dramane intoned a song about hunting elephants:

Hey, the powder is tough, the elephant-killing powder is
tough in Tagbana!
[*He mugu ma ja, samafagamugu ma ja Tagbana na!*]

But to no avail. Mamadou failed to kill an elephant for the rest of my stay in Côte d'Ivoire, assuring a continued "breach between" him and Kombedougou.[28]

For almost two and a half years I noted Mamadou's absence from dozo events. Drissa Koné speculated that he had vanished because he had failed to fulfill his promise. Then, on August 17, 1997, a few months before I returned to the United States, I saw him at a Benkadi meeting in Odienné. He wore a cotton leisure suit, the only dozo in non-dozo clothing. After the meeting, he greeted me warmly. Without my asking, he told me that hunting an elephant takes time, confirming, to me, that a dozo's promise to a singer—like dozos' dancing, firing of volleys, and fierce gazes—did more than represent the hunt. It enacted it, or in the case of Mamadou's agitated response, failed to enact it.

Disarming Mamadou: Sorcery, the State, and Benkadi

By the song's end, Dramane had serenaded, antagonized, and reassured all three of his audiences so thoroughly that his song's structure verbalized their spatial and moral relationships. He proceeded concentrically, focusing on non-dozos at the compound's periphery, and momentarily on senior dozos at its center, in act 1 (see fig. 21). In act 2, he focused on the dozos seated or dancing within the compound and, momentarily, on non-dozos at the end. In act 3, he focused exclusively on dozos and Mamadou. He ended each scene by returning his focus to Mamadou. Throughout the song, he moved back and forth among the parties he targeted, both rhetorically and physically. He juxtaposed his audiences syntagmatically and paradigmatically—through concentric progressions and recurrent parallelisms, respectively—to nurture agreement among them by dramatizing Mamadou's and all dozos' ethical accountability to non-dozos and to each other.

Dramane castigated Mamadou for disrupting this relationship: for inspiring non-dozos to argue about his hunting skills (lines 3, 7–8, 15–18, 60–62), for using sorcery on himself rather than on game (lines 21–34), and for refusing to hunt that night (lines 47–48). These behaviors, especially Mamadou's slashing at himself, threatened the agreement needed to placate the dead dozo's spirit (lines 35–36). Instead of directing violence against game, Mamadou targeted it against his own body as proof of his dozo prowess, channeling it away from any productive use for non-dozos or Dramane. Mamadou appealed to the sorcery of *dozoya* as a form of power beyond any accountability, whereas Dramane praised sorcery as a mere aspect of *dozoya*, useful for helping kill game for others (lines 49–50, 55–57, 67–68, 82–83). Through sorcery, Mamadou momentarily suspended his vulnerability to the same check on his authority that legitimized it: the praise and criticism of dozo singers like Dramane. He tried instead to bolster his reputation by risking the "bare life" of his arm (see Agamben 1998, 8–11, 142), which was not his to risk. Mamadou's illusion of a sui generis dozo power contradicted Dramane's vision of dozos embodying a respectful (*bɛn*) collaboration between dozos (lines 51–52) and non-dozos. Mamadou remained untouched by his violence because sorcery protected him. Most non-dozos lacked such protection. To the extent that Mamadou incarnated a reciprocal ethical relation with non-dozos, his assault on his own body was an assault on theirs, just as his attacks on animals' bodies offered nourishment *to* theirs, in the cycle of generalized exchange between the forest and compound (lines 87–89). While reinforcing his reputation as a sorcerer, Mamadou distracted himself from the hunting he should have been engaged in. His error, according to Dramane, was to substitute a display of sovereign power absent any concern for the welfare of non-dozos in place of a concrete act of assistance (lines 30–31, 35, 38–39, 62, 64–65, 73, 80–81).

By hesitating to hunt at a *kozi,* Mamadou did indirectly what errant dozos did on patrols when they attacked civilians and civil authorities. Dozos who beat, tortured, raped, or murdered Ivoirian citizens or residents assumed the exceptional status of the Ivoirian state, which continued to overlook dozos' exactions on the population as long as they were not so egregious as to draw media attention. Given dozos' alliances with national power brokers, it became increasingly difficult for individual dozos to challenge such arbitrary uses of power, although Dramane could still appeal to his near monopoly on public discourse at *kozi*s and *tonsigi*s to reinforce dozos' accountability to the moral expectations of *dozoya.* To assume that no internal critique of Benkadi existed among dozos, or that they had to express it in the idiom of human rights to be legitimate, would be naïve.

No less a Benkadi enthusiast than Dramane Coulibaly criticized Benkadi as directly in his personal remarks to me as he did indirectly in his songs. He regularly used the expression, "Politics is no good," *Politiki man nyi,* when we spoke about Benkadi, AE, and their leaders. His use of the French-originated word *politiki* (from *la politique,* "politics") connoted the disagreeable way that Benkadi dozos had reconfigured power among themselves by allying with francophone politicians like Inza Fanny, Édouard Coulibaly, and local officials whose networks of influence extended well beyond *dozoya.* Given these alliances, along with Benkadi's popularity and dozos' deferential way of relating to each other, it is no surprise that dozos who were critical of Benkadi refrained from overtly voicing their dissent. But dozo discourse on Benkadi was far from homogenous. When one compares the Benkadi work of dozos in northern Denguélé, in Odienné, in other major cities, and under the aegis of either Afrique Environnementale or the National Hunters' Association, one notes widely different scales of integration with state authorities, degrees of violence toward lay people and state security agents, and levels of accountability to non-dozos. And at the core of *dozoya,* in the sung relationship between dozos, dozo singers, and non-dozos, one finds a moral compass by which to evaluate dozo integrity in any milieu.

Singing the Hunt

The image of *dozoya* that Dramane portrayed referred to more than killing game. It recalled a range of tasks and skills—from knife wielding to sorcery to trekking—that featured in every aspect of *dozoya,* from hunting, to fighting sorcerers, to guarding fields, to healing, to patrolling against crime. Because hunting demanded the most challenging integration of dozos' talents, it became the "root metaphor" of *dozoya* (Turner 1975, 26) for eliciting an ethical response to the challenges that dozos faced in any domain. *Dozoya* transcended Benkadi, retaining an autonomous existence within it. Even sorcery, as Dramane sang to Mamadou, was not *dozoya* but something that dozos did. But because hunting encompassed everything that dozos did, Dramane used hunting-related imagery to elicit action from and to critique dozos in regard to Benkadi. To every dozo, the *ngɔnun* player stood as "an opponent . . . who would draw from him the full exercise of all that was in him; one who would evoke him . . . to an answering response of exertion beyond [his own] known limits" (Lee 1976, 19). The hunt epitomized this exertion, the singer its source or *sababu*, a "cause" or "intermediary" who brought beneficial change to people's lives by bringing mutually interested parties into collaboration.

At *kozi*s, singers brought dozos and non-dozos into agreement before the dead to reestablish a productive exchange between them. At *tonsigi*s, they brought dozos and non-dozos into collaboration to restore the moral reciprocity disrupted by theft and banditry. Singers were the guarantors of these collaborations. Their presence at both *kozi*s and *tonsigi*s dramatized dozos' ability to shift the uses of *dozoya* by applying their hunting-related skills to new projects. Such critical acumen reminded dozos that *dozoya* was ultimately a relationship of moral accountability to non-dozos and to each other. But even Dramane's repeated critiques of dozos could do little to prevent the outbreaks of violence that characterized Benkadi in the 1990s and that spread on a greater scale after 1999. I will turn to these dynamics in the final chapter.

NINE

Conclusion: From Civic Duty to Civil Unrest

Hunters as Soldiers

In this book, I have tried to show how dozos adopted the security prerogatives of the Ivoirian state as a result of a long history of migration and ongoing tensions with state security agents due to national hunting laws. As a result of migration, dozos transferred their protective responsibilities as hunters, antisorcerers, and crop guardians in northern rural Côte d'Ivoire to southern urban and rural areas. They used the sacrifices that structured these responsibilities to respond to a national crime wave in the 1990s in ways that made crime analogous to the dangers they encountered as hunters. They did so through the same mimetic aesthetic that their stories of Manimory illustrated and that reconciled them with Islam. By imitating the state and its laws, they gained power within it, just as Manimory mastered the forest by assimilating to it through sacrifice. Dozos created their own laws, security measures, and criminal trials in the same spirit, imposing their authority on civilian contexts where state authorities failed to do so, just as dozos historically intervened in domestic contexts where the expected rules of moral reciprocity had disintegrated; their village became the nation. Dozos did so in response to a self-critical ethos best expressed in their hunting songs that singers performed at hunting- and Benkadi-related events. But their increasing entanglement with the state, and the state's growing

antagonism toward Benkadi, eventually created too great a gulf for even dozos to bridge.

On December 24, 1999, less than two years after interior minister Bombet confined Benkadi to northern Côte d'Ivoire (see chap. 7), a group of military officers overthrew the regime of President Henri Konan Bédié (Keiffer 2000, 26). They called on General Robert Guéï, the former army chief of President Houphouët-Boigny, to lead the country. As president, Guéï called on dozos in Abidjan to "guard public places and commercial areas to prevent looting and rioting" and to guard the presidential palace, where dozos "were issued with automatic weapons while on guard duty" (Bassett 2003, 19) and where they guarded the highway north of the city. Abidjan's senior dozos reportedly "pledged their support to the government and their political neutrality" in meetings with the president (19).

Once more, an unstable state of questionable legitimacy called on dozos to consolidate power during a time of transition. And once again, the state disavowed them. In February 2000, Laurent Gbagbo, the leader of the opposition Ivorian Popular Front (FPI), denounced dozos as a "potential militia force at the disposal of [Guéï's] rival, Alassane Ouattara" (Bassett 2003, 20). General Lassana Palenfo, a "junta member and Minister of State responsible for security," threatened dozos with prosecution unless they ceased their security work (20), which they did. Benkadi's brief return only confirmed that its national presence was exemplary of, rather than exceptional to, the state's modus operandi at the turn of the twenty-first century.

This final chapter offers a brief, selective overview of key events in Côte d'Ivoire between 1999 and 2009 to contextualize my interpretation of Benkadi within more recent Ivoirian history. I review Ivoirian politics in relation to *dozoya* from 1999 to 2007, through General Guéï's rise to power to Gbagbo's assumption of the presidency to the beginning and aftermath of the country's rebellion. I interpret the rise of other paramilitary groups under President Gbagbo as resulting from conditions similar to those that opened the way for Benkadi. I conclude by relating lessons learned from Benkadi to current strategies for resolving the rebellion.

Guéï, Gbagbo, and Belligerents

When General Guéï came to power in December of 1999, he dissolved the National Assembly and suspended political parties (Contamin and Losch 2000, 120). For the first time in Côte d'Ivoire's history, the state was ex-

plicitly a state of exception. Previous presidents had arbitrarily rewritten or skirted existing laws. President Guéï abrogated the constitution altogether and reinstituted Bédié's politics of *ivoirité* (Langer 2004, 28–30). Subsequently, like Houphouët-Boigny, he had the constitution rewritten, this time by the Electoral and Constitutional Advisory Commission (Commission consultative constitutionnelle et électorale; Dozon 2000, 46–47). But unlike Houphouët-Boigny, Guéï submitted it to a national referendum. It passed (Le Pape 2002). Although its most controversial change involved modifying the criteria of eligibility for candidates to run in presidential elections, the new constitution did little more than transfer the language of Bédié's electoral code to the constitution itself (Aggrey 1995a, 2000; cf. Dozon 2000, 46). Article 35 now required that all presidential candidates be born of parents both of whom were Ivoirian by birth. It also held that no candidate should have ever assumed non-Ivoirian nationality. Guéï seemed as determined as Bédié to eliminate Alassane Ouattara as a presidential rival.

Guéï continued Bédié's politics of ethnicity in other ways as well. He purged the army of Baoulé and "northern" elements whom he believed might be loyal to Bédié or Ouattara (Dozon 2000, 53; Langer 2004, 28–30; O. Dembélé 2003).[1] He arrested, reprimanded, and expelled soldiers who had served as bodyguards for former Prime Minister Ouattara and who subsequently helped him come to power in 1999. Many of them took refuge in Burkina Faso.

Guéï also chose his ministers along ethnopolitical lines. He eliminated Bédié's Democratic Party of Côte d'Ivoire (PDCI) from his first government and doubled the component from his own Yacouba or Dan ethnicity in his second government (Langer 2004, 28).[2] Due to an apparent de facto alliance with opposition politician Laurent Gbagbo and his FPI party, Guéï increased the number of FPI ministers while reducing the number of "northern" Syenara-speaking ministers (Langer 2004, 29; see Dozon 2000, 54–55).[3] The number of Mandenkan-speaking ministers remained the same, but three of the four endorsed Ouattara's exclusion from presidential elections, and one, Prime Minister Seydou Diarra, had no party affiliation (Langer 2004, 29).

On October 22, 2000, Guéï ran for president against Laurent Gbagbo, his sole opponent. Guéï's regime had disqualified all other potential challengers on various arbitrary grounds. But on October 24, when it became clear that Gbagbo was winning the election, Guéï dissolved the electoral commission and proclaimed himself president. Gbagbo responded by calling his FPI supporters into the streets (Le Pape 2002). Clashes between the army and civilians followed. Two days later, on October 26, Gbagbo was sworn in as president, and Ouattara's RDR party organized demonstrations in Abidjan to call for new elections. Gbagbo used gendarmes, police, and violence to repress the demonstrations, just as Ouattara had repressed demonstrations led by Gbagbo in 1992. That same night, dozos "repulsed an attack on Alassane Ouattara's private residence by a mob of FPI supporters backed by gendarmes" (Bassett 2003, 22). The next day, dozos "provided security to RDR supporters at a demonstration in Odienné . . . During a confrontation in which gendarmes fired at the crowd, the [dozos] fired back. Three people were wounded, including a gendarme" (22).

Political circumstances had now overtly polarized dozos' identity vis-à-vis the state. Benkadi appeared unambiguously as a political militia. So too did gendarmes. On October 27, the bodies of fifty-seven men with "northern-sounding" names and who had been abducted the night before from the district of Abobo were found murdered behind Abidjan's municipal prison in the district of Yopougon. Survivors implicated the gendarmes (Fédération Internationale des Ligues des Droits de l'Homme/Reporters sans Frontières 2000), but a show trial exonerated all eight gendarmes accused of the crime (IRIN 2002). Dozos' ethnic armed resistance to ethnically targeted attacks henceforth defined their interaction with the state.

From 2000 to 2002, tensions only worsened. President Gbagbo intensified ethnic and political antagonisms between FPI and RDR supporters, between "northerners" (*nordistes*) and other Ivoirians (Vidal 2002), and with certain elements in the military. He decommissioned soldiers of the Zinzins and Bahéfouê contingents that had operated under President Guéï (Banégas and Losch 2002, 142). Again Ouattara was excluded from running for office, this time from legislative elections, sparking further violent protests (Le Pape 2002). And Gbagbo further refined the ever-evolving principle of *ivoirité* in the "clearest consecration in the history of the country of the principle of territorial autochthony as the grounds for national identity and citizenship" (Marshall-Fratani 2006, 27). The state began issuing new national identity cards to citizens with the stipulation that "northerners" claim theirs in their ancestral regions of origin even though those "northerners" living in southern Côte d'Ivoire may never have lived in or visited these areas. The process was potentially perilous for participants, depending upon how officials judged their ethnic, religious, and regional identity:

> The enrollment of individuals in the exercise could result in their receiving a foreign resident's card instead of a national identity card . . . The announcement of these poli-

cies only served to reinforce the impunity with which security forces harassed northern populations, often destroying their documents in the process. (Marshall-Fratani 2006, 28)

Being Ivoirian now meant documenting a preexisting affiliation to a village that matched the ethnic sonority of one's family name (*jamu*). The exercise ran counter to the historical mobility that had long characterized Côte d'Ivoire's populations. Its skewed vision of history threatened to undermine rather than consolidate the new president's power.

Early on the morning of September 19, 2002, rebels attempted to overthrow Laurent Gbagbo. The rebels included those soldiers who had fled Côte d'Ivoire for Burkina Faso after being expelled from the army by Presidents Guéï and Gbagbo (Banégas and Losch 2002, 141; Balint-Kurti 2007, 4).[4] During the ensuing battle for Abidjan, state forces assassinated Guéï (Banégas and Losch 2002, 141). Meanwhile, the rebels, who later announced themselves as the "New Forces" (Forces Nouvelles), seized the large northern cities of Korhogo and Bouaké, which became their capital, but they failed to take Abidjan. France placed 3,000 troops in a buffer zone (*zone de confiance*) running west to east along the middle of the country to halt the rebel advance (see fig. 1). They later augmented the number of troops to 4,000 (Chirot 2006, 71). The zone began south of the city of Danané at the Liberian border, continued eastward south of Zuénoula and Bouaké, and ended north of Bondoukou at the Ghanaian border (Bouquet 2005, 121). Ironically, this north-south divide exactly mirrored the ethnopolitical divide first inspired and realized by *ivoirité*.

Guillaume Kigbafori Soro, a Syenara-speaking Roman Catholic from the Korhogo region and former leader of the Student Federation of Côte d'Ivoire (Fédération Estudiantine et Scolaire de Côte d'Ivoire [FESCI]), emerged as the leader of the New Forces (Baxter 2003). From 2002 on, he and President Gbagbo successively engaged and disengaged themselves from a series of summits (in Accra and Lomé), peace accords and resolutions (Linas-Marcoussis in Paris, Accra I-III, Pretoria, and UN Resolution 1633), and prime ministers (N'Guessan, Diarra, and Konan Banny [Gnakalé 2006, 23–57]). Gbagbo's failure to hold elections on preestablished dates, the New Forces' postponement of disarmament, as well as repeated bombings, skirmishes, civilian massacres, and attacks on French soldiers and New Forces ministers kept the country in a continuous state of emergency (Chirot 2006, 72–74).

Meanwhile, Simone Gbagbo, Côte d'Ivoire's First Lady, was reportedly organizing extrajudicial "death squads" (IRIN 2005) that targeted RDR members and sympathizers. And a new group calling themselves the Young Patriots (Jeunes Patriotes) emerged under former FESCI leader and Guillaume Soro colleague Charles Blé Goudé (Marshall-Fratani 2006, 29).[5] The group worked closely with the Gbagbos, "surveying the opposition and denouncing 'suspicious' or 'enemy' behavior, controlling popular neighborhoods, creating a climate of terror throughout the city, and even assisting at times with the notorious 'death squads' responsible for numerous disappearances and summary executions" (30). Like Benkadi, the Young Patriots began as nonstate actors working both beyond the law and side by side with the state. Other pro-Gbagbo militias like the Patriotic Group for Peace (Groupement Patriotique pour la Paix) arose along similar lines (30), "complete with president, treasurer, and posts linked to activities such as security, fundraising, and mobilization" (31). Members of these groups possessed identity cards "proving that they [were] patriots serving their country, with their names, age and village of origin. These cards [were] used as laissez-passer on instructions given by the Préfet" (Chauveau and Bobo 2003, 20, cited in Marshall-Fratani 2006, 31). Pro-Gbagbo groups engaged semi-officially with the state in ways reminiscent of Benkadi were emerging faster than Benkadi had. They too organized themselves bureaucratically and worked with the approval of prefects.

And, just as the Young Patriots began to resemble dozos, perpetrating violence on the president's behalf, dozos began waging war. Shortly after the rebellion began, French journalists reported that in the rebel capital, Bouaké, "800 traditional hunters" had "joined the rebellion" (R. M. 2002) and that "an estimated 50 out of 250 rebel soldiers in the west were dozos" (Hellweg 2004, 19; Agence France Presse 2003a). Dozo involvement had become ubiquitous:

> In [Côte d'Ivoire's] central western region, "war chief" Koné Zakaria, who hailed from the Odienné subprefecture of Séguélon and claimed to be a dozo with dozo followers, captured the city of Vavoua for [another rebel group] the MPCI [*Mouvement Populaire de Côte d'Ivoire*, the Popular Movement of Côte d'Ivoire] (Al Séni 2003). Then, in May 2003, an Ivoirian journalist reported that men wearing dozo uniforms and potentially linked to the MPIGO rebel movement (*Mouvement Populaire Ivoirien du Grand Ouest*) [Ivoirian Popular Movement of the Greater West] had massacred sixty-eight civilians in the western village of Bangolo (Konan 2003). In contrast, a civilian eyewitness implied that dozos, though spied near the scene, took no part in the atrocity (None 2003). Likewise, although some journalists reported dozo involvement in the December 11–12, 2003, attack on Abidjan's television station, others attributed it to a radical pro-government militia ([Agence France Presse] 2003b). (Hellweg 2004, 19–20)

At least one dozo, though, was reported to have murdered captured gendarmes and their children in Bouaké in 2002 (Amnesty International 2003, 9). Ivoirian soldiers, New Forces troops, and national security forces also participated in atrocities (Amnesty International 2003, 2005). Such exactions continued up until at least 2009 (U.S. Department of State 2010).

After fifty years, Côte d'Ivoire had come full circle. Houphouët-Boigny had avoided devolving "authority and prerogative to local, nonstate authorities" (Boone 1998, 10) whereas under Bédié, prefects and subprefects indirectly authorized Benkadi, Afrique Environnementale, and Édouard Coulibaly's National Hunters' Association to help control crime. President Guéï granted such authority directly to dozos. And President and Mrs. Gbagbo worked overtly with non-dozo parastatals. Their involvement with "patriot" groups merely intensified the state's commitment to recruiting nonstate actors to fill quasi-state roles. Despite the Young Patriots' alleged implication in numerous atrocities (Marshall-Fratani 2006, 36), Blé Goudé became a member of the national government in the unlikely role of "peace ambassador" in 2007. Also in 2007, Guillaume Soro, the New Forces' leader, became prime minister (Sapa 2007), giving dozos a presumed ally in high places as well.

The State of Nonstate Actors

I have compared dozos and Young Patriots to highlight a central contention of this book, that dozos' originality lay in a long history of oscillation between contrasting forms of political, religious, geographic, cultural, and communicative idioms: state and segmentary, Muslim and pagan, urban and rural, modern and traditional, literate and oral, respectively. Groups like the Young Patriots cooperated closely with the state as politically motivated militias from the start. In contrast, Benkadi did not originate as an opposition militia. Although it eventually became one in response to opposition political pressure and state aggression, it originally attempted to provide a nonpartisan form of public security. Its small, improvised collaborations were at first minimized or dismissed by Ivoirian and international analysts, diplomats, and policy makers. In retrospect, however, they appear as among the most unexpected yet most frank, most successful, and most telling state/nonstate collaborations in Côte d'Ivoire's history. Marginalized Julakan- and Syenara-speaking peasants and proletarians with little or no schooling managed to provide a service to officials, citizens, and residents by committing no more violence against lay populations than state security forces already did, which hardly made Benkadi any less reprehensible. Local officials, in turn, worked with dozos at the price of compromising constitutional and criminal law, enabling dozos to abuse their newfound authority while ignoring pressure from government ministers to repress Benkadi.

Dozos and officials worked together in the very climate of ethnic and religious discrimination, virulent nationalism, regional inequalities, and emerging violence that led them into conflict against each other. But Benkadi's members, constituency, and claims on the state were analogous if not identical to those of the rebels even before the rebellion. Men of northern descent, mostly Muslims with Christians among them, sought a place as full citizens and legal residents of Côte d'Ivoire under legal and extralegal provisions that denied them this. Benkadi's initial ability to find peaceful ways of relating to the state consequently has important lessons to teach about the lost potential for resolving the Ivorian rebellion before it even began as well as about the minimal requirements for resolving it in the twenty-first century.

Resolving Rebellion

Political scientist Patrick Regan (2009) has outlined three strategies for diffusing the conditions that lead to civil conflict: (1) tolerating cultural and political differences, (2) reducing structural poverty, which he defines as "poverty born of discrimination," and (3) negotiating with rebels to give them the means to pursue the justice they seek without resorting to conflict. In Côte d'Ivoire, dozos and local officials were doing all three before the rebellion, offering an unrecognized, working strategy for keeping the peace.

First, dozos and local officials worked together across multiple cultural and political differences, though at cross-purposes. Local officials sought alternative sources of community policing in the absence of state resources. Dozos sought security for the physical survival for their communities. Their collaborations were more than cynical attempts at mutual manipulation. They continued, and in fact only began in Denguélé, after the emergence of *ivoirité* and Security Minister Koné's call for Benkadi's dismantlement. In fact, it took state officials two more years, from 1996 to 1998, to stop local officials and dozos from collaborating and, even then, only in southern Côte d'Ivoire. Benkadi's success testified to the state's ability to find grounds for compromise with armed potential enemies.

Second, Benkadi's collaboration with local officials had economic consequences. Denguélé, like the rest of the north, was among the poorest, most underpopulated, and most rural of Côte d'Ivoire's regions. One might have expected, like Fanon (2007, 84), that peasants there would have been among the first to rebel because they had the least to lose and were "the first among the exploited to discover that only violence pays." Dozos in the south were also poor and working-class. But dozos' work with Benkadi in both the north and south enabled them to eke out a living or at least enough of one to forestall for these men "the grinding poverty that can motivate individuals to take risks they might otherwise avoid" (Regan 2009). Benkadi, in other words, proved a momentary, useful fix.

Third, Benkadi and its alliances with power brokers like Inza Fanny and Édouard Coulibaly enabled dozos to negotiate a position for themselves on the state's margins. As the collaboration between local authorities and Afrique Environnementale's office in Denguélé showed, such negotiation was an ongoing, even disappointing state of affairs, but it sustained the sense that dialogue between state and nonstate actors was possible and productive. But instead of seeing Benkadi's collaborations with local officials as a potential model for conflict prevention, the state finally villainized dozos as subversive Others, overlooking the fact that its own police were similarly subverting state laws and legitimacy. In fact, Benkadi was in a position exactly analogous to that of the politicians who exploited and opposed it. Within the Ivoirian state of exception, ruling elites acted outside of the legal order but were yet somehow a part of it (Agamben 2005, 35). Like them, dozos operated both beyond and beside the law. In this sense, Benkadi amounted to a popular appropriation of the same legal exceptionalism by which political elites ruled Côte d'Ivoire, which may explain why Benkadi proved at first so useful but subsequently so threatening to them.

The parallels go further still. Just as Benkadi stood outside but also beside the state, it existed both beyond and akin to *dozoya*—not as *dozoya* but as "something dozos did." Dozos drew on their repertoire of ritual symbols and practices to assume new roles as unofficial police, retromimetically grounding their legal exceptionalism in the state with their exceptional status in domestic contexts as a result of Manimory's sacrifices.

"*Being-outside, and yet belonging:* this is the topological structure of the state of exception," according to Agamben (2005, 35, emphasis in original) just as it was for dozos, who both belonged to the forest and yet, like Manimory, transcended it. By assuming an exceptional status within the state—as "unofficial police" (an oxymoron)—they assumed a position analogous to the sovereign himself, "only because the sovereign, who decides on the exception, is, in truth, logically defined in his being by the exception" (35). Since the death of Houphouët-Boigny, all three successive Ivoirian presidents have stood, like him, at some remove from the state's constitutional functioning, moving like dozos both within and beyond it—and like Manimory, pragmatically omnipresent but legally invisible. It is, therefore, far from self-evident that Benkadi represented a distortion of statist politics as much as it did a variation on them. The fact that impoverished, semiliterate peasants and proletarians accomplished this variation on their own initiative and, at first, for the most part peacefully, made Benkadi all the more remarkable, especially in comparison to the rise of comparable but more narrowly defined and more immediately violent organizations following the outbreak of rebellion in 2002.

As a result, Benkadi's collaboration with local officials remains instructive even after the supposed end of hostilities in Côte d'Ivoire. As of the publication of this book, no peace accord has definitively resolved the crisis. Any attempt to unify the country must appeal to interests as divergent as the cultural, political, and economic differences that characterized collaborations between local officials and Benkadi before the war (see Tsing 2005, 245–246). What held true for Benkadi's relationship with the state will hold true for relations between Soro, Gbagbo, and their respective camps if they are to achieve lasting peace:

> Usually, scholars think of collaborators as like-minded colleagues who each contribute to a commonly conceived product . . . Of course, there is another meaning of collaboration . . . Collaborators work with the enemy in wartime. These collaborators are not positioned in equality or sameness, and their collaboration does not produce a communal good . . . The more different they are, the more they must reach for barely overlapping understandings of the situation. Their common cause is also a cultural encounter, and the objects on which they appear to agree are most successful when they appeal simultaneously to divergent cultural legacies . . . In the process, they make wide-ranging links possible: they are the stuff of . . . emergent politics: they make new objects and agents . . . (Tsing 2005, 246–247)

In many respects, the Ivoirian state of 2010, ruled by a president who triumphed in a flawed election and, governed by a prime minister who was a former rebel, resembled the unique partnership between local officials and dozos that prevailed under Benkadi. Any definitive peace agreement will have to do what local officials and dozos did: create new forms of local enfranchisement that circumvent the dichotomies of state and nonstate power typical of previous regimes. No coalition government, however encompassing, will resolve the current crisis unless it operates beyond the bounds of state and civil society as usually conceived (see Comaroff and Comaroff 1999; Ferguson 2006).

National reconciliation will likely be achieved not by "searching for seamless consensus or making a point of . . . irreconcilable differences" (Tsing 2005, 262) but through the kinds of cross-cultural engagements local officials and dozos realized under Benkadi. The parties to the current conflict have already been trying, albeit reluctantly and with repeated delays and obstructions, to do justice to each other's demands in these terms. President Gbagbo agreed to allow Prime Minister Soro to begin resolving the legal status of Ivoirians who lacked the documents necessary to apply for national identity cards (Lynch and Calabia 2007). And the New Forces ostensibly began disarming in May 2008 (J. James 2008; Christophe Koffi 2010). But the failure of either process and the continued postponement of presidential elections could prevent a definitive solution to the crisis. So, too, could the failure to integrate former rebels into the military as the state has promised to do (International Crisis Group 2009). Ironically, such integration of nonstate agents into the state is precisely what Benkadi sought in the first place.

Mimesis as Statecraft

Now after more than a decade since Benkadi's last appearance as a public security force in Abidjan, dozos' mimetic collaboration with state officials still stands as a template for resolving the country's crisis. I do not mean that dozos or local officials should oversee or play a leading role in the process. I mean instead that the key to preventing future conflicts in Côte d'Ivoire lies in recognizing and correcting for the underlying conditions that made the mimetic oscillation of legal exceptionalism such an effective if, in the end, destabilizing political strategy for both the state and Benkadi. Since 1960, the Ivoirian state has stood constantly on the "threshold of indeterminacy between democracy and absolutism" (Agamben 2005, 3), acting at one moment or in one aspect as a democracy while in other ways as a dictatorship. The vagaries of international political economy dictated this strategy during the cold war, during the era of structural adjustment, and then under neoliberalism. To offset the unpredictable nature of state policy and resources, local officials and dozos likewise shifted between their respective bureaucratic and ritual idioms to create reliable local alliances in the face of national uncertainty.

Those dozos with the ethical self-control to avoid using violence against officials, citizens, and residents of Côte d'Ivoire, and those officials who collaborated with dozos despite the state's stigmatization of Benkadi, showed that even under the tyranny of legal exceptionalism, everyday people could manage to appropriate it for their own welfare.

Dozos' ritual and occult hunting idioms therefore proved to be more than culturally othered perceptions of political corruption (Geschiere 1997), subterranean sources of empowerment (Ferme 2001a), unconscious strategies of resistance (Jean Comaroff 1985), or capitulations to state hegemony (A. Cohen 1981; Stoller 1995), although they were, at the same time, all of these. Dozos opened new political spaces in which state actors worked beyond state interests as narrowly conceived, and marginalized nonstate actors felt engaged with the state. Far from a liberatory political discourse, the result was a contentious collaboration that operated beyond the conventional stability of state institutions and oversight, sometimes—and ultimately—with disastrous results. Meanwhile, Benkadi revealed that the political ingenuity required to bridge apparently irreconcilable differences might just as well come from local bureaucrats, peasants, and laborers as from diplomats, international NGOs, and national political parties, defying the assumption that a "vertical topography of power" (Ferguson 2006, 89–112) offers the only map worth following for resolving conflicts in Africa or elsewhere—a lesson that top-heavy mediation efforts in Côte d'Ivoire have so far ignored. All this to say that Benkadi's prewar ethos of mimetic hunting and bureaucratic collaboration—grounded in the inventive use of ritual sacrifice—still stands as an original worth copying especially in light of more recent events.

On November 28, 2010, long-delayed presidential elections in Côte d'Ivoire ended with an internationally recognized victory for Alassane Ouattara. But Laurent Gbagbo refused to relinquish power. He and Ouattara both declared themselves president, and new attacks on northern-descended Muslims began. The state's privatization that had begun under Houphouët-Boigny, and consolidated under Bédié and Guéï, now came to full fruition. At last the state revealed itself as the nation's ultimate nemesis. What dozos had divined through sacrifice as a threat had become a positive menace: the state's lack of accountability to any but those who controlled it. It was now apparent that Benkadi had been a symptom of, and reaction to, a deeper, more disconcerting dilemma: how to engage to a state, as citizens, when it moves itself beyond reach, and how to reform that state, as outsiders, without being deformed in the breach.

Notes

CHAPTER ONE

1. Dozos I knew sought to cut the throats of slain animals as quickly as possible after killing them to approximate halal procedure (see Quardhaoui 1990, 53).
2. Phonetically, one would spell Manimory's name *Manimori.* I spell it "Manimory" instead because "Mory" is a common personal name for men in West Africa and, given Manimory's saintly status, because other scholars spell the title for learned West African Muslims in the same way: "mory" (Launay and Miran 2000, 63–84).
3. The franc CFA (Communauté financière africaine) is the currency of most of France's former West African colonies. In 2010, its value was fixed at a constant exchange rate of 100 francs per Euro. Before 1994, the rate was 50 francs per French franc. During my research on Benkadi between 1994 and 1997, it stood at 100 francs per French franc.
4. Ivoirian citizens showed their national identity cards (*cartes nationales d'identité*). Residents showed their residency cards (*cartes de séjour*).
5. In northern Mande languages, to which one may refer as *Mandenkan, bɛn* means "agreement," *ka* is the copula, and *di* means "sweet." In everyday speech, one may say, *bɛn ye nyɔgɔn ye,* to mean, "we agree," or, literally, "agreement is between us." The verb *ka bɛn* also means "to meet."
6. The suffix *-kan* means "throat," "sound," "call," or "language," and the word *jula* means "merchant" or "trader" (see Person 1963, 139–140). In Côte d'Ivoire, *julakan* or "merchants' language" refers to a host of northern Mande languages that are mutually intelligible to varying degrees (Braconnier, Maire, and Tera 1983; M.-J. Derive 1983). These

include the market language and mother tongue, Tagbusikan (Knutsen 2008), and the Mande languages (Koyagakan, Maokan, Wojɛnɛkakan, and Worodugukan) spoken in northwestern Côte d'Ivoire and in the north-central Kong region (Julakan). The word *jula* also has ethnic connotations. It has come to mean almost anyone of northern descent who is Muslim and speaks a northern Mande language or, in the case of Soninke, a western Mande language. The word may also apply to speakers of Gur languages (unrelated to Mandenkan) such as Syenara (commonly called *sénoufo* in French and *Senufo* in English; Knutsen 2008; Skattum 2008).

7. By morality, I denote a discourse by which one determines the value of thought and practice within a given sociocultural context. By ethics, I mean the comparative evaluation of such discourses (see Kremer-Marietti 1987, 4). Fortin (1995, 41–60) notes similar definitions of ethics in the work of Baruch Spinoza, Immanuel Kant, Jürgen Habermas, Paul Ricœur, André Comte-Sponville, and William Frankena.
8. According to D'Andrea (2006, 258), a virtue ethic posits "a table of virtues . . . and a list of proscribed acts or habits of action . . . Law will have a tertiary role in such a well-ordered community: enjoying pride of place will be the goods that the community exists to pursue and to foster. In second place will be those virtues deemed necessary to and or constitutive of the sought-after goods; in third place will be public prescriptions which enumerate prohibitions of significantly harmful or defective acts or habits of action, and which assign rewards of various sorts for contributions to the goods of the community." Dozos and the state approached law from different viewpoints. Dozos privileged the implicit rules of social reciprocity as the primary standard for regulating and restoring community life. The state, in contrast, defined violations against persons and property as transgressions first and foremost against itself, as codified in punitive laws.
9. By ethos, I mean a cultural logic underlying contrasting practices that orients practitioners toward analogous moral ends in pursuing those practices. I build on Benedict (1934), Bateson (1958), Geertz (1973), and Wagner (1986), who have defined "ethos" similarly as an emotive pattern, tone, or standard for multiple kinds of behavior.
10. By "state" in the political sense, I mean the administrative discourse and apparatus defined by the Ivoirian constitution and realized, negotiated, and contradicted by those who occupied the executive, legislative, and judicial offices that the constitution defined. See Trouillot (2003, 79–96) for a concise history of the concept.
11. In Bhabha's (1994, 37) terms, dozo sacrifice was more than an "integrated, open, expanding code." Crime placed it within a "disruptive temporality of enunciation" that "ensure[d] that the meaning and symbols of [dozo] culture [had] no primordial unity or fixity; that even the same signs [could] be appropriated, translated, rehistoricized and read anew." Benkadi belonged neither to the state nor to civil society per se, nor to some static hunting

"tradition." While Benkadi appeared to upset the rule of law and nascent multiparty democracy, it more importantly signaled and attempted to protect in various ways the fragility of both. As Ayers (2006, 321) has argued, "democracy" is often so narrowly defined as to be no more than a watchword for reproducing a "transition to capitalist modernity" regardless of any expansion of people's well-being. Benkadi revealed the gap between democracy's promise and the Ivoirian state's inability to fulfill it.

12. In francophone West Africa, colonizers' collaborations with chiefs foreshadowed analogous power-sharing arrangements after independence between state and nonstate agents (Alexandre 1970).
13. Fox (1985), Guha (1997), Mintz (1989), Ong (1987), Stoler (1985), and Taussig (1980) have documented similar discourses beyond Africa.
14. Discerning the extent to which rituals have done so, however, requires a nuanced discussion of practitioners' intentions (see Seymour 2006).
15. Speakers of northern Mande languages call an initiated hunter *donso* in Guinea and Mali, *dozo* in Burkina Faso, and *dozo* or *donzo* in Côte d'Ivoire. The Mande languages from which these terms come are generally agreed to be a subgroup of the Niger-Congo family (Greenberg 1963).
16. Sory Kourouma, an instructor at the University of Kankan, Guinea, told me in March 2009 that he had witnessed *donso*s guarding the town of Guéckédou against Liberian rebels before rebels overran the city in 2002.
17. He did not imply by this that non-*dozo* men joined Benkadi.
18. Sahlins's (1981) notion of the "structure of the conjuncture" highlights dissonances between performed ritual structures and unforeseen historical events that force agents to alter their rituals. Crespi (1992) locates such conjunctures within human persons as well. In ritual, he might argue, the person her- or himself is the point of resolution between event and structure, agency and constraint. The person's alternation between the possibilities of agency and the imperatives of structure is not just the result of historical contingency but of personal creativity.
19. I use the terms "Sufi" and "Islam" with caution. They "are highly contested terms," (Ernst 1997, xvi), having been "introduced into European languages in the early nineteenth century by Orientalists" (xiv). Neither describes an exclusive or homogenous community (xv).
20. I use the adjective "pagan" in this book as Amselle (1998) does, in its literal sense from the Latin *paganus*, meaning "rural denizen," to describe ritual practices anchored in rural life. I intend no negative connotations such as those implied by the synonym "heathen," which also draws on rural imagery, meaning "heath dweller."
21. The principle is similar to that of sympathetic magic. One accomplishes one's ends by manipulating behaviors or substances similar to or in proximity to those one seeks to influence (Frazer 1922; Taussig 1993, 47).
22. In hierarchies (Dumont 1981), founding principles encompass their contraries.

23. The parallels with retroviral imitation are apparent but unintended (see Napier 2003). Whereas retroviruses seek to destroy their hosts, dozos sought to coexist indefinitely with theirs.
24. See chapter 3 for details on these rituals.
25. These sacrifices commemorated Abraham's near sacrifice of Ishmael.
26. I use the term "sacrifice" in English because it best translates what dozos said in French and Julakan. Following Gibson (1986), I avoid positing dozo offerings as a manifestation of some universal thing called "sacrifice." I refer to the anthropological literature on "sacrifice" in the following pages because it helps explain the particularities of dozo rituals.
27. For Mauss (1967, 18), "Alms are the result on the one hand of a moral idea about gifts and wealth and on the other of an idea about sacrifice . . . [T]he gods and spirits consent that the portion reserved for them and destroyed in useless sacrifice should go to the poor and the children. Originally the Arabic *sadaka* meant, like the Hebrew *zedaqa*, exclusively justice, and it later came to mean alms." Dozo sacrifices extended dozos' protection and their concerns for justice to those to whom they distributed the game they killed.
28. Drissa Koné, personal communication.
29. For Bloch (1992), the power accessed is animal in nature rather than spiritual per se. It is, in any case, extrahuman.
30. Bailleul (2000a, 166–167) defines the Bamanankan cognate *hakili* in French as *intention*, among other things.
31. I discuss incidents of dozo violence in chapters 6 and 7.
32. My focus on dozos' ritual creativity makes me in no way an advocate for their violence. In fact, I discern in their rituals a critique of violence (see chap. 8).
33. When I first arrived in Odienné, everyone I met could understand me when I spoke Tagbusikan, but I had difficulty understanding their replies in Wojɛnɛkakan. The version of Julakan spoken in the Bako subprefecture (Siɛnkokakan), where Nienesso is located, presented further grammatical and lexical differences (see M.-J. Derive 1983).
34. *Selidaga* means "prayer pot." West African Muslims use it to make ablutions before praying and to clean themselves after using the toilet.
35. An extensive artisanal goldmine was located near Ziévasso at the time of my research.
36. So great was the demand that I once had to squeeze through an open window to get seats for Drissa Koné and me on the postal van to Korhogo so that we could arrive there on time for a dozo meeting (see chap. 6).
37. Most Christians living in Odienné were southern Ivoirians or foreign nationals.

CHAPTER TWO

1. Gluckman's (1958) remarks about whites and Zulu in his essay "The Bridge" also reflect the relationship between dozos and the Ivoirian state:

"Zulu and whites are systematically interrelated into a single system, which the [ethnographic] situation creates and reinforces" (Frankenberg 2002, 60). The same was true of dozos and the Ivoirian state. Dozos were as modern and cosmopolitan as the state officials with whom they collaborated (see Fabian 1998; Piot 1999). They used the same strategies to effect sociopolitical change.

2. By "engaged universal," Tsing (2005, 8, 264) means any concept, idea, or practice defined by so-called global institutions or networks as universally valid: discourses of development, environmental protection, or human rights, for example. But these discourses can only be "effective within particular historical conjunctures that give them content and force." Tsing calls this "conjunctural feature of universals . . . engagement" (8). Engaged universals are the means by which global and local, state and nonstate actors collaborate to achieve their ends across difference (246).
3. Mimesis is often an aspect of universal engagement. It is key to understanding the diverse expectations that inform unexpected collaborations. "The ability to mime, and mime well . . . is the capacity to Other," that is, to understand and appropriate another's expectations and behaviors (Taussig 1993, 19).
4. Amin (1973, 66, 48–66, 170–177) described Côte d'Ivoire's situation as "growth without development."
5. These networks stretched "from Senegal to Nigeria and from Timbuktu to the Northern Ivory Coast" (Mundt 1987, 59).
6. The phrase is an English translation of Côte d'Ivoire's national motto, *Union, Discipline, Travail,* which appears on the state coat of arms.
7. The term "Burkinabe" refers to citizens of Burkina Faso.
8. The president's oft-quoted saying, "The future of this country rests on agriculture (*L'avenir de ce pays repose sur l'agriculture*)," was played almost daily on Ivoirian television.
9. Although the Ivoirian constitution of 1960 allowed the formation of opposition parties, Houphouët-Boigny forbade them in practice (Zolberg 1964, 262).
10. The state's lack of resources translated directly into increased insecurity. "As a result of the general insolvency and material devastation" of the state, "the very production of public order" was threatened (Mbembe 2001, 75).
11. Residents of the Economic Community of West African States (ECOWAS) paid 5,000 CFA francs for residency cards, and non-ECOWAS residents paid 50,000 (Koudou 2005, 41). At the time, the US dollar was worth roughly 250 francs.
12. The "coincidence" of Houphouët-Boigny's death with Radio France Internationale's initial FM broadcasts was uncanny (*Fraternité Matin* 1993d, 17; Ozoua 1993, 2).
13. *Fraternité Matin,* December 12, 1993, 3 (see also I. Cissé 2007, 50).
14. *Fraternité Matin,* December 4–7, 1993.

15. Côte d'Ivoire's transporters were mostly of Mande origin (see B. Lewis 1970). Ivoirian politics had long reflected such ethnic cleavages, notably between Houphouët-Boigny's mostly Akan-controlled PDCI and Gbagbo's FPI party, which counted as its primary base the Bété-speaking populations of west-central Côte d'Ivoire and their diaspora in Abidjan.
16. Ouattara's informality was a calculated protest.
17. Bédié's succession was now uncontested.
18. *Washington Times,* October 10, 1996, A17, cited in Ayittey 1999, 170; see also Crook 1997, 226; Toungara 2001, 67–68.
19. The names "Palenfo" and "Coulibaly" have Senufo "resonances" (Langer 2004, 30).
20. Djéni Kobina, who identified himself as Appollonian ("a sub-group of the Nzima," who are Akan speakers), founded the RDR (Crook 1997, 226).
21. Bédié's supporters eventually insisted on a DNA test to prove that Ouattara was the son of his Ivoirian mother (Zoro-Bi 2004, 53).
22. Neither supposition necessarily followed from the situation (see Langer 2004, 30, n. 8).
23. Artexaga (2003, 404–408) defines the "state of exception" as "a social-political space of force ruled by a law beyond the law, where the distinction between fact and law has become blurred . . . The state of exception is not decided by a situation of conflict or chaos, although this is often its discourse of legitimation; rather it is decided to affirm a juridical order in which lawfulness, right, is suspended in the name of law" (404).
24. Mills (2007, 190) notes that the "state of exception or state of emergency" is "the normal situation of politics today." Zolberg (1964, 335) seems to argue that Côte d'Ivoire was governed under a state of exception since its inception: "While in external appearance it is a government of laws rather than of men, these laws, including the constitution itself, have been tailored to suit a specific set of governors and can easily be altered at their discretion."
25. In 1958, Houphouët-Boigny implied that he was ready to take "exceptional measures," not because a "state of emergency" *existed,* "but because such a state of emergency could arise" (Gullì 2007, 219): "Although I am against violence, although I am a democrat . . . I want it to be known . . . that here in the Ivory Coast, we shall not accept license in place of freedom or of democracy" (Zolberg 1964, 253). Houphouët-Boigny's Côte d'Ivoire amounted to a "sovereign dictatorship"—a particular form of the state of exception (see Hirst 1986, 94–95; Loizidou 2007, 99; Paye 2006, 246–248)—where the ruler "aims at creating a state of affairs in which it becomes possible to impose a new constitution" (Agamben 2005, 33). After Houphouët-Boigny, no Ivoirian ruler had to work again to achieve this situation; it was a given. Ivoirian law as employed by subsequent presidents became unthinkable without the possibility of overriding it (51).
26. Amin (1973, 49) claims that the Ivoirian colony acquired its present borders in 1904.

27. Brunie (n.d. a, n.d. b) compiled a dossier of Ivoirian newspaper articles published between 1991and 1995 on crime and Ivoirian security. She did so while working for the Mission Française de Coopération et d'Action Culturelle. I refer to many of these articles in the following discussion. I found her work in the *salle de documentation* of the French Embassy, Abidjan. In cases where page numbers and other publication information are lacking for these sources, either Brunie or I failed to collect it when clipping the articles in question.
28. Houphouët-Boigny fanned the wars in both Liberia and Sierra Leone by supporting Charles Taylor and allowing Taylor and Burkina Faso's president Blaise Compaoré to mount an attack against Liberia from Côte d'Ivoire (Ellis 1999, 159). In this case, rising crime and violence in Côte d'Ivoire was, in part, a matter of the chickens coming home to roost.
29. Conversely, when security forces intervened successfully, they killed members of bandit groups without compunction (L. Kouassi 1993d; *La Voie* 1995a).
30. Urban taxi vans are called *gbakas*, in contrast to those that run in the interior, called *dynas*.
31. In contrast, a farm or construction worker or manual laborer was paid 500 francs for a full day's labor.
32. Two such companies were Vigassistance and Lavegarde. The name of the first combines the concepts of "vigilance" and "assistance." The latter name combines an abbreviated form of the French verb, *laver*, "to wash," and the verb *garder*, "to guard." Both names lend a pleasant aura—of helping or keeping something clean—to the unpleasant, sometimes violent activity of providing security.
33. Houphouët's death so upset one man that he threw himself into the moat surrounding the president's house in Yamoussoukro and was killed by the crocodiles living within it (*Herald* [Glasgow], February 16, 1994, 6).

CHAPTER THREE

1. Fonio millet (*Digitaria exilis*) is *fɔni* in Julakan.
2. Cuello and Robin (2005, 155, n.13) offer a nearly identical etymology for Malian Malinke speakers, for whom the word *dusu* means "initiated hunter": "'Enter into the house', an invitation made to the hunter returning to the village after a long stay in the bush." They dismiss a second etymology: "'*do-so*, horse of knowledge,' an expression that signifies that the hunter holds clear and agile knowledge."
3. I make no claim that Dramane's analogy is linguistically correct. But I follow Amselle's (1998, 176, n. 3) example in discussing the local etymologies of words to give a sense of their connotations, as when Amselle refers to local ideas about the place-name "Wassolon" (176, n. 9).
4. Dozos performed several forms of divination: *bɛrɛla* with small rocks,

koronfirila with tossed cowrie shells, and *ciɛnlala* or *ciŋɛlala*, which involved writing in sand.

5. Here *sogo* means "animal," *ka yɛrɛ* means "to change," and *-ma* is an agentive suffix, together giving "one who turns into an animal."
6. *Su* means "death" or "night"; *-baga* is an agentive suffix. The word means "doer of death" or "doer of darkness."
7. The related word *soma* denotes men who manipulate "power objects" (*boli*). Since dozos used power objects designed specifically for hunting (see McNaughton 1988, 58; Cashion 1984, 1: 180–195), which differentiated them from *somas*—unless the *somas* in question also happened to be *dozos*—and because some "sorcerers" were women, *soma* was no substitute for the word *subaga*. *Somas* also had a reputation in Côte d'Ivoire in the 1990s for being "magicians" and for performing public feats of magic to make money from spectators. Dozos performed such feats at colleagues' funerals, but they did not ask for money for them.
8. Odiennéka described witches as working in covens that recruited new members by feeding them a kind of human "flesh" (*sogo*). The coven then required new members to offer a relative of theirs for consumption in a form of balanced reciprocity. The flesh consumed was a tangible form of a human soul. Witches consumed this substance until the victim collapsed.
9. These stories may express cultural concepts of space more than they describe actual village histories. According to O'Sullivan (1976, vi, 65–69 passim), Mande-speaking farmers, scholars, traders, and warriors began arriving in Denguélé from the fifteenth through eighteenth centuries to settle among indigenous Senufo in a "gradual dispersal of families who spread throughout the region searching for good sites for hunting and agriculture" (67). They established "villages which became important trade foci along the north-south kola nut, salt, and cattle trade" (vi). According to O'Sullivan, a sort of homesteading experience . . . [was] the essential characteristic of the Malinké [Jula] takeover of the region" (69). Kopytoff (1987, 33) has described such frontier situations as political creations rather than geographical facts: "[S]ocieties often define neighboring areas as lacking any legitimate political institutions and as being open to legitimate intrusion and settlement . . . Frontiers tend to be seen as geographical phenomena because empty or sparsely populated areas are usually also the areas that can offer little political resistance to intrusion" (11) In Denguélé, Mande migrants displaced a preexisting Senufo presence to found new settlements. One may therefore interpret stories of dozos founding villages as political arguments about claims by later settlers to land that they may have appropriated from others, although it also seems possible that dozos founded many villages in Denguélé.
10. Delafosse (1955, 473) defines *lu* as the "area inhabited by a family (in the extended sense), the courtyard around which are built the huts or houses which serve as the dwellings of members of the same family . . . the

ensemble of members and servants or clients of a family." Cotten (1969, 27), writing about urban family dwellings in Odienné, similarly defines *lu* as "the inhabited spatial unit of the Malinke [Jula]. It forms an area clearly defined by the houses which open toward the compound's center . . . The word also has a social meaning. Within the compound live members of the extended family who have maintained close ties among themselves." Even in Odienné and many villages where compounds sometimes took the form of rectangular spaces, defined by rectangular cinder block houses with corrugated sheet-metal roofs, the term *lu* still applies. Although M.-J. Derive (1976, 14), citing an unpublished manuscript by Cotten, claimed that *lu* refers more to family ties than to a place of residence, I conclude that the word subsumes both familial and residential connotations.

11. The first-person singular appears here abbreviated as *n'* (from *ne*). *Ka wa* (*ka ta* in the Bamanankan of Mali, mutually intelligible with Ivoirian Julakan) means "to go," and *-tɔ* marks the intransitive future tense.
12. O'Sullivan's (1976, 69) choice of the word "homestead" for *lu* conflates the notion of a particular place with the people living there, connoting a migratory situation. The notion of the *lu* accompanied and structured the Mande diaspora, which progressed "as the possibilities of agriculture and hunting allowed" (69).
13. D. Cissé (1970, 57–76) offers an elegant analysis of Malinke kinship reminiscent of Evans-Pritchard's (1967) and Radcliffe-Brown's (1952) structural functionalist approach, tying lineage, clan, and ethnicity to an underlying agnatic logic.
14. Delafosse (1955, 518) derives the word *jamu* from the suffix *–mu* and the prefix *jan* meaning "length," "long," "to be long," or "to lengthen" (278). He defines *jamu* as "that which honors, that which renders great or goes far back, genealogy, noble title, clan or family name; go back to a noble or distant origin, have noble titles, be honorable; trace or recite the genealogy of, honor, ennoble." Prof. Kandioura Dramé of the University of Virginia proposed an alternate etymology, "sweet [praise] name," from the root of the Mandenkan verb "to be sweet," *ka ja*. When griots (*jeli*) sing one's praises, they sing of one's ancestors who bore the same *jamu*. In Wojɛnɛkakan, the verb *majamu* means "to praise" (Braconnier 1999, 513).
15. In Julakan, the suffix *-tigi* denotes ownership or mastery. *Lutigi* means "owner" or "master of the compound."
16. *ʃemɔn* is the simplified phonetic transcription of the name. I never saw its written form in French.
17. *Ta* is a possessive marker.
18. Such shelters looked like round mud-brick houses absent doors and with holes in the wall near the thatched roof for ventilation.
19. *ʃibon* literally means "sleeping house" or "house where one sleeps." The verb *ka ʃi* means "to sleep."
20. Jènèba and Madénba are now deceased.

21. In Africa, power may be "eaten whole" (Fabian 1990), but when it is not, it can be bitten off in pieces.
22. See Braconnier (1999, 33–34, 181–182) for a discussion of these terms and Leynaud and Cissé (1978, 100–101) for their ethnographic descriptions.
23. From this perspective, depictions of Mandenkan-speaking peoples as strictly patrilineal appear overstated.
24. As Muslims, Odiennéka men could marry up to four wives, but polygyny was exceptional in Denguélé, given the resources necessary to sustain it.
25. When a father died, one group of wife's children could contest the inheritance against the children of the other mother(s). At worst, such fighting could cause a *lu* to split into as many segments as there were groups of mothers' children (see Leynaud and Cissé 1978, 170–171), spurring the formation of new compounds.
26. *Den* also "serves to form the diminutive [of a noun]" (Delafosse 1955, 109). I can now explain the meaning of *fadenmalu* and *badenmalu*, "father's" and "mother's children," respectively. *-Ma* is a postposition indicating similarity or equivalence (Braconnier 1999, 499). The word *tɔgɔma*, for example, joins the root *tɔgɔ* or "personal name" to *-ma* to indicate someone who has the same name as oneself. *-Lu* or *-lugu* is a pluralizing suffix. In Jula the /g/ is sometimes minimized or dropped between identical vowels (*-lugu* may become *-lu*). When added to a proper noun, the suffix forms "an expression designating a group of people linked in one way or another to a certain individual" (497), as in the word *Kulibalilu*, which denotes all those in a given area who share the family name Coulibaly. Similarly, when *-lu*/*-lugu* is added to a common noun, it forms an archaic plural form (497). Dramane often used this form in his songs, addressing women collectively as *musolu* and dozos as *dozolu*. In such cases, he was not just referring to women or hunters in the plural, he was addressing them as a category of persons united by particular qualities or characteristics, such as being women or dozos. *Fadenmalu* and *badenmalu* thus name children belonging to the same group of father's or mother's offspring, respectively.
27. In Dramane's compound, for example, children by his first and third wives differed enough in age—by some two decades—that they had little reason for disagreement or conflict.
28. The epic of Sunjata Keita is an archetypal case. The hero's mother, Sogolon, endured insults and mistreatment from her jealous, senior cowife, Sassouma Berté, whose son seemed sure to be king after his father's death. But after years of personal, political, and military struggle, Sunjata ascended to the throne, vindicating his mother's patience, for "it is one's mother who decides [that] one's future will be bright not only if she suffers, but also if [her] children obey her" (K. Traoré 1994, 95). It follows, Ly (1979, 109) writes, that "all the renowned personages of Mande (from Sunjata to Samory and beyond) were great because of the example their mothers provided." As the proverb states, "All are in their mothers' hands" (K. Traoré

1994): *byɛ y'i ba bolo*, or *byɛ y'i ba boro* in Wojɛnɛkakan. Odiennéka, like other Mandenkan speakers, more often preceded their own personal names (*tɔgɔ*) with their mother's rather than their father's to distinguish themselves from those with the same personal and family names (see Ly 1979, 109). People referred to Dramane's brother, Mamandou, for instance, as *Makura Madu* or "Makoura's Madou" (Madou being short for Mamandou) after his mother, Makoura. They did so to distinguish him from other men named Mamadou Coulibaly. Dramane's taking his father's name as a prelude to his own was rather unique. People called him Chémon Dra.

29. In order, the three offerings are *mamɛnaliworo*, *kɔnɔtɛgɛworo*, and *kofoliworo*.
30. Denich (1974) has argued that, in the Balkans, women's potential to divide male lineages checked male power. The same could be said of women's ability to found their own "mother's houses" in Denguélé.
31. She had children from her first.
32. The use of the word, *dozo*, to denote both "initiated hunter" and "placenta" in Wojɛnɛkakan appears coincidental, although the words are tonally identical (Braconnier 1999, 164). Bailleul (2000b, 234) translates *placenta* in French as *tónso* in Bamanankan, in contrast to the word for "initiated hunter," *donso*.
33. The translation of *si* as *lignage* is likely the result of anthropological ideas introduced by the French colonial administration and subsequent national education system. West Africans appear comfortable thinking about the concept in multiple ways.
34. Gottlieb's (1992) focus on identity and difference among Beng has helped shape my approach to Jula kinship.
35. Children maintained joking relations (*senanguynya*) with their maternal grandfathers (*mamɔgɔcɛ*), grandmothers (*mamuso*), and uncles (*bɛnɔgɔcɛ*), reflecting their prerogative to visit and stay with them and impose upon their hospitality (*mɔgɔsobɛ*) and resources without censure.
36. Some Malian dozos have claimed that an initiate "remains an apprentice to his master until killing three large animals (formerly seven) or for an initiation period of two to three years" (Cashion 1984, 1: 106, 131 n. 42; see Y. Cissé 1994, 55). Dozos in Denguélé seemed to enforce no such schedule, like most Malian dozos: "It seems that one can remain an apprentice to a master for an indefinite period of time. An apprentice may find that his teacher's knowledge is so extensive that only many years of study and learning will provide him with it. This is not to say, however, that one cannot be considered a full-fledged [*donso*] in a relatively short time" (Cashion 1984, 1: 106–107). No dozo I knew in Côte d'Ivoire ever offered a specific period for apprenticeship.
37. Cashion (1984) has summarized the kinds of knowledge dozos sought: "techniques employed to track and kill game, the defenses one uses to prevent needless injury—both to animals and humans, the vital forces (*nyama*) particular to each animal, the ways to control such vital force . . . the various

flora for medicinal uses and the techniques and incantations necessary for their proper exploitation . . . the natures and practices of the different genies [*jina*] believed to inhabit particular trees or bushes or riverbanks . . . [the best use of a dozo's] arms and equipment—for example, the powder charge and type of projectile needed to kill specific animals at specific firing distances . . . [the] knife for cleaning the animal carcass and the knife proper to skinning the animal . . . [and] the rules and practices of [dozos] vis-à-vis other hunters and the society at large" (Cashion 1984, 1: 114–115).

38. Jula also use red kola nuts and chickens in sacrifices to acquire occult power when charging power objects (*jo, boli*) with energy (see Keita 1985, 34–35, 45–46).
39. Similarities among dozo initiations, weddings, and naming rituals should come as no surprise. As van Gennep (1960, 3) wrote, "Transitions from group to group and from one social situation to the next are looked on as implicit in the very fact of existence . . . Since the goal is the same, it follows . . . that the ways of attaining it should be at least *analogous, if not identical* in detail" (emphasis added).
40. He died between 2002 and 2008.
41. Whereas Y. Cissé (1964, 191; 1994, 67–75) writes that *danguns* in Mali were located at the crossroads of paths (see also Keita 1985, 44–45; Dieterlen 1988, 163–165), the *danguns* that I saw in Côte d'Ivoire were not.
42. Not far to the south of the path that led to the *dangun* stood another path parallel to it that led to Nienesso's cemetery (*kaburuso*).
43. The termite mound was a point of contact and communication between dozos and the forest soil into which Manimory had vanished, as if its tunnels channeled dozos' blood offerings directly to him and relayed his responses back to them in turn, much as termites aerate and water the soil through their excavations into it (see Fairhead and Leach 1996, 49, 317, n.4).
44. See Kassim Koné (1996) for a critical engagement with Brett-Smith's (1994) discussion of the gendered use of termite mounds in Mande.
45. Y. Cissé (1994, 58–61) has recorded an elaborate set of questions and responses required of Malian dozo initiates. The process as I observed it in Denguélé was much simpler.
46. *Bawo dozoya a ja ni ye.*
47. *Dozo kana wuya fɔ, o kana fen ʃonya, o kana nyamɔgɔya kɛ, o kana janfa kɛ.*
48. He inserted the knife behind the rooster's arteries so that it cut through them from behind.
49. *Lekɔl* in Julakan comes from the French word for "school," *l'école.*
50. She said that only men could make the initiatory sacrifice and that she would put aside her participation in *dozoya* after getting married.
51. Junior dozos enacted this hierarchy by greeting presumed seniors with a handshake while bending at both knees, often to the point of squatting. They might then massage the calves of senior dozos with both hands.

52. In Mali, dozos called each other "my older sibling" (*n'kɔrɔ*) or "my younger sibling" (*n'dɔkɔ*) to stress their closeness (Y. Cissé 1994, 54).
53. I therefore wish to nuance depictions of dozos as anomalous or marginal in Mande life, either because they exhibit exceptional egalitarianism and cooperation (Cashion 1984; Y. Cissé 1964) or exceptional hierarchy and violence (Bird and Kendall 1980; Leach 2000; McNaughton 1988).
54. Benkadi organizer Moussa Fofana translated the song into French for me while Movaly Fofana was singing it. I was unable to record it but reconstructed it from my notes of Moussa Fofana's translation and from my recollection of the lyrics in Julakan.
55. The "vulture is the symbol of the master hunter, for he is never empty-clawed or empty-beaked, never without a kill" (Cashion 1984, 1: 245).
56. The verb is *ka bɛn*, "to agree," "to get along with."
57. Amadou Hampaté Bâ characterized this approach as that of a good researcher: "The true scientific attitude, isn't it that of the researcher who knows how to forget what he knows in order to have a chance to learn what he does not?" (Bâ 1972, 46).
58. In Certeau's (1984, 117) terms, families and dozos transformed places into meaningful spaces through their practice to create the shared substances of both kinship and *dozoya*.

CHAPTER FOUR

1. For MacIntyre (1984) and Aristotle (2000), "The bond of a moral community . . . is not . . . the rule of law; it is the antecedent bond of a common set of loves or desires, and the friendship resulting from an acknowledgment of these shared valuings" (D'Andrea 2006, 257). Similarly, the generalized exchange that dozos maintained by hunting on behalf of non-dozos offered a source of morality on which dozos could draw to supplement a national legal system that lacked effective enforcement.
2. Dozos offerings were "qualisigns" (Pierce 1955, 101) of the relations they sustained through sacrifice and hunting. Munn (1986, 16) uses the term to refer to a sign "that is part of a more comprehensive whole and conveys some fundamental aspects of that whole." Qualisigns "exhibit something other than themselves *in* themselves" (74, emphasis in original). The "whole" in this case is the generalized cycle of exchange between dozos and non-dozos that gives rise both to *dozoya* and to domesticity as complementary, contrasting realms.
3. Sacrificers sometimes tossed kola nuts repeatedly until they fell the way dozos hoped they would to indicate Manimory's approval. Drissa Koné told me that during a sacrifice he attended at a Benkadi meeting in San-Pédro, Manimory refused a dozo's initiation despite repeated kola tosses. The initiation was indefinitely postponed.
4. Braconnier (1999, 288) and Bailleul (2000b, 177) define the Mandenkan

word *hɔrɔnya* as *liberté* in French—"freedom." It denotes the quality of being born into the family of an independent farmer and landowner or *hɔrɔn*, as opposed to being a slave (*jɔn*) or member of the occupational status groups (*nyamakala*) who historically depended on *hɔrɔn* patrons. *Dozoya* conferred such freedom because dozos from all backgrounds treated each other as *hɔrɔn*, whether born *hɔrɔn* or not.

5. This is not to say that dozos never sell game meat to restaurateurs, business people, or government functionaries. Those dozos who lived in and around Odienné did so often, but when they did, they called it "business" (*commerce*) or "poaching" (*braconnage*), not *dozoya*.
6. This might, for instance, be another dozo who fired a second shot to fell the animal.
7. Dozos discarded other parts of the genitalia.
8. Samka died in December 2000 or January 2001.
9. Delafosse derives the word *hakili* from the Arabic *'aql* (Delafosse 1955, 303).
10. Drissa Koné offered this etymology. I offer another in Hellweg (2001, 152). I defer to Drissa's.
11. He used the verb *ka foron* to say "throw." I recorded my English translation of their remarks in writing as we spoke.
12. Perspectivism is the notion "according to which the world is inhabited by different sorts of subjects or persons, human and non-human, which apprehend reality from distinct points of view" (Viveiros de Castro 1998, 469).
13. See Shaw (1992, 45–48, 51–52) and Goody (1962, 107–108, 129) for similar instances elsewhere in Africa.
14. Almost every dozo sacrifice involved two sacrificers, a *jibɔla*, or "water pourer," who addressed Manimory verbally, poured libations of water, and tossed kola nut halves to him, and a "throat cutter" (*kantɛgɛla*). Sometimes they were one and the same.
15. See Charry (2000, 63–89) for a detailed discussion of Mande hunters' music. He describes the *ngoni* as coming from the Wassolon region. Dramane said that *dozoya* originated in Wassolon, the region where southern Mali, northeastern Guinea, and northwestern Côte d'Ivoire converge.
16. *Ka fɔ* also means "to speak."
17. Odiennéka also used the word *ngɔnunfɔla*, "*ngɔnun* player," to refer to dozo musicians. The suffix *-fɔla* means "player," from the verb "to play." The suffix *-la* corresponds to the English agentive suffix "-er."
18. According to Dramane Coulibaly, dozos formerly used antelope gut to make the strings.
19. The *ngɔnun* contrasted with the oblong-based *ngoni* (Hale 1998, 149–153) played by *jeli*s ("griots"), but the Julakan word *ngɔnun* appears to derive from the Mandenkan word *ngoni*.
20. This does not mean that singers always played the *ngɔnun* while performing. Dramane Coulibaly usually left *ngɔnun* playing to his apprentices.

21. The *dagalabirin* names one aspect of the *yaladon*, but dozos also used the word as a synecdoche to name the entire rite.
22. The suffix *bɔ* here comes from the verb *ka bɔ*, meaning "to come out of" or "leave," "take out of," or "extract." When combined with the word *saraka*, it gives a word meaning something akin to "sacrifice extraction."
23. Five thousand francs was about ten dollars at the time.
24. *Baraka* comes from the Arabic for "grace" in the religious sense. In West Africa, it connotes the kind of power that makes one invulnerable to spiritual attack from outside forces.
25. Like trailblazing in the forest, *matɛgɛli* cleared the way for successful hunting.
26. In Hellweg (2009), I misidentified this *kozi*'s location as Somokoro.
27. I was thirty-one at the time.
28. The pot and termite mound were both made of earth. Like termite mounds, the pot potentially signaled the passage of insects from below the soil to the surface. Each vessel was a point of contact between living dozos and the earth into which the dead decayed.
29. In contrast to my initiation, Laciné answered no questions and made no vows, at least not in my presence, perhaps because his father's vows also stood in for his.

CHAPTER FIVE

1. Such scenarios illustrate Viveiros de Castro's (1998) notion of perspectivism.
2. More recent versions of the epic circulated as cassette recordings in Odienné's main market. I use Fofana's transcribed version (M.-J. Derive 1978) because it is available in published form with the original Julakan text.
3. Abbink (1998, 119) details a similar "religious oscillation" and "non-exclusivist identification" between Islam and Christianity in Ethiopia.
4. Abraham's faith in Allah made him a *hanif*, a pre-Jewish, pre-Christian, pre-Muslim monotheist (Gibb 1982, 26).
5. "Wahhabi" Muslims consider themselves to be Muslim reformers inspired by nineteenth-century theologian Shaykh Muhammad Ibn 'Abd al Wahhāb (1992). But I follow Miran (2006a) in distinguishing between "Wahhabis" and "Reformist" Muslims in Côte d'Ivoire because Wahhabis were not the only Muslim reformers in Côte d'Ivoire, and their version of reform was distinctive in its search for religious purity.
6. Widespread Muslim practice began only relatively recently in Denguélé. The first Muslim settlements in Denguélé (Fèrèfougoula, Samatiguila, and Tiémé) began winning converts at the end of the nineteenth century (O'Sullivan 1976, 83, 92).
7. For Mosko (2005, 24), "The term 'fractal' refers to phenomena of 'self-similarity,' or the tendency of patterns or structures to recur on multiple levels or scales." Dozo mimesis recurred at the level of hunting, Islam, and the state.

8. The English imperfect makes the most sense for the context in which Drissa made the remark. We had just returned from hunting.
9. The American English slang exclamation , "Sweet!" captures the relevant meaning.
10. Dozos claimed that animals occasionally identified and explained the novel use of plants to dozos in exchange for being spared from death.
11. Appatam was a weekly interview and entertainment program. Journalists interviewed celebrities on a set designed to resemble the round, open-air, thatched roof *appatam* under which Ivoirians gathered for meals, meetings, and conversation.
12. In Hellweg (2001), I referred to Dramane Coulibaly, Gbaga Soungalo, Fofana Lansiné, and Drissa Koné with pseudonyms: Samka Soumaoro, Zaki Camara, Yacou Koné, and Issa Traoré, respectively. In this book, I use their real names, for which they originally gave me their permission.
13. But then, power is almost universally morally ambiguous. I doubt that Bird and Kendall (1980) or McNaughton (1985) meant to imply that Mande societies are unique in this. They meant only to qualify simplistic readings of the morality of Mande epic heroes. McNaughton (1985) argues that Sunjata Keita and Soumaoro Kanté engaged in duplicity, pillage, and murder in their attempts to vanquish each other. But today, those who hear their tales revere them just as others revere Catherine the Great, Mao-Tse Tung, or Houphouët-Boigny, all of whom had blood on their hands (see S. Diarra 1997 for Houphouët-Boigny). Moral ambiguity always coexists with morality, or there would be nothing "ambiguous" about it.
14. Nor does *nyama*, in Denguélé, seem to be a basis for categorizing together the occupational status groups referred to in Mali as *nyamakala* (Bird, Kendall, and Tera 1995). In Denguélé, the term *nyamakala* refers to bards alone (Toungara 1980).
15. Here Soungalo played on two senses of the word *dangun* in Julakan, that of a crossroads, where Y. Cissé (1994, 67–74) claims that Malian dozos located their *danguns*, and that of the dozos' ritual area per se.
16. Thoyer (1995, 131–175) and Cashion (1984, 2: app. 2) recount Malian *donso* stories with themes similar to those of Manimory's stories.
17. A person, in contrast, would see the dozo in human form in a subversive play on perspectivism (Viveiros de Castro 1998).
18. The incantation compares the chameleon's ability to shape-shift to a dozo's. Note that the first line attributes such abilities to Allah, reconciling sorcery with Islam.
19. Equating a woman with a hyena may express male fears of deception behind the semblance of marital fidelity or indicate that a wife can subvert her husband's prerogatives over her. Female hyenas stand at the top of their social hierarchy. And see Sapir (1981) for other symbolic associations with hyenas.

20. Wassolon is populated mostly by sedentarized Fulbe who speak Madenkan. Diakité, Diallo, Sangaré, and Sidibé—all Fulbe family names—are prevalent in the region.
21. As in domestic contexts, associating over time at a particular place forms close bonds.
22. Malian dozos provided alternate origin stories for this agreement among dozos. These stories make reference to a female Sânin or Sânènè and a male Kontron or Kondoro (Y. Cissé 1994, 37–38; see also Cashion 1984, 1: 104–106; Y. Cissé 1964, 176–181; Herbert 1993, 176–178 passim; Travelé 1928). Y. Cissé (1994, 39–49) also reports an entirely different dozo origin story that also ends in agreement.
23. For Amselle (1998, 121), "[a]ny effort to isolate pagan elements from their Islamic envelope becomes invalid."
24. The Qur'an makes no mention of Esau, but ninth-century Persian Qur'anic exegete al-Tabari (1987, 136–138) notes Esau as the son of Isaac and brother of Jacob, not Ishmael.
25. The prophet Muhammad reached beyond Judaism and Christianity for a precedent for Islam in the person of Abraham, whose existence preceded these other religions and which Qur'anic revelation purportedly superseded (Gibb 1982, 26, 31). Like *dozoya,* Islam took a retromimetic approach to religious pluralism.
26. "In this region, as elsewhere," Amselle (1998, 121) writes, "he is Moslem who considers himself as such."
27. In some cases, precolonial Muslim authorities appear to have gone so far as to condone human sacrifices practiced by local non-Muslim leaders (Person 1968, 143).
28. Just as Sufis accessed divine "grace" (*baraka*) in proximity to saints (Brenner 1988, 34–36; Robinson 2004, 19), dozos communed with Allah through Manimory.
29. Delafosse (1955, 512–513) noted that parents named boys "Mori" who were born with the help of diviners' prayers.
30. Freeborn Muslims were often enslaved in West Africa, generating controversies among Muslim jurists and scholars about the proper criteria for enslavement (Robinson 2004, 65–69).
31. Robinson (2004, 68) writes: "Scholars and traders were concerned that some Muslims were being enslaved and that they might be held accountable for that fact. In reality, there was little inspection and accountability."
32. Samatiguila is the village which Amselle (1998, 77, 122, 123, 137) calls "Sanbatigila" and "Sambatikila." The name means "place of the elephant hunter or elephant owner" in Julakan (O'Sullivan 1976, 68–69).
33. A Wahhabi Muslim community existed in Odienné. Its imams and scholars criticized "traditional" Islam both at their mosque and at the Qur'anic readings they conducted at local funerals.

34. Using the now standard recension of Hafs via ‘Asim (1924 Egyptian version), Lewis would be citing sura 5, verse 35.
35. Like Nabi Inzu, Nabi Youssouf had a double identity, as both Jewish and Egyptian.

CHAPTER SIX

1. States justify the enforcement of laws on two grounds, deontological and teleological, or some combination thereof (Schmidtz 1996, 84–85). In a deontological approach, laws serve as moral goods in themselves. In a teleological approach, the good intentions behind laws can only realize themselves in the laws' application, which the state assures (see Aarnio 1987, 188, 208). Both approaches contrast with that of virtue ethics, which focuses on the cultivation of moral persons from whom right legal conduct automatically flows (cf. Burtness 1999, 60, 76–78).
2. I learned most of what I report on the National Hunters' Association of Mali from an audiocassette that a Malian *donso* by the name of M. Diarra (n.d.) let me record while he was passing through Odienné.
3. For a more recent overview of Malian *donso*s' activities, see Davis (2000, 302–304).
4. I use pseudonyms for the dozos and villages through whom and by which Benkadi came to Côte d'Ivoire, save for Yaya Cissé, N'golo Bamba, Gbèya, Goulia, and Toudougou.
5. Because Moussa Fofana, Odienné's main dozo organizer, accompanied me to Borosso and Yorojan, I was able to interview dozos there. His presence established my credibility with them.
6. Kemba said that he and other Yorojan dozos had heard of Benkadi before Borosso dozos ever contacted them. He said that Malian dozos had already invited him to attend Benkadi meetings in Mali. Their communication reflects well-established transnational links between Ivoirian and Malian dozos. I infer that dozos on both sides of the border knew each other from hunting together and attending each other's dozo funerals. Marriage, kinship, and market ties must also have linked them.
7. Moussa Fofana could not accompany me to Gbèya, the home of N'golo Bamba, another early Benkadi organizer. N'golo appears to have brought Benkadi to Gbèya before Borosso and Yorojan adopted it. Word of Benkadi seems to have spread to Borosso and Yorojan from Gbèya.
8. To my knowledge, Benkadi in Mali never assumed the national police presence that it did in Côte d'Ivoire (see Davis 2000).
9. But according to Kemba, at some point between the establishment of the Malian National Hunters' Association and Malian *donso*s' arrival in Gbèya, Malian *donso*s must have assumed police roles of some sort, at least with regard to livestock theft.
10. Toudougou is the name of a precolonial polity that became an administra-

tive unit (*canton*) under French rule. Today the area corresponds roughly to Denguélé's Goulia subprefecture.

11. According to Kemba, Yaya Cissé owed much of his initial success at establishing Benkadi in Côte d'Ivoire to the fact that Malian dozos had introduced it. Whenever someone suggested change or reform from within, Kemba claimed, others saw the move as a means to avenge past quarrels or advance a personal agenda. Because Malians had proposed Benkadi, Kemba said, Denguélé dozos saw the suggestion as impartial.
12. See Leynaud and Cissé (1978, 310–312) for an etymology of the word. *Ton* also means "law" in Wojɛnɛkakan.
13. This exclusive use of the word *dozoton* surprised me. Malian *donsos* referred to *donso* networks in general as the *donsoton* (Thoyer 1995, 14). But in Denguélé and the rest of Côte d'Ivoire, I never heard the word used to denote anything but Benkadi.
14. The format reminded me of a doctor's radio call-in show—minus the radio and phone.
15. After dozos had assembled in the *dangun* to discuss the health-related matters already mentioned, the most senior ones—less than twenty—left the larger gathering to talk in private about the sorcery attacks. They invited me to join them.
16. Moussa Fofana referred to them as the "grand masters" (*les grands maîtres*).
17. This evidence seems to undermine the idea that the subjugation of game gave dozos a precedent for such torture (see Richards 1996, 181), with the application of pepper to suspects' bodies to extract confessions resembling the way dozos applied plant substances to animals' corpses to dispel *nyama*. The albino man's treatment was particularly unsettling given the historical place that albino persons played as victims in precolonial royal Mande sacrifices (Dieterlen 1988).
18. In this sense, dozos participated in the same "aesthetics of vulgarity" that Mbembe (2001) claimed structured the state.
19. *Sobisi* appears to denote gonorrhea.
20. Kemba added that women who removed uncovered pots from fires might give birth to deaf-mutes. He implied that dozos wanted to educate women about the problem in order to prevent it. Leaving food open to exposure by disease-causing elements opened babies' mouths and ears to congenital damage.
21. Futu (*foutou*, in French) is a dish made of pounded plantains or yams. One typically divides it into fist-sized ovoid portions. One consumes it by removing small clumps, partially impaling each one on the middle finger of one's right hand, dipping it in the accompanying sauce, and plopping it into the mouth.
22. An interesting parallel lies in the ethnicization of hometown associations in Côte d'Ivoire as described by Woods (1994, 479–480). The connections that Benkadi established between local citizens and officials, on one

hand, and national authorities, on the other, resembled those established previously among these same parties by migrants' hometown associations. Benkadi was hardly exceptional or original in organizing state-citizen ties along ethnic lines. The fact that Benkadi's members were armed made its case different, although dozos' initial reasons for arming had little to do with ethnically based political claims.

23. Inza Fanny died c. 2001.
24. They may have had the National Hunters' Association of Mali in mind.
25. Fanny did so hoping to win international funding for AE projects.
26. The government published its approval of AE as an NGO on June 18, 1992 in its official record of legislative and executive acts, the *Journal officiel de la République de Côte d'Ivoire* (République de Côte d'Ivoire 1992b).
27. As Tsing writes (2005, 13), "There is no reason to assume that collaborators share common goals." Dozos shared only a minority of Fanny's environmentally related aims, and the security-related aims they did share went unarticulated in written form.
28. Fanny's goals vaguely reflected the contemporary discourse of global ecological activism that links the exploitation of the environment to global sociopolitical problems (cf. Smith and Vivekananda 2007).
29. Tsing (2005, 13, 246–247) notes that global collaborations almost always occur between parties working at cross-purposes, just as dozos, Fanny, and the Ivoirian government appeared to be doing. "The more different they are, the more they must reach for barely overlapping understandings of the situation." Such mutual misunderstandings made dozos' alliance with AE and Benkadi's alliance with the state temporary marriages of convenience.
30. Inza Konaté told me during our interview that Fanny had wooed dozos to join AE by promising to intervene with the state on dozos' behalf.
31. The same prefect made news by reportedly insisting that he arrive at the conference in a four-wheel-drive sports utility vehicle rented by AE after he refused the less expensive Peugeot R12 that AE had proposed. He allegedly described the latter as "unworthy of his rank" (*Nouvel Horizon* 1993).
32. Minister Koné came from the northern city of Katiola.
33. Given Mr. Coulibaly's reluctance to discuss Benkadi matters, I avoided asking to tape-record our conversation. Afterward, I wrote down what I remembered of his remarks. We spoke in French.
34. I saw Fanny at his home in Yopougon on June 24, 1997, the day he met with government officials to discuss AE's future. He seemed deeply shaken by the encounter.

CHAPTER SEVEN

1. Bearpark and Schultz (2007, 85) argue that private security companies provide a useful service as long as it does not "come at the price of further damaging social cohesion whereby security becomes a commodity that

only the wealthy can afford and whereby the disenfranchised remain the disenfranchised." In Côte d'Ivoire, state police were helping only those who could afford them. Here the privatization of security appeared to follow or at least run parallel to its commoditization by those who were charged by law with providing it.

2. See Cashion (1984, 2: 192–193) and McNaughton (1988, 143–144) for discussions of similar objects.
3. Allen (1999, 8) has linked the rise in cannabis cultivation in Côte d'Ivoire directly to falling cocoa prices, and San-Pédro was a major exit point for shipments of Ivoirian cocoa.
4. I made no attempt to help the dozos with their work and felt quite uncomfortable as an observer of the events I am about to describe.
5. Cell phones were not yet widely available in West Africa.
6. The council was a group of thirty-one people elected on the mayoral ballot to deliberate and vote on issues concerning community development, the city budget, municipal investment, public services and salaries, and citizens' general welfare (République de Côte d'Ivoire n.d., 8–13).
7. *Kabla* means "neighborhood" in Wojɛnɛkakan. *Dugu* means "village" or "town." The suffix *-tigi* means "owner," "chief," or "master." *Kablatigi* translates as "neighborhood chief," *dugutigi* as "village" or "town chief."
8. The state accommodated dozos' mostly oral procedures as much as dozos adapted to the state's written ones, mostly to protect itself from establishing a written precedent for Benkadi's activities. The state pursued similar arrangements with dozos across the country.
9. In Hellweg (2004, 19), I mistakenly wrote that patrols began in Odienné in 1996.
10. I remained at the dozos' headquarters at Mr. Fofana's request. We both thought that I might jeopardize Benkadi's status by accompanying dozos, given the prefect's order that dozos bring as little attention to themselves as possible.
11. Coincidentally, Ivoirian pop singer Meiway donned dozo garb to perform at a concert in Abidjan that same night.
12. Tanny's official title was Secrétaire Générale de la Gendarmerie Nationale.
13. The General Administration of National Security (Direction Générale de la Sûreté Nationale), Côte d'Ivoire's national police headquarters, administered national police matters under the Ministry of Security.
14. Elsewhere in Africa, restorative justice has played an official role in national life. South Africa's Truth and Reconciliation Commission is the most famous example (Wilson 2001, 11, 13, 161). In Uganda, "local council" (LC) courts based on "customary law" have officially accomplished what dozo courts unofficially did. "The LC courts . . . operate at the community level, and have the power to order reconciliation, compensation and apology, among other sanctions." Official status has not protected LC courts from criticism for partisanship, corruption, and incompetence, but "the LC

courts do substantially increase access to justice: large majorities of those surveyed find them easily accessible, fast and cheap" (Robins 2009, 65).

15. Hagberg (1998) observed such tensions degenerate into violence in Burkina Faso.
16. The crowd was still assembled when I arrived at the office.
17. The Grands Travaux ("Great Works") supervised civil engineering projects, including the construction of the Basilica of Our Lady of Peace in Yamoussoukro.
18. The dozos who captured the suspect related these events to me shortly after their return to the Benkadi office.
19. This was more than I had ever seen police give the victims of their extortion.
20. Fofana used the word "brothers" to mean same-gendered age mates.
21. *Kɔnyɔ* means "bride," and *ka di* is the infinitive, "to give."
22. I had not previously met Abou.
23. Dozos might have accepted the constitution's endorsement of the Universal Declaration of Human Rights (Aggrey 1995a), given dozos' readiness to adopt state approaches, but the state itself was violating and manipulating the law on a regular basis.
24. Manimory sacrificed his family as the premise for sacrificing himself to protect future hunters so they could gift their families with game meat. Benkadi dozos used excessive violence to enhance their authority. If dozo violence was amoral in the former case, it was immoral in the latter. My aim is to understand the different logics behind these forms of violence regardless of their moral quality (see Schmidt and Schröder 2001; Whitehead 2004).
25. Fofana established a rival dozo organization in Odienné that included only a handful of dissident dozos.

CHAPTER EIGHT

1. When Dramane was young, enemies of Nienesso's *kɔma* association, which Dramane's father led, attacked Dramane through sorcery as a means of injuring his father. The attack left Dramane's right hand and left foot partially paralyzed, causing him to take slower strides with his left foot than with his right.
2. The word *diden* also named the girl or young woman who sang at weddings and young people's performances (*kamberɛntɔrɔn*) in Denguélé. In Niamasso, she held a crescent-bladed axe identical to the one dozos often used. A chorus of adolescents and young adults accompanied her. They sang at intermissions between comic masked skits performed by young men in which male dancers parodied dozo exploits, depicting dozos as bumbling fools chasing more astute animals depicted by men in masks. Such female-associated references to dozo singers are revealing. Recall that

an unmarried dozo offered the neck of slain game to his sister-in-law in the compound and that dozos gave the neck of a sacrificed goat to singers in the *dangun* (see chap. 4). Like the *diden* and the sister of an unmarried dozo, the *ngɔnunfɔcɛ* played both a respectively crticial and supportive role vis-à-vis dozos. The *diden* sang to accompany parodies of dozo behavior while an unmarried dozo's sister-in-law prepared a dozo's meals. Dozo singers played an analogous auxiliary role in securing meat for human consumption.

3. Odiennéka use the related expression, *I ni koŋ ɔ*, to praise the work of non-dozos in the bush (*koŋ*).
4. Yanfolila is a region in southern Mali that borders on northwestern Côte d'Ivoire and eastern Guinea.
5. Dramane only sang the song *mazan*, for instance, at *kozi*s. During this song, dancing was limited to those dozos who had lost their first wife and their first son, like Manimory.
6. October 13, 1996.
7. Chérif Keita informed me of this etymology (personal communication, April 1999, Carleton College, Northfield, Minnesota).
8. Walking onto a farmer's field at dusk with Drissa to hunt usually startled a handful of nightjars from the soil where they were waiting to fly up and devour flying insects.
9. Dramane's poetic technique recalled Turner's (1967, 105) appeal to W. James's (1918, 506) "law of dissociation":

   > [W]hen *a* and *b* [occur] together as parts of the same total object without being discriminated, the occurrence of one of these, *a*, in a new combination *ax*, favors the discrimination of *a*, *b*, and *x* from one another. As James himself put it, "What is associated now with one thing and now with another, tends to become dissociated from either, and to grow into an object of abstract contemplation by the mind . . ."

   Dramane likened the image of the "nightjar's call," *a*—which dozos associated with the power to kill—with *x*, a series of images representing various kinds of dozo power: *dozoya* generally, sorcery, power objects, weapons, and physical endurance. In this way, Dramane singled out *b*, the ability to kill on the hunt, implicit in the nightjar image and underlying all dozo powers, as dozos' most definitive characteristic.
10. Dramane often used the technique of multiple layering in his songs, as did other dozo singers. Hoffman (1995, 40–43) has discussed similar poetic strategies in the songs of Mande griots.
11. He could have used the Julakan synonym, *ferinya*.
12. By "real," Dramane meant something akin to the sense of "being real" or "keeping it real," from African American English. Dramane kept *dozoya* "real" by provoking dozos.
13. After we spoke, I returned to my house in Nienesso and wrote in English

what I remembered of our conversation. I was unable to tape-record Dramane's words, but they displayed the same artful, syllogistic style reflected in my translation. The structure of Dramane's statement made it easier to recall.

14. By "objective," I mean to denote how singers brought dozos to an awareness of themselves and their hunting abilities that could deepen through time. Singers appealed to what Nagel (1986, 4) has called a "method of understanding":

    > To acquire a more objective understanding of some aspect of life or the world, we step back from our initial view of it and form a new conception which has that view and its relationship to the world as its object. In other words, we place ourselves in the world that is to be understood. The old view then comes to be regarded as an appearance, more subjective than the new view, and correctable and confirmable by reference to it. The process can be repeated, yielding a still more objective conception.

    Because Dramane knew the histories of the dozos to whom he sang, he could provoke them to greater and greater achievements. Like sacrifice, singing and listening to songs amounted to technologies of the self (Foucault 1988).
15. I have pursued the ethnopoetic analysis of Dramane's song to the extent that I can to illuminate the parallels between its structure and content, on one hand, and the interactions among its participants on the other.
16. Since Dramane's idiomatic use of Julakan surpassed my linguistic abilities, Drissa Koné transcribed the Julakan texts and translated them into French. I worked from the French and Julakan versions to translate them into English.
17. Numbers correspond to the lines of Dramane's song.
18. Sy Brahima was from the village of Zegbao. He used the interrogative marker *na* as opposed to the *wa* used by most Odiennéka.
19. Spectators made more comments in the scenes to come, but Dramane ignored them in all but one other case, when the remark likewise reinforced his message. I only record those to which he responded.
20. In English, I have rendered the word "Jula" in the plural to express the collective sense of the word that Dramane intended.
21. In Wilshire's (1982, 43) terms, Dramane engaged his audience "explicitly with problems of standing in and involvement"—with the verisimilitude of dramatic portrayal at the heart of performance. Dramane asked non-dozos and dozos whether they were willing to let Mamadou "stand in" for their expectations of what a real dozo should be. This remained to be seen, keeping the audience on edge, especially since such unresolved tensions threatened to undermine the agreeable atmosphere deemed necessary for a *kozi*.

22. Drissa told me that Dramane referred here primarily to Mamadou's apprentices. Anything they might have killed that night would have been attributed to Mamadou. By the same token, Drissa added, any dozo who hunted immediately after Dramane sang to Mamadou would have killed game in Mamadou's name.
23. The verb comes from the French *presser*, "to hurry."
24. Drissa translated *dalulu* as "verses" (*versets*). He meant Qur'anic verses, implying a close link between Muslim and dozo occult knowledge. See McNaughton (1988, 42–43) for more on *daliluw* (the Bamanankan cognate of *dalulu*) in Mali.
25. Odiennéka often avoided direct eye contact with others to show respect, especially before elders and superiors. Powerful dozos had no reason to avert their glance.
26. Soumbala is a pungent spice made from seeds of the néré tree used in cooking and purchased in markets in Côte d'Ivoire and across West Africa.
27. People formerly lit dry bark in tortoise shells to carry fire safely from one place to another.
28. The nearest place that I knew elephants to live was Comoé National Park in northeastern Côte d'Ivoire.

CHAPTER NINE

1. Akindès (2004, 30) has described Guéï's version of *ivoirité* as more inclusive than the implicitly pro-Akan version promoted by Bédié: "It is henceforth less Akan and more disposed to the wider inclusion of those originating in the South, Center, and West" (31). It still stigmatized those of northern descent.
2. Guéï's elimination of the PDCI from his government certainly qualified the purported inclusiveness of his version of *ivoirité* (cf. Akindès 2004, 30–31).
3. Guéï accused Generals Palenfo and Coulibaly of plotting to assassinate him. They went into hiding. Gbagbo imprisoned them after they reemerged following Guéï's overthrow in September 2000 (IRIN 2001).
4. From here they first allegedly tried to overthrow President Gbagbo in an unsuccessful coup attempt perpetrated on January 7–8, 2001 (Banégas and Losch 2002, 143–144).
5. Along with Young Patriot leader Eugène Djué and Martin Kouakou Fofié, the New Forces commander in Korhogo, Blé Goudé is one of three Ivoirian figures who face an international assets freeze and travel ban (IRIN 2006).

References

Aarnio, Aulis. 1987. *The Rational as Reasonable: A Treatise on Legal Justification*. Dordrecht: Kluwer.

Abbink, Jon. 1998. "An Historical-Anthropological Approach to Islam in Ethiopia: Issues of Identity and Politics." *Journal of African Cultural Studies* 11, no. 2: 109–124.

Abiali, P. M. 1992. "Insécurité: Le cri de détresse des commerçants." *Fraternité Matin*, 20 July.

———. 1994. "Sécurité: Ce qui attend le nouveau ministre." *Fraternité Matin*, 3 January.

Abrahams, Ray. 1987. "Sungusungu: Village Vigilante Groups in Tanzania." *African Affairs* 86, no. 343: 179–196.

Adiaffi, Jean-Marie. 1996. "Diversité culturelle, nation et identité ivoirienne." *Ethics* 1 (October): 61–77.

Afrique Environnementale. n.d.a. "Présentation." Typescript (photocopy). Abidjan: Afrique Environnementale.

———. n.d.b. "Recommendations du Séminaire de Kaniasso." Typescript (photocopy). Abidjan: Afrique Environnementale.

———. n.d.c. "Les commissions spécialisées." Typescript (photocopy). Abidjan: Afrique Environnementale.

Agamben, Giorgio. 1998 [1995]. *Homo sacer: Sovereign Power and Bare Life*. Stanford: Stanford University Press.

———. 2005. *State of Exception*. Chicago: University of Chicago Press.

Agence France Presse. 2003a. "Details of Three Ivory Coast Rebel Groups and French Forces." January 12. http://www.reliefweb.int/rw/rwb.nsf/AllDocsByUNID/0f237eb58424e12249256cad000bac7b. Accessed August 29, 2009.

———. 2003b. "Fusillades d'Abidjan: La presse spécule sur l'identité des assailants." December 13. http://www.abidjan.net. Accessed December 13, 2004.

Agence Ivoirienne de Presse. 1995. "Duékoué: Regain de criminalité." *Fraternité Matin*, 10 May.

———. 1996a. "Korhogo: Les dozos traqués par la justice." *Le Jour* 382, 4–5 May, 2.

———. 1996b. "Sécurité: Les Dozos fâchés contre le ministre." *SoirINFO* 635, 10 September.

Aggrey, Albert. 1981. *Code penal.* Abidjan: Juris Éditions.

———. 1994. *La Constitution.* Abidjan: Juris Éditions.

———. 1995a. *La Constitution.* Abidjan: Juris Éditions.

———. 1995b. *Code de la nationalité.* Abidjan: Juris Éditions.

———. 1995c. *Guide des elections.* Vol. 2, *Les candidats.* Abidjan: Juris Éditions.

———. 2000. *La constitution.* Abidjan: Juris Éditions.

Akindès, Francis. 2004. *Les racines de la crise militaro-politique en Côte d'Ivoire.* Dakar: Codesria.

Akpo Kouassi, Karrhel. 1994. "Akoupé: Recrudescence du banditisme." *La Voie*, 17 January.

Akrou, J. B. 1991. "Drogue: Le sergent de police transportait 105 kg de cannabis dans sa voiture." *Fraternité Matin*, 4 September.

Al Séni, D. 2003. "Zakaria Koné (Chef des opérations militaires du MPCI à Vavoua): 'Je ne désarme pas tant que Gbagbo est au pouvoir.'" *Le Patriote*, 26 March.

Alexandre, Pierre. 1970. "The Problems of Chieftaincies in French Speaking Africa." In *West African Chiefs: Their Changing Status under Colonial Rule and Independence*, edited by Michael Crowder and Obaro Ikime. New York: Africana Publishing Corporation.

Allen, Chris. 1999. "Africa and the Drugs Trade." *Review of African Political Economy* 26, no. 79: 5–11.

Amin, Samir. 1967. *Le développement du capitalisme en Côte d'Ivoire.* Paris: Éditions de Minuit.

———. 1973 [1971]. *Neo-colonialism in West Africa.* Middlesex: Penguin.

Amnesty International. 1994. "Legal Concern / Fear of Ill-Treatment." AFR 31/01/94. London: Amnesty International. http://www.amnesty.org/en/library/asset/AFR31/001/1994/en/843e89d8-ec07–11dd-85b9–0939011eabc9/afr310011994en.pdf. Accessed June 10, 2010.

———. 1995. "Fear of Ill-Treatment / Health Concern / Possible Prisoners of Conscience." AFR 31/05/95. London: Amnesty International. http://www.amnesty.org/en/library/asset/AFR31/006/1995/en/c8a3f05a-eb24-11dd-92ac-295bdf97101f/afr310061995en.pdf. Accessed June 10, 2010.

———. 1997. "Legal Concern / Fear of Ill Treatment." AFR 31/01/07. London: Amnesty International. http://www.amnesty.org/en/library/asset/AFR31/001/1997/en/93a61bb9-eeac0–11dd-b6f5–3be39665bc30/afr310011997en.pdf.

———. 2003. "Côte d'Ivoire: A Succession of Unpunished Crimes; From the Massacre of Gendarmes at Bouaké to the Mass Graves of Daloa, Monoko-Zohi and Man." London: Amnesty International. http://www.amnesty.org/en/

library/asset/AFR31/007/2003/en/4dd055a9-d72a-11dd-b0cc-1f0860013475/afr310072003en.pdf. Accessed August 29, 2009.

———. 2005. "Côte d'Ivoire: Threats Hang Heavy over the Future." London: Amnesty International. http://www.amnesty.org/en/library/asset/AFR31/013/2005/en/1f92b6b2-d49f-11dd-8a23-d58a49c0d652/afr310132005en.pdf Accessed August 29, 2009.

Amondji, Marcel. 1984. *Félix Houphouët et la Côte d'Ivoire: L'envers d'une légende.* Paris: Karthala.

Amselle, Jean-Loup. 1985. "Le Wahabisme à Bamako (1945–1985)." *Canadian Journal of African Studies* 19, no. 2: 345–357.

———. 1998 [1990]. *Mestizo Logics: Anthropology of Identity in Africa and Elsewhere.* Stanford: Stanford University Press.

Anderson, Benedict. 1991. *Imagined Communities: Reflections on the Origin and Spread of Nationalism.* New York: Verso.

Antoine, Philippe, A. Dubresson, and A. Manou-Savina. 1987. *Abidjan "côté cours": Pour comprendre la question de l'habitat.* Paris: Karthala.

Aristotle. 2000. *Nicomachean Ethics.* Cambridge: Cambridge University Press.

Arnaud, J. C. 1980. "Dabadougou Mafiéléni: Un village malinké de la région d'Odienné." *Annales de l'Université d'Abidjan, série G (Géographie)* 9: 197–231.

Artexaga, Begoña. 2003. "Maddening States." *Annual Review of Anthropology* 32: 393–410.

Assi, Amédée. 1997 "L'édito: Dibonan, où es-tu?" *Actuel,* 24 March, 1.

Austen, Ralph. 1987. *African Economic History.* London: James Currey.

Ayers, Alison. 2006. "Demystifying Democratisation: The Global Constitution of (Neo)Liberal Polities in Africa." *Third World Quarterly* 27, no. 2: 321–338.

Ayittey, George. 1998. *Africa in Chaos.* New York: St. Martin's Press.

———. 2006 [1991]. *Indigenous African Institutions.* Second edition. Ardsley, NY: Transnational Publishers.

Azam, Jean-Paul. 2006. "The Paradox of Power Reconsidered: A Theory of Political Regimes in Africa." *Journal of African Economies* 15, no. 1: 26–58.

B. K., Lionnelle. 1994. "Recrudescence du banditisme: Les chauffeurs de taxis, proie facile des brigands." *La Voie,* 14 September.

Bâ, Amadou Hampaté. 1972. *Aspects de la civilisation africaine.* Paris: Présence africaine.

Badié, Raphaël. 1994. "Agboville: Le banditisme devient inquiétant." *La Voie,* 18 September.

Badmus, Isiaka. 2009. "Even the Stones Are Burning: Explaining the Ethnic Dimensions of the Civil War in *Côte d'Ivoire.*" *Journal of Social Sciences* 18, no. 1: 45–57.

Bah, Bernadette. 1996. "Polémique autour des 'Dozo': Fologo désavoue Dibonan Koné." *Le Jour* 499, 23 September, 3.

Bailleul, Père Charles. 2000a. *Dictionnaire Bambara-Français.* Bamako: Éditions Donniya.

———. 2000b. *Dictionnaire Français-Bambara.* Bamako: Éditions Donniya.

Bailly, Ferdinand. 1997. "Les dozos battent à sang une famille." *Actuel*, 28 October.

Bailly, Séry. 2005. *Ne pas perdre le Nord*. Abidjan: Éditions Universitaires de Côte d'Ivoire.

Balandier, Georges. 1957. *Afrique ambigüe*. Paris: Plon.

———. 1970. *The Sociology of Black Africa: Social Dynamics in Central Africa*. New York: Praeger Publishers.

Balint-Kurti, Daniel. 2007. "Côte d'Ivoire's Forces Nouvelles." London: Chatham House. http://www.chathamhouse.org.uk/files/9735_ivorycoast0907.pdf. Accessed June 18, 2010.

Bamba, Franck. 1994. "Gagnoa: L'insécurité est garantie." *La Voie*, 7 April.

Bamba, Idrissa. 1997. "Bongouanou: Les dozos, un danger permanent." *Notre Chance* 98, 13–19 March.

Banégas, Richard, and Bruno Losch. 2002. "La Côte d'Ivoire au bord de l'implosion." *Politique africaine* 87: 139–161.

Banégas, Richard, and Ruth Marshall-Fratani. 2007. "Côte d'Ivoire: Negotiating Identity and Citizenship through the Barrel of a Gun." In *African Guerrillas: Raging against the Machine*, edited by Morten Bøås and Kevin C. Dunn. Boulder: Lynne Rienner Publishers.

Banto, D. 1997. "La galère des policiers." *Ivoir'soir*, 13–14 September.

Barry, Josette. 1992. "Trafic de drogue: Les réseaux Inza et Sidibé n'ont pas fonctionné." *Fraternité Matin*, 2 March.

Bassett, Thomas. 1988. "The Political Ecology of Peasant-Herder Conflicts in the Northern Ivory Coast." *Annals of the Association of American Geographers* 78, no. 3: 453–472.

———. 2003. "Dangerous Pursuits: Hunter Associations (*donzo ton*) and National Politics in Côte d'Ivoire." *Africa* 73, no. 1: 1–30.

———. 2004. "Containing the *Donzow:* The Politics of Scale in Côte d'Ivoire." *Africa Today* 50, no. 4: 31–49.

Bateson, Gregory. 1958. *Naven: The Culture of the Iatmul People of New Guinea as Revealed through a Study of the "Naven" Ceremonial*. Stanford: Stanford University Press.

Baxter, Joan. 2003. "Profile: Ivory Coast's Charming Rebel." London: BBC. http:/news.bbc.co.uk/2/hi/africa/2793729.stm. Accessed June 18, 2010.

Bayart, Jean-François, Stephen Ellis, and Béatrice Hibou. 1999. *Criminalization of the State in Africa*. Bloomington: Indiana University Press.

Bearpark, Andy, and Sabrina Schulz. 2007. "The Private Security Challenge in Africa: Problems and Options for Regulation." In *Private Security in Africa: Manifestations, Challenges and Regulations*, edited by Sabelo Gumedze. ISS Monograph Series, 139. Pretoria: Institute for Security Studies.

Beidelman, Thomas. 1966. "The Ox and Nuer Sacrifice: Some Freudian Hypotheses about Nuer Symbolism." *Man* n.s. 1, no. 4: 453–467.

el-Bekri, Abou-Obeïd. 1965. *Description de l'Afrique septentrionale*. Translated by Mac Guckin de Slane. Paris: Jean Maisonneuve.

Benedict, Ruth. 1934. *Patterns of Culture*. Boston: Houghton Mifflin Co.

Benjamin, Walter. 1968. "Theses on the Philosophy of History." In *Illuminations: Essays and Reflections*, edited by Hannah Arendt, 253–264. New York: Schocken Books.

———. 1978. "Critique of Violence." In *Reflections: Essays, Aphorisms, Autobiographical Writings*, edited by Peter Demetz, 277–301. New York: Harcourt Brace Jovanovich.

———. 2005 [1933]. "On the Mimetic Faculty." In *Walter Benjamin: Selected Writings, Volume 2: Part 2*, edited by Michael W. Jennings, Gary Smith, and Howard Eiland. Cambridge, MA: Harvard University Press.

Benot, Yves. 1989. *Les députés africains au Palais Bourbon, de 1914 à 1958*. Paris: Éditions Chaka.

Bhabha, Homi. 1994. *The Location of Culture*. London: Routledge.

Binsbergen, Wim M. J. van. 1981. *Religious Change in Zambia: Exploratory Studies*. London: Kegan Paul.

Bird, Charles, and Martha Kendall. 1980. "The Mande Hero: Text and Context." In *Explorations in African Systems of Thought*, edited by I. Karp and C. Bird. Bloomington: Indiana University Press.

Bird, Charles, Martha Kendall, and Kalilou Tera. 1995. "Etymologies of *nyamakala*." In *Status and Identity in West Africa: Nyamakalaw of Mande*, edited by David Conrad and Barbara Frank. Bloomington: Indiana University Press.

Bledson, Mathieu. 1997. "La dose dozo." *Actuel* 378, 28 October, 8.

Bloch, Maurice. 1991. *Prey into Hunter: The Politics of Religious Experience*. Cambridge: Cambridge University Press.

Boas, Franz. 1974 [1889]. "On Alternating Sounds." In *A Franz Boas Reader: The Shaping of American Anthropology, 1883–1911*, edited by G. W. Stocking, Jr. Chicago: University of Chicago Press.

Bobissi, Christian. 1995. "Terreur sur Abidjan: 23 écoliers assassiné en 2 mois." *La Voie*, 19 May.

Boddy, Janice. 1989. *Wombs and Alien Spirits: Women, Men, and the Zar Cult in Northern Sudan*. Madison: University of Wisconsin Press.

Bombet, Émile Constant. 1996. "Ivoirité et intégration nationale." *Ethics* 1 (October): 135–144.

Bonnassieux, Alain. 1987. *L'autre Abidjan: Chronique d'un quartier oublié*. Paris: Éditions Karthala.

Boone, Catherine. 1998. "State Building in the African Countryside: Structure and Politics at the Grassroots." *Journal of Development Studies* 34, no. 4: 1–31.

———. 2003a. "Decentralization as Political Strategy in West Africa." *Comparative Political Studies* 36, no. 4: 355–380.

———. 2003b. *Political Topographies of the African State: Territorial Authority and Institutional Choice*. Cambridge: Cambridge University Press.

Bouabré, Paul. 1996. "Le ministre Dibonan à Man: 'Les bandits seront dénichés, abattus et filmés.'" *Le Jour* 485, 6 September, 4.

Bouquet, Christian. 2005. *Géopolitique de la Côte d'Ivoire*. Paris: Armand Colin.

Bourdieu, Pierre. 1977. *Outline of a Theory of Practice.* Cambridge: Cambridge University Press.

Braconnier, Cassian. 1999. *Dictionnaire du dioula d'Odienné: Parler de Samatiguila.* Vols. 1–2. Paris: Linguistique africaine.

Braconnier, Cassian, and Sanoussi Diaby. 1982. *Dioula d'Odienné (Parler de Samatiguila): Matériel lexical.* Abidjan: Institut de Linguistique Appliquée.

Braconnier, Cassian, John Maire, and Kalilou Tera. 1983. *Études sur le mandingue de Côte d'Ivoire.* Abidjan: Agence de Coopération Culturelle et Technique/ Institut de Linguistique Appliquée.

Brenner, Louis. 1988. "Concepts of *ṭarīqa* in West Africa: The Case of Qādiriyya." In *Charisma and Brotherhood in African Islam,* edited by Donal B. Cruise O'Brien and Christian Coulon. Oxford: Clarendon Press.

———. 1993. "Constructing Muslim Identities in Mali." In *Muslim Identity and Social Change in Sub-Saharan Africa,* edited by L. Brenner. Bloomington: Indiana University Press.

Brett-Smith, Sarah. 1994. *The Making of Bamana Sculpture: Creativity and Gender.* New York: Cambridge University Press.

Brunie, Valérie. n.d.a. *La Côte d'Ivoire: Un nouveau far west?* Vol. 1. Abidjan: Mission Française de Coopération et d'Action Culturelle.

———. n.d.b. *Combattre l'insécurité.* Vol. 2. Abidjan: Mission Française de Coopération et d'Action Culturelle.

Burke, Kenneth. 1957. *Counter-Statement.* Chicago: University of Chicago Press.

Burtness, James. 1999. *Consequences: Morality, Ethics, and the Future.* Minneapolis: Fortress Press.

Camara, Sory. 1992. *Gens de la parole: Essai sur la condition et le rôle des griots dans la société malinké.* Paris: Karthala.

Campbell, Bonnie. 1995. "L'Ajustement en Afrique: L'expérience de la Côte d'Ivoire." *Canadian Journal of African Studies* 29, no. 2: 290–302.

Carr, Matt. 1995a. *Wojènèkakan, the Jula of Odienné: A Basic Grammar.* Odienné: SIM International.

———. 1995b. *Wojènèkakan, the Jula of Odienné: Dictionary.* Odienné: SIM International.

Carsten, Janet, and Stephen Hugh-Jones. 1995. *About the House: Lévi-Strauss and Beyond.* Cambridge: Cambridge University Press.

Cashion, Gerald. 1984. "Hunters of the Mande: A Behavioral Code and Worldview Derived from the Study of Their Folklore." 2 vols. Ph.D. dissertation, Indiana University.

Certeau, Michel de. 1984. *The Practice of Everyday Life.* Berkeley: University of California Press.

Chabal, Patrick, and Jean-Pascal Daloz. 1999. *Africa Works: Disorder as Political Instrument.* Bloomington: Indiana University Press.

Charry, Eric. 2000. *Mande Music: Traditional and Modern Music of the Maninka and Mandinka of Western Africa.* Chicago: University of Chicago Press.

Chauveau, Jean-Pierre, and Koffi Samuel Bobo. 2003. "La situation de guerre dans l'arène villageoise: Un exemple dans le Centre-Ouest ivoirien." *Politique africaine* 89: 12–32.

Chirot, Daniel. 2006. "The Debacle in Côte d'Ivoire." *Journal of Democracy* 17, no. 2: 63–77.

Cissé, Boubacar. 1997. "Divo: Les dozos rançonnent les populations." *Le Jour* 841, 18 November, 3.

Cissé, Diango. 1970. *Structures des Malinké de Kita.* Bamako: Éditions Populaires.

Cissé, Ibrahima Bacongo. 2007. *Alassane Dramane Ouattara: Histoire d'une vie singulière, légende et épopée.* Abidjan: Nouvelles Éditions Ivoiriennes/CEDA.

Cissé, Youssouf Tata. 1964. "Notes sur les sociétés des chasseurs Malinké." *Journal de la société des africanistes* 34, no. 2: 175–226.

——. 1973. "Signes graphiques, représentations, concepts et tests relatifs à la personne chez les Malinké et les Bambara du Mali." In *La notion de personne en Afrique noire,* edited by Germaine Dieterlen. Colloque international sur la notion de personne en Afrique noire. Paris: Éditions du Centre National de la Recherche Scientifique.

———. 1994. *La confrérie des chasseurs Malinké et Bambara: Mythes, rites et récits initiatiques.* Ivry: Éditions Nouvelles du Sud.

Clough, Marshall. 2003. "Mau Mau and the Contest for Memory." In *Mau Mau and Nationhood: Arms, Authority and Narration,* edited by E. S. Atieno Odhiambo and John Lonsdale. Oxford: James Currey.

Cohen, Abner. 1981. *The Politics of Elite Culture: Explorations in the Dramaturgy of Power in a Modern African Society.* Berkeley: University of California Press.

Cohen, William B. 1971. *Rulers of Empire: The French Colonial Service in Africa.* Stanford: Hoover Institution Press.

Collett, Moya. 2006. "Ivoirian Identity Constructions: Ethnicity and Nationalism in the Prelude to Civil War." *Nations and Nationalism* 12, no. 4: 613–629.

Comaroff, Jean. 1985. *Body of Power, Spirit of Resistance: The Culture and History of a South African People.* Chicago: University of Chicago Press.

Comaroff, Jean, and John Comaroff. 1993. *Modernity and Its Malcontents: Ritual and Power in Postcolonial Africa.* Chicago: University of Chicago Press.

———. 1997. *Of Revelation and Revolution.* Vol. 2, *The Dialectics of Modernity on a South African Frontier.* Chicago: University of Chicago Press.

———. 1999. Introduction to *Civil Society and the Political Imagination in Africa,* edited by John L. and Jean Comaroff. Chicago: University of Chicago Press.

———. 2001. "Millennial Capitalism: First Thoughts on a Second Coming." In *Millennial Capitalism and the Culture of Neoliberalism,* edited by Jean Comaroff and John L. Comaroff. Durham, NC: Duke University Press.

———, eds. 2006. *Law and Disorder in the Postcolony.* Chicago: University of Chicago Press.

Conrad, David. 1995. "Blind Man Meets Prophet: Oral Tradition, Islam, and *funé* Identity." In *Status and Identity in West Africa: Nyamakalaw of Mande,* edited by David Conrad and Barbara Frank. Bloomington: Indiana University Press.

Cosentino, Donald. 1989. "Midnight Charters Muso Wo and Mende Myths of Chaos." In *Creativity of Power: Cosmology and Action in African Societies*, edited by William Arens and Ivan Karp. Washington, DC: Smithsonian Institution Press.

Contamin, Bernard, and Bruno Losch. 2000. "Côte d'Ivoire: La voie étroite." *Politique africaine* 77: 117–128.

Coote, Jeremy. 1996. "Aesthetics Is a Cross-Cultural Category: For the Motion." In *Key Debates in Anthropology*, edited by Tim Ingold, 266–271. London: Routledge.

Cotten, Ann-Marie. 1969. "Le développement urbain d'Odienné: Essai d'explication." *Cahiers d'ORSTOM*, sér. Sci. hum. 6, no. 2: 22–49.

Coulibaly, Moussa, and Takehiko Haraguchi. 1993. *Lexique du dioula*. Abidjan: Institut de Linguistique Appliquée.

Coulibaly, S. Voltaire. 1996. "Bouaké: Dibonan Koné déclare la guerre aux Dozos." *SoirINFO* 634, 9 September, 9.

———. 1997. "Un jeune homme abattu par un dozo: La population s'insurge." *SoirINFO* 729, 3 January, 11.

Courchamp, Raymond. 1995. "Évaluation retrospective des programmes d'appui à la sécurité en Côte d'Ivoire." Unpublished MS, Salle de documentation, French Embassy, Abidjan.

Crespi, Franco. 1992. *Social Action and Power*. Oxford: Blackwell.

Crook, Richard C. 1990. "Politics, the Cocoa Crisis, and Administration in Côte d'Ivoire." *Journal of Modern African Studies* 28, no. 4: 649–669.

———. 1997. "Winning Coalitions and Ethno-Regional Politics: The Failure of the Opposition in the 1990 and 1995 Elections in Côte d'Ivoire." *African Affairs* 96: 215–242.

Crowder, Michael, and Obaro Ikime. 1970. *West African Chiefs: Their Changing Status under Colonial Rule and Independence*. New York: Africana Publishing Corporation.

Cuello, Père Gabriel, and Loïc Robin. 2005. *Les Malinké du Konkodugu (Mali)*. Paris: L'Harmattan.

D. S. 1995. "Hold-up devant la Bicici Cité des Arts: Un client perd 15 millions de francs." *Fraternité Matin*, 28 June.

d'Almeida, Charles. 1995. "Vélos Dibonan = vélos du bonheur." *Soir INFO*, 12 August, 10.

D'Andrea, Thomas. 2006. *Tradition, Rationality, and Virtue: The Thought of Alasdair MacIntyre*. Farnham, UK: Ashgate Publishing.

Dacha, Chris. 1994. "Ferké: Une insécurité de plus en plus inquiétante." *La Voie*, 9 September.

Davis, John Uniak. 2000. "Classrooms of Democracy? The Educational Prospects of Malian Civil Society." In *Democracy and Development in Mali*, edited by R. James Bingen, David Robinson, and John M. Staatz, 289–319. East Lansing: Michigan State University Press.

Debali, Clément, and Mathieu Tagba. 1997. "150 Dozo saccagent et brûlent le domicile d'un planteur." *Le Populaire* 697, 18–19 October, 5.

Deh, Vincent. 1995. "Daloa: Des bandits attaquent: Un mort deux blessés graves." *La Voie*, 17 March.

———. 1996. "Daloa: Des 'Dozos' arrêtes pour meurtre." *La Voie* 1415, 14–15 September.

———. 1997. "Daloa: Un gendarme abattu par des Dozos." *La Voie* 1555, 3 March, 7.

Delafosse, Maurice. 1955. *La langue mandingue et ses dialectes (malinké, bambara, dioula)*. Paris: Imprimerie nationale/Librairie orientaliste Paul Geuthner.

Dembélé, Al Séni. 1996. "Sécurité: Que veut Dibonan?" *Le républicain ivoirien* 208, 11 September, 3.

Dembélé, Ousmane. 2003. "Côte d'Ivoire: La fracture communautaire." *Politique africaine* 89: 34–48.

Denich, Bette. 1974. "Sex and Power in the Balkans." In *Woman, Culture, and Society*, edited by M. Z. Rosaldo and L. Lamphere. Stanford: Stanford University Press.

Derive, Jean. 1978. "Le chant de Kurubi à Kong." *Annales de l'Université d'Abidjan*, série J (Traditions orales), 2: 85–114.

Derive, Marie-José. 1976. *Chroniques des grandes familles d'Odienné*. Abidjan: Institut de Linguistique Appliqueé.

———. 1978. *Bamori et Kowulen: Chant de chasseurs de la région d'Odienné*. Abidjan: Institut de linguistique appliquée.

———. 1983. *Étude comparée des parlers mandings ivoiriens*. Abidjan: Agence de Coopération Culturelle et Technique/Institut de Linguistique Appliquée.

———. 1985. *Étude comparée des parlers mandings ivoiriens*, vol. 2. Abidjan: Agence de Coopération Culturelle et Technique/Institut de Linguistique Appliquée.

Detchi, Martial. 1996. "San-Pédro: Les dozo envahissent la P. J." *Ivoir'Soir* 26 August, 12.

Diaby, Salif. 1994. "Sécurité: Face aux coupeurs de route." *Fraternité Matin*, 31 1 December–2 January, 1995.

Diarra, Mamadou. n.d. Self-recorded history of Malian Benkadi on audiocassette. In author's possession.

Diarra, Samba. 1997. *Les faux complots d'Houphouët-Boigny: Fracture dans le destin d'une nation (1959–1970)*. Paris: Karthala.

Dieterlen, Germaine. 1988 [1951]. *Essai sur la religion bambara*. Brussels: Éditions de l'Université de Bruxelles.

Diomandé, Dro. 1991. "Insécurité: Alerte rouge à Bonon." *Fraternité Matin*, 30 December.

Djezon, Banto. 1997. "Daloa: La galère des policiers." *Ivoir'Soir*, 13–14 September, 4.

Doualy, Abel. 1993. "Le dernier gouvernement de Houphouët a démissionné hier." *Fraternité Matin*, 10 December, 3.

Douglas, Mary. 1966. *Purity and Danger: An Analysis of the Concepts of Pollution and Taboo.* London: Ark Paperbacks.

Dozon, Jean-Pierre. 1987. "Au cœur des ethnies ivoiriennes . . . l'état." In *L'état contemporain en Afrique,* edited by Emmanuel Terray. Paris: L'Harmattan.

———. 2000. "La Côte d'Ivoire entre démocratie, nationalisme et ethnonationalisme." *Politique africaine* 78:45–62.

Dumont, Louis. 1981 [1967]. *Homo Hierarchicus: The Caste System and Its Implications.* Chicago: University of Chicago Press.

Duprey, Pierre. 1962. *Histoire des Ivoiriens: Naissance d'une nation.* Abidjan: L'imprimerie de la Côte d'Ivoire.

Durkheim, Emile. 1965 [1912]. *The Elementary Structures of the Religious Life.* New York: Free Press.

Economist Intelligence Unit. 1989. *Cocoa to 1993: A Commodity in Crisis.* London: Economist.

Eliade, Mircea. 1974 [1949]. *The Myth of the Eternal Return or, Cosmos and History.* Translated by Willard R. Trask. Second edition. Princeton: Princeton University Press.

Ellis, Stephen. 1999. *The Mask of Anarchy: The Destruction of Liberia and the Religious Dimension of an African Civil War.* New York: New York University Press.

———. 2003. "International Elements of West Africa's Wars: The Role of Sub-Regional and Non-African Actors." Unpublished paper from the OECD conference, "Conflict and Development Policy in the Mano River Region and Côte d'Ivoire: The Regional Stakes for Stability and Reconstruction." Paris, 13–14 May. http://www.oecd.org/dataoecd/19/0/33904967.pdf. Accessed 14 November 2005.

Ellis, Stephen, and Gerrie ter Haar. 1998. "Religion and Politics in Sub-Saharan Africa." *Journal of Modern African Studies* 36, no. 2: 175–201.

Engelke, Matthew. 1999. "We Wondered What Human Rights He Was Talking About: Human Rights, Homosexuality and the Zimbabwe International Book Fair." *Critique of Anthropology* 19, no. 3: 289–314.

Ernst, Carl W. 1997. *The Shambhala Guide to Sufism.* Boston: Shambhala.

Evans-Pritchard, E. E. 1956. *Nuer Religion.* New York: Oxford University Press.

———. 1967. *The Nuer: A Description of the Modes of Livelihood and Political Institutions of a Nilotic People.* Oxford: Clarendon Press.

F. N. 1995. "Sommet mondial sur le développement social: Les Ivoiriens face aux défis du chômage, de l'insécurité et de la démocratie." *La Voie,* 9 February.

Fabian, Johannes. 1983. *Time and the Other: How Anthropology Makes Its Object.* New York: Columbia University Press.

———. 1990. *Power and Performance: Ethnographic Explorations through Proverbial Wisdom and Theater in Shaba, Zaire.* Madison: University of Wisconsin Press.

———. 1998. *Moments of Freedom: Anthropology and Popular Culture.* Charlottesville: University Press of Virginia.

Fairhead, James, and Melissa Leach. 1996. *Misreading the African Landscape: Soci-*

ety and Ecology in a Forest-Savanna Mosaic. Cambridge: Cambridge University Press.

Fall, Elimane, with Killian Kra and Ahmed Kouadio. 2001. "Côte d'Ivoire: Les cache-misère." *Jeune Afrique Économie* 325 (19 February–4 March): 6–10.

Fanon, Frantz. 2007 [1963]. "On Violence." In *On Violence: A Reader*, edited by Bruce Lawrence and Aisha Karim. Durham: Duke University Press.

Fédération Internationale des Ligues des Droits de l'Homme/Reporters sans Frontières. 2000. "Côte d'Ivoire: Enquête sur le charnier de Yopougon du 26 octobre 2000." Paris: Fédération Internationale des Ligues des Droits de l'Homme/Reporters sans Frontières. http://www.fidh.org/IMG/pdf/yopoucot.pdf. Accessed June 18, 2010.

Feierman, Steven. 1990. *Peasant Intellectuals: Anthropology and History in Tanzania*. Madison: University of Wisconsin Press.

Ferguson, James. 2006. *Global Shadows: Africa in the Neoliberal World Order*. Durham, NC: Duke University Press.

Ferme, Mariane 2001a. *The Underneath of Things: Violence, History, and the Everyday in Sierra Leone*. Berkeley: University of California Press.

———. 2001b. "La figure du chasseur et les chasseurs—miliciens dans le conflit sierra-léonais." *Politique africaine* 82:119–32.

Ferme, Mariane, and Danny Hoffman. 2004. "Hunter Militias and the International Human Rights Discourse in Sierra Leone and Beyond." *Africa Today* 50, no. 4: 73–95.

Fernandez, James. 1982. *Bwiti: An Ethnography of the Religious Imagination in Africa*. Princeton: Princeton University Press.

Fleisher, Michael. 2000. "'Sungusungu': State-Sponsored Village Vigilante Groups among the Kuria of Tanzania." *Africa* 70, no. 2: 209–228.

Fofana, Mambé. 1997. "Gagnoa: Pour avoir prêché contre des dozos . . . l'Imam Wahabite ligoté." *SoirINFO* 693 (19 November): 11.

Fofana, Moussa. 1996. Letter addressed "To whom it may concern." Typescript (photocopy), dated August 4.

——. 1997. Letter to Inza Fanny on behalf of the dozos of "Binkadi." Typescript (photocopy), dated July 7.

Fortes, Meyer. 1980. Preface to *Sacrifice*, edited by M. F. C. Bourdillon and Meyer Fortes. New York: Academic Press.

Fortin, Pierre. 1995. *La morale, l'éthique, l'éthicologie*. Québec: Presses de l'Université du Québec.

Foucault, Michel. 1988. "Technologies of the Self." In *Technologies of the Self: A Seminar with Michel Foucault*, edited by L. Martin, H. Gutman, and P. Hutton. Amherst: University of Massachusetts Press.

Fox, Richard. 1985. *Lions of Punjab: Culture in the Making*. Berkeley: University of California Press.

Frankenberg, Ronald. 2002 [1982]. "'The Bridge' Revisited." In *The Anthropology of Politics: A Reader in Ethnography, Theory, and Critique*, edited by Joan Vincent, 59–64. Malden, MA: Blackwell.

Frankl, Viktor. 1959 [1946]. *Man's Search for Meaning: An Introduction to Logotherapy.* New York: Washington Square Press.

Fraternité Matin. 1991. "Faits divers: 32 kg de cannabis saisis à Kanton." 22 March.

———. 1993a. "Haut-lieu du banditisme." 8 April.

———. 1993b. "Déclaration du Premier Ministre." 8 December, 1.

———. 1993c. "La Côte d'Ivoire est orpheline: Le Président Bédié: J'assumerai dès maintenant mes responsabilités." 8 December, 32.

———. 1993d. "R. F. I. désormais en F. M." 9 December, 17.

———. 1994a. "Forces de l'ordre: Trois agents tués." 31 August.

———. 1994b. "Nord-est: Criminalité en hausse." 5 October.

———. 1997. "Communiqué: Réunion des chasseurs de Tienko." *Fraternité Matin,* 28–29 June, 21.

Frazer, Sir James George. 1922 [1911]. *The Golden Bough: A Study in Magic and Religion.* New York: Macmillan.

Friedlander, Judith. 1975. *Being Indian in Hueyapan: A Study of Forced Identity in Contemporary Mexico.* New York: St. Martin's Press.

Fuglestad, Finn. 1975. "Les hauka: Une interprétation historique." *Cahiers d'études africaines* 58, no. 15.2: 203–216.

Gable, Eric. 1996. "Women, Ancestors, and Alterity among the Manjaco of Guinea-Bissau." *Journal of Religion in Africa* 26, no. 2: 104–121.

Galy, Michel. 2004. "Côte d'Ivoire: la violence, juste avant la guerre." *Afrique contemporaine* 209, no. 1: 117–139.

Gbagbo, Laurent. 1982. *Côte d'Ivoire: Économie et société à la veille de l'indépendance (1940–1960).* Paris: L'Harmattan.

———. 1991. *Côte d'Ivoire: Agir pour les libertés.* Paris: L'Harmattan.

Gbizihi, Jean Claude. 1994. "Allô police: Des bandits attaquent le commissariat." *La Voie,* 22–23 January.

Geertz, Clifford. 1973. *The Interpretation of Cultures.* New York: Basic Books.

Gendarmerie Nationale de Côte d'Ivoire. n.d. "Présentation générale de la gendarmerie nationale." Typescript (photocopy).

Gennep, Arnold van. 1960. *The Rites of Passage.* Chicago: University of Chicago Press.

Geschiere, Peter. 1997. *The Modernity of Witchcraft: Politics and the Occult in Postcolonial Africa.* Charlottesville: University Press of Virginia.

Geurts, Kathryn Linn. 2002. *Culture and the Senses: Bodily Ways of Knowing in an African Community.* Berkeley: University of California Press.

Gibb, H. A. R. 1982. *Mohammedanism: An Historical Survey.* London: Oxford University Press.

Gibson, Thomas. 1986. *Sacrifice and Sharing in the Philippine Highlands: Religion and Society among the Buid of Mindoro.* London School of Economics Monographs on Social Anthropology. London: Athlone Press.

Giddens, Anthony. 1979. *Central Problems in Social Theory: Action, Structure and Contradiction in Social Analysis.* London: Macmillan.

———. 1984. *The Constitution of Society: Outline of the Theory of Structuration.* Berkeley: University of California Press.

Gluckman, Max. 1958 [1940]. *Analysis of a Social Situation in Modern Zululand.* Manchester: Manchester University Press.

———. 1963. *Order and Rebellion in Tribal Africa.* New York: Free Press of Glencoe.

Gnakalé, Viviane. 2006. *Laurent Gbagbo: Pour l'avenir de la Côte d'Ivoire.* Paris: L'Harmattan.

Gnonsoa, Angèle. 1991. "Repenser notre société." *Fraternité Matin,* 2 August.

Godelier, Maurice. 1999. *The Enigma of the Gift.* Chicago: University of Chicago Press.

Goody, Jack. 1962. *Death, Property and the Ancestors: A Study of the Mortuary Customs of the Lodagaa of West Africa.* Stanford: Stanford University Press.

Gooré-Bi, Hué. 1993. "Campus de Cocody: Un voleur brûlé vif." *Fraternité Matin,* 19 April.

Gottlieb, Alma. 1992. *Under the Kapok Tree: Identity and Difference in Beng Thought.* Bloomington: Indiana University Press.

Gow, Peter. 1996. "Aesthetics Is a Cross-Cultural Category: Against the Motion." In *Key Debates in Anthropology,* edited by Tim Ingold, 271–275. London: Routledge.

Gramsci, Antonio. 1971. *Selections from the Prison Notebooks.* New York: International Publishers.

Greenberg, Joseph. 1963. *The Languages of Africa.* Bloomington: Indiana University Press.

Griffeth, Robert. 1971. "The Dyula Impact on the Peoples of the West Volta Region." In *Papers on the Manding,* edited by Carleton Hodge. Bloomington: Indiana University Press.

Grosz-Ngaté, Maria. 2002. "Memory, Power, and Performance in the Construction of Muslim Identity." *Political and Legal Anthropology Review* 25, no. 2: 5–20.

Gueu, Edison. 1997. "Parce qu'elle a refusé le mari, son beau-père la livre aux dozos." *Ivoir'Soir* 2426 (11 February): 12.

Guha, Ranajit. 1997. *Dominance without Hegemony: History and Power in Colonial India.* Cambridge, MA: Harvard University Press.

Gullì, Bruno. 2007. "The Ontology and Politics of Exception: Reflections on the Work of Giorgio Agamben." In *Giorgio Agamben: Sovereignty and Life,* edited by Matthew Calarco and Steven DeCaroli, 219–242. Stanford: Stanford University Press.

Gumedze, Sabelo. 2007a. "The Private Security Sector in Africa: The 21st Century's Major Cause for Concern?" ISS Paper 133. Pretoria: Institute for Security Studies. http://www.iss.co.za/dynamic/administration/file_manager/file_links/133PDF.PDF?link_id=3893&slink_id=4204&link_type=12&slink_type=23&tmpl_id=3. Accessed August 23, 2009.

———, ed. 2007b. *Private Security in Africa: Manifestation, Challenges and Regulation.* ISS Monograph Series, 139. Pretoria: Institute for Security Studies.

http://www.iss.co.za/uploads/MON0139/FULLPDF.PDF. Accessed August 23, 2009.
———, ed. 2008. *The Private Security Sector in Africa: Country Series.* ISS Monograph Series, 146. Pretoria: Institute for Security Studies. http://www.iss.co.za/index.php?link_id=3&slink_id=6390&link_type=12&slink_type=12&tmpl_id=3. Accessed August 23, 2009.

Hagberg, Sten. 1998. *Between Peace and Justice: Dispute Settlement between Karaboro Agriculturalists and Fulbe Agro-Pastoralists in Burkina Faso.* Uppsala: Acta Universitatis Upsaliensis.

———. 2004. "Political Decentralization and Traditional Leadership in the Benkadi Hunters' Association in Western Burkina Faso." *Africa Today* 50, no. 4: 51–70.

Hale, Thomas. 1998. *Griots and Griottes: Masters of Words and Music.* Bloomington: Indiana University Press.

Hall, Stuart, and Tony Jefferson. 1976. *Resistance through Rituals: Youth Subcultures in Post-War Britain.* London: Hutchinson.

Haltenorth, Theodor, and Helmut Diller. 1977. *Mamifères d'Afrique et de Madagascar.* Neuchâtel: Delachaux et Niestlé.

Handler, Richard. 1988. *Nationalism and the Politics of Culture in Quebec.* Madison: University of Wisconsin Press.

Hannerz, Ulf. 1996. *Transnational Connections: Culture, People, Places.* New York: Routledge.

Hardin, Kris. 1993. *The Aesthetics of Action: Continuity and Change in a West African Town.* Washington, DC: Smithsonian Institution Press.

Heald, Suzette. 2005. "State, Law, and Vigilantism in Northern Tanzania." *African Affairs* 105, no. 419: 265–283.

Hebdige, Dick. 1979. *Subculture: The Meaning of Style.* New York: Methuen.

Hégaud, O. 1994. "Au quotidien: Coupeurs de route." *Fraternité Matin,* 7 June.

Hellweg, Joseph. 1997. "Like the Leaves of the Trees: Hunters Stalk Security in Urban Côte d'Ivoire." *Anthropology Newsletter* 38, no. 5: 61–62.

———. 2001. "The Mande Hunters' Movement of Côte d'Ivoire: Ritual, Ethics, and Performance in the Transformation of Civil Society, 1990–1997." Ph.D. dissertation, University of Virginia.

———. 2004. "Encompassing the State: Sacrifice and Security in the Hunters' Movement of Côte d'Ivoire." *Africa Today* 50, no. 4: 3–28.

———. 2006. "Manimory and the Aesthetics of Mimesis: Forest, Islam, and State in Ivoirian *Dozoya.*" *Africa* 76, no. 4: 461–484.

———. 2009. "Hunters, Ritual, and Freedom: *Dozo* Sacrifice as a Technology of the Self in the *Benkadi* Movement of Côte d'Ivoire." *Journal of the Royal Anthropological Institute* 15, no. 1: 36–56.

Herbert, Eugenia. 1993. *Iron, Gender, and Power: Rituals of Transformation in African Societies.* Bloomington: Indiana University Press.

Heusch, Luc de. 1985. *Sacrifice in Africa: A Structuralist Approach.* Bloomington: Indiana University Press.

Hirst, Paul. 1986. *Law, Socialism, and Democracy.* New York: HarperCollins

Hobsbawm, Eric. 1959. *Primitive Rebels: Studies in Archaic Forms of Social Movement in the 19th and 20th Centuries.* New York: W. W. Norton & Co.
Hobsbawm, Eric, and Terence Ranger, eds. 1983. *The Invention of Tradition.* Cambridge: Cambridge University Press.
Hoffman, Barbara. 1995. "Power, Structure, and Mande *jeliw.*" In *Status and Identity in West Africa: Nyamakalaw of Mande,* edited by David Conrad and Barbara Frank. Bloomington: Indiana University Press.
Holland, Dorothy, William Lachicotte, Jr., Debra Skinner, and Carole Cain. *Identity and Agency in Cultural Worlds.* 1998. Cambridge, MA: Harvard University Press.
Hountondji, Paulin. 1977. *Sur la "philosophie africaine."* Paris: Maspéro.
Howley, Pat. 2003. *Breaking Spears and Mending Hearts: Peacemakers and Restorative Justice in Bougainville.* London: Zed Books.
Hubert, Henri, and Marcel Mauss. 1964. *Sacrifice: Its Nature and Function.* Chicago: University of Chicago Press.
Human Rights Watch. 2006. "'Because They Have the Guns . . . I'm Left with Nothing': The Price of Continuing Impunity in Côte d'Ivoire." New York: Human Rights Watch. http://www.hrw.org/reports/2006/cotedivoire0506/cotedivoire0506web.pdf. Accessed August 29, 2009.
Hunwick, John. 1976. "Songhay, Borno and Hausaland in the Sixteenth Century." In *History of West Africa,* vol. 1, edited by J. F. A. Ajayi and Michael Crowder, 264–281. New York: Columbia University Press.
———. 1985. *Sharia in Songhay.* Oxford: Oxford University Press.
Hutchinson, Sharon. 1985. "Changing Concepts of Incest among the Nuer." *American Ethnologist* 12, no. 4: 625–641.
Hymes, Dell. 1981. *"In Vain I Tried to Tell You": Essays in Native American Ethnopoetics.* Philadelphia: University of Pennsylvania Press.
———. 1985. "Language, Memory, and Selective Performance: Cultee's 'Salmon's Myth' as Twice Told to Boas." *Journal of American Folklore* 98, no. 390: 391–434.
Ibo, Cheick Oumar. 1997. "Divo: Le dozo coupeur de route prend 20 ans." *Actuel* 19, 23 January, 8.
Ibo, F. 1995. "Duékoué: La ville est devenue un nid de bandits." *La Voie,* 12 January.
Institut National de la Statistique. 1996. *Enquête Ivoirienne sur les Migrations et l'Urbanisation. Séminaire de Dissémination des Résultats.* Abidjan: République de Côte d'Ivoire.
International Crisis Group. 2003. "Côte d'Ivoire: The War Is Not Yet Over." November 28. Brussels: International Crisis Group. http://www.crisisgroup.org/en/regions/africa/west-africa/cote-divoire/072-cote-divoire-the-war-is-not-yet-over.aspx. Accessed May 12, 2010.
———. 2009. "Côte d'Ivoire: What's Needed to End the Crisis?" July 2. Brussels: International Crisis Group. http://www.crisisgroup.org/en/regions/africa/west-africa/cote-divoire/B062-cote-divoire-whats-needed-to-end-the-crisis.aspx. Accessed May 12, 2010.

International Monetary Fund. n.d. "Alassane Ouattara: Biographical Information." http://www.imf.org/external/np/omd/bios/Ado.htm. Accessed August 23, 2009.

IRIN. 2001. "State asks for 20 years in army trial." March 13. http://www.irinnews.org/Report.aspx?ReportId=19125. Accessed August 28, 2009.

———. 2002. "IRIN Chronology of Key Events: December 1999-November 2002." December 4. http://www.irinnews.org/Report.aspx?ReportId=40005. Accessed August 28, 2009.

———. 2005. "UN confirms existence of blacklist of human rights abusers." January 31. http://www.irinnews.org/report.aspx?reportid=52848. Accessed August 28, 2009.

———. 2006. "Profiles of Three Ivoirians Facing UN Sanctions." February 8. http://www.globalsecurity.org/military/library/news/2006/02/mil-060208-irin04.htm. Accessed August 29, 2009.

Jackson, Michael. 1988. "In the Thrown World: Destiny and Decision in the Thought of Traditional Africa." In *Choice and Morality in Anthropological Perspective: Essays in Honor of Derek Freeman*, edited by George Appell and T. Madan. Albany: State University of New York Press.

———. 1990. "The Man Who Could Turn into an Elephant: Shape-Shifting among the Kuranko of Sierra Leone." In *Personhood and Agency: The Experience of Self and Other in African Cultures*, edited by M. Jackson and I. Karp. Uppsala: Acta Universitatis Upsaliensis.

James, John. 2008. "Ivoirian Ex-Rebels Begin to Disarm." May 3. London: BBC News. http://news.bbc.co.uk/2/hi/africa/7381704.stm. Accessed August 29, 2009.

James, William. 1918. *Principles of Psychology*. Vol. 1. New York: Henry Holt and Co.

———. 1956 [1897]. *The Will to Believe and Other Essays in Popular Philosophy, Human Immortality*. Mineola, NY: Dover.

Jansen, Jan and Clemens Zobel. 1996. "Kinship as Political Discourse: The Representation of Harmony and Change in Mande." In *The Younger Brother in Mande: Kinship and Politics in West Africa*. Edited by Jan Jansen and Clemens Zobel, 1–7. Leiden: Research School CNWS.

Johnson, John William. 1992. *The Epic of Son-Jara: A West African Tradition*. Bloomington: Indiana University Press.

Joyce, Rosemary, and Susan Gillespie. 2000. *Beyond Kinship: Social and Material Reproduction in House Societies*. Philadelphia: University of Pennsylvania Press.

Kaba, Lanciné. 1974. *The Wahhabiyya: Islamic Reform and Politics in French West Africa, 1945–1960*. Evanston: Northwestern University Press.

Kakapé. 1994. "Notule: Les pilleurs de cars récidivent à Kongodékro." *Fraternité Matin*.

Kam, Elie. 1992. "Cannabis: Trois dealers dans le filet." *Fraternité Matin*, 11 May.

Kambiré, Elie. 1994. "Plein Centre: Un douanier tué, quatre armes emportées." *Fraternité Matin*, 24 February.

Keita, Djigui. 1985. "Le rôle socio-religieux de la cola dans la société malinké (Exemple de Kaaba)." Mémoire de maîtrise, University of Abidjan.

Kieffer, Guy-André. 2000. "Armée ivoirienne: Le refus du déclassement." *Politique africaine* 78: 26–44.

Kikié, Ahou Nazaire. 1997. "Deux papillons pour un seul véhicule le même jour: La prévue du racket policier." *Soir INFO* (December): 12.

Knox, Colin, and Rachel Monaghan. 2003. "Violence in a Changing Political Context: Northern Ireland and South Africa." In *The Meanings of Violence*, edited by Elizabeth A. Stanko, 184–202. New York: Routledge.

Knutsen, Anne. 2008. "Ivory Coast: The Supremacy of French." In *Language and National Identity in Africa*, edited by Andrew Simpson. Oxford: Oxford University Press.

Koffi, Charles André. 1997. "Conseil national de sécurité: La décentralisation pour quadriller le territoire." *Le Démocrate Plus* 103 (24 October).

Koffi, Christophe. 2010. "Côte d'Ivoire: Les ex-rebelles du nord commencent leur regroupement." Paris: Agence France Presse. http://news.abidjan.net/h/367035.html. Accessed June 18, 2010.

Kohon, Landry. 1995. "Yopougon-Aimé Césaire: Les habitants terrorisés par des gangs." *Fraternité Matin*, 16 March.

Konan, André. 2003. "Nouveau massacre à Bangolo: 68 guéré [*sic*] tués par des rebelles." *Le Nouveau Réveil*, May 12.

Koné, Kassim. 1996. Review of *The Making of Bamana Sculpture: Creativity and Gender*. *African Arts* 29, no. 2: 90–91, 102–103.

Koné, Saliou. 1993. "Nouvelle saisie de la douane à l'aéroport: Plus de 2.000.000 de comprimés dans l'avion." *Fraternité Matin*, 12 January.

Kopytoff, Igor. 1987. "The Internal African Frontier: The Making of African Political Culture." In *The African Frontier: The Reproduction of Traditional African Societies*, edited by Igor Kopytoff, 3–84. Bloomington: Indiana University Press.

Kouamé, Jean-Roche. 1998. "Plus de 100,000 armes circulent en Côte d'Ivoire." *Le Jour* 1072 (29–30 August). http://www.africaonline.co.ci/AfricaOnline/infos/lejour/1072NAT1.HTM. Accessed August 31, 1998.

Kouamé, Wilfried. 1994. "Banditisme sur l'axe Gagnoa-Soubré: Cinq cars de transport attaqués." *La Voie*, 5 September.

———. 1995. "Criminalité: Un vendeur de chaussures égorgé." *La Voie*, 12 April.

Kouamouo, Théophile. 2005. *La France que je combats: Itinéraire intellectuel et personnel*. Abidjan: Les éditions *Le Courrier d'Abidjan*.

Kouassi, Emmanuel. 1996. "Une bavure des dozos (Bouaké): Un jeune tué devant sa fiancée." *Ivoir'Soir*, 19 December, 12.

Kouassi, Lobo. 1991a. "Lutte contre la drogue: Cocaïne et héroïne, 102 grammes saisis sur cinq prostituées." *Fraternité Matin*, 18 December.

———. 1991b. "Lutte contre la drogue: 92 boules d'héroïne dans le ventre de Christelle." *Fraternité Matin*, 22 December.

———. 1993a. "Kaniasso: Les chasseurs traditionnels pour la sauvegarde de la faune." *Fraternité Matin*, 8 April.

———. 1993b. "La population à l'écoute des universitaires." *Fraternité Matin,* 9 April, 8.

———. 1993c. "Kaniasso: Recommandations pour un meilleur environnement/ Collaborer avec les chasseurs." *Fraternité Matin,* 14 April, 7.

———. 1993d. "Insécurité dans le nord: Une quinzaine d'embuscades en 1992." *Fraternité Matin,* 27 September.

———. 1993e. "Hold-up à Shell: Un bandit tué." *Fraternité Matin,* 14 December.

———. 1994a. "Coupeurs de route: La terreur des voyageurs de nuit." *Fraternité Matin,* 31 August.

———. 1994b. "Scénario pour une embuscade." *Fraternité Matin,* 31 August.

———. 1994c. "Coupeurs de route: La riposte/Qui sont-ils donc?" *Fraternité Matin,* 1 September.

———. 1996a. "Le Ministre de la Sécurité à Man et à Odienné: 'Dozos, déposez vos armes.'" *Fraternité Matin,* 6 September, 12.

———. 1996b. "Sécurité des personnes et biens: Les policiers sollicitent ... les populations accusent." *Fraternité Matin,* 11 September, 2.

———. 1996c. "La stratégie de combat." *Fraternité Matin,* 11 September, 3.

Kouassi, Y., and A. K. Djidji. 1998. "Conseil des Ministres: Au titre du Ministère de l'Intérieur et de l'Intégration Nationale." *Fraternité Matin* 10062, 2–3 May.

Koudou, Claude. 2005. *Côte d'Ivoire: Pour un nouveau mode de coopération entre l'Afrique et la France.* Paris: L'Harmattan.

Kouliahan, Adolphe. 1996. "Les 'Dosso' ne séviront plus." *Le Populaire* 185, 22 January, 7.

Krassault, Robert. 1993. "Les chasseurs du Nord-Ouest et la protection de la nature." *La Voie* 469, 13 April.

Kremer-Marietti, Angèle. 1987. *L'éthique.* Collection Que sais-je?, no. 2383. Paris: Presses Universitaires de France.

Kuper, Adam. 1988. *The Invention of Primitive Society: Transformations of an Illusion.* London: Routledge.

Kwamkan. 1991. "'Escadrons de la mort?'" *Fraternité Matin.*

La Voie. 1995a. "Kouto: Un coupeur de route tué lors de l'attaque d'un car." 15 June.

———. 1995b. "San-Pédro: La ville vit dans l'insécurité." 29 June.

Laclau, Ernesto. 1996. *Emancipation(s).* London: Verso.

Laidlaw, James. 2002. "For An Anthropology of Ethics and Freedom." *Journal of the Royal Anthropological Institute* n.s. 8, no. 2: 311–332.

Lambek, Michael. 1990. "Certain Knowledge, Contestable Authority: Power and Practice on the Islamic Periphery." *American Ethnologist* 17, no. 1: 23–40.

Lan, David. 1985. *Guns and Rain: Guerillas and Spirit Mediums in Zimbabwe.* London: James Currey.

Langer, Arnim. 2004. "Horizontal Inequalities and Violent Conflict: The Case of Côte d'Ivoire." Oxford: Centre for Research on Inequality, Human Security and Ethnicity, Oxford University. http://www.research4development.info/ PDF/Outputs/inequality/wp13.pdf. Accessed May 11, 2010.

Lanternari, Vittorio. 1963. *The Religions of the Oppressed: A Study in Modern Messianic Cults*. New York: Mentor Books.

Launay, Robert. 1982. *Traders without Trade: Responses to Change in Two Dyula Communities*. Cambridge: Cambridge University Press.

———. 1992. *Beyond the Stream: Islam and Society in a West African Town*. Berkeley: University of California Press.

Launay, Robert, and Marie Miran. 2000. "Beyond Mande Mory: Islam and Ethnicity in Côte d'Ivoire." *Paideuma* 46: 63–84.

Launay, Robert, and Benjamin Soares. 1999. "The Formation of an 'Islamic Sphere' in French Colonial West Africa." *Economy and Society* 28, no. 4: 497–519.

Le Jour. 1995. "Plateau: L'envers du 'Manhattan d'Afrique.'" 8 February.

——. 1996. "Le ministre Koné Dibonan: Les dozos sont dans l'irrégularité."483, 4 September, 2.

Le Pape, Marc. 2002. "Chronologie politique de la Côte d'Ivoire, du coup d'état aux élections." In *Côte d'Ivoire: l'année terrible, 1999–2000*, edited by Marc Le Pape and Claudine Vidal. Paris: Karthala.

Le Populaire. 1997a. "Bongouanou: Un chasseur dozo tire à bout portant sur une femme." *Le Populaire* 532, 24 March, 5.

———. 1977b. "Dabou: Les dozos font la loi." *Le Populaire* 534, 26 March.

———. 1997c. "Issia: Le dozo était un voleur d'ignames." *Le Populaire* 628, July, 5.

———. 1997d. "Kolia: Trois femmes blessées par balles lors de funérailles à Zanasso." *Le Populaire* 709, 3 November, 2.

Le Républicain Ivoirien. 1997. "Séguela: Les dozos interdits d'activité." *Le Républicain Ivoirien* 353, 24 March, 12.

Leach, Melissa. 1994. *Rainforest Relations: Gender and Resource Use among the Mende of Gola, Sierra Leone*. Edinburgh: University Press for the International Africa Institute.

———. 2000. "New Shapes to Shift: War, Parks and the Hunting Person in Modern West Africa." *Journal of the Royal Anthropological Institute* 6, no. 4: 577–595.

LeBlanc, Marie Nathalie. 2000. "Versioning Womanhood and Muslimhood: 'Fashion' and the Life Course in Contemporary Bouaké, Côte d'Ivoire" *Africa* 70, no. 3: 442–481.

Lébry, Léon Francis. 1995. "Comment-taire: Ministre-Dozo." *Fraternité Matin*, 27 December, 10.

———. 1996. "Trois semaines après avoir été braqué: Mgr. Bruno Kouamé raconte son agression." *Fraternité Matin*. 5 March.

Lee, Dorothy. 1976. "Autonomous Motivation." In *Valuing the Self: What We Can Learn from Other Cultures*. Englewood Cliffs: Prentice-Hall.

Lévi-Strauss, Claude. 1966 [1962]. *The Savage Mind*. Chicago: University of Chicago Press.

———. 1971 [1963]. *Totemism*. Boston: Beacon Press.

———. 1982 [1975]. *The Way of the Masks*. Translated by Sylvia Modelski. Seattle: University of Washington Press.

Lévy-Bruhl, Lucien. 1985 [1910]. *How Natives Think.* Translated by Lilian A. Clare. Princeton: Princeton University Press.

Lewis, Barbara. 1970. "The Transporters Association of the Ivory Coast: Ethnicity, Occupational Specialization, and National Integration." Ph.D. dissertation, Northwestern University.

Lewis, Ioan. 1989. *Ecstatic Religion: A Study of Shamanism and Spirit Possession.* Second edition. London: Routledge.

———. 1996. *Religion in Context: Cults and Charisma.* Second edition. Cambridge: Cambridge University Press.

Leynaud, Emile, and Youssouf Cissé. 1978. *Paysans malinké du Haut Niger (Tradition et développement rural en Afrique Soudanaise).* Bamako: Imprimerie populaire du Mali.

Lienhardt, Godfrey. 1961. *Divinity and Experience: The Religion of the Dinka.* Oxford: Clarendon Press.

———. 1985. "Self: Public, Private. Some African Representations" In *The Category of the Person: Anthropology, Philosophy, History,* edited by M. Carrithers, S. Collins, and S. Lukes. Cambridge: Cambridge University Press.

Limam, Ziyad. 1993. "Après Houphouët, qui?" *Jeune Afrique* 1715, 18–4 November, 18–20.

Linden, Ian, with Jane Linden. 1974. *Catholics, Peasants, and Chewa Resistance in Nyasaland, 1889–1939.* Berkeley: University of California Press.

Loizidou, Elena. 2007. *Judith Butler: Ethics, Law, Politics.* London: Routledge.

Lonsdale, John. 1992. "The Moral Economy of Mau Mau: Wealth, Poverty & Civic Virtue in Kikuyu Political Thought." In *Unhappy Valley: Conflict in Kenya & Africa,* edited by B. Berman and J. Lonsdale. London: J. Currey.

———. 1994. "Moral Ethnicity and Political Tribalism." In *Inventions and Boundaries: Historical and Anthropological Approaches to the Study of Ethnicity and Nationalism,* edited by P. Kaarsholm and J. Hultin. Roskilde, Denmark: International Development Studies, Roskilde University.

Loucou, Jean-Noël. 1996. "De l'ivoirité." *Ethics* 1 (October): 19–24.

Lukes, Steven. 2005. *Power: A Radical View.* Second edition. Houndsmill, UK: Palgrave Macmillan.

Ly, Madina. 1979. "La femme dans las société traditionnelle mandingue (d'après une enquête sur le terrain)." *Présence africaine* 110, 2: 101–111.

Lynch, Maureen, and Dawn Calabia. 2007. "Côte d'Ivoire: Address Root Causes of Conflict to Prevent and Reduce Statelessness." Washington, D. C.: Refugees International. http://www.refugeesinternational.org/policy/field-report/côte-d'-ivoire-address-root-causes-conflict-prevent-and-reduce-statelessness. Accessed August 29, 2009.

MacIntyre, Alasdair. 1984. *After Virtue: A Study in Moral Theory.* Second edition. Notre Dame: University of Notre Dame Press.

Mair, Stefan. 2005. "The New World of Privatized Violence." In *Challenges of Globalization: New Trends in International Politics and Society,* edited by Alfred Pfaller and Marika Lerch, 1–12. New Brunswick, NJ: Transaction Publishers.

Makarius, Laura. 1969. "Observations sur la légende des griots malinké." *Cahiers d'études africaines* 4, no. 4: 626–640.

Mamdani, Mahmood. 1996. *Citizen and Subject: Contemporary Africa and the Legacy of Late Colonialism*. Princeton: Princeton University Press.

Mariko, Kélétigui. 1981. *Le monde mystérieux des chasseurs traditionnels*. Paris: Les Nouvelles Éditions Africaines.

Marshall-Fratani, Ruth. 2006. "The War of 'Who Is Who': Autochthony, Nationalism, and Citizenship in the Ivoirian Crisis." *African Studies Review* 49, no. 2: 9–43.

Masquelier, Adeline. 2001. *Prayer Has Spoiled Everything: Possession, Power, and Identity in an Islamic Town of Niger*. Durham, NC: Duke University Press.

Mauss, Marcel. 1967. *The Gift: Forms and Functions of Exchange in Archaic Societies*. New York: W. W. Norton & Company.

Mbembe, Achille. 2001. *On the Postcolony*. Berkeley: University of California.

———. 2006. "On Politics as a Form of Expenditure." In *Law and Disorder in the Postcolony*, edited by Jean Comaroff and John. L. Comaroff. Chicago: University of Chicago Press.

McCall, John. 1995. "Social Organization in Africa." In *Africa*, edited by Phyllis M. Martin and Patrick O'Mear. Third edition, 175–189. Bloomington: Indiana University Press.

McKinnon, Susan. 1991. *From a Shattered Sun: Hierarchy, Gender, and Alliance in the Tanimbar Islands*. Madison: University of Wisconsin Press.

———. 1995. "Houses and Hierarchy: The View from a South Moluccan Society." In *About the House: Lévi-Strauss and Beyond*, edited by Janet Carsten and Stephen Hugh-Jones. Cambridge: Cambridge University Press.

———. 2000. "Domestic Exceptions: Evans-Pritchard and the Creation of Nuer Patrilineality and Equality." *Cultural Anthropology* 15, no.1: 35–83.

McNaughton, Patrick. 1988. *The Mande Blacksmiths: Knowledge, Power, and Art in West Africa*. Bloomington: Indiana University Press.

———. 1995. "The Semantics of *jugu*: Blacksmiths, Lore, and 'Who's Bad' in Mande." In *Status and Identity in West Africa: Nyamakalaw of Mande*, edited by D. Conrad and B. Frank. Bloomington: Indiana University Press.

Mead, George H. 1934. *Mind, Self, and Society: From the Standpoint of a Social Behaviorist*. Chicago: University of Chicago Press.

Meagher, Kate. 2007. "Hijacking Civil Society: The Inside Story of the Bakassi Boys Vigilante Group of South-Eastern Nigeria." *Journal of Modern African Studies* 45, no. 1: 89–115.

Meillassoux, Claude. 1991 [1986]. *The Anthropology of Slavery: The Womb of Iron and Gold*. Translated by Alide Dasnois. Chicago: University of Chicago Press.

Mills, Catherine. 2007. "Biopolitics, Liberal Eugenics, and Nihilism." In *Giorgio Agamben: Sovereignty and Life*, edited by Matthew Calarco and Steven DeCaroli, 180–202. Stanford: Stanford University Press.

Ministère de l'Agriculture de Côte d'Ivoire. 1968. *Code forestière et législation forestière*. Abidjan: Direction des Eaux, Forêts et Chasse.

Ministère de la Protection de la Nature. 1968. *Législation de la chasse et de la protection de la nature.* Abidjan: Direction de la Protection de la Nature.

Mintz, Sidney. 1989. *Caribbean Transformations.* New York: Columbia University Press.

Miran, Marie. 2006a. "The Political Economy of Civil Islam in Côte d'Ivoire." In *Islamic Democracy? Political Islam in Western Africa,* edited by H. Weiss and M. Bröening. Berlin: Lit Verlag.

———. 2006b. *Islam, histoire et modernité en Côte d'Ivoire.* Paris: Karthala.

Missionnaire de la Congrégation du Saint-Esprit. 1906. *Dictionnaire français-malinké et malinké-français.* Conakry: Mission des Pères du Saint-Esprit.

Monteil, Charles. 1977. *Les Bambara du Ségou et du Kaarta.* Paris: G.-P. Maisonneuve & Larose.

Morphy, Howard. 1996. "Aesthetics Is a Cross-Cultural Category: For the Motion." In *Key Debates in Anthropology,* edited by Tim Ingold, 255–260. London: Routledge.

Mosko, Mark. 2005. "Introduction: A (Re)turn to Chaos." In *On the Order of Chaos: Social Anthropology and the Science of Chaos,* edited by Mark Mosko and Frederick Damon. New York: Berghahn Books.

Moussa, Alfred Dan. 1992. "Quelle sécurité pour les Ivoiriens!" *Fraternité Matin,* 1 June.

Mudimbe, V. Y. 1988. *The Invention of Africa: Gnosis, Philosophy, and the Order of Knowledge.* Bloomington: Indiana University Press.

———. 1991. *Parables and Fables: Exegesis, Textuality, and Politics in Central Africa.* Madison: University of Wisconsin Press.

Mundt, Robert. 1987. *Historical Dictionary of the Ivory Coast (Côte d'Ivoire).* Metuchen, NJ: Scarecrow Press.

Munn, Nancy. 1986. *The Fame of Gawa: A Symbolic Study of Value Transformation in a Massim (Papua New Guinea) Society.* Cambridge: Cambridge University Press.

Nagel, Thomas. 1986. *The View from Nowhere.* New York: Oxford University Press.

Napier, David. 2003. *The Age of Immunology: Conceiving a Future in an Alienating World.* Chicago: University of Chicago Press.

Nawayou, L. 1995. "Commissariat de Yopougon Toits-Rouges: Les policiers sont inactifs." *La Voie,* 30 March.

Ndiaye, Bokar. 1995. *Les castes au Mali.* Paris: Presence Africaine.

N'Dri, Bernard. 1996. Dozos: prévenir toute tentative de récupération. *Le Démocrate Plus* 47, 13 September, 2.

N'Guessan, Raphaël. 1994. "Ce que je sais: Question de volonté politique." *Fraternité Matin,* 1 September.

N'Guessan, Solange, Zouzou Bruno, and Allangba Yoboué. 1992. "La peur au quotidien." *Fraternité Matin,* 7 October.

Niangoran-Bouah, Georges. 1996. "Les fondements socio-culturels de l'ivoirité." *Ethics* 1 (October): 45–51.

Niane, Djibril Tamsir. 1989 [1960]. *Sundiata: An Epic of Old Mali.* Harlow: Longman.

Niezen, R. W. 1990. "The 'Community of Helpers of the Sunna': Islamic reform among the Songhay of Gao (Mali)." *Africa* 60, no. 3: 399–424.

None, Serguei. 2003. "Marcellin Oulai (rescapé des récents massacres de Bangolo): Les Burkinabés regroupent leurs victimes avant de les égorger." *Notre Voie,* May 16.

Nouvel Horizon. 1993. "Confidences: Le préfet ne veut rouler ... qu'en Patrol." *Nouvel Horizon* 135, 16 April.

Nyamnjoh, Francis. 2002. "A Child Is One Person's Only in the Womb: Domestication, Agency and Subjectivity in the Cameroonian Grassfields." In *Postcolonial Subjectivities in Africa,* edited by Richard Werbner. London: Zed Books.

Ollman, Bertell. 1971. *Alienation: Marx's Conception of Man in a Capitalist Society.* Cambridge: Cambridge University Press.

Omeje, Kenneth. 2005. "The Egbesu and Bakassi Boys: African Spiritism and the Mystical Re-traditionalisation of Security." In *Civil Militia: Africa's Intractable Security Menace?* edited by D. J. Francis. Burlington, VT: Ashgate.

Ong, Aihwa. 1987. *Spirits of Resistance and Capitalist Discipline: Factory Women in Malaysia.* Albany: State University of New York Press.

Ortner, Sherry. 1984. "Theory in Anthropology since the Sixties." *Comparative Studies in Society and History* 26, no. 1: 126–166.

O'Sullivan, John. 1976. "Developments in the Social Stratification of Northwest Ivory Coast during the Eighteenth and Nineteenth Centuries: From a Malinke Frontier Society to the Liberation of Slaves by the French—1907." Ph.D. dissertation, University of California, Los Angeles.

Overing, Joanna. 1996. "Aesthetics Is a Cross-Cultural Category: Against the Motion." In *Key Debates in Anthropology,* edited by Tim Ingold, 260–266. London: Routledge.

Overing, Joanna, and Alan Passes. 2000. "Introduction: Conviviality and the Opening Up of Amazonian Anthropology." In *The Anthropology of Love and Anger,* edited by Joanna Overing and Alan Passes. London: Routledge.

Ozoua, Marie Chantal. 1993. "Bédié se proclame président de la République: Scénario d'un 'coup d'Etat' de la France." *La Voie,* 9 December, 2.

Parsons, Talcott. 1968. *The Structure of Social Action.* Vol. 1, *Marshall, Pareto, Durkheim.* New York: Free Press.

Paye, Jean-Claude. 2006 [2004]. *Global War on Liberty.* New York: Telos Press.

———. 1968. *Samori, une révolution dyula.* Vol. 1. Dakar: IFAN.

Peirce, Charles S. 1955. *Philosophical Writings of Peirce,* edited by Justus Buchler. New York: Dover.

Person, Yves. 1963. "Les ancêtres de Samori." *Cahiers d'études africaines* 4, no. 13: 125–156.

Piot, Charles. 1999. *Remotely Global: Village Modernity in West Africa.* Chicago: University of Chicago Press.

Placca, Jean-Baptiste. 1994. "L'après-Houphouët: La guerre de succession." *Jeune Afrique Economie* 175 (January): 16–22.

Quardhaoui, Youcef. 1990. "La chasse." In *Le licite et l'illicite en Islam.* Paris: OKAD Éditions.

R. M. 2002. "Trève en trompe-l'œil à Lomé." *Le Nouvel Observateur,* 7 November.

Radcliffe-Brown, A. R. 1952. *Structure and Function in Primitive Society.* New York: Free Press.

Ranger, Terence. 1967. *Revolt in Southern Rhodesia, 1896–97: A Study in African Resistance.* Evanston: Northwestern University Press.

Reed, Daniel. 2003. *Dan Ge Performance: Masks and Music in Contemporary Côte d'Ivoire.* Bloomington: Indiana University Press.

Regan, Patrick. 2009. "The Road to Damascus." In *Sixteen Million One: Understanding Civil War.* Boulder: Paradigm Publishers.

Reno, William. 1998. *Warlord Politics and African States.* Boulder: Lynne Rienner Publishers.

République de Côte d'Ivoire. n.d. *Organisation municipale en Côte d'Ivoire.* Book I. Abidjan: Imprimerie Nationale.

———. 1991. *L'organisation des ministères.* Abidjan: Service des Journaux Officiels.

———. 1992a. "Récépissé de déclaration d'association." No.156/INT/ATAP/AGP/5, 27 March. Abidjan: Imprimerie Nationale de Côte d'Ivoire.

———. 1992b. "Déclaration d'Association." *Journal officiel* 25, 18 June, 520. Abidjan: Imprimerie Nationale de Côte d'Ivoire.

———. 1994. "1994 Actes du Gouvernement." *Journal officiel* 42, 13 October, 778–781. Abidjan: Imprimerie Nationale de Côte d'Ivoire.

———. 1997. *Guide pratique des services de police.* Abidjan: Ministère de la Sécurité.

Richards, Audrey Isabel. 1956. *Chisungu: A Girls' Initiation Ceremony among the Bemba of Northern Rhodesia.* London: Faber and Faber.

Richards, Paul. 1996. *Fighting for the Rainforest: War, Youth, and Resources in Sierra Leone.* Bloomington: Indiana University Press.

Ricœur, Paul. 1981. *Hermeneutics and the Human Sciences.* Edited by John B. Thompson. Cambridge: Cambridge University Press.

Ridler, Neil B. 1993. "Fixed Exchange Rates and Structural Adjustment Programmes: Côte d'Ivoire. *Journal of Modern African Studies* 31, no. 2: 301–308.

Riesman, Paul. 1977. *Freedom in Fulani Social Life: An Introspective Ethnography.* Translated by Martha Fuller. Chicago: University of Chicago Press.

Robins, Simon. 2009. "Restorative Approaches to Criminal Justice in Africa: The Case of Uganda." In *The Theory and Practice of Criminal Justice in Africa.* African Human Security Initiative Monograph, 161. Pretoria: Institute for Security Studies.

Robinson, David. 2004. *Muslim Societies in African History.* Cambridge: Cambridge University Press.

Rodney, Walter. 1973. *How Europe Underdeveloped Africa.* Washington, DC: Howard University Press.

Rotberg, Robert. 2003. *When States Fail: Causes and Consequences.* Princeton: Princeton University Press.

Roure, Georges. 1956. *Faune et chasse en Afrique Occidentale Française: Guide du tourisme de la nature vivante.* Dakar: Éditions GIA.

Sahlins, Marshall. 1976. *Culture and Practical Reason.* Chicago: University of Chicago Press.

———. 1981. *Historical Metaphors and Mythical Realities: Structure in the Early History of the Sandwich Islands Kingdom.* Ann Arbor: University of Michigan Press.

Salih, Mohamed Abdel Rahim Mohamed. 2001. *African Democracies and African Politics.* London: Pluto Press.

Sangho, Diaroukou. 1997. "Haro sur les tracasseries policières: La colère de Bédié." *Fraternité Matin* 16 September, 2.

Sapa. 2007. "New Ivory Coast government 'boost for Gbagbo.'" April 12, 2007. Paris: Agence France Presse. http://www.int.iol.co.za/index.php?set_id=1&click_id=68&art_id=nw20070412095335190C984275. Accessed August 29, 2009.

Sapir, J. David. 1981. "Leper, Hyena, and Blacksmith in Kujamaat Diola Thought." *American Ethnologist* 8, no. 3: 526–543.

Saussure, Ferdinand de. 1983 [1916]. *Course in General Linguistics.* Peru, IL: Open Court Publishing.

Schechner, Richard. 1985. *Between Theater and Anthropology.* Philadelphia: University of Pennsylvania Press.

Schmidt, Bettina, and Ingo Schröder, eds. 2001. *Anthropology of Violence and Conflict.* London: Routledge.

Schmidtz, David. 1996. "Justifying the State." In *For and against the State: New Philosophical Readings*, edited by John Sanders and Jan Narveson. Landham, MD: Rowman & Littlefield.

Schoffeleers, Matthew. 1972. "The History and Political Role of the M'bona Cult among the Mang'anja." In *The Historical Study of African Religion*, edited by T. Ranger and I. N. Kimambo. Berkeley: University of California Press.

Scott, James. 1977. "Protest and Profanation: Agrarian Revolt and the Little Tradition, Parts I and II." *Theory and Society* 4, no. 1: 1–38; 4, no. 2: 211–246.

———. 1985. *Weapons of the Weak: Everyday Forms of Peasant Resistance.* New Haven: Yale University Press.

———. 1998. *Seeing Like a State: How Certain Schemes to Improve the Human Condition Have Failed.* New Haven: Yale University Press.

Serle, William, and Gérard Morel. 1993. *Les oiseaux de l'Ouest africain.* Lausanne: Delachaux et Niestlé.

Seymour, Susan. 2006. "Resistance." *Anthropological Theory* 6, no. 3: 303–321.

Shaw, Rosalind. 1992. "Dreaming as Accomplishment: Power, the Individual and Temne Divination." In *Dreaming, Religion, and Society in Africa,* edited by M. C. Jedrej and Rosalind Shaw. Leiden: E. J. Brill.

Simmel, Georg. 1971 [1918]. "The Transcendent Character of Life." In *On Individuality and Social Forms*, edited by Donald N. Levine. Chicago: University of Chicago Press.

Skattum, Ingse. 2008. "Mali: In Defence of Cultural and Linguistic Pluralism." In *Language and National Identity in Africa*, edited by Andrew Simpson. Cambridge: Cambridge University Press.

Smith, Dan, and Janani Vivekananda. 2007. "A Climate of Conflict: The Links between Climate Change, Peace, and War." http://www.international-alert.org/pdf/A_Climate_Of_Conflict.pdf. Accessed on June 10, 2010. London: International Alert.

Smith, Daniel Jordan. 2004. "The Bakassi Boys: Vigilantism, Violence, and Political Imagination in Nigeria." *Cultural Anthropology* 19, no. 3: 429–455.

Soares, Benjamin. 1996. "The Prayer Economy in a Malian Town." *Cahiers d'études africaines* 36, no. 144: 739–753.

SoirINFO. 1997. "Lettre ouverte à MM. le préfet et le maire de Duékoué." *SoirINFO* 934, 12 September, 9.

Soudan, Françoise. "Ouattara et Bédié: le lièvre et la tortue." *Jeune Afrique*, 16-22 December, 14–15.

Stoler, Ann. 1985. *Capitalism and Confrontation on Sumatra's Plantation Belt, 1870–1979*. New Haven: Yale University Press.

Stoller, Paul. 1989a. *Fusion of the Worlds: An Ethnography of Possession among the Songhay of Niger*. Chicago: University of Chicago Press.

———. 1989b. *The Taste of Ethnographic Things: The Senses in Anthropology*. Philadelphia: University of Pennsylvania Press.

———. 1995. *Embodying Colonial Memories: Spirit Possession, Power, and the Hauka in West Africa*. New York: Routledge.

Strathern, Marilyn. 1988. *The Gender of the Gift: Problems with Women and Problems with Society in Melanesia*. Berkeley: University of California Press.

Suret-Canale, Jean. 1988. "The Geography of Capital in the Parts of Tropical Africa under French Influence." In *Essays on African History: From the Slave Trade to Neocolonialism*. Trenton, NJ: Africa World Press.

al-Tabari. 1987. *The History of al-Tabari*. Vol. 2, *Prophets and Patriarchs*. Translated by William M. Brinner. Albany: State University of New York Press.

Tamari, Tal. 1995. "Linguistic Evidence for the History of West African 'Castes.'" In *Status and Identity in West Africa: Nyamakalaw of Mande*, edited by D. Conrad and B. Frank. Bloomington: Indiana University Press.

Taussig, Michael. 1980. *The Devil and Commodity Fetishism in South America*. Chapel Hill: University of North Carolina Press.

———. 1993. *Mimesis and Alterity: A Particular History of the Senses*. New York: Routledge.

Tauxier, Louis. 1927. *La religion bambara*. Paris: Librairie Orientaliste Paul Geuthner.

Taylor, Christopher. 1999. *Sacrifice as Terror: The Rwandan Genocide of 1994*. Oxford: Berg Press.

———. 2004. "Deadly Images: King Sacrifice, President Habyarimana, and the Iconography of Pregenocidal Rwandan Political Literature." In *Violence*, edited by Neil Whitehead. Santa Fe: School of American Research Press.

Tedlock, Dennis. 1983. *The Spoken Word and the Work of Interpretation.* Philadelphia: University of Pennsylvania Press.

Thoyer, Annik. 1995. *Récits épiques des chasseurs bamanan du Mali.* Paris: L'Harmattan.

Toungara, Jeanne Maddox. 1980. "The Pre-Colonial Economy of Northwestern Ivory Coast and Its Transformation under French Colonialism, 1827–1920." Ph.D. diss., University of California, Los Angeles.

———. 1990. "The Apotheosis of Côte d'Ivoire's Nana Houphouët-Boigny." *Journal of Modern African Studies* 28, no. 1: 23–54.

——. 2001. "Ethnicity and Political Crisis in Côte d'Ivoire." *Journal of Democracy* 12, no. 3: 63–72.

Touré, Abdou. 1985. *Les petits métiers à Abidjan: L'imagination au secours de la conjoncture.* Paris: Karthala.

Touré, Mory-Frey. 1993. "Les chasseurs du Nord-Ouest et la protection de la nature." *Notre Temps* 106, 12 May, 4.

Traoré, Bourahima. 1997. "Tiassalé: Un dozo et un villageois condamnés." *Soir-INFO* 901, 1 August, 12.

Traoré, Karim. 1994. "Bɛɛ y'i ba bolo (Everybody lies in her/his mother's hands): Gender Issues in the Hunters' Songs of the Mande." In *Gender and Identity in Africa,* edited by Mechthild Reh and Gudrun Ludwar-Ene. Beiträge zur Afrikaforschung, 8 (Universität Beyreuth). Münster: LIT Verlag.

———. 2004. "The Intellectuals and the Hunters: Reflections on the Conference, 'La Rencontre des Chasseurs de l'Afrique de l'Ouest.'" *Africa Today* 50, no. 4: 97–111.

Travelé, Moussa. 1928. "Note sur les coutumes des chasseurs bambara et malinké du cercle de Bamoko (Soudan Français)." *Revue d'Ethnographie et des Traditions Populaires* 9, nos. 34–36: 207–212.

Triaud, J.-L. 1986. "Abd al-Rahman l'Africain (1908–1957), pionnier et précurseur du Wahhabisme au Mali." In *Radicalismes islamiques,* vol. 2, *Maroc, Pakistan, Inde, Yougoslavie, Mali,* edited by O. Carré and P. Dumont. Paris: L'Harmattan.

Trimingham, J. Spencer. 1959. *Islam in West Africa.* Oxford: Clarendon Press.

———. 1962. *A History of Islam in West Africa.* Oxford: Oxford University Press.

Trouillot, Michel-Rolph. 1997. *Silencing the Past: Power and the Production of History.* Boston: Beacon Press.

———. 2003. *Global Transformations: Anthropology and the Modern World.* New York: Palgrave Macmillan.

Tsing, Anna Lowenhaupt. 2005. *Friction: An Ethnography of Global Connection.* Princeton: Princeton University Press.

Turner, Victor. 1957. *Schism and Continuity in an African Society: A Study of Ndembu Village Life.* Manchester: Manchester University Press.

———. 1967. *The Forest of Symbols: Aspects of Ndembu Ritual.* Ithaca: Cornell University Press.

———. 1968. *The Drums of Affliction: A Study of Religious Processes among the Ndembu of Zambia.* Oxford: Clarendon Press.

———. 1969. *The Ritual Process: Structure and Anti-Structure.* Ithaca: Cornell University Press.

———. 1975. *Dramas, Fields, and Metaphors: Symbolic Action in Human Society.* Ithaca: Cornell University Press.

United Nations Conference on Trade and Development. 1991. *Prospects for the World Cocoa Market Until the Year 2005: Report.* New York: United Nations.

U.S. Department of State. 1997. "Côte d'Ivoire Country Report on Human Rights Practices for 1996." Washington, DC: United States Department of State. http://www.state.gov/www/global/human_rights/1996_hrp_report/cotedivo.html. Accessed June 10, 2010.

———. 1998. "Côte d'Ivoire Country Report on Human Rights Practices for 1997." Washington, DC: United States Department of State. http://www.state.gov/www/global/human_rights/1997_hrp_report/cotedivo.html. Accessed June 10, 2010.

———. 1999. "Côte d'Ivoire Country Report on Human Rights Practices for 1998." Washington, DC: United States Department of State. http://www.state.gov/www/global/human_rights/1998_hrp_report/cotedivo.html. Accessed June 18, 2010.

———. 2010. "2009 Human Rights Report: Côte d'Ivoire." Washington, DC: United States Department of State. http://www.state.gov/g/drl/rls/hrrpt/2009/af/135949.htm. Accessed June 18, 2010.

Uzendoski, Michael. 2005. *The Napo Runa of Amazonian Ecuador.* Urbana: University of Illinois Press.

Uzendoski, Michael, Mark Hertica, and Edith Tapuy. 2005. "The Phenomenology of Perspectivism: Aesthetics, Sound, and Power in Women's Songs from Amazonian Ecuador." *Current Anthropology* 46, no. 4: 656–662.

Valeri, Valerio. 1985. *Kingship and Sacrifice: Ritual and Society in Ancient Hawaii.* Chicago: University of Chicago Press.

Vauguy, Azo. 1995. "Insécurité à Abidjan: Deux policiers abattus par des bandits." *La Voie,* 3 April.

Vidal, Claudine. 2002. "Deux témoignages abidjanais." In *Côte d'Ivoire: L'année terrible, 1999–2000,* edited by Marc Le Pape and Claudine Vidal, 215–252. Paris: Karthala.

Viveiros de Castro, Eduardo. 1998. "Cosmological Deixis and Amerindian Perspectivism." *Journal of the Royal Anthropological Institute* n.s. 4, no. 3: 469–488.

Vogel, Jerome. 1991. "Culture, Politics, and National Identity in Côte d'Ivoire. *Social Research* 58, no. 2: 439–456.

Wagner, Roy. 1977. "Analogic Kinship: A Daribi Example." *American Ethnologist* 4, no. 4: 623–642.

———. 1981. *The Invention of Culture.* Chicago: University of Chicago Press.

———. 1986. *Asiwinarong: Ethos, Image, and Social Power among the Usen Barok of New Ireland.* Princeton: Princeton University Press.

———. 1991. "The Fractal Person." In *Big Men and Great Men,* edited by M. Godelier and M. Strathern. Cambridge: Cambridge University Press.

Wallerstein, Immanuel. 1964. *The Road to Independence: Ghana and the Ivory Coast.* Paris and The Hague: Mouton.

Weber, Max. 1964. *The Theory of Social and Economic Organization.* New York: Free Press.

Weiskel, Timothy. 1981. *French Colonial Rule and the Baule Peoples: Resistance and Collaboration, 1889–1911.* Oxford: Oxford University Press.

Whitehead, Neil, ed. 2004. *Violence.* Santa Fe: School of American Research.

Willerslev, Rane. 2004. "Not Animal, Not *Not*-Animal: Hunting, Imitation and Empathetic Knowledge among the Siberian Yukaghirs." *Journal of the Royal Anthropological Institute* 10, no. 3: 629–652.

Wilshire, Bruce. 1982. *Role Playing and Identity: The Limits of Theatre as Metaphor.* Bloomington: Indiana University Press.

Wilson, Richard. 2001. *The Politics of Truth and Reconciliation in South Africa: Legitimizing the Post-Apartheid State.* Cambridge: Cambridge University Press.

Woods, Dwayne. 1994. "Elites, Ethnicity, and 'Home Town' Associations in the Côte d'Ivoire: An Historical Analysis of State-Society Links." *Africa* 64, no. 4: 465–483.

———. 2003. "The Tragedy of the Cocoa Pod: Rent-Seeking, Land and Ethnic Conflict in Ivory Coast. *Journal of Modern African Studies* 41, no. 4: 641–655.

World Bank. 1996. *Poverty in Côte d'Ivoire: A Framework for Action.* Abidjan: World Bank.

Y. I. 1994. "Assassins à 15 ans." *Fraternité Matin,* 28 July.

Zartman, I. William, ed. 1995. *Collapsed States: The Disintegration of and Restoration of Legitimate Authority.* Boulder: Lynn Rienner Publishers.

Zartman, I. William, and Christopher Delgado. 1984. *The Political Economy of the Ivory Coast.* Westport, CT: Praeger.

Zéguéla, B. 1997. "Conseil national de Sécurité: La décentralisation en marche." *Ivoir'Soir* 21 October, 8.

Zehr, Howard. 2003 [1985]. "Retributive Justice, Restorative Justice." In *A Restorative Justice Reader: Texts, Sources, Context,* edited by Gerry Johnstone, 69–82. Cullompton, UK: Willan.

Zemp, Hugo. 1968. "La légende des griots malinké." *Cahiers d'études africaines* 6, no. 24: 611–642.

Zobel, Clement. 1996. "Les génies du Kòma: Identités locales, logiques religieuses et enjeux socio-politiques dans les monts Manding du Mali." *Cahiers d'Études africaines* 36, no. 144: 625–658.

Zolberg, Aristide. 1964. *One-Party Government in the Ivory Coast.* Princeton: Princeton University Press.

Zoro-Bi, Épiphane. 2004. *Juge en Côte d'Ivoire: Désarmer la Violence.* Paris: Éditions Karthala.

Index